W9-DEA-523

P 171

The 1950s

The 1950s

WILLIAM H. YOUNG
WITH NANCY K. YOUNG

American Popular Culture Through History
Ray B. Browne, Series Editor

GREENWOOD PRESS
Westport, Connecticut • London

Library of Congress Cataloging-in-Publication Data

Young, William H., 1939–
    The 1950s / William H. Young, with Nancy K. Young.
      p. cm. — (American popular culture through history)
    Includes bibliographical references and index.
    ISBN 0–313–32393–3 (alk. paper)
      1. United States—Civilization—1945–. 2. Popular culture—United States—History—
20th century. 3. Nineteen fifties. I. Title. II. Series.
E169.12.Y69   2004
973.921—dc22   2003061813

British Library Cataloguing in Publication Data is available.

Library of Congress Catalog Card Number: 2003061813
ISBN: 0–313–32393–3

First published in 2004

Greenwood Press, 88 Post Road West, Westport, CT 06881
An imprint of Greenwood Publishing Group, Inc.
www.greenwood.com

Printed in the United States of America

The paper used in this book complies with the
Permanent Paper Standard issued by the National
Information Standards Organization (Z39.48–1984).

10 9 8 7 6 5 4 3 2 1

Contents

Series Foreword

Popular culture is the system of attitudes, behavior, beliefs, customs, and tastes that define the people of any society. It is the entertainments, diversions, icons, rituals, and actions that shape the everyday world. It is what we do while we are awake and what we dream about while we are asleep. It is the way of life we inherit, practice, change, and then pass on to our descendants.

Popular culture is an extension of folk culture, the culture of the people. With the rise of electronic media and the increase in communication in American culture, folk culture expanded into popular culture—the daily way of life as shaped by the *popular majority* of society. Especially in a democracy like the United States, popular culture has become both the voice of the people and the force that shapes the nation. In 1782, the French commentator Hector St. Jean de Crèvecoeur asked in his *Letters from an American Farmer*, "What is an American?" He answered that such a person is the creation of America and is in turn the creator of the country's culture. Indeed, notions of the American Dream have been long grounded in the dream of democracy—that is, government by the people, or popular rule. Thus, popular culture is tied fundamentally to America and the dreams of its people.

Historically, culture analysts have tried to fine-tune culture into two categories: "elite"—the elements of culture (fine art, literature, classical music, gourmet food, etc.) that supposedly define the best of society—and "popular"—the elements of culture (comic strips, bestsellers, pop music, fast food, etc.) that appeal to society's lowest common denominator. The so-called "educated" person approved of elite culture and scoffed at popular culture. This schism first began to develop in Western Europe in the fifteenth century when the privileged classes tried to discover and develop differences in societies based on class, money, privilege and life styles. Like many aspects of European society, the debate between elite and popular cultures came to the United States. The upper class in America, for example, supported museums and galleries that would exhibit "the finer things in life," that would "elevate" people. As the twenty-first century emerges, however, the distinctions between popular culture and elitist culture have blurred. The blues songs (once denigrated as "race music") of Robert Johnson are now revered by musicologists; architectural students study buildings in Las Vegas as examples of what Robert Venturi called the "kitsch of high capitalism"; sportswriter Gay Talese and heavyweight boxing champ Floyd Patterson were co-panelists at a 1992 SUNY New Paltz symposium on Literature and Sport. The examples go on and on, but the one commonality that emerges is the role of popular culture as a model for the American Dream, the dream to pursue happiness and a better, more interesting life.

To trace the numerous ways in which popular culture has evolved throughout American history, we have divided the volumes in this series into chronological periods—historical eras until the twentieth century, decades between 1900 and 2000. In each volume, the author explores the specific details of popular culture that reflect and inform the general undercurrents of the time. Our purpose, then, is to present historical and analytical panoramas that reach both backward into America's past and forward to her collective future. In viewing these panoramas, we can trace a very fundamental part of American society. The American Popular Culture Through History series presents the multi-faceted parts of a popular culture in a nation that is both grown and still growing.

Ray B. Browne
Secretary-Treasurer
Popular Culture Association
American Culture Association

Acknowledgments

As was true of our companion volume about the 1930s in this series, we knew a work of this size and scope could not be written without the assistance of numerous individuals. In fact many of the people who helped us with that book also rallied to our aid with this study. To get a sense of history, at least remembered history, we distributed a completely unscientific questionnaire to about fifty friends and acquaintances. At least some consensus about cultural trends and the more outstanding personalities of the decade emerged from this effort, and we appreciate the time everyone expended to answer our questions. It gave us some confidence about how people continue to view the 1950s.

Once the actual research into the decade commenced, three libraries deserve mention: first and foremost, we are indebted to director Chris Millson-Martula and his able staff at the Lynchburg College Library in Lynchburg, Virginia. They were always gracious and helpful, no matter how demanding and time-consuming the request. As before, Ariel Myers rose to the challenge of locating every interlibrary loan title we ordered, and there were many requests and many titles. Second, Jan Grenci, along with her associates working in the special *Look* collection at the Library of Congress, made searching for and locating images in this huge store of photographs from the magazine a pleasure, and they patiently walked us through the procedures for obtaining copyright clearances and getting pictures reproduced. Third, Lynn Catanese and Jon Williams at the Hagley Museum and Library in Wilmington, Delaware, uncovered many advertising treasures in their collections, plus the Hagley is just such a pleasant place to visit.

Barbara Rothermel, director of the Daura Gallery at Lynchburg College, showed great generosity with resources, both personal and gallery-connected, that helped give this book its flavor. Irresistible sources for illustrations came from Danny Givens and his staff at Givens Book Store in Lynchburg. Hayward Guenard shared an early 1950s Dumont TV, Tom Cassidy some attic treasures, and Ann Harper amazed us with her intact books of trading stamps. Doris and Bill Ewing also supplied us with some timely items, and Tom and Bobbi Schuler and Mel and Mary Ann Sankovitch regaled us with memories and more artifacts from the decade. A book requires many drafts; Ed Canada spared a small forest by giving us reams of usable scrap paper. Finally, Greenwood Press deserves an appreciative nod. This project has been in the able hands of senior Greenwood editor Rob Kirkpatrick; his astute advice and gracious comments carried it all to conclusion. Of course, any errors, either of commission or omission, remain ours and ours alone.

Introduction

A problem with dividing books arbitrarily into decades is that events do not always fall neatly into ten-year segments. A case in point would be the 1950s; in many ways that important decade commenced with the end of World War II and the return of hundreds of thousands of veterans to the United States. Similarly, it could be argued that the forties drew to a symbolic close with the cessation of hostilities in 1945.

But a series of books must have divisions, and so this volume focuses on those events that occurred in the period 1950–1959. Of necessity, reference will at times be made to movements and styles that arose during the 1940s but did not blossom until subsequent years. Some trends did not reach full fruition when they first appeared; much that began in the 1950s emerged as significant only in the 1960s and 1970s. Not everything can be neatly contained within a decade.

As this volume makes clear, the 1950s witnessed a great expansion of mass and popular culture, especially through the vehicle of television. And yet, at the same time, the decade marked the acceleration of individualization within culture, the demassification of music, film, art, literature, and leisure in order to attract narrower, more specialized audiences. Choices expanded as formats splintered and sought new directions. The mass media disseminated information about all human endeavors at an ever-accelerating pace as records, tapes, radio, film, television, paperbacks, and advertising provided so much information that any traditional boundaries between low, middle, and high culture got blurred. Popular culture, its appetites insatiable, absorbed content from everything; to some critics, this constituted vulgarization, but to many others it simply meant popularization—democracy in action.

The postwar era provided a chance for a second start; with the economic challenges of the Great Depression and the horrors of World War II now past, the nation looked to a future filled with both promise and danger. Pundits proclaimed the 1950s an era of "Big Science," a time when laboratories routinely announced major discoveries that would impact many areas of American life: a cure for polio, space exploration, miniaturization, the introduction of the computer, and color television. Science and technology would lead everyone to a better life. But that same technology and science threatened to run amok, causing others to label the decade "The Age of Anxiety." By the beginning of the 1950s, the nation had lost its nuclear weapons monopoly. Soon thereafter, both the United States and Russia claimed possession of hydrogen bombs, the most fearsome invention of the postwar era. The Soviet Union and China signed mutual defense pacts, North Korea invaded South Korea, a succession of spies were arrested on both sides of the Iron Curtain, Senator Joseph McCarthy found Reds under every bed, American kids had to "duck and cover" at school while their parents dug fallout shelters in the backyard, and so the idea of anxiety did not seem far-fetched. Certainly, no one could plead ignorance about world events, although they might try to ignore them. One of the themes followed in this book is how some aspects of ongoing history, like the Cold War, even became part of American popular culture.

Nuclear threats aside, the 1950s marked a new level of consumer consumption. The majority of Americans had to learn how to be good consumers; the idea of thrift, so endlessly preached throughout the Depression and World War II, had to be discarded as a virtue. Relentless advertising instead urged people to buy, buy, buy. Easy credit, time purchases, and a bursting cornucopia of goods replaced the restraint and shortages of previous decades. Instant gratification of all wants and needs became the rule, and popular culture based much of its content on this promise of fulfillment. A case in point: Detroit's new chariots claimed speed and technical superiority, but they also represented a wave of conspicuous consumption that not even a decade could satisfy. The Cold War might have been the grim background, but daily lives resonated with the expectation that at last the American Dream could become reality.

Despite all the optimism, some labeled the fifties as a time of cultural and intellectual stagnation, a period when nothing of significance happened. The nation's youth even got dubbed "The Silent Generation," a group satisfied with prosperity and the status quo, unwilling to challenge the social and cultural standards of the day. On the surface, the fifties perhaps did give the impression of peace and conformity, the era of "the man in the gray flannel suit." A popular phrase taken from a best-selling 1955 novel, it perpetuates the image of a family with a ranch house in the suburbs, an all-electric kitchen and a station wagon, and children who voraciously consume a variety of goods and services never before seen. Comfort and stability became associated with the decade, but not to the exclusion of all else. Nothing happened? Stagnation? Nothing could be further from the truth.

Some critics noticed that occasional bubbles rose to this unruffled surface—cheating scandals at prestigious colleges, payola among disc jockeys, steadily rising divorce rates along with inflation, juvenile delinquency—but the exterior calm seemed to lull the nation. Beneath that unnatural quiet, however, much was seething, ready to boil up into the social disruptions of the 1960s. Acute observers could already detect cracks and fissures in the national mood, yet a nostalgic haze of consensus lingers over the 1950s, often held by those who never actually experienced the decade. Many might think the fifties came the closest to cultural hegemony of any decade in the twentieth century, but this book argues that the fifties portended great social and cultural changes.

The sweeping popularity of rock 'n' roll alone served as a background for a revision of traditional American values. It promised good times, sex, and freedom from constraints. But rock acted merely as one of the messengers; the changes were already occurring. The rising postwar generation of artists, musicians, and writers served as rebels, not complacent conservatives. Jackson Pollock, Marlon Brando, Elvis Presley, and Jack Kerouac hardly stood for the status quo.

The 1950s shows how the entertainment industries, mass publishing, the electronic media, and the arts responded to the events of their times. Abstract Expressionism receives little mention, and experimental novels, avant-garde plays, and little-seen art films are not examined. These subjects assume importance in any detailed history of the decade, but they play a minimal role in the popular culture of the era. Instead, the book focuses on the general content of mass entertainment, discussing movies, music, and television, best-sellers, the rise of the teenager as a marketable entity, the innumerable dance and fashion fads, design trends, the increase in leisure time and travel—in short, the pop culture that made the decade so memorable.

It is too easy to summarize the 1950s with terms like "strong family loyalty" and "sentimentality," attitudes reinforced by many of the popular TV sitcoms and hit records of the day. True, it was a decade watched over by two older presidents, Harry Truman and Dwight Eisenhower, who strove to be good fathers to their increasingly young and restless brood. Following World War II, Americans reproduced as never before, so the inevitable conflicts between youth and age colored the period. Rock 'n' roll and teenage angst collided with Levittown and Detroit behemoths. These stresses emerged most clearly in the second half of the decade as more and more 1940s babies became adolescents, and so the 1950s closed with an insistent clamor for change and a youthful new president taking the reins in 1960. To characterize the decade as "The Silent Generation" or "The Fabulous Fifties," however, implies good times and few worries and does a disservice to this colorful, conforming, raucous, reticent, daring, timid, and ultimately fascinating chapter in American cultural history.

Timeline of the 1950s

1950

At the opening of the decade, U.S. population stands at 150 million. Life expectancy measures almost 66 years for men and 71 years for women.

The average worker makes about $3,100/year; a new national minimum wage of $0.75/hour goes into effect in January.

Illiteracy reaches a new low in 1950: 3.2 percent.

In January, President Truman orders the United States to move ahead on developing an H-bomb after Russia successfully tests an atomic bomb in August of 1949. In February, Wisconsin Senator Joseph McCarthy claims Communists have infiltrated every level of government, especially the State Department.

On June 25th, North Korea launches a surprise attack on South Korea, precipitating the Korean War and U.S. involvement.

President Truman directs the armed services to racially integrate their various branches.

Sixty million Americans go to the movies each week.

All About Eve, a trenchant, sophisticated movie drama, proves a surprise hit and garners many awards. Two young actors make their film debuts: Marlon Brando in *The Men*, a war drama, and Marilyn Monroe in *The Asphalt Jungle*, a crime picture.

The Colgate Comedy Hour, *Your Show of Shows*, and *The Steve Allen Show* all premiere on network television, and Bob Hope makes the jump from radio to television, one of the first major radio comedians to do so. Soon thereafter, most other radio stars follow suit.

In a clever marketing move, Earl Tupper decides to sell his plastic kitchen containers directly to consumers by way of "Tupperware Parties."

DuPont introduces Orlon, a new miracle fiber, and Xerox produces its first copying machine.

1951

The twenty-second Amendment to the Constitution gets passed in February, limiting presidents to two terms.

The number of American soldiers in Korea swells to 250,000, but in April President Truman relieves General Douglas MacArthur of his Korean command after the general urges invading China. MacArthur retires, and a parade honoring him in New York City draws over three million spectators. He then addresses Congress, and his mention that "old soldiers never die, they just fade away" results in a half-dozen hit records, along with much associated memorabilia.

In late March, Julius and Ethel Rosenberg get convicted of spying; they will be executed in June of 1953.

The nickel telephone call becomes history when most pay phones go to a dime.

Remington Rand begins to manufacture the UNIVAC I, the first commercial business computer.

Health officials recommend fluoridation of public drinking water as a means of reducing tooth decay.

In June, CBS presents the first commercial color telecast.

Edward R. Murrow's *See It Now* premieres on TV, as does a new comedy series titled *I Love Lucy*.

The comedy team of Dean Martin and Jerry Lewis becomes a box-office favorite.

Singers like Tony Bennett, Rosemary Clooney, Nat "King" Cole, Perry Como, Bing Crosby, Doris Day, and Frank Sinatra dominate record sales, effectively ending the reign of the big bands.

DuPont introduces Dacron, another new artificial fiber.

In November, the New Jersey Turnpike opens, one of the first postwar superhighways.

1952

Prices climb, and the nation enters into a prolonged period of inflation.

The Postal Service discontinues the penny postcard; the new rate doubles to two cents.

An April atomic test explosion in Nevada is broadcast live.

In September, Richard Nixon, the candidate for vice president, delivers his famous "Checkers" speech. A record 58 million viewers tune in.

In early November, the Atomic Energy Commission announces the successful detonation of the first H-bomb at Eniwetok Atoll in the Pacific.

General Dwight Eisenhower gets elected president in November, ending the Democratic monopoly on the office held since 1932. He promptly travels to Korea, fulfilling a campaign promise.

During the secure Eisenhower years, the average age for both marriages and divorces falls.

The conservative "man in the gray flannel suit" comes to epitomize both the fashions and lifestyles of the era.

Jonas Salk begins testing of his experimental vaccine to ward off the ravages of polio; in the meantime, the disease strikes over 50,000 people, mainly children.

Fiberglass is introduced.

Dick Clark's *American Bandstand* debuts in January on Philadelphia television; it will become an ABC network offering in 1956. *Dragnet* premieres on TV after a successful radio run, and comedians Jackie Gleason and Ernie Kovacs introduce new shows.

RCA introduces tiny transistors that can replace bulky vacuum tubes; soon thereafter, the Sony Corporation brings out the first transistorized radios.

The Quiet Man, a movie starring John Wayne and Maureen O'Hara, reaffirms the popularity of both actors.

On college campuses across the nation, the first "panty raids" occur.

1953

Senator McCarthy's investigations into Communist influence in government capture the attention of many people.

In June, a Korean armistice is declared for July, effectively ending the war. Peace negotiations will, however, drag on for years.

An unknown guerilla leader named Fidel Castro launches an attack against the Cuban government on July 26th. It fails, and he goes to prison.

At the end of September, Earl Warren takes the reins as Chief Justice of the Supreme Court.

In August, Russia announces that it also possesses the H-bomb.

In a bow to the new medium's success, the Academy Awards get televised for the first time, with Bob Hope serving as host.

Over 300 television stations schedule regular broadcasting, triple the number from 1950.

CinemaScope, a projection technique employing a wider screen and stereophonic sound, is introduced; *The Robe*, a religious epic starring Richard Burton, becomes the first offering using the new system.

Big, string-filled orchestras have a momentary burst of popularity for music fans. Percy Faith, Hugo Winterhalter, Frank Chacksfield, and Mantovani are among the leaders.

IBM introduces its first computer, the Model 701.

1954

In January, Secretary of State John Foster Dulles unveils the defense policy of "massive retaliation."

That same month, the Navy commissions the U.S.S. *Nautilus*, the first nuclear-powered submarine.

In March, the United States explodes the largest thermonuclear blast ever in an experiment at Bikini Atoll.

On June 14th, the phrase "under God" gets added to the Pledge of Allegiance.

The Supreme Court rules in May that "separate but equal" schools (those systems that separate students by race) are inherently unequal, one of the first major legal attacks for segregation.

In a move to stave off bankruptcy, Studebaker and Packard, two old U.S. auto manufacturers, merge in June.

Reflecting a renewed interest in jazz, the Newport Jazz Festival debuts in July.

That same month, Elvis Presley's first commercial recordings are released by Sun Records.

In December, the U.S. Senate censures Senator McCarthy.

"Serious pictures," like *On the Waterfront*, *Rear Window*, *The Country Girl*, and *A Star Is Born* dominate the movies as producers search for films that will lure audiences away from television.

1955

With the recession of 1953 clearly over, Americans purchase almost eight million automobiles.

In April, and after extensive testing, officials declare the Salk vaccine against polio safe and effective, and inoculations of millions of children follow.

At the end of May, the Supreme Court rules that school segregation must end "within a reasonable time."

In July, the first Disneyland opens in Anaheim, California.

In August, the minimum wage rises from $0.75 to $1.00.

"The Pill," an oral contraceptive for women in capsule form, is introduced. More effective than previous birth-control devices, it will help change sexual behavior throughout the country.

"Smog," a combination of smoke and fog, enters the language as a means of describing polluted air. The condition becomes particularly noticeable in Los Angeles, where the exhausts from large numbers of vehicles mix with damp air and cause a thick haze to hang over the city.

Rock 'n' roll begins to attract a mass audience. The August release and success of Chuck Berry's "Maybelline" draws attention, and RCA Victor purchases Elvis Presley's contract with Sun Records.

In September, actor James Dean dies in an auto accident. A cult almost immediately forms around his memory.

1956

Voters overwhelmingly reelect Eisenhower in November, despite his lingering health problems.

Grace Kelly, a popular movie actress, marries Prince Rainier of Monaco in April.

In a test, the United States drops the first airborne hydrogen bomb in May.

In June, Congress passes the Federal Aid Highway Act; it will lead to the Interstate Highway system.

In July, the *Andrea Doria* sinks after colliding with the *Stockholm* off the Massachusetts coast; 60 people drown, but over 1,600 are saved.

In November, the Supreme Court again attacks racial segregation, this time by ruling racially separated seating on public transportation illegal. In the meantime, rioting and protests accompany attempts at school desegregation in the South.

Freed from prison, Fidel Castro retreats to a mountain stronghold and, in December again attacks the Cuban government.

Billed as a "hillbilly singer," Elvis Presley makes his TV debut on a show called *Stage Door*. Noting the publicity the vocalist's appearance inspires, Ed Sullivan books him for his *Toast of the Town*. In the meantime, Presley's "Heartbreak Hotel" proves a tremendous hit.

Country singer Johnny Cash crosses over into the pop charts with "I Walk the Line" in October. The lines dividing musical genres continue to blur.

Disposable Pampers diapers make their first appearance.

1957

Following a dramatic showdown in September, President Eisenhower dispatches U.S. troops to Little Rock after Arkansas defies the courts and uses the National Guard to block entry of black students into a previously all-white high school.

In September, the Atomic Energy Commission begins underground testing of nuclear weapons at its Nevada test site.

In early October, Russia launches an experimental unmanned spacecraft called *Sputnik*. Two months later, the Russians launch a second craft, this time with a dog aboard. The Space Race officially begins, with the United States far behind.

The Ford Motor Company introduces the much-heralded Edsel.

The Bridge on the River Kwai breaks box-office records.

Popular music follows several avenues: traditional (Debbie Reynolds, Johnny Mathis), rock 'n' roll (Elvis Presley, Bill Haley and His Comets), country (Elvis Presley, the Everly Brothers), rhythm and blues (The Platters, Sam Cooke), and mixtures of all the foregoing.

In September, *West Side Story* opens on Broadway.

1958

Unemployment creeps up to an uncomfortable seven percent as the nation enters into another recession.

In January, the United States finally launches its first satellite, *Explorer I*, but the Russians put a much larger *Sputnik III* into orbit. In July, NASA (National Aeronautics and Space Administration) is formed to coordinate U.S. space ventures.

In August, first-class postage goes up a penny to four cents, and airmail follows suit, six cents to seven cents.

In order to avoid integration, Arkansas's governor closes the Little Rock schools in September and classes are held on television.

In October, the Boeing 707 jetliner begins regular New York–Paris flights.

In November, the U.S. successfully tests an ICBM (Intercontinental Ballistic Missile); the Atlas rocket covers 5,500 miles and hits its target.

Angelo Giuseppe Roncalli becomes Pope John XXIII.

Elvis Presley enters the U.S. Army in March.

In April, a young American pianist named Van Cliburn wins the International Tchaikovsky Competition held in Moscow, becoming a star overnight.

A love triangle involving singer Eddie Fisher and two women, his wife Debbie Reynolds and "homewrecker" Elizabeth Taylor, titillates the public for months and results in the divorce of Reynolds and Fisher.

Groups like Danny and the Juniors ("At the Hop"), the McGuire Sisters ("Sugartime"), the Silhouettes ("Get a Job"), and the Champs ("Tequila") begin to hold sway over individual vocalists.

"Beatnik" enters the language; it refers to people who do not conform to perceived proper behaviors. The "-nik" suffix comes from the publicity surrounding Russian successes with space satellites called "Sputniks."

1959

At the close of the decade, U.S. population stands at 179 million, an increase of over 18 percent since 1950, and marking the most rapid growth since 1900.

The average worker earns almost $5,000 a year, a 61 percent increase over 1950 figures.

Alaska officially gains statehood on January 3rd; on August 23rd, Hawaii becomes the fiftieth state.

In January, Fidel Castro overthrows the Cuban government after a lengthy revolution; his new government gains prompt recognition by the United States. Castro pays a friendly visit to the United States in April.

Virginia begins "massive resistance" to integration in January.

"We will bury you," says Russian Premier Nikita Khrushchev, but he also makes a historic visit to the United States as relations warm somewhat.

In June, the United States launches its first missile-firing submarine, the U.S.S. *George Washington.*

The rush to build home bomb shelters accelerates.

The United States makes a big move into the space race with the selection of the Mercury Seven, the first American astronauts: Scott Carpenter, Gordon Cooper, John Glenn, Virgil Grissom, Alan Shepard, Walter Schirra, and Donald Slayton.

Congressional investigations into television quiz show scandals commence in November.

In November, Ford Motor Company ceases producing the Edsel, the costliest failure in automobile history.

PART I

LIFE AND YOUTH DURING THE 1950s

The 1950s

1

Everyday America

At the opening of the decade, the United States found itself in the enviable position of being far and away the most powerful nation on earth. Its industrial base, undamaged and immeasurably strengthened by World War II, manufactured over half of all the world's products, along with producing raw materials like steel and oil in prodigious quantities. Franklin D. Roosevelt's "arsenal of democracy" had grown into a true colossus.

America itself proved the biggest single consumer of this outpouring. Denied many goods during the austere war years, their pockets lined with unspent money, citizens rushed to buy everything that appeared on the new peacetime market. This orgy of self-indulgence created a level of prosperity unseen since the heady days just before the stock market crash of 1929, resulting in a period of unparalleled growth and economic expansion that lasted through the decade.

THE ECONOMY

Between 1950 and 1960, the gross national product (GNP) grew by over $200 billion, escalating from $285 billion to $500 billion in ten years, a remarkable increase by any measure. Although worker productivity doubled, much of this growth stemmed from the changing demographics of the nation: the mid- to late 1940s heralded a nonstop population surge that carried through the 1950s. In 1940, the U.S. census counted 132 million Americans, a figure that rose to 150 million in 1950, and then leaped to 179 million in 1960. More people meant more of everything: jobs, workers, goods, services—all the ingredients for a boom economy that eagerly accepted the challenge.[1]

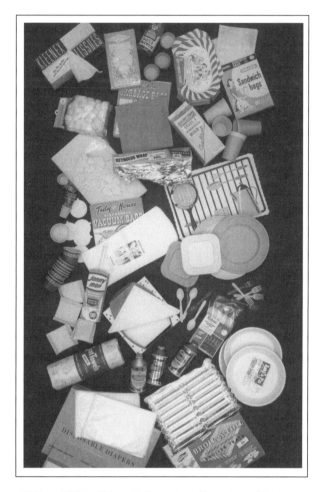

If the 1950s did nothing else, they heralded an onslaught of personal consumption the likes of which the world has never seen. This display shows the wealth of disposable products that flooded the market during the decade, proof that American prosperity was such that people could throw away much of what they used. Source: Hagley Museum and Library.

By 1956, the makeup of the American labor force had undergone a profound change. For the first time, industry employed more white-collar (office) employees than blue-collar (factory) workers. The mechanization and automation of traditional occupations led to the creation of many more office positions. Further, in 1957, the service sector overtook and

In the area of durable goods, Americans went on a buying spree in the 1950s, bringing about the birth of huge, warehouse-like stores to cater to their wants. This picture shows shoppers looking at the latest in television sets, a product that certainly helped spark this phenomenon. Source: Library of Congress.

surpassed the manufacturing portion as the leading component of the national economy. Both industry and service grew increasingly impersonal, as little family businesses became components of large corporations. More efficient levels of service replaced the old, familiar standards, but the folksy touch, the comforting familiarity, was fast disappearing. The small-town face of America, the one portrayed in countless Norman Rockwell covers for the *Saturday Evening Post*, had begun to be supplanted by an urbanized and corporate one.[2]

Most people, however, had little time to look to a nostalgic past; they were too enmeshed in a consumer frenzy to buy and accumulate. Despite rising inflation spurred by rising government expenditures, Americans as a whole directed increasing amounts of their money to whatever they wished, enjoying a level of goods and services never dreamed of earlier. Median family income almost doubled: between 1950 and 1960, it went from $3,083 per year to $5,976 per year. Even factoring in inflation, real wages increased 30 percent, so that food, clothing, and shelter no longer took away so much of each paycheck. New cars (instead of used models), televisions, high-fidelity units, improved telephones, alcoholic beverages, and endless entertainment saw sharply rising sales.[3]

Nevertheless, pockets of poverty persisted in postwar America. Many black Americans still toiled in underpaid, low-status jobs and lived in substandard housing. Neither did a majority of farmers and factory workers immediately share the fruits of rising prosperity. Single women, already laboring in low-paying positions, continued to lag behind their male counterparts.

CREDIT CARDS

Although no one foresaw the consequences at the time, the 1950 formation of the Diner's Club and the issuance of a wallet-sized credit card to members led directly to a fundamental change in American buying habits. At first, the rather exclusive Diner's Club limited its use to restaurants in the New York City area, but the idea caught on and rapidly expanded. In 1958, giant American Express started issuing cards of its own, and a year later Bank of America brought out its first BankAmericard (which later became Visa). This new approach to credit represented a financial, technological, and sociological breakthrough. It meant that those extending credit were guaranteed payment, that only high-speed computers could handle all the millions of transactions, and that individuals no longer had to rely on cash or checks to make purchases.

The credit-card revolution also reflected a profound transformation in attitudes about debt. Prior to World War II, most families owed as little as possible because they were imbued with an ethic that frowned on any indebtedness, plus most merchants demanded full payment for goods. People accepted the rule that you saved until you could afford whatever it might be you wanted; if an item seemed too expensive or your finances would not permit it, you did without. Following the war, the rules changed. Time payments for big-ticket (i.e., expensive) items became more commonplace, and businesses exhibited a willingness to extend credit to their newly affluent customers.[4]

With credit so readily available, people had little reason to deny themselves. The old reservations about accumulating debt got cast aside, especially by younger consumers. A new extravagance replaced the frugality of the past, one that touted "buy now, pay later." For most Americans, this phrase described the fifties accurately; private debt increased sharply, going from $73 billion in 1950 to $196 billion in 1960.[5]

FAMILY LIFE

The family itself changed significantly during this period. Instead of Mom, Dad, and the usual two children, more and more couples opted for three and four children. Not only were there many more people, but many more offspring as well, making the 1950s one of the most youthful decades on record. By 1958, almost a third of all Americans were 15 years old or younger. The parents of all these children—anxious to buy houses, cars, and all the other material goods needed to set up a household and join the ranks of the swelling middle class—emerged as a primary factor in the rambunctious economy. And everyone, young, old, single, and married, had more discretionary cash than at any time in the nation's history.[6]

Divorce rates rose somewhat during the decade, and marriage rates fell slightly. The rush to marry during and immediately following World War II had subsided, and some couples that had wed with the pressures of war reexamined their decisions, a partial explanation of growing divorce figures. Despite the declining marriage totals, surging birth rates more than made up for any differences. "Baby boom" evolved as the term used to describe the skyrocketing numbers of new additions to families. Some 3.6 million births were recorded in 1950; by the end of the decade the figure had grown to 4.3 million; in addition, the birth rate itself surged to 3.51 births per woman by 1959, or up from 2.2 as measured in the late 1930s. This astonishing rise proved an economic bonanza for retailers, but schools and recreational facilities found themselves stretched to their very limits.[7]

Having children was touted as the highest form of happiness; a woman fulfilled herself by bearing children. And, despite a swelling population, the baby boom continued unabated. In the popular television situation comedy, *I Love Lucy*, Desi and Lucy Ricardo, husband and wife, find that Lucy is "expecting." In those more innocent days of TV, network censors considered the word "pregnant" taboo, although they embraced the concept of approaching motherhood. In reality, Lucille Ball, the star of the show, had become pregnant, and so her condition got written into the series. It proved a wise move; audiences followed her progress in one episode after another, culminating in the birth of little Ricky in early 1953 (filming took place in November of 1952). It became one of the most watched events in the history of American television.

In a similar way, shows like *Father Knows Best*, *The Adventures of Ozzie and Harriet*, *Leave It to Beaver*, *Make Room for Daddy*, and *The Donna Reed Show* espoused strong family values. The picture painted of the decade might be unrealistic and rose-colored, but it has persisted as a nostalgic perception of the 1950s. [For more on TV and films of the fifties, see chapter 10, "Performing Arts."]

"TOGETHERNESS" AND "DO IT YOURSELF"

In the 1954 Easter issue of *McCall's* magazine, the term "togetherness" gained some media legitimacy. It meant the family worked as a unit, that Mom and Dad and the kids undertook joint activities. It meant families looked inward, that parents and children learned from one another, and the home became the nexus of sharing. "Do it yourself"—instead of letting outsiders do it for you—emerged as a catchphrase eagerly embraced by suburban families everywhere. Fathers showed sons how to assemble a bookcase, and mothers demonstrated to daughters how to prepare a proper meal. Everyone could work on a "paint-by-numbers" kit in the family room, an area reserved in the modern suburban home for just such activities. As long as the family operated together, all was well with America, or so "togetherness" would have it.[8]

Organized religion also celebrated this emphasis on the insular family. A popular slogan of the time touted "the family that prays together stays together." And so it would seem: Americans attended church in record numbers. About half the citizenry claimed church membership or affiliation in 1950; by 1960, the number had climbed to 69 percent, an all-time high then and now. During his tenure, President Dwight Eisenhower even got baptized in the White House. The new Revised Standard Version (RSV) of the Bible spent an unprecedented three years on the best-seller lists. In 1954, the words "under God" were added to the Pledge of Allegiance, and "In God We Trust" became a part of the country's coinage the following year.

With the government proclaiming a Christian heritage, various evangelists found themselves drawing record crowds into churches and other venues. Chief among them was Billy Graham and his Crusades, but Bishop Fulton Sheen, Norman Vincent Peale, and Oral Roberts also attracted large audiences. Even with togetherness, evangelism, and record church attendance, the 1950s also witnessed the development of tranquilizers, most of which sold in astronomical numbers. By 1957, some 73 brands crowded the market, with Miltown and Equinal among the best known. Although available only by prescription, it soon became obvious a lot of people used them. Beneath an outwardly calm surface, Americans had issues that needed attention, and organized religion seemed unable to solve all of them. For some, masking reality with drugs appeared a possible outlet.

In retrospect, the collective spiritual messages of the day reflected moral complacency, not a call to action. One's concern should be with individual salvation, not social problems. In the nation's quest for some kind of spiritual certainty, writers like Catherine Marshall (*A Man Called Peter*, 1952) and Jim Bishop (*The Day Christ Died*, 1957) obliged. Not to be outdone in the spirituality department, Hollywood released an unprecedented number of quasi-religious films. *The Robe* (1953), *The Silver Chalice* (1954), *The Ten Commandments* (1956), and *Ben-Hur* (1959) drew record crowds and prospered at the box office.

CIVIL RIGHTS

For much of the decade, white Americans remained blissfully ignorant about racism. The fact that their beloved suburbs were often almost one hundred percent white, and likewise their schools and country clubs, did not seem an issue, especially on network television series or the movies. If the era also continued to see lynchings in the South, a complacent majority took such dreadful events in its stride.

Not until 1954 did civil rights develop into a widespread issue. The Supreme Court ruled against the Topeka Board of Education, saying that racially segregated schools and facilities were not necessarily equal, a decision that awakened the nation from its long slumber about justice for all citizens. Then in 1955, a tired Rosa Parks refused to give up her bus seat to a white man, and the nation again had to look at the artificial separation of people by race. When bus boycotts followed, accompanied by the elevation of Dr. Martin Luther King, Jr., into the national limelight, the country slowly realized that racial segregation could not remain a part of the fabric of American life.

In 1957, Arkansas Governor Orval Faubus refused to protect black students attempting to integrate Little Rock High School, compelling President Eisenhower to call out federal troops. By this time, the television cameras had already arrived on the scene, and the national nightly news detailed the unfolding stories of rage and repression. The civil rights movement had shifted into high gear, and American mass media had become an unblinking witness. Dr. King, by dint of almost continuous media exposure, emerged as a spokesman for expanding civil rights, and also became the conscience of the country. By the end of the decade, the nation found itself poised, reluctantly or not, to enter into some of the greatest social changes of the century.[9]

TECHNOLOGICAL CHANGE

In addition to the civil rights challenge, the 1950s witnessed significant technological change. In order to accomplish high-speed computations, a machine called UNIVAC (Universal Automatic Computer, 1951) succeeded a previous calculator called ENIAC (Electronic Numerical Integrator and Computer, 1946). The ENIAC and its variations (about 20 different models) might be called the first real computers, but UNIVAC, because it could store memory, came on the scene as a marked improvement. Remington Rand, which owned the rights to UNIVAC, convinced the U.S. Census Bureau that its computer was the best for calculations and tabulating. Put into service in 1951 in Philadelphia, UNIVAC ushered in the Information Age, although no one at the time foresaw the dimensions of change computers would have on everyday life.

International Business Machines (IBM), a Remington Rand competitor, and best known at the time for its electric typewriters and dictating equipment, also developed a working computer in 1950. In a 1951 advertisement, IBM refers to its computer as an "Electronic Calculator" so that potential customers would not be confused by its function. By 1954, the company had sold only about twenty of the machines, and they were earnestly improving their mainstay typewriters. The firm nonetheless introduced its 700 series of computers in 1955. Machines designed for use by businesses, the new line impressed potential customers, shipping over a thousand units in the later years of the decade. Although IBM would continue to sell far more typewriters than it would computers for some time, people sensed that a profound technological shift was at hand.

Computers may have received most of the headlines in the early 1950s, but the fledgling Xerox Corporation also introduced an office machine destined to transform American business practices. In 1950, the company displayed its first electronic copying machine, and a new word, "xerox," entered the language. The consequences of the Xerox machine would not be realized until a few years later, when copiers became commonplace in offices everywhere.

WOMEN AND THE IMAGERY OF HOUSEWORK

Throughout the fifties, popular media portrayed American women as possibly the best-dressed housekeepers ever seen. In television situation comedies and countless advertisements, women don elegant dresses, high heels, jewelry (the pearl necklace seems almost de rigueur), and smile as they dust and vacuum. Three leading TV examples would be Donna Reed as "Donna Stone" in *The Donna Reed Show*, Jane Wyatt as "Margaret Anderson" in *Father Knows Best*, and Barbara Billingsley as "June Cleaver" in *Leave It to Beaver*. In the ads, some even wear crowns—women as queens of domesticity. It mattered little that many American women chose employment and careers over homemaking; the image perpetuated throughout the 1950s was one of inequality: a woman's role consisted of making her family happy by serving them, providing them all the best consumer goods, and then taking her pleasure in their happiness.

Advertisers played up the idea of ease of use and resultant free time. "Comfort" and "convenience" became the watchwords, and chores like cooking and cleaning got blended into a happy lifestyle. Kitchens—the multipurpose command centers of many new suburban homes—merged with the laundry, dining, and family rooms, as fun and recreation became the focus of modern living. And it took a stable, organized woman to maintain this focus, something reinforced in advertising, magazine articles, and especially television situation comedies. Even when Lucille Ball in *I Love Lucy* appears inept, the humor works because of the audience's familiarity with the popular housewife ideal. Lucy's frustrations with the ideal might be echoed by millions of similarly challenged women, but the whole family could nonetheless be amused. Lucy, of course, would not be satisfied with her failures, and so the series succeeds on the premise that each week she'll come back and try again, no matter how outlandish her approach. As long as she tries, her lack of success can be excused in a humorous fashion. Thus, *I Love Lucy* fits the American myth of hard work and resultant rewards, even if audiences saw few of those rewards attained in the series.

WORKING WOMEN

The media image of the American woman had her staying at home and raising a family. Widely accepted in the popular mind, this comforting and stereotypical picture got challenged in real life as the fifties moved along. Also, while numerous television shows featured stay-at-home moms in their plots, large-circulation magazines countered with articles that extolled the extra earning power of a second income. Doubtless many women felt torn by such mixed messages, and statistics suggest that increasing numbers of them chose a paying job over being a full-time housewife.

In 1940, about 14 million women, or 28 percent of all women, worked. That number swelled with the onset of World War II and defense jobs. At the end of the war in 1945, women were urged to vacate their occupations so returning servicemen could have them. Some did, but many younger women simultaneously joined the workforce, so that by 1950, 18 million held jobs, a significantly higher number than that achieved in World War II. Contrary to popular beliefs, those numbers continued to increase throughout the 1950s. By 1960, over 23 million American women, or 36 percent of all women, had jobs outside the home—a figure that includes 33 percent of all married women. Although they faced limited employment opportunities, they nevertheless worked and did not spend the day at home, despite what the situation comedies, the movies, and advertising would have had one believe.[10]

With growing numbers of women entering the workplace, contradictions about their goals proliferated. Only about one-third of the women who entered college during the decade actually graduated. Further, fewer women went on to graduate or professional schools than was the case in the 1920s and 1930s. The 1950s female college student was more likely to marry, start a family, and put an end to her educational aspirations. As a result, although an unexpectedly large proportion of American women worked, they were conspicuously absent from high-level jobs. They instead settled for the traditional employment outlets: secretarial, clerical, nursing, teaching, assembly lines, and domestic service. Just over ten percent of working women entered a profession, and a minuscule six percent had management positions.[11]

NUCLEAR ANXIETY

In August of 1949, the Union of Soviet Socialist Republics exploded its first atomic bomb. This blast would cast a pall over the entire upcoming decade. A fear of nuclear annihilation, an underlying anxiety that ran counter to the rampant consumerism that many equate with the time, became a part of the American scene. Popular culture, always sensitive to the many moods of the nation, quickly picked up on this uneasiness, and capitalized on it in a variety of ways.

With the news that Russia also had "the Bomb," President Truman announced in January of 1950 that the United States would continue to develop a hydrogen bomb, a much more destructive version of the atomic bomb. Shortly thereafter, the Russians also commenced working on such a weapon. And so, by 1953, both nations possessed H-bombs, and the threat of total war and mutual annihilation loomed ever larger.

Throughout the decade, the United States and Russia frequently tested their stockpiles of nuclear weapons, and news of growing amounts of radioactive materials in the air became more common. By mid-decade, ominous reports of huge Russian intercontinental missiles circulated, and it all came to a head when the USSR launched *Sputnik* in October of 1957. The Russian name means "little traveling companion," and *Sputnik* shook the U.S. out of any technological complacency. No one had expected the Soviets to be the first into space; it served as a disquieting moment for any lingering notions of inherent American superiority. Part of the American response to *Sputnik* involved spending vast sums of government money to catch up. In the spring of 1958, a reluctant President Eisenhower asked Congress to create the National Aeronautics and Space Administration (NASA), and a new component to the ongoing arms race—the space race—was officially on.

Instead of having their fears alleviated by these moves, Americans found their anxieties compounded by other steps taken by the government. Officials put into place a civil defense system that included aircraft spotters and buildings designated as fallout shelters for protection from deadly radiation. Bright yellow-and-black triangular signs were attached to the entrances of stout public buildings, with the instructions to "take shelter in the event of an attack." The now-faded triangles can still occasionally be found on older buildings, a kind of lingering testament to the nation's fears. Even the public schools had their "Duck and Cover" drills. At the news of approaching planes, students were to "duck" (under whatever is close by) and "cover" (arms over the head for additional protection). A generation of 1950s students practiced the exercise—an exercise in futility had there been an actual attack. Commercial radio and television had CONELRAD (*control electromagnetic radiation*); the Federal Communications Commission (FCC) established this system in 1953 that would notify listeners and viewers of impending attack while simultaneously preventing enemy planes from homing in on radio or TV signals. The more familiar Emergency Broadcast System that warns of any dire emergencies eventually replaced it in 1963.

The government also printed many pamphlets and posters that purported to show how to survive a nuclear explosion. They encouraged building backyard bomb shelters, but suggested a reinforced basement room, suitably stocked with emergency items, might suffice. For those unfortunate to be caught outdoors when disaster struck, the instructions were succinct: because most men wore hats when outdoors in those days, they urged tilting the head so the brim will shield the eyes from "heat flash"; for women, they advised wearing hosiery and long sleeves at all times for a similar level of protection. Lacking a hat or hose, jumping face first into nearby ditches and gutters might also provide a modicum of security.[12]

In a series of movies that ranged from the trite *Invasion, U.S.A.* (1952), to the modest *Magnetic Monster* (1953), to the terrifying *Them!* (1954), Hollywood played on fears of mutations, atomic war, domestic spying, and Communist infiltration. Radio provided shows like *Dimension X* (1950–1951) and *Escape* (1947–1954) that used science fiction as a means to explore many contemporary issues. Not to be outdone by their movie and radio rivals, network television weighed in with series like *Alfred Hitchcock Presents* (1955–1965) and *The Twilight Zone* (1959–1964). Neither of these shows appears obsessed with politics or paranoia, but they frequently offered stories that could be seen in terms of ongoing events. People persecuted by overzealous investigators, communities caught up in mass hysteria, and citizens victimized by unseen accusers were among the themes sometimes explored by these offerings. For the most part, however, commercial TV sought to entertain on the most superficial level, and so series like these stood as the exceptions, not the rule.

By the end of the decade, theaters were showing *On the Beach* (1959), a bleak film depicting the end of the world because of radioactive fallout caused by a nuclear war. Mutant ants and radioactive monsters no longer sufficed; civilization stood at the edge of a precipice. With the push of a button, it could destroy itself. People now spoke of "massive retaliation," "mutually assured destruction," and—with a nod to the economy—"a bigger bang for a buck." The nuclear threat was never far from anyone's mind. [For more on media responses to the Cold War, see chapter 10, "Performing Arts."]

THE KOREAN WAR

On June 25, 1950, North Korean forces attacked South Korea, prompt-ing an immediate military response from both the United Nations and the United States. Many U.N. member nations shipped troops to the distant peninsula, all under a unified command. By far the largest contingent came from the United States. For the next few years, a bloody war raged throughout Korea, and the government employed the disingenuous term "police action" to describe the free world's attempt to hold back Commu-nism. In 1953, the parties agreed to an armistice, and peace negotiations dragged on for years thereafter. This war boasted neither victors nor losers, an unsettling fact for Americans used to winning all their encoun-ters with foreign adversaries. During the decade, over 1.8 million U.S. troops saw service in Korea, with more than 33,600 losing their lives in combat and some 103,000 sustaining wounds.[13]

American popular culture hesitated to deal with the conflict, especially given its murky political overtones. Nuclear annihilation was one thing, but an unpopular, misunderstood war in a distant land was another. As a result, the Korean conflict has come down to the present as America's "forgotten war," and it remains relatively unknown to most citizens, de-spite its bloody toll. [For more on how popular media handled Korea, see chapters 8, "Literature," and 10, "Performing Arts."]

McCARTHYISM

For many TV fans, the various Congressional hearings that marked the decade served as some of the most engrossing series on the air. They had all the stuff of good popular culture: drama, heroes and villains, sensation-alism, and even a few surprises. Most prominent were the McCarthy hear-ings into Communist infiltration in the national government. In February 1950, Joseph McCarthy, the junior senator from Wisconsin, loudly pro-claimed that he had evidence that 205 active Communist agents had been employed at the State Department. Leading the Senate Investigations Sub-committee, McCarthy launched a campaign based on fears, innuendo, and smears to track down Communists in government. An outright witch-hunt, the subcommittee often used guilt by accusation to besmirch its victims. By 1957, some six million individuals had been investigated by various related agencies and committees because of alleged sympathies to the Communist cause. Out of those six million, only a small handful ever got convicted.

McCarthy likewise offered no hard evidence for his ceaseless claims, but many people nevertheless took them at their face value. Reelected in 1952, McCarthy began a full-scale assault on anyone and everyone he deemed subversive. Finally, in March of 1954, the esteemed Columbia Broadcast-ing System newsman Edward R. Murrow aired a special program on his

The 1950s witnessed the frightening power of mass media to create celebrities overnight, such as Senator Joseph McCarthy. A relatively unknown politician, at the height of the Cold War he went on a witch-hunting campaign, purportedly to uncover Communists in government. Thanks to ceaseless television coverage, he emerged as a demagogue, cowing his critics into silence.
Source: Library of Congress.

series, *See It Now*. He titled the special "A Report on Senator Joseph P. McCarthy," and he and producer Fred R. Friendly did the show at their own expense. CBS and its sponsors took a hands-off attitude toward the production, and the CBS "eye" logo was not to be seen. Despite its lack of network and commercial support, the presentation gave viewers a rare picture of the senator, most of it in his own words, and most of them damning. His crude, intimidating attacks on individuals and institutions smacked of a tyrant, a browbeater, a thug.

McCarthy responded to Murrow, labeling him a "jackal" and implying that Murrow himself was a Communist sympathizer. But his blustering rejoinder proved ineffective; the damage had been done. Undeterred, McCarthy pushed ahead with his investigations and included the U.S. Army Signal Corps as one of his targets. Televised hearings with the Army followed shortly after his exchanges with Murrow. With millions watching,

McCarthy came across again as a loutish bully. His charges went unsub-
stantiated, and the country soon tired of his demagoguery; his influence
waned, and the investigations drew to a close.

In 1956, the Senate took away his chairmanship of the investigative committee. The Senate eventually censured him and any remaining influence
ended. Joseph McCarthy died in 1957; that same year, the Supreme Court
began earnestly to restore rights taken away from Americans by the "Red
Scare" brought about by his hearings, and the term "McCarthyism" has
come to mean unfair, unsupported attacks on individuals by governmen-
tal groups, especially Congressional committees.[14]

BLACKLISTING

With a distant war in Korea being waged against Communist adversaries, and McCarthy's claims of Communist infiltration at all levels of government, a climate of fear and suspicion descended on the nation. As
McCarthy grew more shrill in his accusations, few would challenge him.
He was aided and abetted by an organization calling itself AWARE, which
in 1950 commenced publishing a newsletter titled *Red Channels*; it purported to identify 151 individuals from the performing arts that the organization found "subversive." No one—from networks to studios to
sponsors—offered to stand up and challenge these vicious attacks, and
innocent people found themselves blacklisted, unable to work in radio,
film, or television. For many, the stigma of the blacklist lingered until well
into the 1960s, and the damage proved permanent.[15]

This divisive atmosphere struck Hollywood particularly hard. The
House Un-American Activities Committee (or HUAC, for short), an investigative arm of Congress, seized on the issue of dangerous influences
corrupting the nation's entertainment center. A number of congressmen,
convinced the content of movies had been colored by subversive elements
intent upon spreading Communist lies and innuendo, enthusiastically
joined the fray. The media have always been suspect in the eyes of some
government agencies and elected representatives, and the chance to de-
nounce what they perceived as treasonous activity proved irresistible.
Hearings were held, and many Hollywood personalities received calls to
testify. Actors, producers, directors, and writers faced a dilemma: whether
or not to inform on their colleagues about possible Communist ties.

During the 1930s and 1940s, the social unrest of the Depression and the
country's alliance with Russia during World War II had caused some
members of the film community to take an interest in the Communist
party. For most, any real party connections proved slight, often the result
of youthful curiosity in years past. The committee felt otherwise, however,
and pursued a selected group of writers and producers with a relentless
tenacity. Ten individuals, destined to be known as the Hollywood Ten,

were indicted for contempt of Congress. They suffered the fate of being blacklisted, an action that put their careers in tatters—unable to write, produce, or otherwise participate in the industry. Of course, Russia and China had been American allies in World War II, and now, in an ironic twist, the two countries were demonized as America's implacable enemies. Those persons with past or present associations with either one found themselves branded traitors.

Only with time and the lifting of the climate of fear that so preoccupied Hollywood did things return to normal. A sensitive film that addresses the issue of informing is director Elia Kazin's *On the Waterfront* (1954). One of the bedrock beliefs in American culture is a distaste for "telling" on one's friends, and yet that was exactly what the HUAC investigators wanted their subjects to do. In a splendid performance, Marlon Brando burnished his acting reputation portraying a young boxer who must deal with conflicting loyalties. Kazin had been deeply involved in the hearings and did indeed offer evidence that proved detrimental to some of his colleagues, and the film indirectly comments on the whole process and its impacts on belief systems.

Don Siegel's *Invasion of the Body Snatchers* (1956), another disturbing film from the period, works on a different level. Mysterious pods from outer space descend on a community, ingeniously taking over the physical appearance of the inhabitants. Who can be trusted? Who can be believed? Who is what he or she appears to be? The script plays well into McCarthy-era fears and the Red Scare they precipitated.

For example, in 1953, the popular syndicated columnist Walter Winchell asserted that none other than Lucille Ball, star of *I Love Lucy* and one of the most popular women in America, had been a Communist. This occurred during the McCarthy hearings, when such claims could sink a career. In a moving denial, her husband Desi Arnaz addressed the charge publicly—on television, just before the beginning of one of the *I Love Lucy* shows. In response, the audience gave him a standing ovation, and the matter disappeared. More often, the taint of Communism proved fatal, true or untrue. Had Ball's show not been the most popular one on television, it seems doubtful she would have received any support.

CRIME IN AMERICA

Estes Kefauver, a young senator from Tennessee, played alongside McCarthy in an entirely separate Congressional investigation. He looked into organized crime and racketeering in the spring of 1950 and did so on national television. His committee's findings heightened public awareness about criminal activities in the United States. They also led to a spate of books, magazine articles, and movies that purported to show the extent of crime and corruption within the country. Most of the called witnesses did not do well under the TV lights. In the minds of viewers, they appeared guilty on the basis of their conduct on the stand. The unblinking eye of television revealed their reluctance to testify, and their body language reinforced viewer perceptions. And, for most Americans, the witness's testimony verified the existence of the Mafia—"the Mob," "the Syndicate"—a fact reinforced in television shows like *The Untouchables* (1959–1963) and a string of movies like *Murder, Inc.* (1951), *Hoodlum Empire* (1952), *New York Confidential* (1954), *The Brothers Rico* (1957), and *Al Capone* (1959).

Another Congressional group, the McClellan Committee, also investigated organized crime. Chaired by Arkansas Senator John L. McClellan, it focused more on the infiltration of racketeering into some labor unions. Considerable labor unrest marked the 1950s, a situation brought about by raging industrial demand and worker discontent about wages and benefits in such a prosperous economy. Union rolls swelled, and numerous strikes occurred as labor strove to be treated more equably in the postwar years. The McClellan Committee began its work in early 1957, and names like Teamster's Union president Dave Beck, Jimmy Hoffa (Beck's successor), and investigative lawyer Robert Kennedy became commonplace in general conversation. Although little changed in the unions, the exposure of corruption did make them more open about their finances.

Both the Kefauver and McClellan hearings served to elevate the celebrity status of J. Edgar Hoover. Director of the Federal Bureau of Investigation since 1924, Hoover made no secret of his animosity toward crime, disloyalty, subversion, and overly liberal courts. Buoyed by the popular press he was receiving during the hearings, he seemed independent of any controlling agency. Neither Eisenhower nor the Justice Department did much to rein in Hoover, and he therefore amassed great power, including the creation of secret files on American citizens. Given his autonomy, Hoover closed out the decade as one of the most feared men in government. But in long-running radio shows like *The FBI in Peace and War* (1944–1958) and *This Is Your FBI* (1945–1953), the Bureau was presented as above reproach. Television crime offerings occasionally included federal agents in their plots, but did not get around to an actual FBI series until 1965. No such hesitation occurred in the movies; from *"G" Men* back in 1935, a succession of films rolled out of Hollywood celebrating the Bureau and, by extension, Hoover. For the 1950s, the titles ranged from *FBI Girl* (1951) to *The FBI Story* (1959), with a number in between. For popular media, Hoover and the FBI could do no wrong.

Amid all this adulation, the Bureau instituted its first "Ten Most Wanted" list in 1950. It had grown out of an article about at-large criminals, and Director Hoover thought public familiarity with the faces of such criminals might help bring about their capture. Within a year after their appearance on wanted posters, nine of the ten were caught, and the FBI made The Ten Most Wanted a permanent part of its crime-fighting weaponry. Thanks to brilliant public relations, the public applauded the move, and Hoover solidified his position as the country's number one crime fighter.[16]

THE EISENHOWER YEARS AND
THE RISE OF TELEVISION

With the foregoing as reminders of a threatening, challenging present and future, Americans continued to indulge themselves as never before. Eisenhower, a seasoned military leader, had been elected to the presidency in 1952, and his conservative, patriarchal approach to a dangerous world reassured nervous citizens. He was "everybody's grandfather." His golf

A grand old tradition of American sports involves having the president throw out the first baseball, thus inaugurating the new season. This 1956 shot depicts President Eisenhower flashing his election-winning grin; standing beside him (right) is Yankees manager Casey Stengel, himself an immensely popular sports figure. Source: Library of Congress.

game, his weekend painting, and even his health problems elicited more popular attention than did his abilities as a leader. For most Americans, he presented an image of calm authority. The decade marked, in fact, the increasing use of public relations and advertising techniques in the political arena. That Eisenhower could project such a picture of fatherly confidence overshadowed the difficulties he had articulating issues, and Americans voted their preference for imagery over content in both the 1952 and 1956 presidential elections.

The importance of strong media ties could be seen in the Republican and Democratic national conventions held in July 1952. The first such political conventions to be televised, delegates were aware of cameras and microphones everywhere, and their presence had a clear effect. Little deal making could take place outside the range of the omnipresent cameras, a decided change from the smoke-filled rooms of the past. As Republican enthusiasm for Eisenhower grew, the unblinking gaze of national media helped him win on the first ballot. On the Democratic side, it took three ballots to nominate Adlai Stevenson, but the party did not wish to appear divided to a national television audience.

In the midst of the 1952 campaign, Eisenhower's running mate, California Senator Richard M. Nixon, was accused of improperly using funds and accepting gifts. Alarmists urged Eisenhower to drop Nixon from the ticket. In response, Nixon turned to television and delivered his famous "Checkers" speech, a moment in television history that illustrates the enormous power the medium could wield. An audience estimated at 58 million heard and saw his denials. "Checkers" was a cute cocker spaniel, a gift Nixon challenged anyone to take from his daughters. His somewhat melodramatic defense played well; audiences viewed the charges against him as ham-handed attempts by overzealous Democrats to discredit him. In short, popular imagery overrode any reasoned investigation. Eisenhower retained Nixon in his campaign, and the two savored a strong victory.[17]

THE CULTURAL FERMENT OF THE 1950s

For many American intellectuals, the specter of an undifferentiated mass culture that could lead public opinion seemed far more frightening than any Russian warheads. They saw the nation falling into a kind of mindless conformity, accepting, without question, the nightly offerings of network television, along with Top 40 radio programming and big box-office movies. Those elements, coupled with the paternalistic philosophy of the Eisenhower administration, created undercurrents of dissent and revolt that simmered throughout the decade.

Jack Kerouac set out to rewrite the American novel, Jackson Pollock challenged his fellow artists with abstract "drip paintings," and the suspect insolence of Elvis Presley and James Dean bothered many. Marlon Brando sweated and grunted to the delight of adolescents everywhere, and Charlie Parker and Dizzy Gillespie took jazz places it had never been before. True, Ernest Hemingway's heroes still adhered to a manly code of behavior, Norman Rockwell's *Saturday Evening Post* covers continued to captivate millions, Gary Cooper represented all that was good in the Western myth, Perry Como crooned in a reassuring baritone, and good, old traditional Dixieland Jazz enjoyed something of a revival. Depending on one's focus during the fifties, the decade could seem complacent and conformist, or it could be filled with threatening change and shrill individuals who turned their backs on anything held dear by generations of Americans.

For the average American, however, the intellectual debates of the era occurred offstage, unseen and unheard. With the reality of the Cold War intruding into daily lives, the thought of a cultural consensus sounded reassuring, not threatening. Rock 'n' roll seemed far more challenging to worried parents than discussions of cultural hegemony. Added to that were the changes brought about by civil rights legislation, by school integration, and by a sense of rebellion on the part of youth across the nation. Nothing was as it used to be.[18]

CONFORMITY

In the popular mind, people conformed during the 1950s. The sprawling suburbs of ranch and split-level homes exemplified this social conformity. The typical suburbanite earned slightly more than his city-dwelling counterpart and differing lifestyles reflected this inequality. The suburbs also quietly exploited other, more unfortunate, kinds of conformity: racial, ethnic, and social. Blacks, Hispanics, Asians, Jews, and a host of "others" were kept out of most developments. The "men in the gray flannel suits" were white and Christian, heads of nuclear families, and proudly middle class. Their clothing, their architecture, their jobs, and their leisure all supported this kind of sameness. Hollywood, ever observant of social trends, exploited the move to suburbia in *No Down Payment* (1957), a melodramatic tale of several families and their problems living in what had been promised to be paradise. The title says it all.

Movies, radio, and especially TV usually served as the voices and visions of conformity. These media provided common experience. It came across as middlebrow—neither high culture nor low. Media imagery fostered conspicuous consumption, the idea of keeping up with your neighbors. And because in this imagery men worked and women stayed at home to care for the family, advertisers targeted women as the primary consumers of all the goods and services pouring forth from the bottomless American cornucopia.

The times themselves added to this emphasis on consumption: the United States moved from a devastating world war and immediately into the Cold War, making the 1950s an unsettled decade in international terms. Middle-class Americans, flush with prosperity, responded by retreating into cocoons of secure, look-alike suburbs that preserved traditions and provided a sense of domestic security.

SUMMARY

Outwardly, the decade appeared to be one of confidence, conformity, and prosperity. But appearances can be deceiving; just below the surface of prosperity and complacency lurked dissonance and change, rebellion and anxiety. In retrospect, the cultural upheavals, the sweeping changes, that would characterize the last third of the twentieth century, had been put into place in the 1950s, simmering and waiting to come to a boil.

But popular culture, especially movies and television, also stressed consensus, that opposing voices could reach agreement. An unstated, but nonetheless effective, policy of censorship characterized much popular culture of the 1950s. Americans were expected to have an affirmative sense of their lives, and any darker thoughts ran into resistance. Small wonder, then, that much popular culture espoused this point of view. From small-screen sitcoms to VistaVision spectacles, the center ruled; extremism and dissent had little voice in popular culture, and those challenging the status quo usually saw themselves depicted in a negative way.

The 1950s

2

World of Youth

Because more teens stayed in school after World War II, about three-quarters of all American 16-year-olds still attended classes in the 1950s. Students saw graduation from high school as the ticket to the middle class and a more fruitful life. Thanks to the GI Bill and the influx of veterans returning to civilian life, college enrollments also rose. Because they were not being absorbed into the workforce as readily as before, teenagers emerged as a more identifiable demographic group with a lifestyle distinctly its own. Prosperity gave both children and adolescents the means to enjoy the decade's wave of consumerism, making them a viable force in all areas of popular culture. From cars to movies to music, the youth market exerted a significant impact on American life.

TEEN PROSPERITY

New opportunities for teenagers seeking part-time employment presented themselves as the American economy shifted toward a service-oriented model and away from its more traditional industrial base. Baby-sitting and mowing lawns provided occasional income, but better-paying jobs like clerking in stores, pumping gas, and waiting on customers in the growing fast-food industry proved more popular avenues. Part-time work allowed teens to complete their education and, because many of these jobs were new, they did not threaten established adult workers.

Remaining in school effectively isolated teenagers from most older people. As a result, perceptions about adolescents were based on faulty or incomplete information, and adults often categorized teens as lazy and unproductive, an image popular media reinforced. Hollywood responded

A typical scene repeated across the country during the decade. Books and supplies in front of him, food at hand, and the television set going, an American teenager gets down to the business of homework. Shot in 1954, TV could already be found in over 55 percent of American homes. Source: Library of Congress.

with films like *The Wild One* (1954), *Rock Around the Clock* (1955), and *Rebel without a Cause* (1955), pictures that depict teens as alienated from society, at odds with authority, and generally inarticulate individuals who cared little about anything. Best-sellers included such titles as J.D. Salinger's *The Catcher in the Rye* (1951), John Steinbeck's *East of Eden* (1952), Herman Wouk's *Marjorie Morningstar* (1955), and Warren Miller's *The Cool World* (1959), all novels of loneliness and adolescent angst.

Laws and traditions further hindered young people in any quest for adult responsibility and privilege: voting rights, full-time employment, and social customs like curfew hours and drinking regulations prevented teens from assuming what they viewed as adult roles. Yet, in interviews and sampling, most American adolescents espoused adult values, even if their behaviors at times suggested they participated in some form of revolt against traditional mores. Girls wanted marriage and family; boys wanted good jobs and financial security. And just like their parents, they defined success and security with material goods. The more you had, the happier you were; materialism ruled the day for all ages.[1]

One sector of American life courted young people assiduously: the business community. All facets of commerce saw this growing population as under-realized consumers. On average, American teenagers in the 1950s made more in weekly allowance ($10–$15) alone than many families took in as weekly income during the Depression years of the 1930s. Because of work or generous allowances, their pockets and wallets bulged with spendable cash. Collectively, U.S. teens spent billions every year of the decade, topping out at $10 billion in 1959. And, unlike earlier times, they viewed this money as theirs alone—it was not required to assist in family needs. Since kids could spend their incomes as they pleased, they created a formidable new consumer force, independent and self-directed.[2]

As the buying power of this market became recognized, publishers rushed into print cheap magazines aimed at readers 12–18 years old. The first of this new breed to appear were *Dig* and *Teen*, both of which hit newsstands in 1955. Close on their heels came *Confidential Teen Romances*, *Flip*, *Hepcats*, *Hollywood Teenagers*, *Modern Teen*, *Sixteen*, and in a titling process using "teen" that had to confuse browsers, *Teen Parade*, *Teen Screen*, *Teen Time*, and *Teen Today*. Employing youthful writers and editors, these periodicals made no pretense of adults giving advice to the young; they counseled their hordes of readers on an equal, or peer, basis. Much of it revolved around looks and popularity, two areas of concern to most American teenagers.[3]

Older, more established periodicals also targeted the youth market in both content and advertising. For example, *Seventeen*, a successful magazine geared toward young women, had been founded in 1944. As might be expected, it ran innumerable ads for fashions and cosmetics. But the editors also realized that many of their readers, in keeping with a trend toward earlier marriages in the 1950s, were moving from schoolgirls to young wives and mothers with little time in between. To broaden *Seventeen*'s appeal, the publishers saw to it that appliances, china and silver, furniture, and white goods also got promoted on its pages. On the advice side, the popular Seventeen *Book of Young Living* (1957), an earnest guide to manners and mores that stressed the need for landing the proper spouse and achieving financial security, attracted a wide readership.

One of the shapers of this burgeoning youth market was Eugene Gilbert. He organized thousands of teenaged pollsters to go out and learn about the wants and needs of their peers. His weekly column, "What Young People Are Thinking," ran in over three hundred newspapers and served as required reading for sales and advertising staffers everywhere. Gilbert could assure his business clients that adolescents added billions of dollars to the U.S. economy. With the expertise garnered by his youthful pollsters, he predicted with considerable accuracy trends within this age group. It took time, but a vast array of products and services were marketed directly to eager and youthful consumers.[4]

LEISURE ACTIVITIES

Like their elders, American youth listened to radio at the beginning of the decade, often over four hours a day. Serials dominated in the late afternoon for those 12 and under, and music and comedy shows at any time proved favorites for teenagers. But television entered more and more homes, and young people quickly gave it their full attention. By 1955, this new competitor halved radio listening, as young viewers watched upwards of four hours of TV daily. By 1960, radio served as pure background—almost always music—and television emerged as the preferred medium. Yet, aside from a handful of teenage-oriented shows like *American Bandstand*, most TV programming went to a broad, general viewership. [The remarkable popularity of *Bandstand* and its host, Dick Clark, is covered in chapter 9, "Music."] The absence of shows designed for more specific age groups seemed to matter little to adolescents, however; they watched everything from adult dramas to sitcoms to kiddie cartoons, and even the test patterns. New and novel, TV attracted everyone, and audiences displayed little discrimination in their viewing habits.[5]

The fifties of course offered more than radio and television. Just like youth in previous decades, American teens enjoyed school football and basketball games, parties, and any event that involved dancing. A new generation rediscovered old favorites such as the shag and the lindy, and improvised steps often replaced traditional ones. Along with the frenetic jitterbug and its many variations, young people took to the floor for the Hokey Pokey, the Bunny Hop, Walkin' the Dog, the Madison, the Stroll, the Hand Jive, and Latin numbers like the mambo and the cha-cha. But when the band played a more romantic number, slow dancing ruled— sometimes to the consternation of attending chaperones and others. How close, how entwined, a couple should be while the Penguins harmonized on "Earth Angel" (1955) or Elvis Presley crooned "Love Me Tender" (1956) became a subject of some debate. Some slow steps got tagged with the name "dirty dancing" because of the suggestive ways partners expressed themselves. And in July of 1959, when Ray Charles's rollicking "What'd I Say" soared to the top of the charts, many older people became convinced that modern music and dance had gone too far. The song's blatantly sexual grunts and groans left little to the imagination, a fact not lost on a captivated teenage audience. Shaking their hips and singing along with the record, young people from junior high through college celebrated their freedom from strait-laced traditions.[6]

With the help of a portable record player (center), a group of teens shows off the Bunny Hop. Note the dressiness of the participants—coats, ties, skirts, blouses. This dance fad captivated millions, first surfacing in San Francisco in 1953. It made a big hit of bandleader Ray Anthony's recording by the same title. A form of line dancing, it preceded the heavy beat of rock 'n' roll. Source: Library of Congress.

Along with new dance steps came a new approach to dances themselves: hops. A hop (the name comes from dancing itself; i.e., "hopping") could be highly organized or an impromptu event between classes at lunchtime. It required no more than a gathering place, some records, and a sound system. Several popular hits, such as Danny and the Juniors' "At the Hop" (1957) and Bobby Darin's "Queen of the Hop" (1958), confirmed its immediate popularity. Throughout the fifties, at school gyms and cafeterias, the local YMCA or YWCA, some churches, fraternal halls, or anyplace else that had a level floor, hops became a new social event. If that floor happened to be a polished hardwood basketball court, it became a "sock hop." Dancers had to remove their shoes to avoid marring the surface, but that did little to dampen enthusiasm. What mattered was the music; the rhythms of rock 'n' roll demanded dancing, and hops fulfilled that function with little fuss or expense.

ROCK 'N' ROLL

Prior to the 1950s, most American popular music attracted a mainstream (i.e., white, middle-class) audience. The rise of rock 'n' roll in the 1950s signaled the fragmentation of that traditionally dominant category, and the nation's musical choices expanded markedly. Jazz, classical, mood, big band, easy listening, country, vocal—whatever one's tastes, radio stations, record shops, or television shows could be found that carried those preferences.

If the Cold War or inflation worried adults, rock 'n' roll terrified them. For many older Americans, the roots of this new music seemed particularly bothersome. The most direct antecedent was rhythm and blues, long a staple format among black audiences. But rhythm and blues crossed an imaginary line and got discovered by white youths. And that discovery meant the widespread commercialization of R & B as interpreted (or "covered"—i.e., made more "acceptable") by white groups doing toned-down versions of numbers introduced by black performers. Thus was born rock 'n' roll, the musical and cultural event of the 1950s. The lineage of this new music hardly concerned its enthusiastic fans; what did matter was you could dance to it. It possessed a relentless rhythm, something impossible to lose out on the dance floor. Nevertheless, schools, churches, and parent groups voiced vigorous opposition to rock 'n' roll and they often convinced radio stations to omit it from their playlists.

Despite the protests, the relentless rise of rock 'n' roll served as a kind of cultural and racial barometer. The walls of segregation had begun to crumble in the 1950s, and so did the artificial barriers between white and black music and musicians, especially in the area of pop music. Almost overnight, that infectious backbeat stole across the nation, a heady mix of rhythm and blues, a dash of country, and a leavening of pop. A youthful declaration of independence, the more their elders disliked it, the more the kids loved it. As one song proclaimed, "Rock 'n' Roll Is Here to Stay" (Danny and the Juniors, 1958). And stay it did; for young people, rock 'n' roll proved irresistible. [For more on the rise of rock 'n' roll during the 1950s, see chapter 9, "Music."]

CRUISIN'

With the prosperity that accompanied the 1950s, many teenagers owned cars. Out of this conspicuous wealth came a curious adolescent ritual: "cruisin'." An automobile gave a teen autonomy, and cruisin' provided a means of getting away from anxious adults and mixing with one's peers. Cruisin' indicated no particular destination; it simply meant driving—alone, with a date, or in a car full of friends—from one hangout to another, seeing people, and being seen. Whenever possible, "being seen" meant driving one's own car, not the family vehicle. The automobile emerged as an extension of the driver, or possibly vice versa, as some contemporary psychologists and social commentators would observe.[7]

Young people took to cruisin', and an informal network of places to visit quickly evolved in most communities. Drive-in restaurants proved the most popular, places where carhops served customers directly in their parked automobiles. The thousands of drive-in movie theaters then in business also ranked high in popularity. What played on the screen was secondary to just being there. Because the theaters initially charged the number of people that could be seen in a car, kids delighted in packing trunks or hiding under blankets to try to get in free. It was not long before the drive-ins charged a set price "per carload," whether it was just two people or ten. For some critics, the drive-in deserved its nickname of "passion pit," since the privacy of a darkened vehicle allowed couples to "make out" or "neck." Theater security officers wound their way among the parked cars, tapping on windows that had gotten too steamy, and jokes abounded about "getting caught."

Cruisin' allowed teens, wherever they congregated, an independent sphere of action, a place to escape adult authority. This autonomy enlarged the gulf between adolescents and their parents, one made wider by the easy availability of an automobile. Some saw all this as youth succumbing to a more permissive sexual code of behavior, and it bothered others that young people seemed to get their values from peers and media, not from parents. As a final straw, much youthful behavior challenged the prevailing idea of family-centered togetherness as espoused in TV sitcoms, magazines, schools, and churches.

HOT RODS AND DRAG RACING

Many American teenagers, but primarily males, worked at "customizing" those cars that made cruisin' possible. This involved individualizing the vehicle, making it one of a kind. They might start out with a regular unembellished model bought at a dealer, used or new, and modify it. Or they could take an older auto—commonly called a "jalopy"—and redesign it from the tires on up. Regardless, their physical alterations might create something more akin to a racing car than to a street vehicle. A new vocabulary evolved to describe this addition to youth culture: "hot rods" were "souped up" (i.e., performance exceeded that of a normal car, especially when accelerating); "duals" were dual-exhaust pipes, usually with a throaty roar; "chopping" and "channeling" involved cutting down or removing portions of the vehicle's body; "bull-nosing" meant stripping off exterior hood ornamentation; "skins" were tires; and so on.[8]

In addition to a general fascination with automobiles, there existed a subculture focused on racing hot rods and similarly altered vehicles. The term "drag racing" had entered the language during the 1940s; it meant competing to see whose car could accelerate the fastest over a measured course. If no track, or "drag strip," were available, a lonely road would suffice—and often did. A favorite teen activity involved getting a number of dragsters (or the family sedan, if need be) together and then timing them as they zoomed down the macadam.

As cars proliferated, drag racing became almost a rite of passage for many young people. A frightening variation, but one that caught the attention of adults, law officials, and finally the media, was the game of "chicken." The rules for chicken were simple: two cars got a distance apart and then hurtled straight at each other. The driver that veered away from a head-on collision was, of course, the "chicken." This activity only further convinced most adults that hot rods, drag racing, and anything connected with them, were inherently dangerous and needed to be controlled, another wedge in the widening rift between generations.

By the end of the fifties, dragsters and custom cars constituted a significant part of teenage culture. Even at a high school mixer, their popularity might get recognized with the Hot Rod Hop, a dance number that enjoyed brief popularity around 1955. The booming recording industry should have taken note of this trend by releasing numerous songs celebrating hot-rodding, but remarkably few came out during the decade. Bill Haley's "Rocket 88" (1951), Chuck Berry's "Maybelline" (1955), and the Playmates' "Beep Beep" (1958) have cars as part of their content, but they hardly stand as songs about hot rods and customizing. Only in Hal Singer's 1955 "Hot Rod" did the subject get addressed directly, and the number had no impact, either with audiences or the music business. The designations vocal groups gave themselves proved another matter altogether. Popular cars proliferated, with such names as the Belairs (from a Chevrolet model), the Bonnevilles (Pontiac), the Fleetwoods (Cadillac), the Impalas (another Chevrolet), and the Thunderbirds (Ford's hot-selling sports car of the era).

Hollywood, on the other hand, lost little time in exploiting the automobile-driven aspect of adolescent life. Using the time-tested formula of equating speed and daredevils with misbehavior, a host of movies came out aimed directly at teen audiences. *Hot Rod Girl* (1956), *Hot Rod Rumble* (1957), *Dragstrip Girl* (1957), *Dragstrip Riot* (1958), *Hot Rod Gang* (1958), *Joy Ride* (1958), and *Ghost of Dragstrip Hollow* (1959) served as mindless time killers at drive-in theaters across the land. But the studios also released a handful of more thoughtful productions. One film in particular stands out for its sympathetic portrayal of adolescent alienation: *Rebel without a Cause* (1955). The movie, which catapulted James Dean to stardom, employs a game of chicken in its plot. A disturbing scene to watch, it reinforces the important roles rituals play among the young.

A number of popular magazines oriented toward this growing car culture made their appearance in the late 1940s and into the 1950s. The pioneers— *Road & Track*, *Hot Rod*, and *Motor Trend* (1947, 1948, and 1949, respectively)— at first targeted returning veterans who might want to tinker with automobiles, but soon became more inclusive and reached substantially higher circulations in the fifties. New titles like *Car Craft* (1953–) and *Car & Driver* (1956–) also attracted a wide readership, and teenagers everywhere had to be counted among their most enthusiastic patrons.

COURTSHIP

Americans married at increasingly younger ages throughout the 1950s. Statistics showed that men tied the knot at 22 or so, down from 24, and women wed at 20, down from 22. By the end of the decade, the majority of brides married at 19 years of age. This decrease in years meant that dating commenced earlier than ever before.[9]

Parents, fearful their children would miss out on something, encouraged informal dates in the first teenage years. This emphasis on bringing girls and boys together often resulted in many teenagers "going steady." For junior and senior high school students, rules and rituals soon evolved around steady dating. It gave both partners a kind of social insurance: a regular date and no insecurities about going out instead of waiting for an invitation somewhere. Couples were expected to remain loyal to one another, and young males made a visible sign of commitment, usually with the gift of a ring. Mass-produced, cheap, gold- and silver-plated "friendship rings" often got worn around the neck instead of on a finger. Charms for the girl's bracelet, athletic letter sweaters, or matching articles of clothing also served as indicators that a couple dated steadily. For those in college, the general rules remained the same, but fraternity and sorority pins often substituted for friendship rings. Worn on a blouse or sweater, the pins signified that the wearer had been spoken for. They also represented a kind of pre-engagement, a tangible symbol that preceded the traditional ring.

The music and movie industries quickly acknowledged the phenomenon of going steady. "Too Young" (1951) and "Too Young (to Go Steady)" (1955) served as big hits for singing star Nat "King" Cole, despite the four-year gap in release dates. "A Teenager's Romance" (Ricky Nelson, 1957), "Young Love" (Sonny James, 1957), "Teenage Crush" (Tommy Sands, 1957), and "A Teenager in Love" (Dion and the Belmonts, 1959) lamented the tribulations of romance among the young. If adults listened to their children's music, they could worry about titles like "Let's Elope" (Janis Martin, 1956) and "We're Gonna Get Married" (Lloyd Price, 1959) on the radio. Hollywood chimed in with a couple of forgettable 1958 movies,

Going Steady and *Life Begins at 17*, the plots of which suggest intense dating can lead only to unhappiness. Even more obvious were pictures such as *Unwed Mother* (1958), *Blue Denim* (1959), and *Diary of a High School Bride* (1959).

Going steady meant a forced intimacy between male and female adolescents, a dangerous combination in the eyes of many adults and child psychologists. By 1955, numerous parents' groups were urging that steady dating be discouraged for young persons. They feared an increase in sexual experimentation and subsequent teen pregnancies. As the decade drew to a close, the custom nonetheless remained popular among youth, and their elder's fears became statistics: out-of-wedlock births rose sharply and no one found any easy solutions to the age-old problems associated with sex and adolescence.[10]

JUVENILE DELINQUENCY

For the doomsayers lamenting the evolving teen ethos, it came as no surprise that crime statistics rose throughout the decade, especially violent crime involving young people. Statistically, the arrests of people under age 18 doubled between 1950 and 1959, so there existed some truth in people's fears. A judicially active legal system supported equal protection, but it also championed individual rights. As a result, judges and juries upset many people as the rights of defendants were expanded, and "permissive courts" got blamed for rising crime.

For example, Benjamin Fine wrote *1,000,000 Delinquents* in 1954 and it enjoyed a brief time on the best-seller lists. The number in the title refers to how many teens would be hauled into court during a typical year. But numbers can deceive: admittedly large, it represented only a small percentage of the total teenage population; it ignored the additional hardworking, career-oriented millions who seldom got into trouble.

Mass media picked up on juvenile delinquency as a theme; rock 'n' roll and wild movies only reinforced negative perceptions adults already had about young people. In 1955, the *Saturday Evening Post* declared delinquency "the shame of the nation." Movies with sensational titles like *Crime in the Streets* (1956), *The Delinquents* (1957), *Jailhouse Rock* (1957), *High School Hellcats* (1958), *High School Confidential!* (1958), and *Juvenile Jungle* (1958) only further convinced parents, school administrators, and politicians that the youth of America had indeed embarked on the road to ruin. Even Broadway contributed to the perception of youth run amok. *West Side Story* opened in 1957 and proved to be one of the stage's most enduring musicals. Its plot, a retelling of Shakespeare's *Romeo and Juliet*, involves teen gangs in New York City. Full of violence, the play pits the Jets against the Sharks as they resolve—tragically—issues of territory and identity.

Audiences loved it, especially its score, but *West Side Story* also reinforced the image that teenagers scoffed at laws and good behavior.[11]

Reacting to media sensationalism and worried constituents, the United States Senate convened the Senate Judiciary Subcommittee in 1955 to investigate the causes of, and solutions to, juvenile delinquency. Chaired by the popular Senator Estes Kefauver of Tennessee, the group pored over comic books, watched hours of television, and saw innumerable movies. In 1956, with much fanfare, the committee released its findings. In three separate reports, no concrete links between mass media and juvenile crime could be established. Although all three media were criticized for glamorizing sex and promoting gratuitous violence, the findings proved inconclusive. And, aside from the Comics Code Authority—an industry board of review set up just before Kefauver's hearings—little in the way of media censorship grew out of the committee's activities. In time, the public grew tired of the investigation, and juvenile delinquency faded as an issue of national concern. [For more on the Comics Code Authority, see chapter 12, "Visual Arts."]

THE CRISIS IN EDUCATION

Throughout the fifties, school enrollments steadily rose, both in the percentage of young people staying in school and in sheer numbers enrolled. A million or more new students entered public schools each year of the decade, and the new-student population grew at twice the rate of the general population. In 1950, about 29 million K–12 students attended public schools; in 1959, the number had grown to over 40 million. And, whereas 79 percent of persons aged 5–19 remained in school in 1950, by 1960 the figure had risen to 88.6 percent, or an almost 10 percent jump.[12]

Despite the growth, critics of American education abounded. In 1955, Rudolf Flesch published *Why Johnny Can't Read: And What You Can Do About It.* The first part of the title became almost a cliché, and the sensational book served as a call to arms for many around the country. Flesch urged increased use of phonics and keeping kids away from television. Phonics would familiarize children with word structures, whereas TV stresses images over reading, something he strongly objected to. No resolution could be reached, but the book did bring reading deficiencies to people's attention.

In 1957, Paul Woodring's *A Fourth of the Nation* came out, an indictment of modern educational methods, or, more popularly, "progressive education." In impassioned prose, Woodring argued that subversives had somehow infiltrated the educational community and were substituting meaningless modern courses in place of the traditional reading, writing, and arithmetic curriculum. *Life* magazine joined the fray in 1958 with a five-part series titled "The Crisis in Education." If nothing else, these books and articles convinced many people that American education, particularly at the elementary and secondary levels, was somehow lacking.

In response to this chorus of complaints, Congress passed the National Defense Education Act (NDEA) in the fall of 1958. It provided federal aid to education, something previously left mainly to the states. In addition, it approved loans to college students, and language and science studies received healthy funding increases.[13]

Despite postwar prosperity and swelling attendance, the enrollment of women at colleges actually dropped. Two things were responsible for this phenomenon: most importantly, their places were taken by returning veterans under the generous auspices of the Servicemen's Readjustment Act, or GI Bill, as it was commonly known. For the first time ever, those who served in the military could attend college and the government would pay their tuition. Not only that, but they could also receive supplements if they were married and had families. The second factor involved women dropping out of college. During the 1950s, about two-thirds of entering female college students failed to graduate; usually they left school to marry. With few prospects for a meaningful career requiring advanced education, there existed little incentive to remain in school. Many, men and women alike, perceived college as a kind of hunting ground for finding desirable mates. Perceptions aside, the decade witnessed a boom in college enrollments: by 1953, some 25 percent of the college-age population actually attended a four-year institution, a big increase over past figures, but women made up only 35 percent of the total.[14]

YOUTHFUL VOCABULARY

Young people have always created new words and new meanings for old ones. The fifties seemed especially ripe for this kind of linguistic transformation. Aside from the traditional channel of resourceful teenagers conceiving original words to describe their activities—and thus keeping prying adults in the dark as to what might really be going on—American youth had three unique and rich postwar veins of "insider" language from which to draw: jazz, especially bebop; the so-called "Beat" movement in literature; and the argot of the drag strip. Each of these areas contributed numerous words and phrases that together enriched the language and simultaneously puzzled outsiders. In time, of course, what sounded mysterious or just plain indecipherable either entered mainstream American English or disappeared, any usefulness it might have once possessed forgotten.

For example, teen drinking habits produced such phrases as "church key" to identify a common opener for metal beer cans, since the self-opening kind remained in the future. Getting "bombed" or "stoned" meant getting drunk; "getting carded" signified that a person had his or her age verified before being permitted to purchase or consume alcohol. A "six-pack" consisted of a half-dozen cans or bottles of beer sold as a single unit.

From jazz came a wealth of words, some of which had been employed by earlier generations of musicians, but only gained wide currency in the 1950s. A stylish male could be "hip" (knowledgeable about contemporary trends), as well as "cool" (always composed and seemingly indifferent), or a "cat" (both hip and cool combined). A "hipster" went beyond hip; usually a male, he felt alienated from the manners and mores of normal society and thumbed his nose at convention. Always cool, the hipster personified many who thought themselves part of the so-called "Beat Generation" of the 1950s. [The Beat phenomenon is discussed in more detail in chapter 8, "Literature."]

On the distaff side, a fashionable woman might be called a "chick" and could likewise be cool. Cats and chicks who liked each other said they "dug" one another, just as they could "dig" (understand, appreciate) anything fashionable at the time. "Most" likewise went through a subtle linguistic change: "I dig you the most" implied strong, positive feelings for another person, and to suggest that a movie or a song was "the most" bestowed high praise, indeed.

A quality very much to be avoided was being thought of as "square." A square—the antithesis of a cat, or cool individual—did not dig ongoing trends and thus could not be an insider or "in." Squares were both unfashionable and uninitiated, true outsiders, making them "strictly from dullsville."

Cats and chicks possessing money were said to have "bread," a very cool condition; it would be a "drag" (unfortunate, boring) to be broke. Ample bread usually meant owning an automobile, or "wheels"—the nicer the wheels, the cooler the owner. In fact, it would "bug" (irritate) a cat if his cool wheels failed to impress either the chicks or the squares.

A few other entries in the rich slang of the fifties are:

Crazy: good, wonderful. A crazy set of threads identified a stylish outfit. "Crazy, man, crazy" would be a very strong compliment. "Frantic" served as a positive extension of "crazy." And something just too crazy and frantic might be called "groovy." "Groovy, man, groovy" therefore indicated a more hip—that is, cooler—way of saying "crazy, man, crazy." Clearly, the slang of the fifties took some linguistic facility to speak or interpret correctly.

Far out: something outside the ordinary, or esoteric. A far out pianist would be one who experimented with new and unusual music unfamiliar to even the hippest cats and chicks.

Flip: enthusiastic appreciation or astonishment for music, art, and the like. "I flipped for that jive" ("I really liked that music"). To "flip your lid" means to be head-over-heels (lid equals head) in love with someone or something.

Gas (and gasser): something enjoyable. "The concert was a gas." "That song is a real gasser."

Gone: If something seems too far out, it might be "gone, " as in "crazy, man, that music's gone, gone." If anything is "real gone," it has passed beyond normal experience. "He is one real gone daddy-o" would be someone truly unusual or eccentric.

Hairy: an adjective. "It was hairy, man," suggests a difficult situation, possibly dangerous.

Mary Jane: a popular euphemism of the time for marijuana (from the Spanish *Maria* and *Juana*).

Pad: one's home or apartment.

The foregoing can hardly be thought complete, but serves to introduce some of the inventiveness that characterized the slang of the fifties. In 1956, Bill Haley and His Comets memorialized an expression in a rock 'n' roll hit of the same name penned by Robert Guidry: "See You Later, Alligator!" The phrase comes from various usages dating back to the early nineteenth century, in which alligator denoted both a clever, sly man and the 1930s for a jazz or swing enthusiast.

Properly, a cool person says to another, "See you later, Alligator." Those who were hip would respond, "In a while, Crocodile!" It might all sound like silliness to later generations, but expertise with contemporary slang and wordplay set young people apart, made them a part of the in-crowd, and gave them entrée into the vibrant culture that so characterized their activities during the 1950s. Teens may have gotten unfairly dubbed the "Silent Generation," they may have appeared apathetic about events around them, but in reality they created a vibrant—even revolutionary—culture of their own. The decade served as the rich, fertile breeding ground for all the campus radicalism and protesting that became associated with the 1960s.[15]

SUMMARY

More than any previous generation, the youth of the fifties created a broad, media-based culture they could truly call their own. Prosperous beyond the dreams of past children and teenagers, this new generation had the financial clout to support those whom they felt best represented them. Accordingly, much Hollywood production was aimed at this market. Many mass magazines likewise catered to youthful readers. But nowhere was this generation's economic power more strongly exhibited than in the music business. For all intents and purposes, rock 'n' roll reflected the dreams and desires of America's young people.

PART II

POPULAR CULTURE OF THE 1950s

The 1950s

3

Advertising

In days past, except for an occasional traveling salesman or the print enticements found in newspapers and magazines, the home served as a sanctuary from merchants and their wares. With the advent of commercial radio in the thirties and forties, the haven had been breached. The rise of television in the late 1940s presented a potent new venue. It did not take long for TV to surpass both magazines and radio in advertising volume and profits although, in an era of consumption, the public needed little urging to go out and buy goods and services.

PRINT ADVERTISING AND PACKAGING

As the oldest and most traditional carrier of advertising messages, print can offer clear, glossy pictures, descriptive text, and bright packaging. Because print cannot offer sound or moving images, the presentation of the product takes on major importance. During the 1950s, improved re-production technologies allowed print to continue as a major advertising medium in newspapers and magazines, despite the fierce competition of radio and television. [See chapter 8, "Literature," for more on newspapers and magazines.]

Print advertising allows the reader the luxury to read and reread text that carries both information and emotive content. Radio and TV spots permit no such leisurely return to the message and are therefore limited to one-time responses. It did not take long for advertisers to exploit these media differences. An automobile advertisement in a magazine might mention exact horsepower and engine specifications; the same vehicle in a TV spot would instead give images of speed and power, with little

These Avon Cosmetics can make your summer!

There's nothing like self-assurance to make a girl's summer a success . . . the assurance of a clear and lovely complexion, achieved with Avon's Strawberry Cooler . . . lips aglow with color via Long Life Lipstick . . . nails glamorous with the gloss of Pearlescent Nail Polish . . . hair beautifully managed with Avon's new Hair Cosmetic . . . every inch of you fresh and fragrant with Persian Wood Mist. These and other Avon Cosmetics and Fragrances are brought to you by your Avon Representative. In the privacy of your home, she discusses your beauty needs and wants with you, and gives you friendly guidance. "Avon Calling" means a rewarding visit with your Avon Representative. You will be wiser and lovelier for it!

.AVON cosmetics

Available only through your Avon Representative who calls at your home

you saw it in *seventeen* — june, 1957

Although television was emerging as a dominant advertising force in the 1950s, traditional print ads, like this 1957 Avon example, still enticed readers. This teenager, with her ponytail and lineup of Avon cosmetics, epitomized the youthful thrust of much advertising during the decade. Source: Hagley Museum and Library.

accompanying information. Similarly, food promotions in print, while they could give an attractive picture of the item, would also tell the reader about nutrition and might even include a recipe. That same food, on television, would be presented in such a way as to make the viewer salivate, but the likelihood of much detailed information would be slim.[1]

The fifties, the dawn of this new era of merchandising, witnessed extraordinary growth among those manufacturers responsible for all the bottles, aerosols, bubble-packs, cartons, and boxes: by 1959, packaging stood alongside print advertising as a significant industry in its own right, consuming prodigious quantities of raw materials to create ways of making products more marketable. Food featured zip-lock bags or pressurized cans, with eye-catching slogans like "quick 'n' easy," "heat 'n' serve," "bound to please," and "ready in no time." Hand lotion flowed from dispensers with pumps, thumb tacks were displayed in fancy blister packs, drugs arrived in brightly labeled plastic vials, liquor sparkled in decanters, and underwear came wrapped in cellophane packs of three.

Because many contemporary items exhibited little outward difference, it became imperative that the ads promoting the product or the package holding it bring recognition and a positive response, thereby justifying the costly design process. Both must speak to the consumer. Customers had to be persuaded that the product was now "more convenient," "easier to use," "stronger," "neater," "cleaner," "fresher," "extra dry" (or "extra moist"), or possessed any of a hundred other "improvements." Even standard sizes went through semantic shifts, with "large" becoming "economy size" and "small" evolving into "personal size"; "super economy size" (larger than "economy") and "giant size" (presumably larger than "super economy size") entered the shopping lexicon.

Self-service increasingly emerged as the way consumers purchased goods in stores; the once-knowledgeable and friendly grocery clerk or shop owner ready to help the shopper disappeared into history, replaced by people responsible for many things, but not trained to assist customers. Consumers therefore relied on advertising for both information and the impulse to buy; packaging at times assumed greater significance than the item itself. The product package had to attract the eye, relay some information, and convince the would-be buyer that it was superior to the competition.

RADIO ADVERTISING

Radio found itself sandwiched between print and television. As an advertising medium, radio underwent a significant decline during the fifties; it fell from 9 percent of all ad dollars in 1952 to stabilize at approximately 6 percent in 1959. Advertisers looked to new outlets for their clients, and television emerged as the big winner. As radio slumped, TV advertising rose from 6 percent of all ad dollars in 1952 to 13 percent in 1960. Without text or pictures, radio could offer only voice, music, or sound effects.[2]

Short, catchy jingles, long a staple of radio commercials, continued as a primary means of capturing listeners' attention, albeit sometimes on a background, or subliminal, level. Ad agencies occasionally used the same jingle on both TV and radio, such as those used by Pepsi-Cola and

Coca-Cola. Familiarity became the key, and media repetition achieved it. The heady days of radio's advertising dominance may have come to an end in the 1950s, but the medium remained an important carrier of commercial messages.[3]

EARLY TELEVISION ADVERTISING

Unlike previous media, television came into being as a vehicle to carry advertising; transmission of the first spot occurred in 1941. In addition to images and sound, television offered something neither print nor radio possessed: moving pictures. At first, those pictures came only in black and white, but by the end of the decade several hundred thousand households had color sets and the number was skyrocketing. Advertisers nonetheless came warily to television in the early fifties. The charges for sponsoring a show seemed astronomical compared to radio, as much as ten times higher. But the production costs for TV commercials greatly exceeded those charged in radio or print media, plus advertisers and their agencies had to master television; a visual TV ad could not be equated with an aural radio version.

In the early days of TV, sponsors and their ad agencies took the primary responsibility for the packaging of shows. That power led to abuses, especially in the area of censorship. A car manufacturer might object to a competitor's vehicles being shown, or a cigarette company might reject the sight of anyone smoking pipes or cigars. The situation changed toward the end of the decade, sparked by the quiz show scandals of 1958–1959, a time when the networks took over more of the decision making about what to present. The creation and production of new series fell more and more to packagers that had no connection to sponsors or networks. Ultimately, ad agencies found themselves reduced to buying time and had little control over content. [For more on television and the quiz scandals, see chapter 10, "Performing Arts."]

The commercials themselves reflected the growth of television. The early 1950s witnessed a variety of cartoons and animations as producers capitalized on television's ability to show movement. Ajax Cleanser had its Pixies, little creatures who demonstrated the product's effectiveness; Valleydale sausages had marching pigs; and Autolite featured endless rows of marching sparkplugs, thanks to stop-action filming techniques. Later, Speedy Alka-Seltzer showed how a "plop, plop, fizz, fizz" would make a person feel better, and the Jolly Green Giant's "Ho, ho, ho" echoed throughout homes everywhere. Charlie the Tuna epitomized the cool hipster, right down to his beret, and Mr. Clean's muscled strength could overcome the worst spills and stains. And everyone thought the Pillsbury Doughboy personified cuteness, while Sharpie, the

Gillette parrot, squawked "Look Sharp!" during televised ball games and boxing matches.

Among the cleverest commercial figures were Bert and Harry Piel, two cartoon brothers who used low-key humor and the familiar voices of radio humorists Bob Elliot and Ray Goulding to pitch Piel's Beer, a New York product that quickly acquired national fame and sales. One short and one tall, Bert and Harry traded jokes and quips, more about each other than about the product, and viewers loved them. Not to be outdone, Hamm's Beer featured a friendly cartoon bear that cavorted in the woods while a chorus sang of the "land of sky-blue waters." Not as humorous as the Piel's series, Hamm's nevertheless got away from the gorgeously photographed glass of beer held by a serious announcer to a more lighthearted approach to commercials.

Live action figured prominently in the formative years of TV commercials. The Men from Texaco introduced Milton Berle, the star of *Texaco Star Theater* (1948–1953), one of television's first real hits. Equally memorable were the Old Gold Dancing Packs, oversize cigarette packs with shapely (human) legs that sported white cowboy boots and danced about the stage. Frequently, a diminutive dancing matchbook (with a child inside) accompanied them. In 1951, the famous Budweiser Clydesdales came to television. Although they had represented the brewery since the nineteenth century, they proved an instant hit and have been appearing in Budweiser commercials ever since. That same year saw the debut of Mabel, a barmaid who brought thirsty patrons Carling's Black Label Beer whenever patrons called out, "Hey Mabel! Black Label!" The live Mabel got replaced later in the fifties with an animated version, but she had already become an icon by then. Unfortunately, few of these early commercials survive. No one saw any reason to preserve them, so aside from some snowy kinescopes, a visual record of an important part of popular culture will always remain incomplete.[4]

GROWTH IN TELEVISION ADVERTISING

By mid-decade, American television served as an electronic shopping mall, with advertisers lined up at network and local station offices to buy time, eager to pitch their wares. Americans mastered, via television, a new language of consumerism, and they learned their lessons well in the 1950s.

This incessant growth brought certain costs. Most television commercials in the early 1950s ran for a full minute, sometimes more, allowing mini-stories to be told, ideas worked out, humor developed, a wealth of details included. But time on television costs money and commercials do not come cheap; by the end of the 1950s, producers spent, on average, anywhere from $10,000 to $20,000 for a one-minute filmed ad. In contrast, a minute of content for an entertainment show cost around $2,000. As a result, the luxurious minute shrank to 30 seconds of airtime, still a virtual eternity by current ten- and fifteen-second standards. Many of the classic commercials of the 1950s would be too long (i.e., too expensive) to be aired today.[5]

Annual U.S. spending for advertising rose from $5.7 billion in 1950 to almost $12 billion at the end of the decade. Newspapers and television together consumed almost two-thirds of the advertising dollar; the remainder was divided among magazines, radio, direct mail, outdoor, and other miscellaneous outlets. These figures become even more meaningful when one considers that television managed only a paltry $41 million in ad revenues in 1950. By 1952, that $41 million had swelled to $336 million and was closing in on radio's ad income ($473 million). Further, TV could reach a truly national market in its advertising, whereas both radio and newspapers served more local clients. At mid-decade, television achieved the distinction of becoming the leading carrier for national advertising; by 1959, a single national TV spot could penetrate 90 percent of American homes, something no other medium could accomplish. Ad revenues had surged to over $1.5 billion; only newspaper advertising surpassed in dollars what TV earned.[6]

Automobiles counted among the most heavily promoted products during the 1950s; out of the top ten TV advertisers, nine manufactured motor vehicles. General Motors reigned as the biggest single advertiser in the United States, although giant Procter & Gamble did place second in overall expenditures. Individually, however, Procter & Gamble's ads for Camay, Crisco, Prell, Tide, and a myriad of other brands did not equal the amounts spent on Chevrolets, Oldsmobiles, and Buicks. [For more on automotive advertising, see chapter 11, "Travel and Recreation."][7]

To a degree never envisioned by radio, American television exploited the renown and talents of major show business personalities: Eddie Fisher sipped Coca-Cola; Henry Fonda touted beer; Dinah Shore sang about Chevrolet; Frank Sinatra crooned about shampoo; Jack Benny plugged just about anything; Loretta Young had a box of detergent in view; and Lucille Ball and Desi Arnaz, TV's most popular couple, smoked Philip Morris cigarettes on camera. Even acclaimed film director Alfred Hitchcock, the sardonic host of *Alfred Hitchcock Presents* (1955–1965), entered into the commercial side of television production. He made deprecating remarks about Bristol-Myers, his longtime sponsor, and viewers loved it—as did Bristol-Myers—because his put-downs of the company's ads made them memorable. The seemingly daring jabs amused his audiences, and no one informed them that they had all been carefully scripted; in the meantime, the sponsor happily watched sales increase. The endless endorsements of celebrities like these created a strong link between consumerism and entertainment, and celebrities emerged as effective salespeople.[8]

MEDIA AND THE MESSAGE

Regardless of the medium carrying the message, American advertising during the 1950s presented endless images of the good life. An ad for floor wax might be staged in a kitchen that most consumers only dreamed of; but the imagery came across clearly: use this product and your kitchen will resemble the one in the ad. Fantasy, social values, and the hard sell came together unlike they had in any previous era. Borrowing a device long employed by car manufacturers and the fashion industry, promoters of a wide range of consumer goods began to espouse planned obsolescence in their ads. The product might not really need replacement, but the new model had to be an improvement over the old version. Or, if not an improvement, it possessed more style, more pizzazz. Watch makers recommended having a "wardrobe" of timepieces, one for every occasion. Appliance manufacturers began to make their previously all-white washers and dryers in a rainbow of fashionable colors—they might not wash or dry any better, but they fit more into the modern home than plain old white. With their wallets bulging with discretionary cash, consumers accepted the implicit promise that this year's yellow range surpassed last year's pale pink model.

With all the emphasis on gratifying desires immediately, installment buying and the use of credit replaced the old American trait of paying in full for goods. "No money down, attractive terms!" lured buyers to live beyond their means. But with incomes rising and the economy booming, it seemed a reasonable way to accumulate goods. Ads promoted trading old furniture for new, along with carpeting, appliances, and a host of other products. They modeled their appeals on the concept of the automobile trade-in. "Why be tied down to old, out-of-style furniture [or anything else]?" the argument went. "Trade-in now and get the latest styles." Real-estate agents trumpeted moving every four years, with the idea that each move would be to a bigger, better dwelling. Even the old dream of owning a home free and clear lost its luster as eager consumers sold their mortgaged houses to acquire new ones with even larger mortgages. A cultural groundswell had occurred, and the old maxims about thriftiness and restraint were discarded in a rush to keep up with the neighbors.

QUESTIONING THE MESSAGE

A downside to the decade-long buying spree of the fifties involved customer dissatisfaction with many of the products bought. In their rush to keep store inventories up, manufacturers sometimes skimped on the quality of the merchandise. Jokes about appliance repairmen abounded, and discarded toasters and mixers could be found in any garbage fill. New homeowners had to contend with leaks and faulty wiring as construction crews rushed to finish tract houses. Relentless consumer demand caused most manufacturers and distributors to deem such complaints minor annoyances. Unfortunately, the broad questions of quality and assurance went largely unaddressed during the 1950s as developers and contractors tried even harder to sell more goods, shoddy or not.

Author Vance Packard released *The Hidden Persuaders* in 1957. This bestselling book claims that all manner of colors, shapes, concealed symbols, and other devious devices in advertising manipulate the consumer under the guise of "Motivational Research" (MR), a term the ad industry coined that means investigating human behavior in order to discover what appeals to consumers. Packard's work serves as a damning indictment of advertising, and led to calls for investigations into industry methodologies. The thought that advertising might affect people on a subliminal level stimulated considerable public debate. Packard asserts that motivational research dictates that, in a marketplace crowded with similar products, manufacturers distinguish themselves by appealing to the consumer's subconscious. Instead of selling a specific product, advertisers sell hope, vitality, youth, prestige, respect, and dozens of other abstract concepts.[9]

Packard's claims were not really new—other books and articles had come to the same conclusions—but *The Hidden Persuaders* struck a responsive chord. Despite their ferocious consumerism, a majority of Americans tended to distrust the very ads that urged them to buy, buy, buy. But little, beyond debate that revealed some popular misgivings about the advertiser's trade, came from the book's revelations. Hollywood echoed this unease and attracted wide audiences with *Will Success Spoil Rock Hunter?* a popular 1957 spoof on the profession and its products.

Mainstream novelists also took on the advertising business with *The Last Angry Man* (Gerald Green, 1956), *The Detroiters* (Harold Livingston, 1956), *A Twist of Lemon* (Edward Stephens, 1958), and *The Admen* (Shepherd Mead, 1958). One title in particular summed up the popular image of the advertising executive: *The Man in the Gray Flannel Suit* (Sloan Wilson, 1955). Although the hero of this best-selling novel actually works in public relations, its title contributed a phrase to the language. It also furthered the popular apprehension that advertising and public relations, or "Madison Avenue," the New York street commonly associated with many such agencies, were inherently manipulative and dishonest.

For example, the Food and Drug Administration, the government licensing apparatus for new medicinal and health products, rarely rejected a new cold cure or pain pill. As long as the so-called "remedy" caused no obvious harm, it did not have to prove how efficacious it might be. As a result, the fifties saw all manner of medicines and drugs come into the market that claimed to promote weight loss, cure a nagging cough, cease smoking, stop constipation, increase vitality, decrease nervousness, and so on. These ads continued an age-old practice of quackery in American advertising, one that capitalized on the public's never-ending search for panaceas and placebos, and the industry's insistent reproaches to that public for failure to employ these omnipresent solutions to problems. Advertising of all kinds, but especially TV ads, provided endless fantasies about how these nostrums were superior to all other such remedies. In the process, both the patent medicine and the pharmaceutical industries grew into multibillion-dollar entities. The mass media were more than mere channels; they had become the marketplace.

ADVERTISING AND WOMEN

Throughout the twentieth century, the overwhelming bulk of shopping and spending—upwards to 80 or 90 percent by most estimates—was done by women. Men produced, women consumed. Taking advantage of that truism, many ads of the 1950s targeted women. Most advertising agencies consisted of men, a discrepancy that led to copy written by males but meant for women. American advertising exhibited rampant stereotyping and gender bias throughout the decade, and the idea that a woman should live for her husband and family became a dominant image. It all fit in with the outward conservatism and conformity that many felt characterized the period.[10]

By emphasizing the image of women as housekeepers, ads depicted women as virtual servants, serving meals, doing dishes, cleaning, dusting, and vacuuming. Some humorously asked, "Who does all this work?" and then answered the question with a picture of an attractive, well-dressed, aproned, high-heeled woman of indeterminate age. The woman of the 1950s, at least in much American advertising, functioned as little more than stylish help.

But domestic help with a difference: her portrayal also includes decision making. Not only does the American woman shop in 1950s advertising, but she also decides what will be purchased. Big-ticket items, like appliances, television sets, and even automobiles are displayed with a fashionable woman choosing this or that model. Males may be present, but they function as background filler, not as major players. Manufacturers and their advertising agencies eagerly bought into the concept of the woman as primary selector and arbiter of family wants and needs.

Mom, in charge and decisive, presides over a happy home; she does not go to an office. When she ventures forth, she goes shopping—to buy more goods. In truth, by 1957, women comprised a third of the workforce, so the happy housewife with endless time to shop existed as a part of popular mythology. But the ads of the day show immaculately coiffed and dressed women shopping for food, preparing it in a modern, well-equipped kitchen, and then serving it to an appreciative family. From start to finish, according to thousands of print and television inducements, the woman controls her world, but it exists as make-believe, a world removed from reality.

In 1954, artist Saul Steinberg did a series of cartoons promoting Jell-O. In his distinctive style, Steinberg drew a cutaway of a woman's brain, illustrating household tasks and unending work. But at least instant Jell-O would save a little time, just as the endless array of canned, frozen, prepackaged, precut, precooked food available at the local supermarket would. Advertisers might ignore the limited time available to the modern woman, but their products increasingly spoke to these very stresses. From toilet bowl cleaners to dish detergents, images of ease and economy predominated. Housework existed as an accepted part of life, and the ads directed their energies at the women who would be watching or reading them, a public affirming its behavior through advertising imagery.[11]

The push for ease and efficiency led to many advertising campaigns in the 1950s, both print and electronic, that involved not just items for the kitchen. Automatic transmissions in cars, wrinkle-free clothing, self-pasting wallpapers, and quick-drying paints could be counted among the many products aimed at the busy woman. One campaign that produced mixed results involved extension telephones. The Bell System urged homemakers to add extra phones in various rooms, particularly the bedrooms of their teenage daughters. Manufacturers of such unrelated products as watches, furniture, and carpeting launched their own humorous ads depicting teens talking endlessly on their new telephones. The stereotype of the adolescent girl, receiver to her ear, became a part of youth culture, and Bell installed untold thousands of extensions, many in new decorator colors, across the prosperous nation.[12]

CHILDREN AND ADVERTISING

Next to women (and often posed with them), children occupied an important niche in 1950s advertising. The ages of consumers made little difference, and children were seen as especially vulnerable to persuasive messages. For example, Ovaltine, a venerable chocolate drink, targeted the youthful viewers of its popular television series, *Captain Midnight* (1954–1956), a show that had previously run as a popular serial on radio (1939–1949). The use of premiums to lure larger audiences dated back to early broadcasting, and Ovaltine chose to carry on the tradition. Viewers, just like a generation of avid listeners, could obtain decoder rings that deciphered secret messages, badges, identity cards, and official membership certificates by purchasing jars of Ovaltine and saving the labels that could be cashed in toward these gifts. Only a handful of other sponsors followed suit, however, and the practice declined during the decade. [For more on radio and television serials and premiums, see chapter 10, "Performing Arts."]

Advertising aimed at children also freely used cartoon figures, such as Fresh-Up Freddie, a character that pushed Seven-Up. Created by the Walt Disney studios in 1955, Freddie approached the soft drink humorously, a trait displayed by most cartoon hucksters. In like fashion, giant cereal maker Kellogg's employed the talents of Tony the Tiger for Frosted Flakes in 1955, and then added Snap! Crackle! and Pop! for Rice Krispies, Coco for Cocoa Krispies, and Sugar Pops Pete for Sugar Pops. These were but the first of a vast menagerie of animated characters that would entice children on television screens and packages for decades to come.

The helpless, or hapless, father-male lurks in the background of many ads featuring children. He can beam proudly, but his role remains clearly a secondary one. He cannot, it would seem, comprehend the intricacies of maintaining a proper home or possess the skills needed for successful child rearing. Whether the child is an infant or a strapping teenager matters little; audiences—particularly those audiences composed mainly of women—were drawn to images of competent mothers and happy children, or so advertisers felt.

The usual products, such as baby food, candy, bath powders, soaps, toys, and games, consistently employed children as the focus of their advertising. But less likely products—automobiles, tires, television sets, appliances, furniture—also showed children to broaden their appeal, especially to women. Stereotyping, however, continued to plague such advertising using children. Little boys get depicted roughhousing, playing sports, or working with tools, whereas little girls serve tea from miniature pots, pretend to clean house, or play nurse. Ads with adolescents continue in this mode; the idea of gender-appropriate behaviors, so ingrained in the American psyche, saw little change during the 1950s. Teaching daughters that proper homemaking surpasses any professional goals they might entertain remained a standard component of advertising imagery. [For more about marketing to youth, see chapter 2, "World of Youth."][13]

MEN AND ADVERTISING

Despite the emphases placed on advertising to women, men appear in many ads of the 1950s, more often than not doing "manly" things. This means racing cars, slugging baseballs, hunting, or building something—and usually in the company of other men, a man's world. Although women in the world portrayed in American advertising excel as housekeepers, shoppers, or consumers, they somehow seem at a loss when it comes to comprehending how complex things work. It still takes male expertise—traditional male authority—to conquer the inner workings of mechanical devices or to explain complex topics, like current events or finances.

For example, popular newscaster John Cameron Swayze, in a long-running series of ads commencing in 1952, touted the indestructibility of Timex watches ("it takes a licking and keeps on ticking"), insinuating it takes more than style to market a wristwatch. Actor Ed Reimers for many years told people that they were in the "good hands" of Allstate insurance, his rich baritone assuring viewers that a man understands a whole life policy. In these instances, the actors carried on a theme present in American print advertising for many years—that of the square-jawed, decisive, and self-sufficient male. Women, when placed in these situations, became dependent on their husbands. Males served as agents of authority, knowledgeable about a certain range of non-household things, who then gave their stamp of approval to the purchases made by women.

Women, if present at all in this kind of ad, usually appear subservient. They look on, but they seldom participate. On the other hand, when 1950s advertising deals with domestic themes and deigns to include men, the situation reverses: it is the man who becomes the nonparticipant. He loafs on a chaise lounge while his wife gardens, or he is ensconced in an easy chair, inactive, while household activities occur around him. For whatever reasons, advertisers seemed reluctant to portray men as assisting in the duties of the home.

BETTY CROCKER

General Mills's maternal trademark underwent a facelift in the 1950s. It did not mark the first time her matronly face had been altered, nor would it be the last, but marketing experts at the huge company wanted a countenance that somehow expressed a warmer, less professional look than the one then gracing boxes of cake mix. They sensed that in an age of "togetherness" (a popular phrase used to describe the happy family in the fifties) their corporate logo should suggest everyone's image of "mother," but a more stylish one, a helpful, loving person who could dispense advice without intimidating.

General Mills ran a nationwide search for suitable artists to draw the new Betty Crocker. Finally, in 1955, Hilda Taylor won the coveted assignment. Her version had a touch of gray at the temples, a broader smile, and she seemed happy. This woman enjoyed cooking; she embodied a healthy approach to the chores of the kitchen, and the company hoped homemakers across the country would sense this happiness and purchase General Mills products, smiling as they did so.[14]

In response to changing media demands, Betty Crocker also took to television. *The Betty Crocker Television Show* ran in 1950–1951, and *The Betty*

Crocker Star Matinee came along in 1952. Impersonated by actress Adelaide Hawley, millions of viewers accepted her as "real," a situation that reflected the power of repeated advertising.

BETTY FURNESS AND WESTINGHOUSE

The postwar era promised new and wondrous appliances, and major manufacturers like Westinghouse, General Electric, Frigidaire, and Whirlpool did their utmost to convince consumers the time had come to modernize their old-fashioned kitchens. Westinghouse chose as their television spokesperson Betty Furness, an attractive Hollywood actress who had never quite reached stardom.

Furness began her career in commercials in 1949 for *Studio One*, a prestigious dramatic series sponsored by Westinghouse. In those days, both the shows and the commercials were broadcast live, and Furness had to

As advertisers flocked to television, a number of their spokespeople emerged as minor celebrities. Above is Betty Furness pointing out the advantages of a Westinghouse refrigerator. Many of the commercials were done live, so mistakes did happen, but personalities like Furness developed a following and a high level of consumer trust.
Source: Library of Congress, photo by Jim Hansen.

make her pitch without any errors. In addition, the Teleprompter remained a few years down the road, so she had to be prepared with her lines since she could not read them. Not until mid-decade and advancing technology did TV move to tape and film for most commercials. In spite of these restrictions, she came across as cool and confident—the ideal housewife in the idealized kitchen. In short order Betty Furness herself emerged as a minor celebrity, and Westinghouse sales boomed.

National political conventions had first been televised in 1948; in 1952, Westinghouse sponsored much of the Republican National Convention. With Betty Furness as their visible representative, Westinghouse ran over four-and-a-half hours of commercials during the week. She would appear 20 or more times each day as she demonstrated refrigerators, washers, and ranges, and gained more airtime than any of the candidates. The walls around entertainment, information, and commercialism were crumbling.

The Westinghouse commercials helped define the consumerism that would characterize the 1950s. When Furness pointed out the latest frills on a frost-free refrigerator, she encouraged buying, not based on need, but instead on the principle of consumption for its own sake.[15]

But no one rules forever, and Betty Furness's reign ended in 1956. Dethroned by another actress, Julia Meade, Furness remained on the small screen, but in a diminished capacity. Meade, on the other hand, sold Lincolns, hair products, and *Life* magazine, causing her recognition and income to soar. The success of both women showed the increasing attention advertising agencies paid to selling to women. Other examples of this trend would include Dinah Shore for Chevrolet and Polly Bergen for Pepsi-Cola.

MINORITY ADVERTISING

One area of advertising stereotyping that changed in the fifties involved the depiction of black Americans. With blacks breaking previously inviolate color lines in sports and entertainment, and with civil rights beginning to inch forward, people found the old derogatory images—the shuffling, cartoonish figures of the recent past—offensive. Words like "Sambo," "Uncle," and "pickaninny," along with demeaning uses of dialect, gradually disappear from ad copy of the 1950s, although companies continued to wrestle with how best to portray minority groups. Most major advertisers chose not to depict black Americans at all. As a result, a significant portion of the population received no acknowledgment, rendering it all but invisible. When blacks did receive some recognition, it occurred too often around products with racial associations, such as hair straighteners and bleaching creams, items that appeared primarily in limited (i.e., nonwhite) markets.

CIGARETTE ADVERTISING

At the opening of the decade, Lucky Strikes, Camels, and Chesterfields led all other brands in sales. Change had also come to the tobacco business: by 1951, most major American cigarettes could be purchased in both regular and king sizes, and king-sized had emerged as the fastest-growing segment of the market. Kool cigarettes introduced their "cool" owl in 1954, a reference to their use of menthol as a flavoring agent. Finally, in response to scattered reports about links between smoking and disease, Lorillard introduced its Kent brand in 1952, a cigarette with a cellulose filter on one end. People delighted in their introduction, thinking they were now safe from illness. Their joy, however, would be short-lived.

Surveys done in the postwar era showed just how widespread smoking had become. Almost half of all Americans—60 percent males, 30 percent women—smoked at least a pack of cigarettes a day. In 1954, however, the prestigious American Medical Association issued a study based on the smoking habits of 188,000 men. In it, the AMA established a link between smoking and the incidence of cancer. The gist of this report ran in the high-circulation *Reader's Digest*, forcing an immediate response from the tobacco industry. In full-page newspaper ads, spokesmen denied any correspondences between smoking and cancer.

With the grim medical news, Kent's filter monopoly was brief; in 1954, Winston Cigarettes appeared, backed by the slogan "tastes good, like a cigarette should." Much to R.J. Reynolds's delight, the grammar upset some purists (the "like" should be "as"), and Winston emerged as a major brand in a crowded field and soon occupied the top spot among filter brands. Other manufacturers began a full-scale push to promote filtered cigarettes, along with lower concentrations of tar and nicotine. By 1959, and thanks to incessant industry advertising, filtered cigarettes had gained 50 percent of total sales. The medical profession, however, continued to rail against tobacco use, but the industry repeatedly rebuffed any complaints, assuring the public that modern cigarettes were safe. Not until 1964, when a Surgeon General's report reinforced what doctors had been saying, and a subsequent 1971 ban on cigarette advertising on radio and television, did the numbers of smokers in the United States begin to drop.[16]

In the meantime, Old Gold cigarettes promised, in a memorable 1951 phrase, "a treat, instead of a treatment," an approach that depicted happy women smoking such a mild cigarette. Some brands even had doctors endorsing the use of cigarettes to relieve itchy throats. Another classic ad campaign that occurred at this time involved the Marlboro Man. Marlboro cigarettes had originally appeared in 1924, marketed as a cigarette appropriate for sophisticated women. Their paper wrapper came in a pale pink, and the "beauty tip" had a dark red shade, the better to hide lipstick prints. The brand never did particularly well, and so Phillip Morris, the makers of Marlboros, decided to redo their faltering product in 1954. The Leo Burnett advertising agency accepted the challenge of making Marlboro a top seller in the competitive filter-tip field.

In 1955, the revamped Marlboros came out; advertisements pushed them as "masculine," a smoke for "rugged men" with "man-sized flavor," and packaged in a sturdy "flip-top box" that would not cave in and could be opened with one hand. The ads featured weathered male models with prominent tattoos on the backs of their hands. Thanks to a massive saturation campaign, the Marlboro Man—a tall, lean Westerner in leather and denim—soon evolved into a national icon. Immediately identifiable, his smoking was associated with manly pursuits, and Marlboros rose to become one of the most popular cigarette brands in the United States. To reach that lofty pinnacle, of course, they also had to appeal to women. For whatever psychological reasons, the macho Marlboro campaign also struck a chord among women, proof that gender-based advertising can at times have unanticipated results.[17]

TOOTHPASTE ADVERTISING

Some of the most hotly fought ad campaigns of the fifties involved toothpastes. At the beginning of the 1950s, Colgate-Palmolive's Colgate Toothpaste led the way with the jingle: "It cleans your breath while it cleans your teeth." For most of the decade, Colgate outsold all others. In 1956, Pepsodent, one of many competitors, employed another memorable slogan: "You'll wonder where the yellow went." The phrase helped sales only a little and, despite its cleverness, failed to unseat Colgate.

For their part, Procter & Gamble brought out Crest toothpaste in 1955. The new brand enjoyed heavy advertising, but sales languished. Searching for a gimmick to attract the public, Procter & Gamble discovered "Fluoristan." In the early fifties, the government had moved to include sodium fluoride in most municipal drinking water. Fluoride had been demonstrated an effective dental decay preventative. Despite the fears of a few, the compound lived up to expectations, reducing the number of cavities among Americans with fluoride-treated water by 50 percent. Wisely sensing the public goodwill toward fluoride, Procter & Gamble in 1956 began marketing Crest with the claim that it included stannous fluoride, or "Fluoristan," as they christened it.

When Fluoristan was coupled with a memorable phrase in 1958, Crest took off in sales. "Look, Mom! No cavities!" allowed Crest to outsell Colgate in the closing years of the decade. Numerous photographers, along with the immensely popular illustrator Norman Rockwell, created a series of magazine and newspaper ads of delighted kids proclaiming their absence of cavities, and happy children shouted it out on television commercials. The phrase caught on immediately, ingratiating itself into public consciousness. The Food and Drug Administration soon gave the toothpaste its seal of approval, but millions had already been buying Crest for several years, and the federal agency's blessing only heightened its success. Thanks to an unforgettable phrase and the undeniable benefits of fluoride, Crest had risen to become the sales leader almost overnight.[18]

DAVID OGILVY AND HUMOR IN ADVERTISING

Much advertising in the 1950s, especially that aimed at the newly affluent middle class, used deadpan humor. Because readers could linger over them, such ads more often appeared in magazines. Television exposure was deemed too brief for appropriate understanding, although that attitude softened as the decade progressed and viewers became more media-literate. Liquor, food, clothing, automobiles, cosmetics—many examples exist that seem outwardly serious, but possess a sophisticated, humorous edge. At times this approach came off as bizarre or incongruous, but frequently it worked, and well.

For example, in 1956 the first Clairol advertisements appeared that sported the now-famous line, "Does she . . . or doesn't she?" Despite the clever innuendo, the question referred to the use of hair coloring, and "only her hairdresser knows for sure." Not only was the copy unique, so too the subject: in the 1950s fewer than ten percent of women would admit to coloring their hair. A throwback to earlier, more strait-laced times, critics objected to the use of hair color on moral grounds, just as they had once fulminated against women smoking or drinking. In response, most magazines refused to run hair color ads, but Clairol persisted, and millions of women came around to their point of view. Both the ads and the product were runaway successes, and Clairol would dominate the field until almost the end of the century.

But Clairol was hardly the first to employ humor. Advertising executive David Ogilvy gets credited with possessing one of the most original minds in the business. He cooked up the memorable "Man in the Hathaway Shirt" print campaign in 1951. C.F. Hathaway and Company, an old Maine-based shirtmaker, seemed a perennial runner-up to industry leader Arrow Shirts. In a series of tongue-in-cheek ads, a handsome, gray-haired gentleman, a connoisseur of everything and who also happens to sport a black eye patch, graced magazine pages wearing a Hathaway shirt. He examines fine shotguns, observes polo matches, prices works of art, and follows other pursuits of the rich and leisured. Would wearing a Hathaway shirt give a man access to that lifestyle? Probably not, despite the implications, but the ads were fun to look at. Soon thereafter, Hathaway overtook Arrow in sales.

In 1953, Ogilvy created Commander Whitehead, an urbane, bearded naval officer who in many ways mirrored the Hathaway man. Instead of shirts, however, Whitehead represented Schweppes Tonic Water, a heretofore-unknown carbonated beverage. He touted "Schweppervescence," a neologism that suggested bubbles, but people equated the immaculately dressed Whitehead and his product with elegance and sophistication. In no time, Schweppes had become a leader in tonics and carbonated waters. Sometimes the soft sell worked as well as the hard variety, and no one understood the concept more clearly than David Ogilvy.[19]

TRADING STAMPS

A Denver grocery store began offering S&H Green Stamps in 1951. Trading stamps had first appeared at the end of the nineteenth century, a device to promote sales among participating merchants. They flourished during the Depression years, but their use fell off with World War II. The idea came around again in the 1950s and found shoppers eager to collect them. The early success of S&H Green Stamps spurred the giant Kroger supermarket chain to join with six other firms to introduce their own Top Value Stamps in 1955.

By the end of the decade, more than 80 percent of all American families were collecting trading stamps, receiving one stamp for every ten cents spent. Redemption centers sprouted like weeds, and every enterprise, from gas stations to department stores, offered them. The little three-inch-by-five-inch books of stamps became a ubiquitous part of American shopping. As a rule, it took 1,200 stamps to fill one book, or $120 in purchases. The cash value of a filled book was about $3, so people had to redeem a lot of books for even small items. Nonetheless, some two hundred fifty to five hundred different stamp companies operated during the 1950s, generating over a half-billion dollars in revenues.[20]

PUBLIC RELATIONS

Not really advertising, but certainly a close relative, as well as being a part of American popular culture, public relations enjoyed phenomenal growth during the 1950s. This profession promotes corporate and organization identity instead of products or services. With effective public relations, the image of the parent company becomes as important as the product and a new term entered the language: "image advertising." Many manufacturers had contented themselves with pushing specific brands, but others wanted to stress the company itself, especially those that made a multiplicity of products. For example, a Dodge is an automobile, but it is also a brand of car manufactured by the Chrysler Corporation. Which should be stressed, and under what situations?

A merchandising fad of huge proportions, trading stamps were awarded to consumers for their purchases. Ten stamps equaled a dollar in sales. People put their stamps in booklets, as shown, and they could turn them in for merchandise at redemption centers located just about everywhere. S&H Green Stamps, Top Value, Gold Bond, and a host of other series tempted the public to buy more so they could collect additional trading stamps.

The DuPont Corporation, a giant chemical conglomerate, sponsored both *The DuPont Theater* (1956–1957) and *The DuPont Show of the Month* (1957–1961) on television. In carefully nuanced messages instead of traditional commercials, DuPont spokesmen talked of corporate responsibilities, commitment to excellence, and the role of a large company in serving its employees and families. General Electric, in like manner, spent millions on *The General Electric Theater* (1953–1962) extolling its many roles within the community, not the least of which was that of a major defense contractor dedicated to the security of the nation. Incidentally, GE featured Ronald Reagan as the genial host of the series, a position that catapulted him to political fame. AT&T, General Motors, U.S. Steel, Standard Oil, Ford Motor Company, and numerous other large industrial leaders took similar approaches, intent on getting out a message that cast a positive light on their activities.

The Container Corporation of America sponsored a print campaign titled "Great Ideas of Western Man." Using striking graphics by leading designers, they presented, in sharply condensed form, statements found in the writings of some of the world's most illustrious thinkers. The connections between glass jars and philosophical thought might be difficult to make, but the ads conveyed the image that the Container Corporation of America was a good corporate citizen, concerned about the advancement of learning and the wide dispersion of knowledge. It remains a memorable public relations campaign; whether it had any real impact on company sales would be difficult to verify.

POLITICS, PUBLIC RELATIONS, AND ADVERTISING

Politics serves as an area that blurs the lines separating advertising, public relations, and popular culture. The 1952 presidential campaign, pitting Republican Dwight Eisenhower against Democrat Adlai Stevenson, marked the first large-scale use of both print and electronic appeals for candidates and parties. This innovation became especially apparent in Eisenhower's quest for the presidency. General Eisenhower had, in 1948, authored a best-selling book titled *Crusade in Europe*. Written prior to his candidacy, the book chronicled the Allies' victory in World War II and his role as Supreme Commander, and its popular success brought him further public acclaim.

Eisenhower's run for the presidency employed the resources of Batten, Barton, Durstine, and Osborne (or BBD&O), a large New York advertising firm. Immediately capitalizing on the popularity of the general and his book, his candidacy would be called a "Great Crusade," and BBD&O began to focus on images instead of issues. Eisenhower—or "Ike," as millions fondly remembered him from his days during the war—was presented as a trusted soldier, one whose fatherly wisdom could simplify complex issues. But not too fatherly: the image-makers wanted Eisenhower also to be personable and appear in full command of his powers. In his TV spots, he read from large cue cards, so he would not have to wear glasses and appear elderly, and the familiar "We Like Ike" became the cheer for his supporters.

Stevenson, on the other hand, attempted to discuss the problems of the day, saying there existed no easy choices, no pat explanations, in the Cold War era. But he came across as too smart, too distant. He lacked the folksy touch BBD&O worked relentlessly to associate with Ike. One commentator dredged up an old term used to denigrate an overly learned person: "egghead." It stuck, and Stevenson could never shake the image of an intellectual out of touch with the people.[21]

Eisenhower won in a landslide. The campaign illustrated to all the power of image-based advertising, especially in politics and on television. The candidates spent tens of millions of dollars getting their messages out, far more than in any previous presidential race. Henceforth, American election campaigns and American politics would never be the same.

SUMMARY

Advertising traditionally plays to the perceived needs and desires of consumers, not to the reality of their behaviors or circumstances. The 1950s proved no exception to this convention. All advertising flourished during the prosperous decade, but the rise of television brought commercial messages into the home more forcefully than ever before.

4

Architecture and Design

After 16 years (1929–1945) of depression, recession, and war, Americans stood poised to embark on the biggest building and buying binge the world had ever seen. The return of millions of veterans, stoked by pent-up demand and available money, set the stage. As industry turned back to civilian needs, builders and developers could barely meet the demand for new housing; everyone, it seemed, wanted a part of this postwar version of the American Dream. The result was the mass production of standardized middle-class dwellings in huge suburban tracts. The ubiquitous ranch house emerged as a popular icon of the 1950s, while commercial architecture and innovative design frequently took a back seat in this rush to build.

ARCHITECTURE

Residential Building

The triumph of the suburbs and the building of thousands upon thousands of new homes overshadowed all other architectural endeavors. Virtually everything that occurred in American residential architecture and design in the immediate postwar years came to fruition in the 1950s. New technologies allowed architects freedom to create new spaces in house interiors, stronger building materials promised greater durability and weather resistance, and the quest for economical housing meant these advances would be employed on a vast scale.

"Houses of the Future" became a minor fad during the postwar years. Usually sponsored by suppliers and trade groups, these for-display-only homes were shown across the country and drew large crowds. They tended toward the avant-garde in their design, but they incorporated such prefabrication details as plywood for walls, laminated roofs, metal trusses and wall framing, preassembled windows, gypsum-board ceilings, and a host of other innovative structural details. Despite their pioneering designs, neither developers nor the public felt comfortable with anything quite so modern; few such houses were constructed in any significant numbers. Nevertheless they influenced domestic design, especially in the large picture windows and open interior areas that would characterize so many ranch houses in the ballooning suburbs. What people oohed and aahed at and what they built differed sharply. Most potential buyers wanted something that, on the exterior at least, looked traditional and resembled the other houses in a neighborhood. Many building advances might be incorporated into these new homes, but they would not be obvious to passersby.

Despite the reluctance on the part of homebuyers to move into anything the least futuristic, architects continued to display their modernistic con-

Among the numerous "houses of the future" that took shape in the 1950s, this futuristic pedestal example attracted a lot of attention. Built of molded plastic and glass by the Monsanto Chemical Company in 1957, it was erected at Walt Disney's "Tomorrowland" section of Disneyland in California. Despite public curiosity, none got built, since most Americans preferred more traditional housing. It was finally demolished in 1967, already a relic of an earlier time. Source: Library of Congress.

cepts. Perhaps the most famous of these varied designs was the all-metal Lustron House. Manufactured between 1948 and 1950, this functional dwelling featured a steel frame with porcelain-enameled steel panels available in six colors. The Lustron House cost roughly $7,000 at the time, a very reasonable price, and about 2,500 were built, some of which remain in use.

Other conceptual homes of the era included the 1948 *Look* House, sponsored by the popular *Look* magazine. *House and Garden* erected a "House of Ideas" in 1952, and in the following year *Life* magazine underwrote "The Trade Secrets House." *Arts and Architecture*, another influential magazine, organized the "Case Study House Program"; it commissioned architects to design and build modern dwellings that featured the latest in construction details and furnishings. Monsanto's experimental "House of the Future" (1954) enjoyed wide notice, if not impressive sales. This cruciform-shaped structure, constructed of molded plastic, fiberglass, and concrete, became a permanent exhibition at Disneyland in 1957. Major manufacturers furnished the dwelling with futuristic furniture and appliances. The curious gawked at it, but they went home and built brick-and-wood ranch houses with Early American detailing. Probably the most significant result that came from these varied designs was an increased utilization of prefabricated components.[1]

Ranch Houses and Split-Levels

A postwar power grid that took transmission lines into the open countryside surrounding built-up areas, coupled with a growing highway system second to none, made the relentless growth of suburbs possible. Because most adults had access to automobiles, the distance between urban and rural space ceased being an important consideration. Sprawling subdivisions soon sprang up around the perimeters of cities and towns, occupying areas once thought of as "too far away" from city life.

The home design most favored by developers, realtors, and buyers alike has come to be called the ranch house. One component of the American Dream, at least as envisioned in advertising and much popular media, has long been that of a modest house on its own lot in a bucolic setting. For the 1950s, both the suburbs and ranches fit the Dream admirably.[2]

In the years surrounding World War II, early examples of the style had begun to appear in the San Francisco Bay area, giving rise to the name "California Ranch." In reality, however, many elements contained in the design can be traced to the long, low residences, or Prairie Style homes, that Frank Lloyd Wright and his followers pioneered in the early part of the twentieth century. Original or derivative, the fifties ranch is basically a one-story rectangle, with the long side facing the street. Employing simple frame construction methods, ranch houses could be easily and economically assembled on site. As a rule, a carport, a kind of open, roofed garage at one end, served to shelter the all-important automobile.

No wild, untrimmed areas assault the eye in the neat, controlled environment of 1950's American suburbia. The ranch house might seem to co-exist with its surroundings, but it relies on a deception; the building is far more important than the yard, and landscaping enhances the structure, not the other way around. Ranches suggest a unity with the adjoining natural world, but any unification also presupposes that nature has been tamed.

An inefficient picture window on the street side lets in heat during the summer and cold during the winter, but it nonetheless became a basic part of the house because homebuyers wanted them. As a result, the sales of air conditioners and bigger heating systems also surged. In a neighborhood of ranch homes, everyone looks out at one another, and everyone can likewise look in. But it exists as a sealed environment; ranches do not extend a greeting to those on the street. They have a front entry, but no front porches, once an opening and welcoming component of American house design. Activities are instead oriented to the backyard and privacy, with a tiny patio behind the house emerged as a place for outdoor family entertaining and dining.

To the millions who bought them during the 1950s, the ranch house symbolized an informal lifestyle. The term "cookout" entered the national vocabulary at this time, and almost overnight, a cheap, portable charcoal grill became a necessity. The ubiquitous kettle version made its first appearance in 1952, and the aroma of steaks being grilled on the patio became commonplace. It all fit an image of family "togetherness" that seldom tolerated significant differences.

Most ranch houses possessed less square footage than the designs they replaced, the foursquares, bungalows, and revivals of the 1920s and 1930s. But they give the illusion of being spacious and open, and housewives did not have to repeatedly climb stairs to a second floor. Developers marketed them as efficient, pleasant, and casual—attributes homebuyers wanted in the 1950s.

Old favorites like Cape Cods and Colonial Revivals still were built during the decade, but the ranch house and its variants emerged as the overwhelming favorite for the new American suburb. Inexpensive plans abounded: *Better Homes and Gardens* published its "Better Homes for All America," and *House and Garden* had "Hallmark Houses." In glowing articles, they espoused the advantages of leisurely living and offered economical blueprints. Its low cost and simplicity made the ranch the ideal starter home, and the prosperity of the fifties allowed more and more Americans to become first-time homeowners.

By the mid-fifties, a popular variation on the style emerged. Called a "split-level" house, the design allows for a central entrance and landing at mid-level; one section of the house stands two stories in height, and

As the suburbs grew, two primary residential designs gained primacy: the Ranch (top) and the Split Level (bottom). They replaced the boxy Cape Cods of the postwar 1940s, and they promised roominess and modern efficiency. Since both could be constructed easily and economically, huge tracts containing mixes of each design sprang up as Baby Boom families fled the crowded cities for suburban spaciousness and the implied promise of a better life.

consists of private bath and bedroom areas on the upper floor, and informal areas like the family room and kitchen on the lower level. The other section consists of one story and tends to be more formal and contains the living room and dining room. Split-levels provide designated living (public) and sleeping (private) areas and became a favorite in the late 1950s. While managing to retain the simplicity of the ranch style, they accommodate more rooms and increase overall floor space than do ranch houses, yet both can be erected on cramped suburban lots.[3]

House Trailers and Mobile Homes

Not everyone owned a spanking new ranch house. In the immediate postwar years, about 8 percent of the population lived in house trailers, a carryover from emergency wartime housing. During the 1950s, trailers grew into "mobile homes"; they went from eight feet in width to ten feet, and could hardly be called mobile. The travails of living in this kind of structure are depicted in *The Long, Long Trailer*, a 1954 movie comedy starring Lucille Ball and Desi Arnaz. Riding a crest of popularity because of their hit television series, *I Love Lucy* (1951–1957), the couple tackles any and all stereotypes about trailer living in the film. *The Long, Long Trailer*, however, also acknowledges that a significant portion of the audience would be familiar with many of the plot situations.

Trailer parks, later renamed "Mobile Home Parks" in an attempt to impart a sense of greater permanence, became a part of the American landscape. In terms of modern housing, trailers and mobile homes exemplified true factory prefabrication. And, for those unable or unwilling to make the move into more traditional housing, they provided an alternative.[4]

Suburban Growth

If the ranch house served as the dwelling of choice during the 1950s, the suburbs became the place where more and more Americans chose to live. The Great Depression and World War II interrupted the strides being made toward universal homeownership in the United States. In 1945, at the conclusion of the war, about 40 percent of Americans owned homes. That year saw six million men and women discharged from the armed forces; in 1946, another four million left the services. Over 50 percent of the new homes sold during most of the decade therefore received financing through VA (Veterans Administration) or FHA (Federal Housing Administration) mortgages. With these incentives, builders erected almost fifteen million homes, a new national record. By 1960, 60 percent of Americans owned their own homes, a testament to the impacts of government largesse in this area.[5]

In fact, demand exceeded availability and the late 1940s witnessed a housing shortage, particularly for certain groups. The government limited its role to a handful of financing plans, with the result that some developers and local officials ignored an important segment of the U.S. populace: black Americans. Most middle-class people saw real salary gains and increased buying power, but not black citizens. During the decade, their median incomes lingered at about 40 percent of what white people earned. As whites fled to the welcoming suburbs, blacks found themselves confined to the cities, making do with older, often inferior, housing. Some developments even had "whites only" clauses built into their contracts, and not until later would these restrictions be dropped. Playwright

Lorraine Hansberry captured this dilemma in *A Raisin in the Sun* (1959). An American classic, the play (also a movie in 1961) treats realistically the inequalities that remained manifest in this otherwise prosperous decade.

Levittown

Across the country, new suburban towns rose seemingly overnight. Communities like Lakewood (outside Los Angeles), Park Forest (outside Chicago), Lexington (outside Boston), and a number of other huge subdivisions built thousands of homes in the early fifties. But the largest, the most ambitious of all, had to be Levittown. For many, the name has become synonymous with American suburbia.

In reality, three separate Levittowns exist in the United States. The name acknowledges William J. Levitt, a builder who pioneered in mass production and interchangeable parts for home construction. Levitt and many of his fellow builders gained practice during World War II assembling tracts of temporary housing for defense workers and military families. They saw home building as ripe for the methods of mass production, instead of the more traditional one-house-at-a-time approach. Prefabrication, whenever possible, became the rule. Preassembled components were trucked directly to sites, where cheap, unskilled workers could put them together. By employing techniques he learned during the war, Levitt reduced the need for expensive skilled labor to about a quarter of the tasks. The construction process, refined and simplified, ranged from painting (each color a separate step) to tile laying. At its peak, a new home went up in Levittown every 15 minutes.[6]

Levitt commenced building his suburban communities in 1947. The first Levittown appeared just below Hicksville, Long Island, on what were once potato fields; it consisted of over seventeen thousand homes, almost all of them built in a similar one-and-a-half-story Cape Cod style. They provided eight hundred square feet of living space on a small (sixty feet by one hundred feet), barren lot. Minimal housing by any standard, but people nonetheless flocked to the development. By using a traditional Cape Cod design as his first model, Levitt unwittingly encouraged both the Early American and do-it-yourself crazes that swept the suburbs in the 1950s. Although the typical dwelling had no spare space for a home workshop, enterprising woodworkers found a niche in the unfinished attic or in a corner for projects. Reproduction Colonial furniture kits and plans became immensely popular, and innumerable home handymen built hutches, cobbler's benches, cradles, cup racks, and a host of other "authentic" reproductions of pre-Revolutionary artifacts.

Despite the initial success with Cape Cods, the public's desire for ranch houses predicated Levitt's second phase. In then-rural Bucks County, Pennsylvania, just north of Philadelphia, he created the next Levittown in 1951. As he had done on Long Island, Levitt built some seventeen thousand ranches, along with schools, parks, and stores. The third and final Levittown, sited just across the Delaware River from Philadelphia in Willingboro, New Jersey, also consisted of ranch-style homes, about eleven thousand of them; construction began in 1958.

Those seventeen thousand Cape Cods shared almost identical floor plans, just as did the twenty-eight thousand ranches ; it kept costs down. The exteriors varied only by degree: a few minor changes in detailing and some choices in colors. As the first Levitt version of the American suburban Dream House took shape in the late forties, it provided buyers a kitchen, bath, living room, and two bedrooms. Upstairs, an unfinished attic space could be converted to additional bedrooms. In an admission of television's growing influence, these early Cape Cods included a built-in twelve-and-a-half-inch TV set. In addition, they featured a washing machine already hooked to water lines. Building the TV into a wall and connecting the washer to plumbing made them parts of the house, not separate purchases by the buyer, and qualified them to be part of the mortgage. Major kitchen appliances, like a refrigerator and a stove, also were included in the original purchase price of around $7,000–$8,000.[7]

Levitt's choice of a ranch style for his subsequent developments reflected changing consumer needs. Slightly more spacious than the earlier Cape Cods, it cost more, going for about $9,000. These homes boasted three bedrooms, a necessity for the bigger families most suburbanites desired. "Family rooms," spacious areas that allowed for everyone to come together, became a demand item. Likewise, utility rooms designed to hold an automatic washer and a dryer reflected the buying power and consumerist bent of 1950s families. The once ubiquitous backyard clothesline became a relic of the past, as did the old wringer washing machine.

Certainly, conformity characterized the new postwar American suburb. To some, suburbia in general seemed sterile; it possessed no center, no charm, no tradition. The original Levittown even stipulated that homeowners keep their tiny lots tidy and well mowed. And mow they did; in the 1950s the powered rotary mower replaced the old-fashioned hand-powered reel mower. For some, the lawn became an end in itself, a celebration of the final taming of nature. In order that no backyard detract from its neighbors, laundry could only be done on certain days in certain neighborhoods, and it was to be dried on identical metal racks, not hung from clotheslines. The rules forbade fences, so yards flowed into one another, contributing to the overall anonymity of the development.[8]

In his appropriately named novel, *The Crack in the Picture Window* (1956), author John Keats launched an acerbic attack on the conformity he observed in American suburbs. The book attracted a momentary following and sold briskly, but soon disappeared from the best-seller lists. The suburbs, however, continued their extraordinary growth for many years. By

1960, fully one-third of all Americans could be classified as suburbanites. Farm population decreased by half during the decade, and urban growth slowed. Long after Keats's novel had been forgotten, the ranch house, picture window and all, maintained its dominance.[9]

Home Fallout Shelters

As fears about nuclear war increased during the 1950s, many families decided to construct fallout shelters either in their basements or backyards. Supposedly such a move would give protection from nuclear explosions and radioactive fallout to any users. These shelters ranged from elaborate multiroom underground facilities well stocked with food and water to simple cave-like excavations designed to protect a family at the time of the initial blast. Whatever shape the shelter took, the idea gave people

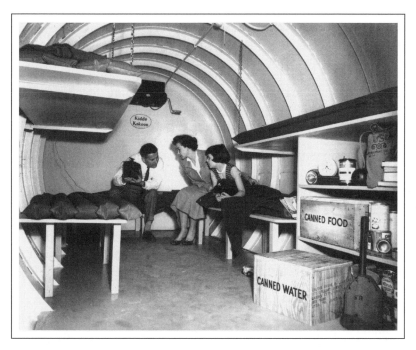

Fear of atomic warfare led many citizens to construct fallout shelters, both crude do-it-yourself models and professionally built ones. Usually sited underground, they normally were provisioned for three to five days of cramped living, and came as equipped as those owning them wanted. In this example, a commercial design, note the boxes of canned food and water—and the dressiness of its occupants. The fad endured into the 1960s.
Source: Library of Congress.

pause. Leading popular magazines like *Life* ran articles complete with detailed plans to accommodate this interest, and the government obligingly provided pamphlets with titles such as "You Can Survive," "The Family Fallout Shelter," and "Atomic Attack." One of the most popular campaigns focused on "Grandma's Pantry." Put together by the National Grocer's Association, pharmaceutical firms, medical groups, and the Federal Civil Defense Administration, it stressed readiness in dealing with any disaster, particularly a Soviet nuclear attack. If a shelter held the items prescribed in "Grandma's Pantry," the pamphlet suggested the lucky family would survive any atomic strike. Now relics of the Cold War, untold thousands of fallout units were built by fearful citizens.[10]

Commercial Architecture

For most Americans, any growth in commercial architecture during the 1950s seemed incidental to their primary interest: acquiring a home of their own. Nevertheless, the decade-long construction boom consisted of more than just personal residences; the skylines of most cities also underwent change.

Elite architects like Philip Johnson, Eero Saarinen, Edward Durrell Stone, Frank Lloyd Wright, and the firm of Skidmore, Owings & Merrill (featuring Gordon Bunshaft, in particular) busily signed contracts and watched their works rise across America. For the fifties, among commercial structures large and small, the glass box emerged as the dominant form. In academic terms, it signaled a continuation of the International Style, spare and unadorned. For the average person, however, such titles meant little; simplified manifestations of this kind of design appeared in shopping centers and office complexes, but most observers saw them as little more than "modern architecture."

Despite public indifference, the glass-fronted office or shop became commonplace, a direct outgrowth of the International Style, but the majority lacked any particular distinction. Extruded aluminum framing, maybe an inset panel or two of colored anodized aluminum, along with glass and anonymous detailing characterized these diluted interpretations of the style. But it served as a cheap, fast way to create commercial spaces, and people liked the openness it gave the businesses enclosed within. Supermarkets, banks, insurance firms, loan agencies, car dealerships, gas stations, department stores, and myriad other commercial establishments quickly adapted to this kind of modernism.

The Shopping Center and the Shopping Mall

Retailers discovered, in the years immediately following World War II, that Americans would shop for virtually anything. Voracious demand and extra dollars signaled that consumers wanted quantity, variety, and convenience. Also, the continuing move to the suburbs by so many middle-class families meant they lived a distance from urban downtowns, the traditional location for shopping. Out of all this grew two things: first emerged big urban and suburban shopping centers consisting of vast paved parking lots with innumerable structurally related shops and stores lining their perimeters; second came more sophisticated shopping malls, an architectural original that clustered stores around a central hub and often featured a climate-controlled environment.

Throughout the 1950s, outlying rural property that bordered cities could still be found in most places at reasonable prices. Open tracts outside the cramped city offered endless free parking, the space to build huge stores featuring an abundance of goods, and an array of specialty shops. The thirties and forties had seen the rise of the strip shopping center, usually a small parking area and a long row of businesses that abutted a street or highway. The new shopping centers and malls of the fifties, however, took that simple concept much further, with many more establishments including large "anchor tenants," such as department stores and supermarkets. Fancy restaurants—as opposed to fast food—located in them also. Many included movie theaters, and some offered multiple screens toward the end of the decade. The space allotted for parking grew geometrically, often covering acres of flattened land, further proof of how the automobile has restructured American society. Endless automobiles could crowd onto these mega-lots, which of course encouraged the erection of still more stores.

Victor Gruen, an architect and designer, pioneered in developing the modern-day mall. Outside Minneapolis, Minnesota, he created Southdale, a commercial center that challenged old ideas about such complexes. An immediate success, it opened in 1956. Gruen still allowed for all the cars that would come daily, but he enclosed the entire development under a single roof, giving shoppers constant air-conditioned and/or heated comfort. In addition, he made it a place for socializing and entertainment. People strolled, conversed, ate in a large food court, and rediscovered the pleasures of being pedestrians. Its widespread acceptance led other communities to demand malls of their own; although the old perimeter and strip developments continued to be built, for the late 1950s everyone's favorite shopping experiences revolved around these new enclosed malls.[11]

Roadside Architecture and the Highway

New high-speed, multilane highways increasingly defined American life. With millions of additional vehicles coming onto American roads throughout the 1950s, the architectural challenge—as it has been since the introduction of the automobile—was how to capture the motorist's attention. People zoomed past commercial establishments and seldom slowed down. Easy access became paramount, and a sophisticated system of signs and symbols guided drivers in their quest for goods and services.

The superhighways linking the nation also brought with them innovative designs for roadside services. The earlier structures shaped like giant pigs, ducks, coffeepots, and flying fish that so intrigued motorists just years before, had begun to disappear. Their replacements reflected postwar aspirations to be "modern" at all costs. Some employed unusual and bizarre shapes and colors, along with plastics, stainless steel, fiberglass, lots of neon tubing, and anything else their developers thought would be eye-catching. Triangles instead of rectangles, boomerangs instead of triangles, abstractions instead of boomerangs—everything had to be scaled to the moving automobile, not to the strolling pedestrian.

After the 1956 launch of the Russian space vehicle *Sputnik I*, shapes that somehow suggested the space race became immensely popular. Rocket-like imagery, along with hints of satellites, planets, suns, stars, and constellations appeared with great profusion. No one ever questioned what a rocket or a satellite had to do with a hamburger; space occupied a part of the public mind and the public loved hamburgers. Atomic designs followed close behind—atoms, complete with rotating neutrons and protons, sparkled above even the most mundane of enterprises.

Collectively, this constituted an architecture of wonder, almost anti-gravitational in its effects, and brought about by advances in building technology. Plastics led the way; their malleability, the ease with which they could be molded into infinite shapes, lent them to creative design. Nowhere was freeform architecture better displayed than on the trend-setting West Coast, especially in drive-in restaurants and diners. Burgers and fries might be a staple across the country, but back in the East, the staid White Castles and White Towers could not hold a candle to their more frivolous Western counterparts. When Walt Disney in 1955 laid out the first Disneyland in Anaheim, California, he did not hesitate to incorporate this kind of futuristic approach in Tomorrowland.[12]

This period also marked the beginning of the age of the franchise: franchised hamburger stands, motels, gas stations, bowling alleys, dry cleaners, supermarkets, convenience stores, and variety stores. The parent organizations strove to make the businesses instantly recognizable, and in a sea of clutter and distractions, the order proved a daunting one. But once recognized, the franchisee promised predictability; the unrecognized business, on the other hand, usually folded.

The Sign as Symbol

In another bow to the highway, commercial signs grew to monumental size in order to be seen from greater distances while traveling at high speeds. In fact, architects conceived of the entire structure as an integrated sign—from the orange roofs on a Howard Johnson's to the golden arches of a McDonald's. Broad expanses of glass allowed a view into the interior and all that transpired there, a kind of billboard to advertise function. This openness suggests a democratization of architecture and a reproach to elitism. Transparent walls mediate between the exterior and the interior, and private space and public space blend into one.

An example of the iconic role signs play can be found with the familiar green and yellow roadside emblem that announced a Holiday Inn during the fifties. Founded in 1954 and still new to many people, the chain's towering sign—the "Great Sign" as some called it—featured an exploding star, a huge boomerang arrow, the words "Holiday Inn" in a distinctive script, and a marquee of such dimensions that it could simultaneously advertise coming events, meal specials, perhaps a birthday or anniversary, and ongoing activities within. Its sheer size demanded recognition, and the sign itself became an icon, a visual magnet, one promising food, shelter, and economy.

Holiday Inns of America, the corporate owners of the chain, recognized the value of their sign and registered it as an official trademark. Although its design and dimensions have changed over the years, the sign is never sold; franchise holders lease it, allowing it to remain the property of the corporation.[13]

Another illustration of the iconic sign would be the famous Golden Arches of McDonald's hamburger stands. They really do not mean or represent anything; they exist simply as shapes—parabolas, to be exact. But they have become associated with the company, with fast food, and have assumed a symbolic meaning of their own. The work of architect Stanley Meston and first introduced in 1953 at a new McDonald's in Phoenix, Arizona, the Golden Arches immediately garnered attention. The growing firm saw to it that they got replicated in all subsequent stands. By the end of 1959 the firm had 145 outlets dispensing burgers and fries to eager consumers. With time, the arches have diminished in size, but they continue to symbolize the company and have become the corporate logo. Originally, McDonald's also had a mascot named Speedee, a bulbous, neon-lit figure tucked into the apex of each of the arches. Speedee represented the speed and economy of the chain, but when marketers later learned that people identified McDonald's with the arches and not with the mascot, the company unceremoniously dropped him in 1962.[14] [See chapter 6, "Food and Drink," for more on the rise of McDonald's.]

DESIGN

Designers

Heretofore anonymous, a number of designers established names for themselves in association with their products. People like Harry Bertoia (wire furniture), Charles and Ray Eames (laminated plywood and molded plastic "Eames Chairs"), George Nelson (storage systems and platform benches), Eero Saarinen (molded fiberglass "Tulip Chairs"), and Russel Wright (plastic and ceramic dinnerware, including the popular "American Modern" line) became known to the public. Advertising promoted their names along with their designs, and it was chic to buy a product designed by someone famous and respected.

Furthering this trend, New York's Museum of Modern Art sponsored, from 1950 to 1955, annual "Good Design" shows that exhibited the best in contemporary home accessories by the leading figures in the field. To have the prestigious museum's "Good Design" label attached to a product served as a badge of honor, one recognized by savvy consumers.

Kitchens and Appliances

The immensely popular ranch houses of the 1950s gave considerable attention to kitchens, especially the appliances that would be found there. As a result, this once-neglected room emerged as an important display area for modern design. Because most ranches put a premium on available space, the kitchen became home to built-in cabinets and appliances. This emphasis signified a blend of the technologically new and the traditional. Cabinets faced in Early American knotty pine with wrought-iron hardware might share space with an advanced, all-electric range.

General Electric experimented with horizontal refrigerators that hung from wall studs. Perhaps too daring or different for most homemakers, they lasted only a couple of years. Other manufacturers introduced swing-down burners for stoves, ranges on wheels, and eye-level controls. Functionalism was stressed, but in a bow to the prevailing automobile culture, the ranges of the 1950s boasted as much chrome—burner rings, handles, accents and trim—as the latest models from Detroit. In addition to the chrome touches, major appliances clad in stainless steel instead of enamel finishes made their debut, along with a host of other innovations for the consumer. [For more on American automotive design in the 1950s, see chapter 11, "Travel and Recreation."]

Much commercial design of the 1950s carried over the Streamline Moderne characteristics developed during the late 1930s and 1940s, but designers found themselves pressed to create a distinctive 1950s look in small appliances and dinnerware. They responded with plain, unadorned pieces, especially in the case of casual china. Featuring hourglass and tulip shapes in cups and pitchers, they gave saucers and plates sharp, dynamic lines instead of the curves and rounded edges that so characterized Streamlining. Accessories that dispensed with ornamentation quickly became the favorites of consumers. Flatware likewise was redesigned, often becoming sculptural in its lines, with stainless steel emerging as a new favorite at the expense of traditional silver. Even prosaic pots and pans enjoyed a facelift, displaying crisper lines and more ergonomically shaped handles.

Polyethylene, a durable but flexible plastic and one of the technological advances of the postwar era, was used to make everything from refrigerator containers to garbage cans. It would not crack or break, resisted cold, and could be cheaply mass produced in a rainbow of colors. Names like Tupperware and Rubbermaid attracted millions of shoppers, and Tupperware parties in private homes proved a novel and effective way to merchandise their modern-looking polyethylene containers.[15] [For more on the Tupperware phenomenon, see chapter 6, "Food and Drink."]

Melamine, another sturdy plastic, gained renown as a revolutionary new product for dinnerware in 1952. Virtually unbreakable, and available in white and pastels, it complemented the appliances and furnishings found in the modern kitchen. Formica, a plastic laminate for countertops, introduced its "Skylark" pattern in 1950. This popular choice echoes the abstract forms found in modern Abstract Expressionist painting, although few consumers realized the connection. Even the lowly sink received a new look. The basin could be had in stainless steel, and plumbing manufacturers offered faucets that mixed hot and cold water from a single, moveable spigot.[16]

Modern kitchens received an unanticipated emphasis from television. Cooking shows, cheap and easy to produce in the early days of TV, usually featured a lineup of shiny new appliances loaned by willing merchants. A spacious work island might constitute the entire set. In addition, the major networks often employed kitchens as props in their situation comedies. Many of these series, such as *The Donna Reed Show* (1958–1966), *Father Knows Best* (1954–1962), *Leave It to Beaver* (1957–1963), and *Ozzie and Harriet* (1952–1966) set numerous scenes in sparkling, well-equipped kitchens.

Although "Mom" (Donna Reed as Donna Stone, Jane Wyatt as Margaret Anderson, Barbara Billingsley as June Cleaver, and Harriet Hilliard as herself) frequently appeared at the sink or stove, she made her entrance impeccably coiffed and dressed, looking more like a model than a mother. The kitchen served as her territory, and she was firmly in command when there. "Dad" (Carl Betz as Alex Stone, Robert Young as Jim Anderson, Hugh Beaumont as Ward Cleaver, and Ozzie Nelson as himself) bumbled in and out, clearly out of his element. And thus were gender roles—along with the latest in appliances—promoted. Viewers could compare their kitchens with those they saw weekly on these popular shows. Of course, the same could be said for other areas of the house, but the kitchen often seemed the center for both drama and humor.

Interior Decoration

Because most postwar homes and apartments had less floor space than did prewar buildings, many suburban houses featured open interior main floors. The device of eliminating walls also cut costs, and at the same time it encouraged "togetherness," a term that grew in popularity throughout the decade. It suggested that families should do things together, that group activities created families that stayed together. The typical suburban house did in fact force upon the family a kind of shared space, and by the middle of the decade, the "family room," something new in American housing, had become a standard part of the typical ranch dwelling. It served as a communal room for watching TV, listening to the hi-fi, playing games, reading (but not alone), snacking, and so on. The very ubiquity of family rooms in much suburban construction testified to their popularity with the public.

Given this emphasis on openness, furniture groupings instead of walls often delineated the uses of space. A large, formal table and six or eight matching chairs identified the dining area. Easy chairs, a couch or two, and maybe a coffee table and some small end tables said that a particular space served as the living room. Because furniture often had to be moved around to adapt to activities, designers tended to opt for lightweight, portable pieces. The overstuffed sofa became a dated relic; furnishings often constructed of slender pieces of wood or fabrics suspended on metal frames replaced the massive tables and chairs formerly in style. Open and flexible storage units supplanted the bulky armoires of years gone by. The activities of the modern house flowed from area to area, and only the bedrooms and bathrooms were walled off and built with doors.

Offices, too, had to contend with the concept of openness. Freestanding dividers created semi-private cubicles for employees. In addition, the flexible accordion wall came along in the 1950s; it allowed large spaces to be divided into smaller ones, or vice versa, as needs arose.

Color became an important part of modern design. Because most new structures displayed little applied ornamentation, decorators called for bold colors as visual compensation. Both the interiors and exteriors of homes and office buildings saw the application of bright, cheery hues. "Color consultants" analyzed the psychological properties of colors; they purportedly revealed how warm tones (reds, yellows, creamy whites) and cool ones (blues, greens, grays) affect people's moods. These studies at times lacked much scientific validity, but they sold millions of gallons of paint.[17]

Furnishings

Modern furniture slowly caught on during the fifties, especially that labeled "Scandinavian" or "Danish Modern." Three Scandinavian countries—Denmark, Finland, and Sweden—led this movement, with

In the postwar 1950s, the concept of Scandinavian furniture design took hold. Many people liked the plain, no-frills look of "Danish Modern." Its austerity was lessened, however, by the warmth of natural woods, especially teak and walnut. Note the latest home furnishing in this 1952 photograph: the addition of a cabinet-style television set. Source: Library of Congress.

Denmark, at least in American eyes, being the leader, innovating in furniture, textiles, jewelry, and ceramics. Much of the furniture came in exotic woods like teak and rosewood, and it emphasized both traditional craftsmanship and modern lines. It could be easily disassembled for shipping; it was durable, comfortable, and fit in with many decors.

American manufacturers picked up on the Danish/Scandinavian look, and soon marketed products as varied as air conditioners and kitchen ranges that sported oiled teak and clean lines. Two companies in particular led the move toward progressive American furniture design: Herman Miller, Inc., and Knoll International. Both brands became popular with the public, and they pioneered in the mass production of affordable contemporary furniture. In time, consumers looked for "American Modern," a term signifying functionality and low price. Such furniture often employed molded plastics, metals, and laminated woods and veneers. By 1952, some 50 to 60 percent of all new furniture sold in the United States could be labeled modernistic, although traditional designs continued to attract a significant following.

Plastics, often seen as substitutes for other materials, became stylish in their own right. Instead of trying to imitate marble, wood, and so on, plastics took on their own identity. For example, consumers in the 1950s discovered Naugahyde, a trademarked kind of flexible vinyl that can replace leather and other natural upholstery fabrics. Cheap and relatively carefree, Naugahyde quickly became a favorite for chairs, sofas, bar stools, and decorative trim.[18]

Accessories

The freestanding hooded fireplace, ideally suited for family rooms, made its first appearance in 1953 and it immediately caught on. "Atomic clocks" sold well throughout the decade. They featured round faces representing the nucleus of an atom, and radiating numbers on spokes that symbolized the rotating particles. Pole lamps (also referred to as "pogo lamps") were so called because they relied on a spring-loaded pole that created a snug fit between floor and ceiling. Adjustable reflectors up and down the length of the pole directed light as needed. For the open spaces of a modern house, these fixtures could be placed almost anywhere. Because high-fidelity sound attracted a wide following, the various components—amplifier, tuner, turntable—often led the way in Scandinavian design and the free use of teak.

The basic concepts for the classic rotary desk telephone began to evolve in 1946; the work of designer Henry Dreyfuss, it was commercially introduced in the early fifties. Because AT&T and Bell Laboratories then held a monopoly on all telephones in use, virtually every American home had at least one of these black plastic instruments. Almost indestructible, there existed no other piece of technology better known to the general public, and its sleek, contemporary lines resonated with the times.

Similarly, the Rolodex rotary card file came out in 1958. Completely manual—flip the cards until the desired information comes up—they could be updated or edited easily. Its polished metal and plastic holder seemed to symbolize the modern office. Although the Rolodex predated the personal computer, it remains a valuable tool that employs minimal technology.

The gaudy 1950s jukeboxes, particularly in the models created by Paul Fuller for the Wurlitzer Company, tend to sum up much of the decade's design trends. Brightly lit, with cascading and blinking colors, lots of shiny surfaces, and angles that suggest Detroit's cars of the era as much as anything, their flashiness and pizzazz epitomize the era. For just a few nickels, these machines encouraged conspicuous consumption and leisure pursuits, two activities forever associated with the fifties.

By the middle of the decade, the initial demand for many domestic products had been satisfied. With wartime shortages a thing of the past, manufacturers now found themselves experiencing declining sales in a wide range of durable goods. Companies therefore urged their designers to come up with new ideas and motifs on a yearly basis, thus taking the concept of planned obsolescence, so successfully employed by the automobile industry, into the home. Consumers did not necessarily need a new refrigerator, but this year's model in pink certainly seemed an improvement over last year's off-white one, or so the marketing people would have potential buyers believe. In this way, consumerism continued to be encouraged and the postwar buying spree had no end in sight.

SUMMARY

In a minor building boom that went almost unnoticed because of all the Levittowns, malls, and skyscrapers that were being erected at the same time, architects and designers collaborated on some of the most outrageous, flamboyant, and fanciful building of the decade. This was the age of the drive-in, both the food kind and the movie variety; it also saw restaurants, gas stations, specialty shops, banks, motels, supermarkets, car washes, and bowling alleys conspiring to distinguish themselves in a sea of commercial development.

Rejecting any futuristic designs, residential architecture on the other hand remained traditional, with one important exception: the modest ranch house, low and somewhat open, emerged as the home of choice during the decade. In terms of popular culture, the most important aspect of architecture and design was the 1950s housing boom that led to the Great American Suburb, repeated subdivisions built on the fringes of towns and cities across the land.

5

Fashion

In the postwar years, via insistent marketing and advertising, manufacturers convinced consumers of the necessity of updating their wardrobes. New items constantly appeared on the racks, rendering their once-stylish predecessors obsolete. In a similar manner, products ranging from automobiles to waffle irons went through model changes, making the 1950s the first true era of planned obsolescence. But, with more disposable income than ever before, Americans gleefully accepted this obvious manipulation; it grew from the austerity of the Great Depression and the shortages of World War II. People could go on a spending binge, and an endless array of fashionable choices made the shopping fun.

SYNTHETIC FIBERS

Touted as "an age of science," the 1950s stand as a time when technology and creativity combined to make life easier and better. For clothing manufacturers, this promise meant an array of synthetic fibers that would be adaptable to any kind of apparel; in fact, one could wear outfits that contained few or no natural fibers. Led by the giant DuPont chemical corporation ("better things for better living" read the company slogan), acrylics and polyesters came on the market, revolutionizing what people wore. Orlon, a DuPont acrylic, went into production in 1952 and emerged as the material of choice for sweaters and other casual wear; it felt soft and resisted pilling. Thanks to Dacron, DuPont's name for a polyester fiber introduced in 1953, shirts, blouses, suits, and dresses, usually wrinkled and limp after one wearing, could be tossed in the washer and hung to dry, emerging fresh and crisp in a matter of hours.

The huge DuPont chemical corporation developed a
number of new, man-made fibers during the 1950s. One of
the most popular was Orlon, which, as this 1952 ad points
out, made for soft, washable sweaters and skirts.
Presumably the sweater worn by the admiring male is also
woven from Orlon. Source: Hagley Museum and Library.

These man-made fibers made possible significant fashion changes, and
because they were synthetic, they could be mass-produced in bold, fluorescent colors, a trend that carried over into bright costume jewelry. Consumers discovered a few disadvantages with these early synthetics: if not
cleaned regularly, they took on an unpleasant chemical odor. And, for
some wearers, polyesters and acrylics possessed a cheap, artificial look—
too crisp, too bright—but most people nevertheless shopped eagerly for

clothes made from "no-iron, drip-dry" fabrics. The durability and the little care such items required assured them great and enduring popularity.

In the late 1940s, a Swiss hiker named George de Mestral became annoyed with the various burrs that clung to his clothing when he was outdoors. But an examination of those burrs led de Mestral to the conclusion he could create a product that would rival the ubiquitous zipper. He noted that the burrs used an ingenious hook-and-loop locking process to catch onto clothing, and from this came Velcro. By the mid-1950s, he had a nylon locking tape in production. He chose "vel" from velvet, and "cro" from crochet, and a new fastener came on the market.[1]

MEN'S FASHION

Gentlemen's Attire

American men tend to be inherently traditional in their clothing choices, and the 1950s proved no exception. The conservative, three-button suit dominated business wear. It had narrow lapels, straight legs with cuffs, and most likely featured shades of gray or other somber colors, eschewing flashiness of any kind. Shirts generally came in white or pale blue broadcloth, either in button-down or spread-collar styles. Author Sloan Wilson had typified male tastes as "the man in the gray flannel suit," also the title of his best-selling 1955 novel. For the remainder of the decade, this phrase held true for the overwhelming majority of white-collar men.

Narrow ties decorated with subtle patterns or stripes usually accompanied these sedate suits, although equally sober bow ties might be worn. A few males tried wearing ascots (a knotted scarf that goes inside an open shirt collar) in place of the long-established necktie, but the majority saw them as an affectation. Ascots never became a part of any basic wardrobe.

If the weather threatened rain, a tan or beige raincoat sufficed. Plain and serviceable, it reinforced the uniform look that so characterized male fashion. Rain or shine, a hat completed the outfit, usually a felt fedora for most weather, and maybe a Panama style when temperatures rose. Snap-brim hats (the brim is smaller and less pronounced than in, say, fedoras) also enjoyed a certain vogue, as did tweedy and velour hats that were variations on the snap-brim design. Style leaders might sport a British cap, but most men preferred to go with tradition. Regardless of what he wore, a properly dressed man in the 1950s still had to don a hat.

Men's Leisurewear

For the more casual male, Bermuda shorts gained acceptance as warm-weather alternatives to long trousers. Until 1953, such an item of clothing simply would not have been found in a man's closet. Why Bermuda shorts, or "walking shorts" as some called them, became so popular is anyone's guess, but staid, conservative American males liked them. A few daring souls even showed up at the office in jacket, tie, and Bermudas, but that went too far in the minds of most men. Many restaurants and hotels attempted to ban them, and fashion arbiters derided them. As sales moved steadily upward, however, Bermudas moved from audacious to traditional; by 1959, most people considered them entirely appropriate leisurewear, just another item in any well-stocked closet.

As the decade drew to a close, more and more men's slacks, both casual and dress, lost their bagginess, becoming straighter and slimmer, and the unpleated, cuffless look dominated. For reasons never entirely understood, a small, nonfunctional belt and buckle appeared on the backs of many pants. Sewn directly onto the material, just above the rear pockets but below the regular belt around the waist, it became a minor accessory on slacks and shorts in the later 1950s. This unusual attachment soon fizzled out, however, relegated to the category of failed fashion fads.

The success and acceptance of rock 'n' roll, especially as personified by Elvis Presley, helped usher in denim as an adult leisurewear fabric. Denim jeans, also called blue jeans or dungarees, had long been associated with low-paid laborers and juvenile delinquents. Schools forbade them, commentators railed against their bad influence, and adolescents everywhere wanted them. Seen increasingly in movies and on television, jeans continued to carry their negative connotations for many, but for an equally large number they represented freedom from dress codes, a new appreciation of leisure. By the end of the decade, the stigma attached to blue jeans was wearing off, and more and more men had taken to adding denim to their leisure wardrobe.[2]

Male Hair Styles

Throughout the decade, short hair dominated—crew cuts, flattops, butch cuts (the last thought to go with a tough-guy image), or just simple short haircuts. The crew cut, as casual and carefree as it looked, actually required some attention. Many men took to applying moustache wax to their hair. This product, which goes on as a soft paste but dries hard, allowed the hair in a crew cut to stand erect for the day. Of course, the closer the crew cut, the less any need existed for waxes or pomades.

Sideburns were often equated with gangsters and hoodlums. But when Elvis Presley and a number of other rock 'n' roll stars sported sideburns, some men quickly affected them, although overall the hair remained short. As the decade drew to a close, more hair "on the sides and top" became fashionable, pushing aside the crew-cut look.

WOMEN'S FASHION
Women's Wear

Following trends established during the depressed thirties and wartime forties, the vast majority of American women no longer looked to Europe, especially France, for fashion inspiration. A growing number of young and energetic domestic designers provided plenty of attractive designs, most of which were quickly translated into inexpensive, ready-to-wear items available at the nearest dress shop or department store. These styles finally gained a name of their own: the "American Look," and its success marked the end of European dominance in haute couture as far as the U.S. market was concerned.

European designers continued to have some, albeit limited, impact among more wealthy clients. The French design houses, especially those of Christian Dior and Givenchy, along with the Spanish Balenciaga, exported the "New Look" in the early years of the decade. Cinched waists and billowing skirts characterized this import, and costly materials and complex construction put the New Look out of the financial range of many women. In 1956, the "sack dress" (or chemise dress, as it was also known) appeared on American shores. Initially a subject of ridicule because of its basic shapelessness, women nonetheless bought the design, often in inexpensive knock-offs manufactured domestically, in sufficient numbers to make it a trendsetter for the period. Many women liked its lack of a defined waistline. But men did not appreciate the "sack," and the jokes ensued, but so did the sales. In the later fifties, manufacturers began labeling it a "shift," working with the idea this new term might be more acceptable and less liable to ridicule than "sack." Whatever its name, the sack/shift/chemise continued as a favorite for women around the nation. Easily duplicated and simple, it became an enduring part of American popular fashion for years.

A career woman, however, did not put on a sack when going to work; she wore tailored wool suits over silk blouses. She also donned gloves and a hat in the early fifties, both customs carryovers from earlier times. To be "dressed up," no woman would think of leaving the house without the proper accessories. The pillbox hat dominated as the choice for the decade. Her shoes, equally dressy, often came with thin stiletto heels. In cool weather, a clutch coat finished off the ensemble. The simple frocks worn by Mamie Eisenhower more accurately represented the mass market. Despite derision by many fashion commentators, the president's wife epitomized middle-class tastes and values, and her simple wardrobe illustrated the conservative fashions most women chose to wear.

Business executive or housewife, women still found themselves saddled with heavy and binding underclothing. Bras had wires, complex stitching, and padding. Virtually all women wore girdles or corsets. At the beginning of the decade, these "foundation garments" tended to be cumbersome and uncomfortable, with elastic, Lastex, stays, and even lacing to constrict the body into certain contours. Synthetics made possible new, streamlined girdles that, in turn, allowed for tight, straight, slim skirts and slacks. Garter belts, panties, stockings, liners, slips, and possibly even a large number of petticoats, starched and stiffened, added to the burden. For most of the decade, women suffered in the name of fashion, and fashion was sometimes a harsh mistress.[3]

Films and Fashion

Even with the triumph of the American Look, Hollywood remained infatuated with the mystique of Paris and high fashion. Such frothy movies as *Lovely to Look At* (1952), *The French Line* (1954), and *Funny Face* (1957) allowed endless displays of designer styles. For example, the high-powered casting of Audrey Hepburn and Fred Astaire in *Funny Face* caused the film to do well at the box office, not its costuming. In the eyes of producers, however, its success perpetuated the notion that American women wanted high European style and conveniently ignored the reality of booming sales of American sportswear and ready-to-wear.

A contrast between the New Look and the American Look can be seen in the styles worn by actresses Audrey Hepburn (*Roman Holiday* [1953], *Sabrina* [1954], *Love in the Afternoon* [1957], etc.) and Marilyn Monroe (*Gentlemen Prefer Blondes* [1953], *The Seven Year Itch* [1955], *Some Like It Hot* [1959], etc.) in most of their movies. The first represents innocence; the other exudes glamour. Hepburn is chic; Monroe is Hollywood. An extension of that equation can be found in the work of Grace Kelly (*Rear Window* [1954], *High Society* [1956], etc.) and Jayne Mansfield (*The Girl Can't Help It* [1956], *Will Success Spoil Rock Hunter?* [1957], etc.). Kelly personifies classic beauty, whereas Mansfield plays on traditional sex appeal. On the male side, a similar contrast can be found between singers Elvis Presley and Pat Boone. It is a case of "Blue Suede Shoes" versus white bucks, grease, and close-cropped hair.

Both Hepburn and Kelly donned expensive gowns, stylish dresses, and classic leisurewear. In fact, Hepburn frequently enjoyed the able assistance of Edith Head with her wardrobe. Head, the leading costume designer in Hollywood throughout the 1950s, boasted over thirty Academy Award nominations during her long career. Her trademark elegance showed in those pictures starring Audrey Hepburn.

On the glamour side, Monroe and Mansfield presented an image of sex, using their well-endowed figures—along with costumes to accentuate them—as part of their movie presence. Revealing décolletage and tight outfits served as their stock in trade, styles that few American women would, or could, imitate. In fact, the basic black dresses and sailor tops Audrey Hepburn wore became the most copied of all Hollywood costumes during the fifties, fitting in nicely with the simplicity that characterizes the American Look. Marilyn Monroe might have had her legions of fans, but the appearance most women strove for emulated Hepburn's gamine/pixie appeal. Perhaps many young women saw the glamour of Monroe as unattainable, but the elegant class Hepburn displayed became a more realistic goal.[4]

Singer/actress Doris Day mediated between Audrey Hepburn and Marilyn Monroe. In a series of successful comedies—*Lucky Me* (1954), *Teacher's Pet* (1958), *The Tunnel of Love* (1958), *It Happened to Jane* (1959), and *Pillow Talk* (1959)—Day came to epitomize the 1950s American woman/girl. Immaculately dressed and coiffed, but in very American fashions that neither glamorized nor hinted at high styles, Day plays an attractive young woman who, despite the best intentions, gets herself into goofy situations. But she also gets out of them, with her honor always intact. Doris Day would, on many levels, find her television counterpart in comedian Lucille Ball. As more and more Americans watched television, their exposure to celebrity fashions increased proportionally, and they quickly imitated what they saw on sitcoms and variety shows. This imitation helps to explain the dressiness of much clothing, even that designed for doing housework or cooking.

Women's Hair Styles

Younger women frequently wore their hair pulled back in a manner dubbed a "ponytail." Many others, however, wore their hair cut short in a "poodle cut," the perfect clip to accompany a poodle skirt. Both the ponytail and the poodle cut emphasized a girlish appearance, but the poodle cut required bi-weekly trims and many curlers at night. In honor of Mamie Eisenhower, the president's popular wife, and her long-established style of bangs on the forehead, "Mamie Bangs" became an overnight sensation for many women.

Both Toni home permanents and Miss Clairol hair coloring came along in 1950. The famous Clairol advertising slogan, "Does she or doesn't she?" appeared in 1956. Because of their impacts, beauty shops across the nation noted a fall-off in business. The enormously successful *Gentlemen Prefer Blondes* (1953) cast Marilyn Monroe (blonde) and Jane Russell (brunette), and the movie suggested that gentlemen indeed did prefer the blonde look, with the result that three out of every ten brunettes dyed their hair blonde.[5]

In the late 1950s, bouffant hairdos began to capture a number of admirers. The "Bouffant Look" involved putting one's hair in elaborate curlers, or rollers, and applying generous amounts of hairspray to preserve the look. Revlon, in a clever marketing ploy, introduced various sprays for different hair types. It all resulted in lacquered hair that stood out from the head and could be arranged in numerous styles. Bouffants, however, took patience and they were somewhat fragile. For women with time and the inclination, however, the bouffant marked a change from all the girlish, natural styles that had flourished earlier in the 1950s.

The rise of the bouffant meant the decline of the hat. As long as a hairstyle remained uncomplicated, a hat could be worn. But the fragility of a bouffant almost always precluded a hat. Only the simplest berets and pillboxes survived, and even they often looked strange atop mounds of lacquered hair.

In the areas of hygiene and makeup, roll-on deodorants gained an immediate following in 1955; "no-smear" lipsticks also came out in 1955 and sold well. Throughout the decade, Max Factor had legions of cosmetic customers; the firm's pancake foundation emulated Hollywood, giving a woman an unblemished appearance. Eye shadow and eyeliner also became commonplace applications, further proof that the beauty business, like everything else, was booming.

THE YOUTH MARKET

Unlike prior decades, young people in the fifties constituted a formidable consumer force. They had money and few qualms about spending it, making teenage and young adult fashions one of the most profitable postwar lines of attire. Styles for both children and adolescents became ever more elaborate and varied as manufacturers awoke to the potential market before them. They were not to be disappointed.

Perhaps the most significant aspect of youth fashion involved the myriad ways it rejected the more conservative and traditional clothing worn by adults. Instead of owning outfits that mimicked adult styles, young people in the fifties delighted in putting on clothes they could call theirs and theirs alone. For the first time, a unique, identifiable style emerged, and designers jumped at the opportunities presented by this prosperous youth culture.

Young Men's Clothing

When it came to dressing up or dressing down, males in every walk of life, from junior high onward, desired a look dictated by evolving fashion codes for the young. Two primary styles evolved: the conservative, or "preppy," Ivy League look, and the cool "greaser" look. Class and economic lines often determined the choice.

Those bound for college or white-collar jobs opted for the Ivy League style: for formal, dress-up wear, the suit possessed three buttons, often

For the well-dressed male, the look was tight and
buttoned-down, or "Ivy League." This grouping—
appropriately posed in front of Columbia University's Low
Library—shows the dressier side of the style, emphasizing
even in casual clothing the need for a conservative, well-
groomed appearance. Source: Library of Congress.

included a vest, and the trousers had unpleated fronts and straight legs.
The shirt collar came in a proper oxford button-down, the tie featured rep
stripes or a muted paisley, and the shoes tended to be businesslike wing-
tips. The trend clearly aimed toward a kind of elegance, from close-
cropped hair to a faultlessly tied Windsor knot on a narrow tie. In fact,
the young men of the fifties frequently attired themselves more carefully
than did their fathers, who persisted in wearing versions of the nonde-
script suits of the thirties and forties.

Ivy League males readily accepted a uniform casual look: tweedy sport
coats, unpleated cotton khaki slacks, and oxford-cloth button-down shirts,
usually in a solid pastel, with pink a particular favorite. Some might fancy
a bold waistcoat or vest. These tended to be two-sided, reversible garments, with a bright paisley on one side and a more conservative solid
color on the other; they were worn with ties and never left open, in keeping with the tight, buttoned look of the decade. Sweaters featured either
a V-neck or crewneck. Penny loafers—a shiny penny could be inserted into
a space provided on the leather instep—or carefully scuffed white bucks
or "dirty bucks" (the leather came in a tan or light brown color) completed
this studied casualness.[6]

Many junior and senior high school–aged males, along with those who decided against college or engaged in blue-collar trades, bowed to the imagery found in much mass media, choosing the "greaser" or "hood" look. Although it has come to be associated with working-class youth, it also signified rebellion against parental and societal restrictions imposed on youth in general. But fashion rebellions can go only so far. The 1950s still demanded that all males wear neckties for most social affairs, and because people associated Ivy League propriety with college and white-collar pursuits, a different look evolved for those young men who chose other avenues of fashion. Shaped suits and sport coats often came in charcoal gray or pastel tones, and emphasized long lapels that plunged dramatically to the waist; the jacket closed with either a single or double button slightly below the belt line. Slacks, often called "rogue trousers," occasionally sported set-in side seams of contrasting colors; most featured double and triple pleats and pegged bottoms (taken in at the cuff). Highly polished shoes, preferably cordovans, the name of an expensive leather then much in vogue, finished the outfit.

Often a billowing roll collar highlighted dress shirts, and French cuffs with huge, showy cufflinks provided the finishing touch. For the truly stylish, these shirts came in bright pink or black, graced by a slender red or black necktie. The young men wearing these outfits presented an intriguing link to their zoot-suited brothers of the 1940s, although nothing so daring as the zoot suit carried on into the 1950s.

More memorable, however, was the casual dress of the hoods and greasers, a look that swept through the ranks of American adolescents. Tight blue jeans, T-shirts, leather motorcycle jackets, wide garrison belts, boots, slicked hair, often styled in a ducktail (or "D.A.", so called for its resemblance to the tail feathers on the rear end of a duck), along with sideburns, characterized the look. The more radical, controversial hood costume included such touches as rolling up a pack of cigarettes in the sleeve of a T-shirt and wearing chains and studs. Its most famous manifestation came in 1954's *The Wild One*, a teen-oriented movie starring Marlon Brando. The outfits worn on screen evolved into a virtual uniform for everyday wear and critics associated such dress with juvenile delinquency and a host of other social ills.

School administrators around the country attempted to ban all vestiges of the hood look. Although there was nothing intrinsically wrong with motorcycle jackets and garrison belts, the connotations said otherwise. Anyone wearing that garb had to be rebellious and a nonconformist, and looking tough suggested juvenile delinquency to worried parents and officials.

Singers Elvis Presley and Carl Perkins both had big hits with the same song, "Blue Suede Shoes," in 1956. The result was a rush to buy suede shoes, preferably blue, of course. Country vocalist Marty Robbins made the charts with "A White Sport Coat (and a Pink Carnation)" in 1957, spurring another buying spree. But they were not alone in celebrating teen fashions. In 1955, the Cheers had a minor hit with "Black Denim Trousers"; the Clovers likewise attracted attention with "Blue Velvet" in 1955. Eddie Fisher crooned "Dungaree Doll" in 1955, and Billy Vaughn orchestrated "Petticoats of Portugal" in 1956. A final contribution to the sartorial scene came with "Tan Shoes with Pink Shoelaces," by Janet King in 1959. Rockers like Presley, Little Richard, Jerry Lee Lewis, and Chuck Berry began affecting all sorts of trademark costumes that teens everywhere admired. Adolescents might not emulate every item of clothing a star wore, but they were aware of the connections between fashion and music, particularly rock 'n' roll.

Young Women's Clothing

Trendsetting magazines like *Vogue* and *Seventeen* helped to usher in the new teenage market. By running constant features that stressed youthful fashions instead of "young adult" or "women's" styles, they targeted the growing numbers of teens in the country. Department stores stayed close behind, setting up teenage departments to cater to this new clientele.

Just like menswear, approaches to youthful fashions differed among various groups. Everyone seemed to agree that turned-up jeans, complemented by a too-large white shirt belonging to Dad or Big Brother and never tucked in, but with the tails sometimes tied, served well as a virtual uniform for teenaged girls outside of school. They finished off the outfit with bobby sox and loafers or saddle shoes. In all, it served as a comfortable, inexpensive, and very popular style.[7]

The preppy look of the early fifties emerged as a major style success. It featured a full skirt with a tiny waist, the fullness emphasized by many starched crinoline petticoats beneath and maybe even a four-foot diameter hoop to keep it all symmetrical. Crinolines may not have been practical, but they enjoyed a wide following. The poodle skirt, a flaring skirt often constructed of felt with poodle appliqués and a cinched belt, also burst onto the scene. It proved only a momentary variation, but nonetheless won many adherents. Popular footwear included flats (no heels), ballerina shoes that resembled slippers more than anything else. Some young women wore white bucks, just as did innumerable males. But most carried a chalk bag to keep theirs spotless; the "dirty buck" look existed primarily for men.

A few teenaged girls took on the trappings of a feminine greaser look, or "tough" image. Heavy makeup, tight sweaters over an obviously padded bra, and a general air of lawlessness characterized their appearance. Male or female, the greaser look served more as a statement about rebellion than about fashion.

Both men and women wore Bermuda shorts during the 1950s, and the style had many fans. But some women saw Bermudas as inherently unattractive; they emphasized the knees, arguably the least flattering part

The look for women was dressy and formal. This photograph shows a young woman wearing a feminine version of the Eisenhower Jacket, a short, tight-fitting battle jacket worn by millions of troops in World War II. Her single strand of pearls and white gloves give no hint of military dress, but they were just as much a uniform as the khaki worn by soldiers. Source: Library of Congress.

of the leg. As an alternative to Bermudas, shorter shorts, or even "short shorts," gained popularity. By 1957, this new article of clothing aroused hot debate among school administrators and public authorities. It centered on what constituted "too short." Adolescents loved the squabble, and a record, "Short Shorts," by the Royal Teens briefly made the charts in 1958. Although the debate would continue long after the fifties were over, dress codes began to appear in junior and senior high schools across the nation.

If a woman disliked Bermudas, preferred not to wear full-length slacks, and lacked the courage or confidence to wear abbreviated shorts, she could always turn to Capri pants. Pants that reached only to midcalf, Capris came in a variety of bright colors and could be worn with virtually any top, qualities that quickly made them a hot-selling item. Capris also were called "pedal pushers" because they had no cuffs to catch on a chain when riding a bicycle. In 1958, Carl Perkins's "Pink Pedal Pushers," could be heard on jukeboxes across the nation, musical testimony to their popularity.[8]

Teenagers also discovered ankle bracelets as a fashion accessory. They signified going steady or, for the cynical, being chained to someone. This latter attitude led to the phrase "slave bracelet." Another minor fad involved Pop-It beads. By popping two beads apart, and then adding or deleting beads, the owner could lengthen or shorten a strand at will.

Children's Styles

Durability and practicality characterized most children's clothing. Blue jeans, such a contentious item for adolescents, did not achieve widespread

The phenomenal success of Walt Disney's *Davy Crockett* TV series (1954–1955) precipitated a boom in children's clothing. As shown, the fringed jacket and pants proved big sellers, but the runaway hit was the raccoon cap, complete with striped tail. Merchants sold millions, especially to boys, and little frontiersmen could be found in every neighborhood. Source: Library of Congress.

acceptance for kids until the 1960s. Instead, tradition ruled, and items like sun suits, jumpers, and overalls outsold anything new or controversial.

Hardly a fashion or a style, beanies with plastic propellers mounted on their tops became a fad for youngsters in 1952. Completely nonfunctional, the propeller rotated in a breeze or when the wearer walked or ran. For some mysterious reason, the gimmick caught on, and children everywhere wore them. [For more on this craze, see chapter 7, "Leisure Activities."]

With the growing popularity of Westerns on television, it came as no surprise that cowboy outfits for boys and girls enjoyed a new life. Fringed jackets, embroidered shirts, jeans, vests, Stetson hats in kids' sizes, and cowboy boots all sold well, with Hopalong Cassidy and Roy Rogers ensembles being particular favorites. But in 1954 and 1955, *Disneyland*, a popular and long-running (1954–1990) show, ran a five-part miniseries depicting the life and times of Davy Crockett. Each segment entertained millions of viewers, and set off a merchandising craze for Crockett-inspired items. By far the most successful was the coonskin cap reputedly worn by the woodsman. By 1956, the fad had run its course, but prior to then every little boy had to have one. [For more on Cassidy and Crockett, see chapter 7, "Leisure Activities."]

SUMMARY

In a decade of outward propriety, most men went about tightly suited and buttoned down, and women found themselves girdled and padded. For males, jeans and a leather jacket gave a hint of menace; for women, about the only allusion to sexuality came through a celebration of buxomness. Movie stars like Marilyn Monroe and Jayne Mansfield, among a number of others, flaunted their bosoms in endless pinups and films. Clearly they did not present themselves as conservative examples of American womanhood, and most women chose not to imitate them. The healthy good looks of Doris Day and the innocent high style of Audrey Hepburn instead dictated popular fashion choices.

The 1950s

6

Food and Drink

FOOD

After the belt-tightening of the Great Depression and the rationing of the war years, Americans felt ready for good food, and the prosperity of the postwar period gave them the freedom to indulge themselves. In response, food manufacturers and distributors offered a cornucopia of new tastes, new recipes, and new ways of preparing dishes of all kinds

Throughout the decade, Americans—particularly young people—ate more and consumed more calories than ever before. An increasing proportion of women worked, placing greater reliance on high-calorie processed and/or prepared foods in the home. TV dinners became a staple for many families. As fast-food restaurants proliferated in the later years of the decade, and with greater available cash for food outside the home, burgers 'n' fries supplanted salads and other more healthful menus. Medical specialists observed that American kids were out of shape; these findings came to a head with the creation of the President's Council on Youth Fitness in 1957, an organization that gained headlines but did little to improve anyone's physical heath, other than spurring interest in organized sports.

The Kitchen as Cultural Symbol

The 1950s may be remembered as the decade that rediscovered the kitchen, often making it the symbolic center of the modern house. With a return to peace, millions of women had been released from their wartime work in order to make room for discharged servicemen, but this created the problem of making use of time once taken by a job. Writers, columnists, and advertisers sought to glorify the role of the housewife in this new society. These commentators assumed that women would find their primary fulfillment in being mothers, wives, cooks, and hostesses. Endless articles claimed that the work that awaited women in the home provided far more rewards than any occupation they might have previously held. In addition, keeping a good home allowed women a means to express their love for their families. Nowhere could this love be articulated more fully than in the kitchen. From radio soap operas like *Ma Perkins* to television situation comedies like *Father Knows Best*, the image of the homemaker, ensconced in her spotless kitchen, surrounded by shiny new appliances, became commonplace. Father might know best when in the den or out in the backyard, but Mom presided when at the stove or counter.[1]

One clever way to celebrate kitchen skills involved having competitions among homemakers. An important part of the marketing strategies for Pillsbury Flour occurred when the company inaugurated its annual Bake-Off in 1949. Designed to promote their flour products, these well-publicized contests also allowed cooks to show off their talents—a reinforcement of the idea that a woman's place was in the kitchen, even if she spent her time there creating new cakes and muffins for competition. The act of cooking, of preparing food for consumption, demonstrated both nurturing and culinary skills, an attitude enhanced in much popular imagery of the 1950s.

Cookbooks

In order to make homemaking, especially cooking, more attractive, publishers, appliance manufacturers, and food processors worked on methods of preparing and serving ever easier and faster meals. The leading cookbooks of the period stressed creativity and modernity, themes that translated into guides urging the contemporary homemaker to take advantage of new technologies. The competent use of rotisseries, grills, blenders, immersible electric skillets, portable mixers, chafing dishes, electric can openers, and all the other postwar appliances flooding onto the market signified a modern, efficient kitchen. With the right equipment, there existed no reason why a housewife could not play canasta in the morning, go shopping in the early afternoon, chauffeur the kids after school, or do a dozen other personal chores and still put an attractive, nutritious meal on the table come dinner time.

With frozen and freeze-dried foods sometimes encompassing entire dinners, and canned goods of every variety available, the old image of slaving over a hot stove and laboriously preparing each dish lost validity, at least in the view of a new generation of cookbooks. Even the traditional casserole was glamorized and modernized, thanks to recipes designed to take advantage of preprepared ingredients and easy cooking.

Books like *Betty Crocker's Picture Cook Book* (1950; many editions), *The Complete Small Appliance Cookbook* (1953), and *The Complete Book of Outdoor Cookery* (1955), along with magazines like *American Home, Woman's Day,* and *Ladies' Home Journal,* featured shortcuts and practical hints on using the latest foodstuffs available at the local supermarket. They proved so popular that sales and circulations soared; *Betty Crocker's Picture Cook Book* alone had sold over a million copies by 1951. One best-seller, 1952's *The Can-Opener Cookbook,* went through several revisions and editions during the decade, and its title spoke volumes about what modern cooks really wanted. In fact the Udico electric can opener, the first of its kind, responded to that want when it came out in 1956 [2]

Incomes also rose rapidly during the 1950s, but the percentage budgeted for food rose even faster. Prepared foods, frozen dinners, snack items, and a wide range of exotic canned goods cost more than traditional groceries. Although the processing costs were considerably higher than those incurred with raw ingredients, homemakers displayed a willingness to spend the additional dollars to save some additional time. They desired the speed and efficiency that advertisers and columnists said characterized the contemporary, jet-propelled era.

Supermarkets

To accommodate this increased spending for food—and to adapt to changing demographic patterns, especially the growth of the suburbs—new, more modern supermarkets sprang up across the land. Between 1948 and 1958, the number of supermarkets in the United States doubled to over 2,500, with most of the expansion occurring outside central cities. The affluent suburbs benefited most, because the middle-class families moving there tended to spend more for groceries.

At the beginning of the decade, American supermarkets, although in the minority among grocers, accounted for about a third of all sales. By 1959, they claimed roughly 70 percent of all sales, and yet still comprised only 11 percent of all grocery stores. At the same time, they grew in size: by the early 1950s, a typical supermarket carried about four thousand items, or two to three times as much as they stocked just before World War II. Their usable floor space doubled during the decade, and their hours lengthened until some in more populous areas stayed open twenty-four hours a day, seven days a week.[3]

Suburban supermarkets provided vast parking lots, air conditioning while shopping, bright fluorescent lighting, and endless displays of their huge inventories. It all seemed a far cry from the cramped, stuffy, mom-and-pop stores most consumers remembered from their days in the city.

The modern supermarket became an icon, a showcase for the abundance of America. When England's Queen Elizabeth II visited the United

The prosperity of the 1950s meant that Americans ate better—and more—than ever before. This typical 1951 family stands amidst a cornucopia of foodstuffs, and the photograph attempts to show what four people would consume in a normal year. Note the hundreds of glass milk bottles—the plastic carton still lay in the future. Source: Hagley Museum and Library.

States in 1957, one item on her itinerary was a stop at a typical supermarket. Soviet leader Nikita Khrushchev likewise wanted to see one during his 1959 tour. This modern-day successor to the traditional grocery store had emerged as a weapon in the Cold War. To many, its vast array of goods symbolized the triumph of capitalism. But this U.S. institution also functioned as a testament to 1950s consumerism, a time when individual prosperity reached new, unheard-of heights.

Barbeques

In 1951, Sears, Roebuck and Company offered a new item: a rectangular charcoal grill on an aluminum cart; the age of the home barbeque had arrived. A competing firm added a hood to the basic design; it protected the grill from the weather, while also reflecting heat for faster, more even cooking. By 1957, grills using gas instead of charcoal appeared, and a wondrous array of utensils, aprons, and cooking aids could be purchased. The grill moved cooking to the backyard, making this exterior space an extension of the house. But because cooking on the grass lacked sophistication and class, concrete or brick patios were designed for grilling sites. "Patio dining" became stylish, and furniture makers rushed to design new lines of outdoor accessories to accommodate the fad.

Where once people considered a half-inch-thick rib-eye steak a luxurious cut of beef, the popularity of grilling made two-inch-thick marbled sirloins the last word. Grilled food tends to be hearty fare, so the job of cooking all these steaks, sausages, and roasts fell to men, a chore they readily accepted. Males who would not be caught in a kitchen donned aprons, fireproof mitts, and chef's hats as they concocted secret sauces and marinades for their specialties. It proved a curious role reversal, but one most men seemed to enjoy. Perhaps it evoked the mythic West, with cowboys gathered around the chuck wagon beneath a starry sky. At outdoor parties, the male guests congregated with the chef over drinks and offered advice, while the women stayed in the kitchen for small talk. Of course, the man grilled only the main meat dishes; a woman set the table, prepared the salads and potatoes as well as beverages and desserts indoors, and probably had primary responsibility for cleanup after the guests departed. But legions of proud males endured smoke, heat, and insects in their quest for the perfect steak. Not incidentally, beef consumption rose sharply during the 1950s, a rise led by the more expensive cuts.

Food Introductions

Throughout the 1950s, many new food products came into the marketplace. Some touted taste, but more stressed timesaving preparation and easy cooking. In the late 1940s, Post Cereals introduced a product called Post Sugar Crisp. Little did they know that a revolution in children's breakfast habits was at hand. Sugar Crisp was promoted, on the box and in advertisements, by cartoon bears named Handy, Dandy, and Candy. The use of such characters presaged nothing new—Little Orphan Annie, Buck Rogers, Donald Duck, Mickey Mouse, and many others had earlier promoted various foodstuffs—but the resulting onslaught of sugar-coated breakfast cereals could not have been predicted. Perhaps the wide availability of sugar, after its strict rationing during World War II, awakened a sweet tooth in the American public, and these new, candylike concoctions helped satisfy it.

Rival manufacturers quickly climbed aboard the sugar bandwagon. Kellogg's Sugar Pops could be found on grocery shelves in 1950, followed closely by the same company's Sugar Frosted Flakes. Tony the Tiger served as the spokesman, telling kids everywhere that "they're gr-r-reat!"

In case they missed any finicky children, Kellogg's followed their own lead with Sugar Smacks in 1953; by this time, the sugar content had reached 56 percent, and Cliffy the Clown smiled at youngsters from the box.

Rocky and Bullwinkle, hits in a popular television cartoon series called *Rocky and His Friends* (1959–1961), touted Trix, a new General Mills cereal that boasted a 46 percent sugar content. And, to be on the safe side, General Mills also had Frosty-O's, this time with the Frosty-O's Bear lending encouragement. Kellogg's returned yet again with Frosted Krispies, a spin-off from their traditional, unsugared Rice Krispies. In fact, Snap! Crackle! and Pop! the figures long associated with Rice Krispies, found themselves drafted as the advertising icons for the sugar-coated version.

The sugar sweepstakes intensified as the 1950s progressed, leading to such inventions as Kellogg's Cocoa Krispies and General Mills's Cocoa Puffs (Rocky and Bullwinkle exclaimed they "make breakfast taste like chocolate!"). In order to retain their market share, other cereals both old and new were likewise enlisting comic and cartoon characters to endorse their brands. Kixie and Nixie touted General Mills' Kix; the Bran Bees buzzed happily for Kellogg's Raisin Bran; Post Grape Nuts employed an animated boxing glove (Grape Nuts "pack a wallop!"), as well as Li'l Abner from the comic pages. The Post Toasties Marble Boy reflected a brief marbles craze in the early fifties, and the Trailer Twins echoed a trailer fad for Post Raisin Bran.

The food tie-ins did not end with cartoon figures; the rise in popularity of television brought out endorsements from many new TV celebrities. Hopalong Cassidy, a favorite cowboy in early television, represented Post Raisin Bran, Howdy Doody stepped in for Rice Krispies, and Tom Corbett, Space Cadet, appeared on three Kellogg's brands: Pep, Corn Flakes, and Raisin Bran. Sugared or unsugared, the breakfast cereal business emerged as a multibillion-dollar enterprise in the 1950s, and manufacturers eagerly sought promotional help from the ranks of entertainment figures, real or created. Dull old shredded wheat had metamorphosed, becoming a part of the complex connections between food and popular culture.[4]

In a reversal of the above, and in a bow to dieters and fashion, sugarless products also made their debuts during this time period. Sugarless chewing gum appeared in 1951. Its success prompted imitation: in 1952, No-Cal Ginger Ale came along, the first of the sugar-free soft drinks. By 1958, Diet Rite Cola graced grocery shelves, and for sweetening all manner of things, Sweet 'N Low, an artificial sugar replacement, was marketed in handy single-use packets.

The 1950s witnessed an episode where politics affected the foods Americans consume. The dairy industry had long campaigned to have butter as the primary table spread in American homes, and they enjoyed success in their battle. Margarine suffered discriminatory taxation, along with a number of nuisance restrictions, such as forbidding the sale of colored margarine. Because margarine possesses a natural white color in contrast to the yellow of butter, manufacturers provided packets of food coloring that had to be kneaded into the gelatinous block, a laborious task that hindered sales. In a surprise move, President Harry Truman signed the Margarine Act in 1950, ending these discriminatory laws against "the other spread." Almost instantaneously, margarine sales took off, and by 1958, for the first time ever, the consumption of margarine exceeded that of butter and the American diet underwent a significant change.[5]

Kraft introduced pasteurized, processed sliced cheese in 1950, a move that helped gain broad acceptance for cheese in general. Two years later, Kraft brought out Cheez Whiz, another processed cheese product, and one that became an instant hit. Because Cheez Whiz came packaged as a spread, its viscous consistency made it adaptable to many dishes. In short order, cookbooks appeared on the market proclaiming the hundreds of uses homemakers had found for Cheez Whiz.

Minute Rice stands as another product introduced to make cooking easier and faster. Available in grocery stores in 1950, it eliminated the tedious boiling of rice and the strong possibility of over or undercooking it. A year later, Ore-Ida potatoes, made from powdered potatoes (presumably from Oregon and Idaho) were asvertised as a similar "Heat and Eat" product. The slow process of cooking rice or potatoes had been superseded by new agricultural technology.

Continuing the quest for speed in the kitchen, Gorton's Fish Sticks came along in 1953; they allowed fresh-tasting fish to be served in almost no time as a main course. For dessert, venerable Jell-O introduced a line of instant puddings. Initially available in chocolate, vanilla, or butterscotch, the quick desserts promised no mixing or other preparation. Then came Rice-A-Roni (a mix of fast-cooking rice and pasta) in 1958 for yet another quick, effortless meal. The 1950s pointed the way to an endless array of food that could be put on the table, piping hot, in just minutes. Where speed and efficiency were concerned, the decade heralded a revolution in the way Americans prepared their meals.

Frozen Foods

Most of the problems associated with freezing foods and preserving their freshness and tastiness had been solved by the early 1950s. Thereafter, the frozen-food industry boomed, growing fourfold during the decade. One of the most visible manifestations of its health came with the inception of some 2,500 different frozen-food plans across the country that involved home delivery of specified frozen foodstuffs. Participants checked off the desired fruits, vegetables, TV dinners, desserts, and so forth, from handy lists, called in the order, and the items would be delivered to their doorsteps. Of course, supermarkets also carried ample displays of frozen products, but the plans attracted consumers with the promise of lower prices and greater variety. Eventually, the novelty wore off, but not before many homes had purchased large, chest-type freezers to hold all the bags and boxes of frozen foods they accumulated.[6]

The TV Dinner

In 1951, the Omaha-based Swanson Company began selling frozen turkey potpies nationally. They had a surplus of turkey, and took a gamble that homemakers would like the convenience of a meal that required only heating before serving. The potpies did well, and in 1954 Swanson expanded their line to include a turkey dinner that came in a stamped aluminum tray divided into sections that held dressing, potatoes, and buttered peas along with the turkey. They also trademarked the name "TV Dinner," a phrase that has long since entered the popular language and denotes any frozen, preprepared meal available from numerous manufacturers. To reinforce the idea that this dinner had been designed for eating while watching television, the box it came in resembled a TV screen. The "picture" represented the meal inside, and the "knobs" allowed for product information. By the time the giant Campbell Soup Company bought Swanson in 1955, the Nebraska firm was shipping twenty-five million TV dinners a year.

When Swanson first started distributing its potpies and TV dinners, few dining rooms or kitchens contained television sets. The popularity of TV dinners in general prompted the design and mass production of TV trays—small, collapsible metal or plastic trays that could be set up in the living room in front of the television receiver. Consumers bought millions of them during the 1950s, which meant they could bypass the kitchen or dining room and eat supper while watching their favorite shows, a telling comment about both the impact of television and the growing informality that characterized the decade.[7]

Popcorn and Other Snack Foods

If not actually eating dinner from a TV tray, people got into the habit of nibbling during their periods of watching television. As a consequence, snack foods entered the national diet as never before. For example, popcorn has been around for thousands of years. American Indians reputedly ate the cooked kernels long before the arrival of Columbus, and it had long been a familiar item on grocers' shelves. But the popcorn of the early 1950s also had its drawbacks: as corn loses its water content, it also loses its unique quality of expansion, or "popping." Consumers therefore expected a fair number of "duds" or "old maids," as unpopped kernels somewhat quaintly were called. In 1952 an agronomist named Orville Redenbacher created a hybrid corn that retained moisture and thus popped more evenly. Redenbacher could not persuade any of the major popcorn labels to take on his new product, so he began marketing, under his own name, his improved version in the mid-fifties. An immediate success, it served as an ideal product for the new age of TV and snacks.

Of course, not everyone liked popcorn, and in 1952 General Mills discovered that their Wheat Chex, a popular breakfast cereal, when mixed with salt, nuts, pretzels, and other tasty additions, made a fine snack. By 1955, the ingredients had been formalized into Chex Party Mix. Other snacks followed: dried soup mixes, especially Lipton's Onion Soup, when combined with sour cream, created a flavorable dip for potato chips. For the fifties, these treats provided the perfect accompaniments to a cocktail party.

Appliances and Other Kitchen Helpers

The 1950s not only witnessed a number of new foods and approaches to their preparation, but also a rapid expansion of kitchen technology. For example, Tupperware, a line of storage containers made from flexible polyethylene, took off in 1951 with the clever marketing ploy of the "Tupperware Home Party." The containers themselves, invented in 1940 by Earl S. Tupper, had been available in stores since 1945, but sales and interest lagged. In 1951, Tupper hired Brownie Wise to oversee home parties where Tupperware products would be sold directly to individuals. Wise capitalized on the idea of women working and socializing simultaneously. A unique direct selling system, known as the "Hostess Plan," had evolved in the 1930s with several home products firms, and Wise adapted the concept. She used churches, clubs, and sororities, as well as friends and neighbors, to sell to one another. Tupperware Parties became an overnight success, and soon the versatile plastic could only be obtained this way—the pastel bowls with the tight lids had been withdrawn from stores.

The Tupperware Party symbolized the suburban 1950s, and Wise herself emerged as a savvy businesswoman. In 1954, she became the first woman ever to appear on the cover of *Business Week*. Tupperware, available in popular 1950s colors, affirmed the machine aesthetic, a utilitarian product that could be economically mass-produced, and it caught the imagination of millions of consumers.[8]

Although Tupperware containers could be found in many a refrigerator, another practical way to store leftovers involved wrapping them up in some way. Wax paper and aluminum foil were already available, but in 1952 the Dow Chemical Company introduced Saran Wrap. The first of many flexible plastic wraps, it gave an airtight seal around just about anything.

Faster cooking seemed to be on the horizon in 1950, when the Raytheon Company brought out the Radar Range, the first gasless, flameless cooking device on the market. The invention cooked foods by bombarding them with microwaves, silent and invisible rays whose concentrated energy has the capacity to cook food. The Radar Range, however, did not do well commercially; its large, bulky size and high price tag made it impractical for home use. Finally in 1952, smaller, more affordable microwave ovens appeared in appliance stores. Manufactured by both Tappan and Hotpoint, these compact units, so new and so different, took time to gain public acceptance, but the companies persevered and eventually microwave ovens could be found in many modern kitchens.

Refrigerators, on the other hand, had by 1950 become a standard appliance. The challenge for manufacturers involved not acceptance, but how to improve on a product, thereby rendering existing refrigerators obsolete in their owners' eyes. Here again the idea of planned obsolescence did not limit itself to the automotive field and yearly model changes; the enormous appliance market likewise entertained the concept. In 1951 Westinghouse introduced a line of refrigerators that automatically defrosted themselves. By 1954, General Electric advertised models available in several colors instead of just white.

Not to be outdone, Kelvinator in 1955 introduced the first side-by-side refrigerator, the "Foodarama." Instead of a freezer and a refrigerator served by a single door, their model featured a door for each function. Three years later Whirlpool extolled their first frostless model, a design so advanced that it eliminated defrosting of any kind.

An American chemist at the DuPont Company created Teflon in 1938, but not until 1948 did the company begin to employ it for industrial purposes. No one thought the nonstick surface would have any uses outside the laboratory. A French inventor, however, perfected a way to make the plastic adhere to aluminum, and his discovery was marketed abroad as Tefal in the 1950s. Teflon-coated pans finally made their way across the Atlantic late in the decade, but the response to Teflon/Tefal remained tepid, although shortly thereafter such cookware would become all the rage.[9]

Teflon or not, cookware and dishes still required washing, and soaps and detergents abounded, all promising to do the job best. In 1951, Procter & Gamble had introduced Joy, the first of many liquid detergents. Joy and its counterparts had been designed for washing dishes by hand in a sink, but the 1950s also saw a sharp rise in the number of electric dishwashers in American kitchens. Never a company to miss a trend, Procter & Gamble released Cascade, a powdered, low-suds detergent for automatic dishwashers. Thanks to effective promotion and the growing popularity of the dishwasher, Cascade became a success and immediately had numerous competitors.

Fast Food

As Americans moved to the suburbs, their jobs more often than not remained in the city itself. This trend may have added to the nation's mobility, but it also meant people traveled farther to work and spent more time on the road and less time with their families. Increased activities (Little League, dance classes, lodges and clubs, shopping, and so on) took young and old away from their homes, and a rush to eat began to characterize the typical suburban kitchen. No more the sit-down dinner with everyone present; families ate in shifts, with frozen dinners and other prepared foods the main courses, often consumed on the run or alone in front of a television set because the rest of the family had other pursuits.

This speeding up of American life did not limit itself to the home; when they were on the road, people wanted restaurants that offered food in a hurry; they did not want to waste dwindling time in dining. In response, the restaurant industry promoted fast food, food that could be prepared and consumed, literally, in minutes. It marked a profound change in American living, but one that fit the patterns of life as they evolved in the 1950s.

Throughout the 1950s, diners continued to be favorite eating places for millions of Americans, especially for breakfast and lunch. They became more streamlined and polished in the 1950s, as this chrome, stainless steel, and plastic example illustrates. Source: Library of Congress.

The Development of Some Prominent Fast-Food Chains during the 1950s

Year	Establishment	Location
1950	Dunkin' Donuts	Quincy, Massachusetts
1951	Jack in the Box	San Diego, California
1952	Church's Fried Chicken	San Antonio, Texas
	Kentucky Fried Chicken	Corbin, Kentucky
1953	Sonic (Top Hat Drive-In)	Shawnee, Oklahoma
1954	Shakey's	Sacramento, California
	Burger King (InstaBurger)	Dade County, Florida
1955	McDonald's (Ray Kroc)	Des Plaines, Illinois
	Mister Donut	Revere, Massachusetts
1957	Gino's	Baltimore, Maryland
1958	Pizza Hut	Wichita, Kansas
	Burger Chef	Indianapolis, Indiana

In 1954, salesman Ray Kroc peddled a product called Malt-A-Mixer, or Multimixer, a device for making multiple milkshakes in restaurants. On a visit to the McDonald Brothers' hamburger stand in San Bernardino, California, inspiration hit: he envisioned a restaurant that mass-produced not just milkshakes, but all the other items that have come to be associated with fast-food establishments. The McDonald brothers had already franchised eight of their stands, one as far away as Phoenix, Arizona. After some negotiation, Kroc acquired future franchising rights to expand the number of McDonald's stands, although the brothers retained their original operations. Following some management disagreements, Kroc purchased the entire chain from the brothers in the late 1950s, along with their name, and proceeded to create the hamburger empire that still calls itself McDonald's. The distinctive golden arches, the company trademark, had first appeared in 1953. Six years later, Ray Kroc had some 145 McDonald's stands spread across the nation, with thousands more to come.[10] [For more on McDonald's, see chapter 4, "Architecture and Design."]

Success guaranteed competition: Sonic began in 1953 as the Top Hat Drive-In in Shawnee, Oklahoma. In 1959, the name changed to "Sonic" to echo the fascination with speed (i.e., "supersonic") then so prevalent in the nation—or, as the company put it, "service with the speed of sound." Colonel Sanders's Kentucky Fried Chicken made its franchise debut in 1955, and briefly claimed more restaurants than McDonald's. Harlan Sanders, the patriarchal-looking gentleman in the white suit and silver goatee, had developed a pressure method of frying chicken in the early 1950s. He struggled to make a go of his business in Corbin, Kentucky, but the opening of Interstate Route 75 diverted traffic from his eatery. A friend persuaded Sanders to franchise his idea, merchandising the product as "Kentucky Fried." The concept caught on, thanks primarily to the colorful Sanders himself and some dogged salesmanship. By effectively marketing the "Colonel," a new fast-food purveyor arrived on the scene, and could boast two hundred locations by the end of the decade.[11]

Florida served as home for another hamburger chain with the unwieldy name of InstaBurger King Company. In 1954, the firm had opened it doors in the Miami area, and the success of their specialty burger, "The Whopper," allowed them in 1957 to grow into the now-familiar Burger King chain. But not all fast food consists of chickens, burgers, and fries. In 1958, Pizza Hut opened its first fast pizza restaurant in Wichita, Kansas. Spurred by the success of chains like Shakey's and Gino's, pizza had by this time become a rival to hamburgers as a favorite meal or snack.

Collectively, these new fast-food chains deeply influenced American eating habits. For example, the purchases of frozen potatoes, usually in the form of french fries, soared. In a similar manner, ketchup and pickle consumption also rose dramatically. Even iced tea and soft-drink sales were affected by this phenomenon. The fast-food stands may have provided more outlets for dining, but they also encouraged conformity in eating. The "burger, fries, and a Coke" quickly emerged as standard fare for millions of Americans.

Haute Cuisine, Gourmets, and American Tastes

As food grew increasingly convenient, the inevitable cost was taste. For most—but not all—Americans, that seemed an acceptable trade-off. A minority, however, opted for flavor and a more aesthetic approach to food. With so much kitchen technology available, why be merely a cook when one could be a chef?

The reasons behind this shift in attitude evolved slowly, and often had little to do with food. For example, the 1950s saw transatlantic air travel become a reality available to many people. And, with broadened horizons and exposure, more and more Americans experienced true foreign foods, not their Americanized imitations. Popular travel books and guides devoted considerable space to dining abroad, with the result that larger supermarkets and specialty stores began to stock items from distant shores, something new for the grocers' shelves.

For both the traveler and the stay-at-home, magazines like *Gourmet* (founded in 1941) offered exotic recipes and advertising that tempted both eye and palate. Their circulations rose, prompting the publication of

Samuel Chamberlain's *Bouquet de France* (1952) and Fernande Garvin's *The Art of French Cooking* (1958), two cookbooks that appeared on best-seller lists. *Gourmet* built its reputation on articles extolling French cuisine, offering up complex recipes that required hours of preparation and hard-to-find ingredients, an approach that flew in the face of the speed and efficiency so important to most homemakers. At the same time, newspaper and magazine columns brought food experts like James Beard and Craig Claiborne a measure of popularity, and their appearances on television cooking shows introduced more foreign fare to millions.

The Continental, a late-night show on CBS television during part of 1952, starred Renzo Cesana as a suave European gentleman who served candle-lit dinners to imaginary women guests. Overdone and ripe for later parody, it nevertheless introduced many Americans to sophisticated dining and came as a far cry from the usual steak and potatoes seen on network sitcoms.[12]

In terms of popular culture, the 1950s witnessed a demassification of culinary standards, a division of tastes that ran from the simple to the complicated. For a majority of Americans, familiar, unimaginative cookery sufficed, but a segment of the population had grown a bit more adventuresome. Fast food could be tasty and quick, but a lavish multicourse dinner, consumed carefully and slowly, also had its supporters, and the food and restaurant industry strove to satisfy all camps.

Ruth Moble's *A Guide to Distinctive Dining* (1954) attempted to acquaint American diners with elegant cuisine, perhaps something on a higher plane than that usually found in a restaurant. Most of the recommendations in her book, however, revolve around steak and basic seafood ("surf and turf") instead of more complex menus. She mentions only a handful of European restaurants, and even their "foreign" dishes tend to be well-known Italian and French fare. Provincial in the eyes of the rest of the world, Americans did not take easily to international cuisine, but the 1950s nevertheless witnessed a broadening of tastes. Despite these efforts, however, the nation's favorite meal for the decade consisted of fruit cup, vegetable soup, steak and potatoes, peas, rolls and butter, and pie á la mode.[13]

Summary

The sales of prepared foods increased by leaps and bounds in the 1950s, as homemakers sought efficiency in the kitchen. With more women working, coupled with the popular expectation that a woman had the responsibility to provide tasty, healthful meals, the food industry worked to market products that required minimal preparation and attention, as well as pleasing the palate. At the same time, quickly prepared items from a limited menu began to characterize the burgeoning fast-food outlets dotting the landscape.

DRINK

Almost twenty years had passed since the repeal of Prohibition, and the opinions of Americans toward the consumption of alcohol had mellowed. In addition, millions of people served in the armed forces during World War II, exposing them to cultures with more permissive attitudes about drinking. At home, virtually everyone consumed soft drinks, and an overwhelming majority also drank coffee or tea. By mid-decade, almost two-thirds of the adult population would accept a drink containing alcohol, with more men (70 percent) than women (58 percent) condoning alcoholic beverages. Relentless advertising and promotion of drinking further softened resistance to the use of alcohol.

Alcoholic Beverages

During the 1950s, the "hard liquors"—whiskey, Scotch, gin, vodka, rum, and the like—gained wide acceptance. Consumption of liquor in general rose from 190 million gallons to 235 million gallons between 1950 and 1960. For example, gin production went from 6 million gallons to more than 18 million gallons within the decade. Vodka likewise rose, from virtually nothing to 9 million gallons produced in 1959. Beer also climbed in favor, and per capita consumption jumped from 12 gallons to 17. Hollywood capitalized on the implied stylishness of drinking in movies like *All About Eve* (1950), *The Tender Trap* (1955), *My Man Godfrey* (1957), and *Auntie Mame* (1958). These films vividly celebrate the conviviality associated with the use of alcohol, adding to the mystique surrounding liquor, fashion, and elegance.[14]

Overall, the cocktail epitomized drinking and the 1950s. As long as they did not seem too exotic or outlandish, cocktails ruled as the drinks of choice for the middle class and above. Martinis, manhattans, gimlets, old-fashioneds—all were served in restaurants, classy bars, and even in suburban homes. For example, the martini, a potent concoction made from gin and vermouth, emerged as a status drink during the decade. To many, a well-made martini represented sophistication and the pursuit of perfection. A popular assumption insinuated that those on the way up, or those who had already gotten there, drank martinis. And if media imagery had any validity, men and women in equal numbers consumed them. Cocktails, either at home or in a lounge, became an American ritual, with "cocktail time" recognized as a special hour.

Throughout the decade, books, movies, recordings, and magazines regularly depicted drinking, an explicit endorsement of the practice. In *The Catcher in the Rye* (1951), J.D. Salinger's classic adolescent novel, even the youthful Holden Caulfield visits a cocktail lounge because he knows drinking signifies an important rite of passage in America. [See chapter 8, "Literature," for more on the book.]

A melodramatic movie like *Written on the Wind* (1957), filled with overblown characters who seem focused on self-destruction, can still take time out for references to martini-mixing. Prowess with alcohol seemed to be a comment on sophistication, regardless of any other problems.

Not all creative works, however, focused on the cool, worldly-wise side of drinking. In the film *The Big Hangover* (1950), star Van Johnson exhibits a peculiar weakness for alcohol, more of an allergy than an addiction. One sip and he goes out of control, which makes for a silly commentary on imbibing, but the point about the dangers inherent in alcohol consumption nonetheless are driven home. *Days of Wine and Roses*, presented on television's *Playhouse 90* in 1958, takes a much more serious view of problem drinking. Starring Cliff Robertson and Piper Laurie, the story involves an upwardly mobile young couple who begin a descent into alcoholism. Sophistication slides into degradation as they find themselves powerless to fight their addiction.

Songwriters also addressed drinking issues, often memorably. Back in 1943, Hollywood released a forgettable film called *The Sky's the Limit*. A vehicle for singer/dancer Fred Astaire, the movie includes "One for My Baby (and One More for the Road)," a mournful lament penned by Harold Arlen and Johnny Mercer. Astaire does his best with the lyrics, but the song languished until some ten years later when it became almost an anthem about the drinking life. In 1954, the equally forgettable *Young at Heart* appeared in theaters. Frank Sinatra and Doris Day share the leads, allowing Sinatra to croon "One for My Baby" and make it his own. Recorded a number of times during the 1950s, "One for My Baby" would henceforth be associated with Sinatra, lost love, and drowning sorrow in a bottle.

Singer June Christy, popular among jazz aficionados in the fifties, also recorded a classic number about drinking with "Something Cool" (1953), in this case a woman on the rebound from a lost love affair. And, because drinking and sadness were often linked, Jackie Gleason released an entire long-playing album of laments with *Music, Martinis, and Memories* in 1957. Gleason, usually thought of as a topflight TV comedian, also fronted a string-filled orchestra for a series of chart-breaking albums during these years.

Not every piece of music dealing with drinking during the fifties focused on the lugubrious side of alcohol. The Clovers, a popular vocal group, recorded "One Mint Julep" in 1951. Bandleader Buddy Morrow cut an up-tempo instrumental version of the song in 1952 that became an instant hit. In a similar vein, "Hot Toddy," performed by the Ralph Flanagan orchestra in 1953, did well on the music charts. Many other areas of popular culture, especially print advertising, endorsed drinking. [For more on liquor and beer ads, see chapter 3, "Advertising."]

Regardless of what they consumed, everyone had beverage preferences. For example, Coca-Cola completely dominated the soft-drink industry in the early years of the decade. *TIME* magazine even had the Coke logo on its cover in 1950, and the accompanying article talked of its amazing popularity around the globe. The company claimed 69 percent of the U.S. market, whereas Pepsi-Cola could only attract about 15 percent. A strong television marketing campaign by Pepsi throughout the fifties narrowed Coca-Cola's lead somewhat, but it remained mired in second place. Coke was truly the drink of choice for millions.

Coca-Cola maintained its dominance in the highly competitive industry by utilizing stylized illustrations of wholesome pretty girls enjoying a Coke. Magazine and billboard print ads, and prominent illustrators like Haddon Sundblom and Gil Elvgren, sustained associations among Coke, youth, attractiveness, and vitality. This work, usually unsigned, was nonetheless recognizable to millions. Always decorous, these ads appeared around the world as the company expanded its bottling and franchising efforts during the 1950s.[15]

The ubiquitous red and white Coca-Cola colors could be found in insulated coolers, on board airliners in special carriers, and of course at the fast-food shops and drive-ins springing up around the country. In 1955, amid great advertising fanfare, the company introduced a variety of larger bottles and cans containing the nation's favorite beverage; the classic six-and-a-half-ounce green bottle also remained, but consumers now had additional choices. With all this marketing, and bolstered by instant recognition, familiarity, and endless celebrity endorsements, Coca-Cola must be seen as one of the most successfully advertised products of the 1950s or any other decade. The pretty model holding up a refreshing Coke emerged as an American icon: life was good, and Coke made it better.

The rise of the supermarket cut into Coca-Cola's sales, because most of the smaller, more traditional grocery stores had for years carried only Coke products. Supermarkets, on the other hand, carried all brands. They granted equal aisle space to Pepsi and others, giving shoppers more choices. In another arena, the two giants competed for exclusivity clauses in the rapidly expanding fast-food chains. For instance, McDonald's served only Coca-Cola, whereas Burger King featured Pepsi products.[16]

In the early 1950s, scientists conducted experiments to find an efficient way to bottle beverages in steel containers. The war in Korea had created some steel shortages, slowing development, but progress occurred toward perfecting an economical steel container that would not impart a metallic taste to the liquid within. Around 1955, steel cans appeared on grocery shelves, often with conical tops and screw-on caps to preserve carbonation. Three years later, the Coors Brewing Company introduced an aluminum beverage container for its line of beer. These early cans required a separate opener, or "church key" as some called them; the popular pull tabs would not appear until the 1960s.

In keeping with the move toward greater speed and ease in the kitchen, a host of new powdered beverages came on the market. In 1952, consumers could dissolve Pream, a nondairy creamer, in tea or coffee to taste. In 1954, Carnation Instant Nonfat Dry Milk (with "Magic Crystals") became available. Lipton Instant Tea, mixed with boiling water, provided the 1958 consumer a quick cup of tea; the following year, a glass of juice could be made by mixing Tang with cold water.

Summary

Commonplace throughout the 1950s, images of drinking glamorized the use of alcoholic beverages, giving it a veneer of sophistication and style. The media mixed text and pictures, breaking down most of the remaining legal and societal barriers to the acceptance of public consumption of alcohol. In the meantime, the competition among soft-drink manufacturers remained fierce, and the food and drink industry introduced a host of new beverage substitutes.

The 1950s

7

Leisure Activities

With the war behind them and industry back on a peacetime schedule, Americans relaxed, comfortable in their new prosperity and ready for novelties. The fads that characterize the fifties may seem silly to later generations, but they lack the desperation and underlying anxieties of the outlandish stunts and daredevil antics that had marked the thirties and forties. The fifties, by and large, represent youthful high spirits.

FADS

College Pranks

Colleges across the nation weathered several fads that gained considerable press attention. First and foremost would be panty raids, a spring ritual in which male students "raided" the co-eds' dorms, expecting—and receiving—undergarments tossed from the windows as their trophies. The raids first emerged as a campus rage in 1952, and remained popular for the rest of the decade, much to the chagrin of administrators and to the delight of undergraduates everywhere.

In the late fifties, instead of cramming for exams, students crammed into anything small, from telephone booths to Volkswagen Beetles. The idea involved getting as many people as possible jammed into an allotted space. The unofficial record for people in a phone booth claimed that twenty-four students had successfully wedged themselves into the cubicle. It seemed like a good thing to do on a warm spring day, and certainly caused no harm.[1]

Chlorophyll

A food additive that caught the public fancy during the early 1950s, chlorophyll initially appeared in a few items like chewing gum and breath mints. A naturally occurring component of green plants, adherents claimed it eliminated bad breath when consumed. In America's endless quest for hygiene and attractiveness, chlorophyll proved a marketer's dream come true. It was soon added to everything—toothpastes, cough drops, deodorants, shampoos, clothing, a few pet foods, and even a couple of brands of cigarettes. Most of these products (but not the cigarettes) displayed a bilious green hue, supposedly the result of the beneficent presence of chlorophyll.

Science finally weighed into the debate, and the result dampened the public enthusiasm for the wonder ingredient. No demonstrable evidence could be found that chlorophyll minimized breath odors, or any other kind of odors. By 1953, the rush to include chlorophyll in every imaginable product abated, although a few believers remained, along with a handful of green products boasting the additive, but they had negligible sales. The fad had lasted only two years, but it exposed a national concern about personal cleanliness and offensive odors, a fact that advertisers would seek to exploit long after chlorophyll's heyday.[2]

Flying Saucers and UFOs

People spotted UFOs (unidentified flying objects) everywhere throughout the decade. The trend began in 1947, when a pilot reported objects that resembled saucers flying outside his plane. From there, the sightings multiplied. Between 1950 and 1959, citizens filed an average of 650 reports yearly, with 1952 being the banner year at 1,500 sightings. The Air Force spent over $500,000 investigating reports, although it never could definitively identify anything as a true extraterrestrial object. In a lengthy document issued in 1955, the government denied that flying saucers or other UFOs had ever violated U.S. airspace. Instead, authorities tried to explain them away as weather balloons and other scientific materials that happened to be seen by an anxious public.

The lack of proof served as little deterrent to the film industry. A spate of movies sharing the common thread of extraterrestrial visitors ensued, including *The Flying Saucer* (1950), *The Day the Earth Stood Still* (1951), *The Thing* (1951), *It Came from Outer Space* (1953), *The War of the Worlds* (1954), *Earth vs. the Flying Saucers* (1956), *UFO* (1956), and *20 Million Miles to Earth* (1957). By the end of the decade, however, the UFO fad had exhausted itself, and Hollywood, along with most other carriers of popular culture, had found new avenues to explore.

Hula Hoops and Frisbees

Not exactly a game, not really a toy, but certainly a fad, the hula hoop, along with the Frisbee, was introduced to an unsuspecting American public in 1957. Both products of the Wham-O Manufacturing Company, they proved runaway best-sellers for kids of all ages. For a time, nothing came close to the hula hoop in sales; one cost only $1.98, and dealers could not keep them in stock. An Australian invention, hula hoops (bamboo rings, in this case) helped teach agility and balance in physical education classes. The originals caught the eye of Wham-O, and the firm fashioned their own models out of lightweight polyethylene plastic so they would float. Because of the hula hoop's simplicity, Wham-O found it virtually impossible to protect any patents, and dozens of imitations soon crowded the market. For about a year, hula hoops sold in enormous numbers and apparently everybody made money. Touted on TV, the plastic ring demonstrated the considerable sales potential of the upstart medium.

The Frisbee, on the other hand, did not enjoy such a sensational beginning as the hula hoop. But it provided Wham-O steady sales, one of those products for which demand always seems to exist. It received its unusual name, so the story goes, from the Frisbee Baking Company of Bridgeport, Connecticut. Customers would sometimes keep the aluminum pie plates from the bakery, sailing them in the air for fun. Walter Morrison, a California carpenter, refined the pie plate concept into the plastic disc so familiar today. Morrison peddled his invention at county fairs, calling it "Li'l Abner," a popular hillbilly comic-strip character. Wham-O bought out Morrison and attempted to market his disc as a "Pluto Platter," but the public persisted in calling it a Frisbee. After a year or so, Wham-O relented; they trademarked the word "Frisbee" in 1959 and the name has stuck.[3]

Both the hula hoop and the Frisbee were simple toys whose time had come. No one could have predicted the long-range success of these two novelty items, and they reflect the playful side of the 1950s.

GAMES

As in all periods of American life, people enjoyed games. Indoor, outdoor, athletic or intellectual, for young and for old, new introduction or old favorite, games constituted an important part of the nation's leisure activities.

Canasta

A card game that found favor everywhere, canasta traced its roots to rummy, another popular game. The name means "basket," and refers to

The game of canasta emerged as one of the most popular new leisure pastimes for the period. A Latin-American import involving two decks of cards (note the large hand held by the woman), the rules encouraged players to take, discard, and lay down their holdings. The tray in the center of the table is called in Spanish a *canasta*, or basket, thus the name of the game. Source: Library of Congress.

the tray full of discards that players vie to win. Canasta landed on American shores in 1949, an import from Uruguay, and gained legions of fans almost immediately. In 1950, Oswald Jacoby, a respected expert on many card games, published *How to Win at Canasta* and it quickly climbed the best-seller lists. Other books followed, and a merchandising boom accompanied them. The game required two standard decks of 52 cards plus jokers—exactly what comes in any regular double box of playing cards. But "special" canasta decks soon went on sale, along with molded plastic trays, or "baskets," and they sold well. As the fad grew, fertile minds created "canasta covers" for card tables, an item that presumably replaced the "bridge covers" from a few years earlier. Canasta clothing, score pads, coasters, and anything else entrepreneurs could imagine tempted fans. Enthusiastic players formed clubs, and canasta quickly surpassed bridge as the nation's favorite card game.

Canasta's dominance began to falter around 1952; the fickle public was ready for something new, and the timing could not have been better. A word game developed in the 1930s was already waiting in the wings.

Scrabble

Despite its relatively advanced age, Scrabble had never really caught the public fancy. The creation of Alfred M. Butts, an unemployed architect, Scrabble struggled in a kind of limbo from the time of its invention until word of mouth and determined marketing finally got people excited about it 20 years later. In its early years, Butts called his invention "Lexico"; in 1938 he christened it "Criss-Cross." Obviously, clever names do not guarantee success.

By 1947, with no interest and no sales, Butts went into a partnership with friend James Brunot who renamed the game "Scrabble" in hopes of generating some public curiosity. The word means to scratch or to scrape, as in the soil. In the game, players "scratch up" small wooden tiles with letters on them in hopes of creating combinations that will form words. This vocabulary association, however, did not seem to work, and Butts and Brunot found themselves faced with unsold boards and lots and lots of tiny wooden tiles. Then, in 1952, the game suddenly took off for no apparent reason. The two men could not keep up with demand, and Selchow & Righter, a large game manufacturer, took over, a move that allowed for mass production. By the mid-fifties, millions of Scrabble games sold each year, with no end in sight. The little wooden tiles, the geometric board, and Double and Triple Word Scores soon became a familiar part of the American family game scene.[4]

TOYS

A buying binge in the prosperous 1950s soon replaced the austerity of World War II. Toys of every description flooded a market grown accustomed to inferior cardboard and poorly cut wood imitations of the metal and cast toys of the past. Symbols of peacetime prosperity, such as construction vehicles, scale models of civilian cars, commercial airliners, steamships, houses, and gas stations replaced war-oriented toys. Metal, rubber, and plastics, all materials in short supply during the fighting, became the materials of choice for the postwar market, although the Korean conflict (1950–1953) did cause some momentary disruptions.

Toys and Television

Reflecting the growing popularity of television, Marx Toys introduced the Milton Berle Car in the early 1950s. Because Milton Berle ranked as the leading comedian on TV during this time, the tie-in seemed an obvious one to guarantee sales. This same car actually appeared earlier as a G.I. Joe Jeep and a Rodeo Joe Car in the late forties, so it served as a versatile toy that the company could adapt to whatever or whomever seemed popular at the moment.

In a similar vein, the Disney organization produced an elaborate portable Television Playhouse in 1953. The set contained plastic figures of Disney characters, along with a stamped metal theater so children could reenact episodes of shows they had seen on ABC's popular *Disneyland*.

Captain Video, a long-running (1949–1957) TV science-fiction series, along with *Tom Corbett, Space Cadet* (1950–1955), inspired many toy manufacturers to work out licensing agreements with the two shows so they could capitalize on their popularity among children. Rings, flashlights, ray guns, and rockets, and space vehicles of all kinds counted among the items released.

Hopalong Cassidy and Davy Crockett, however, proved more popular than any of the foregoing. In 1934, the beginnings of a Western dynasty almost went unnoticed. But sixty-five movies and thirteen years later, people had become aware of William L. Boyd, better known as Hopalong Cassidy. By the late 1940s, Hollywood already felt the impacts of television, so Hopalong, his white horse Topper, and crew moved to NBC-TV and the small screen in 1949. At first, the network merely recycled the old films, but in 1951 they commenced producing the actual television series, creating an additional fifty-two episodes. Despite Boyd's advanced age of fifty-six, *Hopalong Cassidy* galloped away from the competition of the day and emerged as a marketing bonanza: a radio show, a syndicated comic strip, and merchandise galore. Hopalong Cassidy cowboy outfits become the rage for little boys, complete with six-guns, holsters, and spurs. Other toys, towels, raincoats, pajamas, rugs, bedspreads, candy, and miscellaneous items appeared bearing "Hoppy's" name. The pioneering television show carried on until 1954, but then Boyd retired and kids had to look for new heroes.[5]

They did not have to look long or far. At the end of 1954, *Disneyland*, Walt Disney's own show on ABC television, began a five-part serialized series to tell the stories of frontiersman Davy Crockett. Overnight, this character from the nation's past surpassed even Hopalong Cassidy. The episodes made a star of Fess Parker, and immediately captured the imaginations of young viewers everywhere. The show's theme, "The Ballad of Davy Crockett," was released as a single record and sold in the millions. Countless books recounting the hero's adventures enjoyed similar sales. Virtually anything that could be stenciled with the name "Davy Crockett" found a market, from toys to camping gear. In all, the Disney studios marketed over three thousand items. Today, most people recall the Davy Crockett hat, a replica of a coonskin cap, complete with a dangling tail. The hat used both real and imitation raccoon fur, and for a brief period any Crockett gear leaped to the top of children's wish lists.

In 1955, Hollywood rushed out *Davy Crockett, King of the Wild Frontier* and followed that with *Davy Crockett and the River Pirates* (1956). These movies in reality consisted of the television episodes strung together into feature-length productions. But, like all fads and merchandising dreams, the bubble burst. By the end of 1955, *Disneyland* had moved on to other things and "Davy Crockett" disappeared from the lineup. Across the country, storeowners faced unsold inventories of raccoon caps, victims of a fickle public that had turned to new and different sensations.[6] [For more on the Crockett phenomenon, see chapter 6, "Fashion."]

Educational Toys

Formed in 1950, Creative Playthings provided children with educational toys that expanded their imaginations. Packaged as well-finished wooden pieces that represented cars, boats, airplanes, and the like in a non-detailed way, they allowed children the freedom to construct in their minds the missing elements. Throughout the decade, the company did well and came to be associated with quality playthings.

On the other hand, die-cast scale models of cars, trucks, and other wheeled vehicles, manufactured under the name of Matchbox Toys, provided realistic and educational detail. The products of an English firm, Lesney Products & Co., Ltd., these faithful replicas of the real thing had first appeared in 1947, but sales did not soar into the millions until the 1950s. Although generations of kids loved them, the Matchbox miniatures proved to be as much for display as for play, and attracted fans and collectors of all ages.

Slinky

The timeless Slinky, in reality a 1945 toy, took off in popularity during the 1950s. Simplicity itself, a Slinky consists of a flexible coil, or spring, that has provided endless entertainment for generations of kids and their parents. Things went slowly at first for a toy that could descend stairs, crawl over objects, and finally come to rest in an upright position. Although it took five or six years to capture the popular imagination, Slinkies sold in the millions throughout the rest of the decade.

Silly Putty

Another surprise, this malleable mix of silicone also gained big sales in the fifties. First developed in 1945 by the General Electric Company in the course of a search for synthetic rubber, no one knew quite what to do with it until a marketing expert sensed its potential as a toy. Tens of millions of egg-shaped containers of the stuff sold between its introduction in 1949 and the end of the 1950s. After its initial appearance, however, Silly Putty came under criticism because of its tendency to stick to clothing and hair. Engineers revamped the formula so the silicone no longer would adhere to almost anything. Once the public discovered the fun of molding shapes in the gooey substance—"The Real Solid Liquid"—the market seemed to know no limits.

Mr. Potato Head

The first toy ever heavily advertised on TV, Mr. Potato Head achieved runaway success in 1952. Made by Hasbro, Mr. Potato Head initially used a real potato (supplied by the consumer) for the head. Hasbro provided the eyes, mouths, ears, and other facial adornments. In 1953, Mr. Potato Head wed Mrs. Potato Head in a widely promoted ceremony. Offspring, or "small fries," soon followed. Hasbro sold the last originals in 1964; after that, the growing family became all plastic and no longer involved real potatoes.

The saturation advertising that Hasbro employed on television for all its products, especially on Saturday mornings when kids watched cartoons, brought about the toy's popularity. Their huge sales volume soon convinced other toy manufacturers to imitate this new promotional approach, making television the primary ad outlet for children's items.[7]

Propeller Beanies

Another illustration of the power of television in influencing buying patterns can be found with *Beany and Cecil* (1950–1955), a low-budget, syndicated children's show. Its stories revolved around the adventures of two hand puppets, one of whom—Beany—at times wore a beanie festooned with a plastic propeller on the crown. The youthful audience seemed quite taken with this unique headgear, and its popularity soon achieved fad proportions.

Toy manufacturers began to produce them, and cereal giant Kellogg's offered propeller beanies to those who sent in a certain number of box tops. Soon, the caps could be seen everywhere, particularly in schoolyards atop the proud heads of boys. By the end of the 1950s, the craze had run its course, *Beany and Cecil* was canceled, and kids had turned to other interests.[8] [For more on propeller beanies, see chapter 5, "Fashion."]

Powered Toys

Major changes occurred in the toy market when Japanese imports began to appear with battery-powered motors during the early fifties. These cheap intruders featured miniature power plants that allowed movement and mobility. American manufacturers, unable to compete with low Asian prices, began marketing their own imported lines, complete with motors and batteries. It marked a profound change for domestic companies that had once felt secure against foreign competition.[9]

When Russia launched its *Sputnik* satellite in 1957, the toy industry responded with innumerable space-oriented offerings. The Japanese manufacturers took the lead in futuristic toys. Robots, adapted from such hit movies as *The Day the Earth Stood Still* (1951) and *Forbidden Planet* (1956), proved especially popular. Robby, the clever robot in *Forbidden Planet*, emerged as something of an icon in the toy industry, but all manner of mechanical figures that could walk, move their limbs, and imitate other human behaviors fascinated children.[10]

Barbie

Although her real impacts would not be felt until later decades, it is worth mentioning Barbie in the context of the fifties. This famous doll, along with an initial selection of very 1950s-style clothing, made her first appearance in toy stores at the beginning of March 1959. The creation of Ruth Handler, one of the founders of Mattel Toys, Barbie became a favorite doll almost immediately.

Barbie's uniqueness rests with her always-stylish wardrobe. Unlike most toys that remain fixed in time, Barbie reflects the present. And, for a decade that encouraged consumerism, Barbie represents the quintessential consumer. Not only must her considerable wardrobe be constantly revised and updated, so must all her accompanying accessories. Mattel, from the beginning of course, stood ready to sell the latest in fashion for their slender, stylized doll.[11]

Playpens

Not exactly a toy, but a product nonetheless designed for infants and little children, the modern playpen dates from 1955. Until then, these practical contrivances for limiting the activities of the very young came assembled with wooden slats. Arranged in an accordion fashion that formed an open box, the slat construction resulted in a heavy, cumbersome unit in which tiny fingers got pinched, plus it demonstrated an annoying tendency to collapse. Finally, the Play-A-Round pen was unveiled. Consisting of sturdy nylon mesh stretched on a simple tubular frame, parents bought the device in astounding numbers. The success enjoyed by this innovation meant that strollers, carriers, and a host of other baby necessities soon came on the market featuring new, lightweight materials and ease of assembly.

HOBBIES

In a culture that values work and productivity, the concept of spending time in worthwhile pursuits is strongly supported. A hobby should be a pleasurable but worthwhile leisure activity, not the whiling away of precious time. Good hobbies endorse a work ethic and provide socially acceptable leisure, something that advertisers and entrepreneurs exploited in their marketing campaigns.[12]

"Do It Yourself"

From a home-built fallout shelter out in the backyard to a pine umbrella stand for the front hallway, do-it-yourself supported projects of every kind. So widespread became the idea of creating, building, modernizing, repairing, and sprucing up things around the home without professional help that *Time* magazine devoted an August 1954, cover story to the popularity of "doing it yourself."

Almost overnight, home workshops from simple to sophisticated became commonplace. The home itself emerged as a primary hobby—its proper upkeep and improvements occupied many a do-it-yourselfer's time. The sales of multipurpose power tools like the Shopsmith, a five-in-one combination woodworking machine introduced in 1947, skyrocketed, creating a new generation of craftsmen. Simpler power devices, like table saws, jigsaws, lathes, and drills also enjoyed surging popularity, along with quality hand tools. By the mid-1950s, power tool sales exceeded $200 million a year, and they continued their stratospheric climb for the remainder of the decade.[13]

Lumberyards and home supply stores flourished, urging on the public with attractive displays of plywood, free how-to brochures and plans, plus much in-store advice. Husbands saw their shops as male redoubts, even if they got tucked into a closet or a corner of the garage. Advertising emphasized father-son bonding, but seldom did mothers or daughters appear, at least in the idealized workshop. Despite the gender bias found in most depictions of woodworking and carpentry, home improvement and the do-it-yourself craze eventually transcended such barriers when it came to projects outside the confines of the home shop.

For example, remodeling a room brought the concept of "togetherness" into play. In the best of all worlds, husbands and wives jointly planned projects. Males might be allowed to exert a strong influence on interior design because they usually laid out and constructed such projects. The woman's role in improvements involved final decorative touches, like paint colors, wallpapers, and drapery and fabric choices.

To assist families, the home improvement industry brought out such laborsaving innovations as pre-pasted wallpaper and complete paper hanging kits. Paint rollers, patented back in 1869, did not come into widespread use until the early 1950s. Latex paint was introduced in 1949; its easy soap-and-water cleanup made it an instant hit with do-it-yourselfers. By mid-decade, most paint stores featured color-mixing machines, devices that easily allowed for an infinity of hues.

As homeowners flocked to new homes in the burgeoning suburbs, and as city-dwellers spruced up older dwellings, the idea of doing all the repairs and remodeling without professional assistance took hold. "Do it yourself" saved money and supposedly made the family a tighter unit as they worked together, although this 1955 picture—admittedly contrived—would argue that it was never as easy as it seemed.
Source: Library of Congress.

Such traditional women's magazines as *American Home, Better Homes and Gardens, House & Garden, House and Home, House Beautiful, McCall's,* and *Woman's Home Companion* wisely devoted considerable space to do-it-yourself projects of every imaginable kind. Now a woodworker could craft a frame to hold the paint-by-number canvas someone had patiently labored over for many hours. In fact, frame kits could be purchased that would accommodate specific canvases, and a home magazine might provide helpful hints about correctly hanging pictures on a living-room wall. [For more on the paint-by-numbers phenomenon, see chapter 12, "Visual Arts."]

Not just women's magazines, however, supported the popularity of the do-it-yourself concept. *Popular Mechanics, Popular Science Monthly*, and *Mechanix Illustrated*, journals that had long enjoyed a largely male readership, also jumped on the bandwagon. They moved from their traditional articles about science and mechanics to an increasing emphasis on how-to pieces. In no time, they watched their circulations rise. For example, 1951 saw the launch of a magazine called *The Family Handyman*. Within a few issues, it had attracted over 200,000 readers. *The Better Homes and Gardens Handyman's Book*, also first published in 1951, quickly soared to number five on some nonfiction lists for the year. Fawcett Publications issued a number of magazine-like paperbound books such as *How to Use Power Tools* and a series of *Build It!* plan books. One magazine, *Profitable Hobbies*, stressed making money from projects, an approach that caused some hobbyists to become entrepreneurs—often with the result that leisure turned into work. At hobby shows across the country, many home-crafted items could be found for sale, not just for display.

Collecting as a Hobby

By the mid-twentieth century, the terms "hobby" and "collecting" enjoyed interchangeable use. Whether it involved stamps, paperweights, bubble gum trading cards, or cigar bands, people saw collectors as hobbyists. For women, such a list might include buttons, theater programs, and autographs; collecting remained a gender-biased activity. Traditional collecting continued to be popular for all ages, but new hands-on hobbies like woodworking, home decoration, and kit assembly often overshadowed them as people found both time and sufficient prosperity to indulge them.

Model Making

Model airplanes of every description came in easy-to-assemble formats. At first, old firms like Cleveland and Strombecker dominated the field, with kits made from wood, usually balsa, an extremely lightweight variety. A single-edge razor blade, glue, and some tissue paper, along with patience, allowed both kids and adults to construct aircraft, some of which actually flew with rubber bands or small gasoline motors. As the 1950s progressed, the introduction of effective glues for plastic permitted firms like Monogram and Revell to create hundreds of intricate, detailed models

Instead of the traditional balsawood that had to be laboriously carved with a razor knife, model kits comprised of pre-cut, molded plastic parts had become all the rage by mid-decade. A tube of plastic glue and space to spread out all the tiny pieces was all it took. Anything, from World War I biplanes to postwar jets, could be quickly assembled and contain a wealth of detail. Source: Library of Congress.

of cars, trains, ships, and airplanes from all eras. Modelers forgot the traditional balsa and tissue models in the rush to assemble the precision replicas that flooded the market in the later fifties.

If planes and ships held no appeal, one could always turn to model railroading. By the early 1950s, more than one thousand model railroad clubs existed in the United States. Just like model airplanes, people viewed it as a male pastime, with women and their daughters permitted only on "visiting days." The clubs existed more as fraternities, meant for male bonding.

Crafts

Women were not forgotten in the hobby boom. The makers of paint-by-number kits, buoyed by high sales, introduced other craft supplies that they marketed directly to women. Toleware, an old art involving lacquered or enameled metalware, usually with an applied design, became a big seller. The hobbyist applied premixed paints directly to prepared metal plates, waste cans, clasp purses, and many other items to complete the design. A kind of elaborate version of paint-by-numbers, the toleware packages proved a popular hit.[14]

Mosaic sets, in which colored stones, already supplied in the kit, are arranged according to a carefully rendered drawing, likewise flourished. This kind of do-it-yourself artistry constituted but a small part of a much larger 1950s phenomenon. It appealed to an innate urge to create, to take one's hand to something and make an "original" work. Not everyone possesses artistic talents, so the proliferation of kits of all kinds gave a little boost to those who might be intimidated by a blank canvas or a metal plate with no design. In addition, the decade saw would-be artisans flock to woodworking classes, stained glass lessons, ceramics courses, and a host of other hands-on experiences. Any product that could be marketed to this "do-it-yourself" mentality had a good chance of doing well.

SPORTS

Overall, the health of Americans had never been better. By the late 1950s, the increased use of antibiotics lessened the seriousness of many illnesses. For example, the Salk and Sabin vaccines diminished polio's damaging effects markedly. Doctors nevertheless observed that American youth seldom did as well as their European counterparts in various tests of physical fitness, concluding that American kids were out of shape. These findings came to a head with the creation of the President's Council on Youth Fitness in 1957. Although this high-sounding group actually did little to improve anyone's physical heath, it did spur the development of Little League teams and other kinds of organized sport. The pickup game on a back lot had been supplanted by a bureaucracy. However, greater organization meant the loss of a certain spontaneity for games and sports.

In the realm of professional athletics, the American and National Leagues in 1950 agreed to allow the World Series to be televised. NBC, the network making the request, in turn paid the leagues $6 million for the privilege, thereby ushering in the era of big money, sports, and television. At the same time, the beginning of the end for racial segregation in most professional sports also occurred.

Baseball

Willie Mays made his debut with the New York Giants in 1951, as did Mickey Mantle with the New York Yankees. At the same time, Joe DiMaggio retired, but the Yankee dynasty continued: from 1949 to 1953, the team won an unrivaled five straight World Series. In 1954, the Cleveland Indians made the record books by winning 111 games during the season; then, in irony of ironies, they lost the Series in four straight to the New York Giants.

During the 1956 World Series between the New York Yankees and Brooklyn Dodgers, Yankee Don Larsen pitched a perfect game (no hits, no runs), the first time this extraordinary event had occurred in Series play, and only the second time in organized baseball since 1922.

The advent of cross-country air travel, especially by jet in the later 1950s, made truly national teams in any sport a reality. Improved transportation signaled the movement of teams westward, something that commenced in 1953 when the Boston Braves shifted to Milwaukee and continued in 1955 with the Philadelphia Athletics going to Kansas City. The St. Louis Browns, however, defied the trend and headed east to become the Baltimore Orioles in 1956. At the conclusion of the 1957 season, New York lost two of its three legendary franchises: "Dem Bums," the Brooklyn Dodgers, moved to Los Angeles, and the New York Giants transferred to San Francisco.

Despite the shifting allegiances of teams, baseball maintained its hold as the "national pastime" on millions of fans. And, supporting a trend apparent since the 1930s, Hollywood continued to produce films about the game. *The Jackie Robinson Story* (1950) found Robinson playing himself in a movie about his making history as the first black player in the major leagues. In spite of its good intentions, the plot builds on clichés— the supportive wife, fickle fans, and finally the Big Game, but Robinson gives a solid performance and the film does not shrink from its underlying story of prejudice.

On an equally contemporary note, *Fear Strikes Out*, the story of the emotional problems suffered by Jimmy Pearsall of the Boston Red Sox, came out in 1957. Starring the popular Anthony Perkins as the troubled outfielder who endured a mental breakdown, it hardly resembles the usual baseball movie. *The Winning Team* (1952), the story of pitcher Grover Cleveland Alexander (played by Ronald Reagan), served up more traditional baseball fare. Another pitcher, Dizzy Dean of the St. Louis Cardinals, was profiled in *Pride of St. Louis* (1952).

Basketball

For the most part, basketball remained essentially regional in its appeal. In 1950, a number of leading college teams, including the University of Kentucky, Bradley University, and New York University, received stiff penalties for violating recruiting rules. The scandal dampened public enthusiasm for the sport and led to a Hollywood film entitled *The Basketball Fix* (1951). But good players still played the sport; in 1954

Furman's Frank Selvy set a record by scoring one hundred points in a single game.

In an effort to speed up play, the relatively new (1950) National Basketball Association, or NBA, adopted the 24-second shot clock in 1954. This rule stipulated that a team in possession of the ball must shoot within 24 seconds, thus cutting down on stalling and boring, low-scoring games.

On a more popular level, the court and ball-handling wizardry of the all-black Harlem Globetrotters inspired two films, *The Harlem Globetrotters* (1951) and *Go, Man, Go!* (1954). Neither picture carries much plot, relying instead on the comedy routines the famous team had made their own. The movies, however, gave audiences unfamiliar with the story of the Globetrotters a chance to see them in action. At a time when black actors had few chances in mainstream films, these two pictures did well at the box office.

Bowling

By 1950, bowling found itself in the position of being the country's leading participation sport. It had moved from seedy alleys with human pinsetters, usually boys, to bright, modern establishments that featured fully automatic machines. As the decade wore on, it continued its growth, with leagues of every description forming across the nation.

Don Carter and Marion Ladewig stood out as the two biggest bowling stars of the era. Carter ruled as Bowling Proprietors' Association of America (BPAA) Male Bowler of the Year in 1953, 1954, 1957, and 1958; even more remarkable, Ladewig captured the women's title in 1950, 1951, 1952, 1953, 1954, 1955, 1958, and 1959.[15]

Boxing

In a nationally televised bout, Jersey Joe Walcott became the oldest heavyweight champion in history by defeating Ezzard Charles in 1951. Thirty-seven at the time, he enjoyed a short-lived reign. In September of 1952, Rocky Marciano, after brutally beating an aging Joe Louis in 1951, knocked out Walcott and gained the heavyweight title. The victory marked Marciano's forty-third straight win with no losses. He held the championship for the next four years, finally retiring undefeated (49-0) in 1956, the first heavyweight champion to do so. In a November match to determine the new champion, Floyd Patterson defeated Archie Moore. But then Ingemar Johansson of Sweden knocked out Patterson in a 1959 title bout, and the decade ended with boxing's most prestigious championship no longer residing in the United States.

Although boxing fans traditionally pay the most attention to the Heavyweight Division, in the fifties the middleweights also captured the headlines. Sugar Ray Robinson, a graceful, colorful fighter, won the crown in 1951. He proceeded to win and lose the title four times during the decade. But his presence, along with a number of other talented fighters in that class—Rocky Graziano, Jake LaMotta, Gene Fullmer, and Carmen Basilio—made the middleweights considerably more interesting and popular than the heavyweights.

The Joe Louis Story came out in 1953; it features Coley Wallace as the most popular heavyweight champion ever. The film does a modest job of recounting Louis's trials in private life and his glory in the ring. A more ambitious picture is *Somebody Up There Likes Me* (1956). Paul Newman plays middleweight Rocky Graziano, portraying him as a complex, thoughtful person, instead of just a slugger. The film explores Graziano's Italian-American roots, and a fine supporting cast raises this picture above the general run of boxing epics. Finally, *The Harder They Fall* (1956) provides an unsparing look at the underside of boxing. With Humphrey Bogart as a cynical sportswriter, the film chooses not to glorify the ring, but instead shows the exploitation suffered by most prize-fighters and how money corrupts virtually everyone connected with the sport.

Many people knew about the problem of drug addiction and the ring in the 1950s, but Hollywood, because of Code restrictions, practiced caution when depicting it. In 1957's *Monkey on My Back*, actor Cameron Mitchell turns in a fine performance as boxer Barney Ross. Ross, who fought in the 1930s, held the lightweight, junior welterweight, and welterweight titles at various times during the decade. But he also suffered an addiction to morphine, and the movie shows Ross's courage in both the ring and in his continuing battle against drugs.

The Gillette Safety Razor Company, on its *Gillette Cavalcade of Sports* (1948–1960), spurred popular interest in boxing with televised bouts on Friday nights. The long-lived series had such a level of success that occasionally other evenings also telecast sponsored matches. For a time, boxing occupied an important niche in prime-time television.

Football

During the 1950s, professional football surpassed college games in popularity for the first time ever. In December of 1958, the Baltimore Colts defeated the New York Giants, 23 to 17 in overtime, to win the National Football League crown in a nationally televised game. With the popular quarterback Johnny Unitas leading the Colts, this game is thought by many to be among the greatest football contests ever. The ratings success of the broadcast did not go unnoticed, and professional football became a regular part of television sports coverage. People everywhere could follow their favorite teams, and individual players emerged as stars in the growing professional leagues. Because football consists of a period of planning and then a burst of energy all within a small, prescribed place, it proved a format ideally suited to television with its alternating schedule of shows and commercials.

Just as collegiate basketball had its problems, a major 1951 cheating scandal at West Point resulted in the dismissal of several key football players. Similar improprieties were discovered in other college teams, affecting a considerable number of athletes. Despite the scandal, bright spots continued to shine, for both players and coaches. In 1957, rookie Jim Brown of the Cleveland Browns began a systematic attack on the football record book, rushing for over nine hundred yards in his first season. The following year he almost doubled that figure, and continued to rush over 1,000 yards annually well into the 1960s. As a final note, Vince Lombardi, destined to become a football legend in his own time, took over the coaching responsibilities for the Green Bay Packers in 1959.

Golf

The fifties have been called the Ben Hogan era; his attention and devotion to golf brought legions of admirers to the sport. But it took a personable young player named Arnold Palmer to transform golf into the popular game it has become. Palmer led the Professional Golfers Association (PGA) in winnings during 1958; he collected over $42,000 for the year, a new high, and his easygoing manner made him the darling of the fans and helped golf take its place as a major sport on television.

Given the slow pace of the game, golf has seldom attracted moviemakers. But *Follow the Sun*, a 1951 biography with the dour Glenn Ford as Ben Hogan, attempts to bring some drama to the sport. Fans argued that too much emphasis on Hogan's private life and not enough on golf robbed the movie of its potential.

Tennis

Despite its position on the lower tiers of public interest through much of the 1950s, tennis nonetheless enjoyed a few moments of popular acclaim. In 1953, American Maureen Connolly (or "Little Mo" as her fans dubbed her) captured the women's "Grand Slam" by winning the Australian, French, English, and U.S. singles titles. In 1957, New Yorker Althea Gibson won both the Wimbledon Women's Singles and the U.S. National, the first black to win those crowns. Newspapers, however, devoted more space to Gussie Moran during the early 1950s. She shocked staid galleries by wearing an outfit that included lace panties. For women's sports attire, a new level of casualness had announced itself.

A new generation of professional golfers arose in the 1950s. Among the best was Ben Hogan, a real favorite for most fans. Here he exhibits his flawless form. With prosperity and more leisure time, Americans took to golf courses in record numbers, making the sport a much more popular pastime. Source: Library of Congress.

Horse Racing

In 1953, Native Dancer piqued public consciousness by winning the Preakness and the Belmont, two of racing's premier events. Although "The Gray Ghost," as he was nicknamed, failed to win the Kentucky Derby and thus the Triple Crown, he endeared himself to millions. The photogenic horse had personality to spare—he played with kittens in his stall and seldom paid much attention to his jockeys—and went on to win twenty-one of his total twenty-two starts. *TV Guide* magazine claimed he ranked next to Ed Sullivan as a television attraction, and fans plucked at his mane and tail to get some "souvenirs" whenever they had the opportunity. For a few years during the 1950s, Native Dancer raised horse racing to a popular sport of interest to all.[16]

Track

As a rule, track generates little popular attention, but the early fifties witnessed unprecedented interest in the sport. Milers from many nations were inching up on a mark once considered impossible to achieve: the sub-four-minute mile. Finally, in May of 1954, Britisher Roger Bannister ran a 3:58.8 mile, the first to crack the four-minute barrier. With the feat finally accomplished, the under-four-minute mile became almost commonplace. Attention shifted from when to who would be the first American to do it. At last, Don Bowden salvaged some national honor with a 3:58.7 mile in the summer of 1957. No other American would repeat that feat during the 1950s.

Swimming

In a series of movies that revolved around her prowess as a swimmer, Esther Williams emerged as one of only a handful of noted swimmers during the decade. In her films, which relied on spectacle more than on plot, Williams dived, water-skied, and splashed her way to stardom. Her pictures include *Pagan Love Song* (1950), *Skirts Ahoy!* and *Million Dollar Mermaid* (both 1952), *Dangerous When Wet* and *Easy to Love* (both 1953), and *Jupiter's Darling* (1955).

Florence Chadwick, another of the era's swimmers, decided in 1948 that she would conquer the English Channel and began rigorous training. In 1950 and 1951, she succeeded in swimming the treacherous waterway, first from France to England, and then from England to France. These feats granted her celebrity, and she proceeded to swim the Catalina Channel in 1952 and the Straits of Gibraltar in 1953, breaking records previously held by men. The subject of much media attention, pictures of her, covered with grease and emerging from her latest record challenge, became a part of regular newspaper coverage. She went on to conquer the straits of the Dardanelles and Bosporus, making her the greatest long-distance swimmer of the decade.

Despite their interest in Chadwick's celebrity, most Americans had little yen to emulate her style. But they nonetheless had a great interest in swimming, or more specifically, swimming pools. As innumerable families moved to the growing suburbs, the home swimming pool became a popular status symbol. From just a few thousand installations in the late 1940s, well over one hundred thousand pools were gracing suburban homes by the end of the decade. Sometimes they served as well-used recreational accessories; for many, however, the swimming pool functioned as another emblem of material success. Regardless of purpose, the boom in home swimming pools can be traced directly to the 1950s.[17]

The Olympics

American Bob Mathias, just seventeen and fresh out of high school, won the decathlon gold medal in the 1948 Summer Olympics in London. In 1952, the Games moved to Helsinki, Finland, where Mathias repeated his feat, and the press promptly declared him "the world's greatest athlete," an unofficial title. Out of his success came a movie, *The Bob Mathias Story* (1954), starring the medal-winner himself in the title role. The film helped stir interest in the postwar Olympics and doubtless spurred a few young men to practice harder for the 1956 Melbourne games.

What captured the most public attention in Helsinki, however, involved the political overtones of the event. The Cold War was being fought on Finnish playing fields. The Communist bloc nations insisted on totaling points and accumulating medals, thrusting aside individual competition as unimportant. Most press coverage of the events focused on how many medals Russia or the United States would gain by winning the competition. It brought an unfortunate politicizing to the Games, something that has carried forward ever since. Individuals no longer won medals, nations and ideologies did.

SUMMARY

The leisure activities of Americans can be divided among many differing pursuits. In the 1950s, some people got caught up in the fads of hula hoops and tossing Frisbees, while others preferred the more cerebral pleasures of canasta and Scrabble. Television made its impact felt in the marketing of toys; silly items like Mr. Potato Head and propeller beanies might not have been so visible without their presence on TV. One of the most successful and long-lasting activities involved doing just about anything by oneself. Home workshops became commonplace, and the marketplace rushed to create—and satisfy—demand for tools and do-it-yourself supplies. Both collegiate and professional athletics felt the first incursions of television, and no one individual or team completely dominated popular media. The Yankees won in baseball, Native Dancer captivated racing fans for a while, and relative unknowns like Bob Mathias, Florence Chadwick, Roger Bannister, and Althea Gibson savored their brief moments of fame. However they spent them, Americans had both time and money, a combination that made leisure a big business for the era.

The 1950s

8

Literature

In case they had forgotten, the decade reminded Americans about two of their greatest writers, William Faulkner and Ernest Hemingway. Faulkner won the Nobel Prize for Literature in 1950; four years later, Hemingway received the coveted award. This international recognition briefly boosted their appeal and made them the subjects of considerable popular attention.

By and large, Faulkner and Hemingway were supplanted by the usual run of best-sellers and assorted ephemeral titles that sold in astronomical numbers and then disappeared. Mysteries, lurid novels, social studies, along with self-help and how-to books galore, dominated the trade lists. The reading public looked for escapism and instruction, and the works of prize-winning authors could not begin to equal the sales generated by *Peyton Place* or *The Power of Positive Thinking*.

BOOKS

Paperbacks

Paperback (or paperbound, softback, softbound) books rose to dominance in popular publishing, accounting for over one-third of all the books sold in the United States, and showed no signs of slowing down. Pocket Books, founded in 1939, had by 1950 become the leading publisher of the less expensive paperbound titles and they continued to maintain a $0.25 cover price.[1]

The success of Pocket Books led to an expansion of publishing imprints. Cardinal Editions, a subsidiary of Pocket Books, came along in 1951; in a bow to inflation, Cardinals cost $0.35. In 1954, the Pocket Library was created; cover prices ranged from $0.35 to $0.50. This proved a profitable move; the Pocket Library consisted of reprints of earlier Pocket Books and Cardinal Editions titles, but at higher prices. At the end of the decade, the Pocket Library evolved into the Washington Square Press, but continued to offer reprints. In the meantime, the cover price of a typical paperback kept inching up; by 1957, the $0.25 paperbound existed no more; $0.50 and even $0.75 titles had become the norm.

Other publishers, envious of the paperback empire Pocket Books had created, wasted no time in launching their own series. Avon Books debuted in 1941, and throughout the forties and fifties its garish covers, most featuring semi-clothed women, rivaled anything the cheap pulp magazines displayed on newsstands. By 1951, Avon released a dozen new titles a month.

Penguin Books, a well-established English firm that had published paperbacks abroad since 1935, came into the burgeoning American market in the early forties. The imprint did well, and they soon added the Pelican line of nonfiction. Newcomers Bantam Books, Dell Books, New American Library (which included Signet for fiction and Mentor for nonfiction), and Popular Library also were introduced in the mid- to late forties and became significant parts of the deluge of paperbacks that saw print in the fifties.

Still more paperback firms, some new and some boasting fresh imprints from established houses, appeared during the fifties. Familiar names like Ace (1952), Ballantine (1952), Beacon Books (1954), Berkley Books (1955), Crest (1955), Fawcett Gold Medal (1950), Monarch (1958), Perma Books (1950), Premier (1955), and Zenith (1958) commenced publishing. The dominance of the expensive hardcover book had ended, and popular, mass-market writers found expanded outlets for their work.

The covers on many 1950s Popular Library titles, as racy as anything published by Avon, have become collector's items. The content within is almost irrelevant. Responding to complaints, Congress formed a committee in 1952 to investigate the supposedly prurient covers on paperback novels; the committee recommended that the postmaster general ban from interstate or international shipment any books with covers deemed pornographic, a move that gave the U.S. Post Office censorship powers over book illustration. The paperback publishers themselves toned down their product, so that from the mid-fifties onward, the pictures may be tamer, but they also lose a kind of raucous originality that had briefly made them unique.

Covers aside, by the beginning of the 1950s, paperbacks constituted a thriving part of the publishing industry. Some of the larger houses even released original titles, not just reprints of hardcover books. Many mystery novels made their debuts in a paper format; because most people bought the cheaper paper editions anyway, it seemed foolish to go to the

Dr. Norman Vincent Peale, a mainstream Protestant minister, was
one of the most popular religious figures of the decade. His upbeat
book, *The Power of Positive Thinking* (1952) was a long-time best-
seller, and his *Guideposts* newsletter reached millions.
Source: Library of Congress.

expense of a hardcover binding only to then release the same book in
paper covers. Publishers expanded this practice to include such popular
genres as Westerns, science fiction, thrillers, fantasy and horror, romances,
and much in sports and humor.

In 1950, the ABC television network aired *The Adventures of Ellery Queen*,
a series based on a fictional detective whose adventures proved popular
during the 1930s and 1940s. It ran for two unspectacular years and was
canceled in 1952, but NBC brought the durable private eye back for the
1958–1959 season. In like manner, novels featuring Perry Mason, outwardly a lawyer but in actuality another sleuth, had enjoyed considerable
acclaim in the preceding two decades. Capitalizing on that popularity, CBS
Radio ran *Perry Mason* from 1943 to 1955, but Mason's greatest fame came
in 1957 when the network moved the series to television, creating one of
the most successful shows in TV history. It would run until 1966. Naturally, the publishers of both Ellery Queen and Perry Mason promptly
issued fresh paperbound editions of their adventures, introducing a new
generation of readers to the popular mystery series.[2]

Best-Sellers

Despite the inroads made by the ubiquitous paperback, most best-seller lists continued to spotlight hardback titles. And for the prosperous 1950s, plenty of books of both kinds attracted large audiences. Simplistic religious literature boomed as people sought an easy spiritual security. Norman Vincent Peale, the popular pastor at New York's Marble Collegiate Church, wrote *The Power of Positive Thinking* (1952), a consistent best-seller for several years. The book argues that material wealth and an optimistic outlook go hand in hand. Although it did not originate with Peale's work, the motto "the family that prays together stays together" gained wide credence during the 1950s, and its message found support in *The Power of Positive Thinking*. His success assured, Peale also published *Guideposts* magazine and wrote a weekly column for *Look* magazine

The long-awaited Revised Standard Version, or RSV, of the Bible came out in 1952. The work of thirty-two biblical scholars, the project spread over fifteen years, with people everywhere applauding it as a needed updating of the King James Version. Although dissenters abounded, for two consecutive years, 1952 and 1953, it overwhelmed everything, fiction and nonfiction, with over three million copies sold. By 1954, sales had slowed, but only a bit; the RSV still led all nonfiction with close to another million copies purchased.[3]

The evangelist Billy Graham emerged as a multimedia phenomenon in the 1950s. He joined the religious writers' ranks with *America's Hour of Decision* in 1951. The book prospered and he followed it with *Peace with God* in 1953 and *The Secret of Happiness* two years later. In 1956, Graham began a newspaper column, *My Answer*, that quickly received nationwide snydication. He participated in two periodicals, *Christianity Today* and *Decision Magazine*. If all that were not enough, he had incorporated in 1950, creating the Billy Graham Evangelistic Association. This organization then produced films, along with radio and television broadcasts, the most popular being *Hour of Decision*. His star clearly on the rise, Graham led one of the largest religious crusades New York City had ever seen, drawing nearly two million people to Madison Square Garden in the summer of 1957. He also became a personal friend and confidant to President Eisenhower, a role he would consistently play with succeeding presidents.[4]

This religious/spiritual enthusiasm—some likened it to a new awakening—carried over into film, radio, and television. Monsignor Fulton J. Sheen gained fame as a prelate by virtue of his long-running NBC radio show, *The Catholic Hour* (1930–1961). In 1953, the network broadened his radio program to include television. The televised *Catholic Hour* evolved into *Life Is Worth Living* (1953–1955) and then into *Mission to the World* (1955–1957). The television exposure, along with his good looks, low-key delivery, and common-sense values, made Sheen a show business celebrity. Prime-time scheduling put the bishop up against comedian Milton

Berle, and although he could never topple the popular Berle, he did well, and the two referred to one another humorously. [For more on the religious films of the era, see chapter 10, "Performing Arts."]

J. D. Salinger

Just as the movies had their teen stars in the fifties, so did the publishing world. Holden Caulfield, the lonely hero—or antihero, as contemporary critics delighted in calling him—of J. D. Salinger's *The Catcher in the Rye* (1951) captivated audiences everywhere, and came to epitomize contemporary youth. The novel attracted a large public and soon appeared on required reading lists in innumerable high schools and colleges. Holden's distrust of adults and simultaneous yearning for the security and stability of family served as a good metaphor for the decade. It suggested the difficulty of any successful resolution, but its optimistic ending, with Holden returning to his home, posits the idea that contradiction symbolizes modern times and must be accepted. Salinger followed this work with a popular collection of briefer pieces titled *Nine Stories* (1953).[5]

Ernest Hemingway

Established writers like William Faulkner (*The Mansion*, 1959), Ernest Hemingway (*The Old Man and the Sea*, 1952), and John Steinbeck (*East of Eden*, 1952) continued to produce significant works, but only Hemingway succeeded in reaching a truly large audience. *Life* Magazine published his *Old Man and the Sea* in its entirety, so certain were the editors that millions would be attracted to the brief, allegorical work. On September 1, 1952, one week before the book's publication, the magazine printed five million copies, a record number. The editors had guessed correctly; *Life* sold out and the book shot up onto best-seller lists everywhere. The Book-of-the-Month Club featured it, and Hemingway enjoyed the largest single audience he would ever have. In 1958, Hollywood released a film of the novel, with Spencer Tracy taking the lead role. Hemingway continued to write and bask in the role of literary celebrity, but nothing else ever came close to the success of *The Old Man and the Sea*.

Mickey Spillane

American readers might profess admiration for the likes of Hemingway, Faulkner, and Steinbeck, but when they bought books, their purchases suggested their tastes ran toward authors writing in a more violent and graphic style. In sheer sales, no one could top Mickey Spillane, the creator of detective Mike Hammer. Hammer, a private eye only outwardly cut from the mold established by Raymond Chandler, Dashiell Hammett,

The 1950s proved a banner decade for best-sellers. They ranged from sociological studies of the time (*The Affluent Society, The Lonely Crowd, The Organization Man*) to serious, enduring novels (*The Catcher in the Rye, East of Eden, Invisible Man*) to ephemeral novels of the time (*The Man in the Gray Flannel Suit*) to sensational, often lurid, fare (*The Case of the Fiery Fingers, Vengeance Is Mine*). Whatever the subject, the publishing business did well.

and other "hard-boiled" writers of the thirties and forties, is crude and brutal, but neither he nor his creator seems to care a whit. In addition, Hammer functions as a strong anti-Communist and a rampant homophobe, and some would add misogynist. In Hammer's primitive code, sexual deviance leads to moral weakness, and that makes a person a target of Communist infiltrators ready to pounce on any human frailty. Certainly,

Mike Hammer performs as an individual who suffers none of the angst so fashionable in fiction of the time. His attitudes therefore made him the darling of many conservatives, fighting as he does their darkest fears.

The first of the Hammer stories, *I, the Jury*, came out in 1947 and took off like a rocket. By 1952, Spillane's titles—such as *My Gun Is Quick* (1950), *Vengeance Is Mine* (1950), *One Lonely Night* (1951), *The Big Kill* (1951), and *Kiss Me Deadly* (1952)—accounted for one-quarter of all paperback books sold in the United States. Hollywood quickly rushed out dark, moody versions of *I, the Jury* (1953; remade in 1982), *Kiss Me Deadly* (1955), and *My Gun Is Quick* (1957).[6]

Spillaine's work generated so much excitement that he coauthored (with Ed Robbins and Joe Gill) a comic book series titled *From the Files of . . . Mike Hammer* from 1953 until 1954. Radio followed close behind with *That Hammer Guy*, a Mutual Network offering that also ran during those two years. Television lagged a bit in hitching onto the Spillane bandwagon, but 1958 saw a syndicated series titled *Mickey Spillane's Mike Hammer*. Starring Darren McGavin as the tough investigator, it ran for seventy-eight half-hour episodes.

Grace Metalious

Another prominent writer of the period is Grace Metalious. Her claim to fame rests with one blockbuster novel, *Peyton Place* (1956). The book introduces readers to a complex, interrelated cast of characters that move from one steamy episode to another. It took a long time for Metalious to find a publisher, but a small New York house finally picked it up. Thanks to effective prepublication publicity, the book already showed on the trade lists when it appeared in bookstores. Giant Dell Publishing quickly took on the novel, and the combined paperback and hardcover editions made publishing history. Since its release in 1956, the novel has established itself as one of the all-time American best-sellers, with over 12 million copies sold.

Originally written to challenge every sexual taboo in America, in its final form *Peyton Place* was somewhat toned down. Metalious rewrote a few of the more lurid passages, but even with editing, *Peyton Place* manages to include adultery, incest, illegitimacy, and graphic sexual descriptions—certainly sufficient for 1956, and more than enough to make it a "must-read" for millions.

Thanks to its notoriety and huge sales, *Peyton Place* appeared on the big screen in 1957. Metalious, not happy with what editors had done to her work in both novelistic and cinematic terms, nonetheless wrote a sequel, *Return to Peyton Place* (1959). Panned by critics, the book sold well on the strength of the original *Peyton Place*, and likewise became a movie in 1960.[7] [See chapter 10, "Performing Arts," for more on the movie version of the book.]

Over the years, the novels of both Mickey Spillane and Grace Metalious have been disdained by the critical elite and devoured by the general public. Recently, however, critics have begun to reexamine the authors' books, giving them a grudging level of acceptance. What many then saw as "dirty" or "too graphic" has since become quite tame, even quaint; times change, along with standards.

Vladimir Nabokov

With the publication of the Mike Hammer thrillers and *Peyton Place*, plus several other controversial novels, America's sexual innocence drew to a close. The release of Vladimir Nabokov's *Lolita* in 1955 hastened that closure. First published by the Paris-based Olympia Press, the book finally found an American house willing to carry it in 1958. Never officially banned in the United States in either its European or American editions, the novel stunned critics, drove would-be censors wild, sold millions of copies, and dominated best-seller lists soon after its release. The story involves the adventures, both comic and sexual, of a 12-year-old girl and her ardent middle-aged suitor, Humbert Humbert. Nabokov contributed two new words to the language: "Lolita" and "nymphet." Both refer to underage girls who are sexually wise beyond their years. The author until this time had been noted mainly for dense, academic novels that had little to do with eroticism, so *Lolita* came as a surprise and had the book world talking for years after its publication.

Emboldened by the reputation and success of the novel, Hollywood released a film called *Baby Doll* in 1956. A deliberate exploitation of the concept of precocious sexuality by the distinguished playwright Tennessee Williams, the climate engendered by both *Baby Doll* and the reputation of *Lolita* indicated audiences were intrigued by the steamy subject matter, despite the howls of would-be censors. *Lolita* did not make the screen until 1962, but the story has outlived its detractors and ensconced itself as one of the major novels of the twentieth century.[8]

The Beat Generation and Jack Kerouac

Analogous in some ways both to Abstract Expressionism in the visual arts and progressive jazz in music, the work of the so-called "Beat Generation" stands as a cultural phenomenon, The writing that poured forth from this literary movement favored an improvisational approach, and its supporters claimed that true spontaneity in the arts outweighed a text in which the author carefully positions every word. In their eyes, emotion (or the expression thereof) supplanted traditional craft, an attitude that put them in league with many of the Abstract Expressionists then active in painting. [More on Abstract Expressionism can be found in chapter 12, "The Visual Arts."]

Like their counterparts in other arts, the Beat writers rejected much of modern mass culture, claiming that it was sterile and lacking in any substance. Their work first manifested itself on the West Coast, especially in the coffeehouses and bistros of San Francisco. No one seems absolutely sure where the term "beat" originated; these artists would have been called "Bohemians" in an earlier age. Some say it derives from "beatitude" and ideas of mysticism, but others prefer "beat"—suggesting tired or beaten down by the forces of materialism and conformity. Either way, the word quickly entered the language, denoting novelists, poets, and other creative types of the 1950s who were in rebellion against the status quo.

After the successful Russian launch of the *Sputnik* spacecraft in 1957, the suffix "–nik" took on a certain cachet and was added to the word "beat." The resultant "beatnik" veered away from the original; it carried negative connotations, implying a person loafed, possessed a beard (but seldom long hair in those days), wore scruffy clothes and sandals, and displayed numerous bad habits. In the meantime, "beat," without any suffixes, virtually disappeared, along with any redeeming qualities it might have previously suggested.

Poet and publisher Lawrence Ferlinghetti ran the City Lights Bookstore in San Francisco, and there many of the more famous Beat writers and poets congregated. A motley crew, membership in the fraternity seemed often a hit-or-miss affair. But novelists William S. Burroughs (*The Naked Lunch*, 1959), John Clellon Holmes (*GO!* 1952), and Jack Kerouac (*On the Road*, 1957), along with poets Allen Ginsberg (*Howl*, 1956), Gregory Corso (*Gasoline*, 1956), and Kenneth Rexroth (*In Defense of the Earth*, 1956), emerged as prominent members.[9]

Kerouac in particular came to symbolize this free-spirited movement. Not much noticed by the critics at the time, Kerouac published *The Town and the City* in 1950. This novel presaged much of his later work. He called his technique of unpunctuated, stream-of-consciousness prose "sketching," a nod to its similarities with the ongoing art scene. In 1957, *On the Road*, his best-known novel, appeared. Written in the early 1950s in his seemingly spontaneous, nonstop, impulsive style, it attracted a wide range of readers. *On the Road* was followed in 1958 by *The Subterraneans* and *The Dharma Bums*, two novels that added some weight to the claim that Kerouac spoke for the Beat Generation, but their success also relied in large part on the reputation earned by *On the Road*.

A question that often arises in discussing the work of Kerouac, at least in terms of popular culture, is: How often did people actually read his books? Although *On the Road* sold in considerable numbers, and other titles by the author enjoyed modest success, the challenge of staying with his demanding stylistics suggests that Kerouac stood on the fringes of popular culture, a figure destined to be a footnote to American writing in the postwar period.[10]

Poetry

A few established poets like Robert Frost and Carl Sandburg could still attract a handful of readers, but serious poetry held little popular appeal in the 1950s. Robert Lowell, perhaps the best of a new, postwar generation of poets, enjoyed the praises of critics, but that kind of recognition failed to generate any wave of public acclaim or sales.

One exception in the poetry doldrums concerned Allen Ginsberg's long, rambling poem *Howl*. Published in 1956 by City Lights Press and initially released in San Francisco, the local police deemed it obscene and seized all copies. Their heavy-handed action gave the work more publicity than it might otherwise have received. A trial ensued, and both Lawrence Ferlinghetti (as publisher) and his store manager (for selling a copy to a law officer) were cleared, while *Howl* reaped huge sales and became the top-selling book of poetry in the United States for the 1950s.

Nonfiction

A profusion of nonfiction titles purporting to analyze the social changes taking place in contemporary America marked the decade. Many of these works found large, receptive readerships, a fact that encouraged continuing debate and self-examination. David Riesman's *The Lonely Crowd* (1953; with contributions from Nathan Glazer and Reuel Denney) stands as a trailblazing sociological study that suggests Americans could lose their individuality in a quest for "togetherness," a favorite term of the time. The authors argue that people, increasingly "other-directed," conform to values forced on them, rather than being "inner-directed," or holding to personal beliefs and values. The book maintains that Americans, more and more subjugated to the will of a faceless majority, live anonymous, undirected lives, and that newfound prosperity—signified by the acquisition of material goods—deadens any responses to this situation.

Neither nonfiction nor objective science, Sloan Wilson's *The Man in the Gray Flannel Suit* (1955) is a look at contemporary mores clothed as a novel. The book's hero, and wearer of the title's attire, works in a large corporate atmosphere, vaguely aware of his own unhappiness. He sees himself as part of an army of similar automatons, going to work each day, but spiritually empty. Hollywood, quick to pick up on such themes, released a film version of the novel in 1956. Gregory Peck, one of the most popular actors of the day, plays the lead, and the movie did well, suggesting that audiences responded to the relevance of the subject.

Author William Whyte further examined the question of an oppressive work environment in his best-seller, *The Organization Man* (1956). Whyte argues that American businesses force their employees into a kind of unthinking conformity; the title became a phrase to describe almost anyone working in a white-collar job. Whyte's thesis says that Americans, particularly American men, have lost touch with the spirit of individualism and self-reliance. Instead, the modern corporation imposes a self-serving philosophy of cooperation and loyalty to the company, and their millions of "organization men" wallow in a kind of sameness and conformism.

Tied to all the foregoing was a concern about growing materialism. In a pair of studies, Vance Packard attacked the rampant consumerism of the 1950s. *The Hidden Persuaders* came out in 1957. Using many examples, he attempts to show how manipulative advertising has convinced Americans to purchase goods based on psychological needs instead of the more historic ones of scarcity and insufficiency. He followed that with *The Status Seekers* in 1959, an extension of the earlier work. *The Status Seekers* criticizes a society driven by acquisition for its own sake. Packard claims that consumerism bestows status on those with the most goods, but at the expense of traditional social values.

On an altogether different plane, Alfred Kinsey's much-awaited *Sexual Behavior in the Human Female* made big publishing news with its 1953 release. A companion to his controversial *Sexual Behavior in the Human Male* (1948), readers found much to discuss in the two volumes. His findings indicated that Americans, especially American women, were not quite so proper as some would have them. From outrage to enthusiastic support, with all colors in between, the responses readers gave the new work drove it up the best-seller lists and kept it there for much of the year. For an essentially dry academic treatise on behavior, its popular success came as a surprise.

The Great Books Program

The middle class has traditionally viewed self-education in a positive light, picturing it as an old, desirable American trait. In 1947, Robert Maynard Hutchins, the president of the University of Chicago, along with philosopher Mortimer J. Adler and others, initiated what they called the *Great Books of the Western World*, or the Great Books Program. Owing as much to marketing as to education, the program caught the public interest and in 1952 became available as a 54-volume series. Sold under the auspices of the Encyclopædia Britannica publishing group, the Great Books promised those readers who purchased the series a library of works deemed by Adler and Hutchins as basic to what a well-read person should know. Included in the undertaking were over five hundred works by writers ranging from Aristotle to Virginia Woolf. A clever two-volume

Syntopticon served as a guidebook, or outline, to the wealth contained within the thousands of pages of text.

The series enjoyed a modest success, at least in sales, during the 1950s. The nicely bound volumes had color-coded spines (e.g., red for philosophy and religion) and the publishers marketed them as a handsome addition to any home library. Purchasers were encouraged to meet informally with other buyers to have group discussions, or "Great Conversations," as Hutchins put it. No doubt the introduction of a program like the Great Books reflected vague feelings about deficiencies in American reading patterns. The affluent 1950s allowed consumers—both of culture and attractive books—to own something that spoke to aspirations and economic status.[11]

Dr. Spock and Gaylord Hauser

If some aspired to greater knowledge, others merely wanted advice on raising children and healthy diets. Pediatrician Benjamin Spock published his first edition of *The Common Sense Book of Baby and Child Care* in 1946, and the postwar baby boom caused it to become a perennial best-seller, especially in the 1950s. The book served as a bible for millions of young mothers; on only thirteen pages of the over three hundred in his book, does Dr. Spock specifically address fathers and fatherhood. Generally speaking, Spock recommends flexibility and restraint when dealing with infants and children, in contrast to the sterner messages of earlier advice manuals. Many conservative commentators blamed him for a host of social ills like juvenile delinquency and teenage pregnancies, but the overwhelming majority of his devoted readers accepted his messages of tolerance, and *The Common Sense Book of Baby and Child Care* became one of the most popular books in the annals of American publishing.[12]

While Dr. Spock preached common sense, pseudo-science weighed in with Gaylord Hauser's *Look Younger, Live Longer* (1950), a discussion about the virtues of a healthy diet. Already well known because of his widely read health column in the Hearst newspapers, and a familiar figure on radio talk shows, Hauser's book proved a sensational best-seller; by 1953 it had sold over 500,000 copies.

Hauser advises eating five "wonder foods": blackstrap molasses, powdered skim milk, wheat germ, brewer's yeast, and yogurt. If Americans consumed more of these, he argues, many common illnesses would disappear. Readers responded by buying the designated foods in such quantities that grocers found the usually slow-moving items disappearing from their shelves and had to reorder as long as the book remained in vogue. Although little scientific evidence could be marshaled to support his grandiose claims, a second book, *Be Happier, Be Healthier* (1954), also made the best-seller lists, keeping Hauser in the limelight throughout the decade.

Americans seemed ready to part with a few dollars if the advice played to the never-ending quest for youth.[13]

Summary

Book publishing flourished in the 1950s, despite the rise of television and a widespread belief that reading would decline. Paperbacks emerged as a major force in the market, and many new imprints appeared. A popular taste for sex and violence elevated writers like Mickey Spillane and Grace Metalious onto the best-seller lists, but a number of sociological studies about the postwar era also achieved strong sales.

MAGAZINES

In 1950, magazines remained a leading mass medium in terms of advertising revenue. Collectively, they commanded 9 percent of all the advertising dollars in the United States. Television, however, whittled away at this figure, just as it would do with all print media. By 1960 the number had fallen to 7.7 percent, and advertisers had become much more selective about their magazine choices. Adding to their woes, paper and printing costs rose sharply, and postage rates for magazines jumped a whopping 30 percent in 1959. As a result of all these economic pressures, many old, established titles would disappear from newsstands and mailboxes during the decade.[14]

New Magazines

With the realization that advertisers wanted magazines that reflected specific readerships, a flood of new titles came out during the 1950s. Some enjoyed success, and some never survived beyond an issue or two. Most were specialty, or niche, magazines, periodicals that catered to specific interest groups instead of a vague general populace. Finding a blend of materials that would appeal to both the specialist and to the generalist became the challenge for editors.

Playboy

One of the most important new magazines of the era was *Playboy*. The first issue appeared in October of 1953. Almost single-handedly the creation of Hugh Hefner, a former staffer for *Esquire*, *Playboy* attempted to be both spicy and sophisticated. Operating on a true shoestring budget, Hefner published the first issue without a date or number because he was not sure it would go beyond one issue. He need not have worried. *Playboy* overnight cultivated an audience of college males and young men out

As was the case with book publishing, magazines also flourished during the 1950s. A few old favorites died—*American Magazine*, *Collier's*, and *Woman's Home Companion* among them—but their disappearance was caused more by advertising losses than low circulation. They were quickly replaced by numerous new titles aimed at specific audiences, and pointed the direction that periodicals would take for years to come.

in the work world. Of course, the fact that the first centerfold Playmate (a photograph of a nude young woman that appeared each month in the center of the magazine) featured an unclothed Marilyn Monroe did not hurt sales. One of Hollywood's top stars by 1953, Monroe had posed for the shot before her rise to fame in the movies; Hefner obtained the picture through a photo agency.

Espousing a somewhat libertine philosophy of sexual freedom and materialism, the magazine managed to hire the best authors for both fiction and articles. Hefner injected himself into the magazine, writing one lengthy editorial after another justifying the lifestyles portrayed within the periodical's pages. Advertisers, sensing something new and lucrative, flocked to *Playboy*, making it one of the most profitable magazines of any time.

From its inauspicious beginnings, Hefner and his staff expanded from a tiny Chicago office to the Playboy Mansion, a splendid old house where intellect and ribaldry, jazz and parties, could intermix and become models for readers of how the sophisticated male spends his time. It might all have been clever artifice, but for millions of young men around the country, the *Playboy* philosophy seemed a desirable goal. Circulating a profitable one million copies a month by the close of the decade, *Playboy* dominated an important niche market for advertisers: young males with money to spend and tastes honed by the advice provided in their favorite new magazine.[15]

TV Guide

The 1953 debut of *TV Guide* proved as culturally important as the introduction of *Playboy*. The brainchild of publisher Walter Annenberg, the new magazine found its inspiration in the success of a local publication in Annenberg's native Philadelphia that provided complete listings of local television programming. Upon investigation, he discovered some other cities had similar periodicals, including one in New York that called itself *TV Guide*. A wealthy man, Annenberg bought out several of these magazines, including the New York edition so he could have the rights to the name.

By the spring of 1953, Annenberg had ten cities lined up to receive his journal, and the list continued to grow. His staff prepared articles and features for the magazine, along with the all-important network schedules; regional editions of *TV Guide* then added local programming to the listings. The first issue hit newsstands in April, just after actress Lucille Ball delivered her real-life baby. The event had been cleverly worked into her TV comedy series, *I Love Lucy*. In an ingenious marketing move, *TV Guide* capitalized on the enormous public interest about the birth by putting Ball's new son, Desi, Jr., on the magazine's first cover.

Millions of people either subscribed or picked up a copy of the magazine at supermarkets and drug stores. Except for the veteran *Reader's Digest*, *TV Guide* soon enjoyed the highest circulation of any magazine in the country, selling about six-and-a-half million copies a week in 1959.[16]

Sports Illustrated

Yet another new periodical, this one a product of Henry Luce's *Time-Life* empire, made its debut in August of 1954. *Sports Illustrated* reached an audience in excess of 600,000 its first year. Instead of being a specialized journal full of arcane information about a particular sport, *Sports Illustrated* aimed its content at the mainstream fan. It substituted great photography for endless statistics, and frequently had probing articles on events influencing sports, such as illegal gambling. Advertisers liked this nonspecialist approach and supported the magazine generously, making it a profitable addition to the *Time-Life-Fortune* lineup.

Fan Magazines and *Confidential*

As they had done throughout the 1930s and 1940s, Hollywood fan magazines continued to flourish into the fifties. A mix of fact and innuendo, they directed their content primarily at women of all ages eager to read about the makeup secrets and love lives of their favorite stars. The inroads of television may have cut audiences in theaters, but diehard fans continued to buy the magazines in quantity. *Photoplay*, the acknowledged leader among the dozens of such periodicals available at newsstands, boasted a monthly circulation in excess of one million readers.

As the decade progressed, the fan magazines turned increasingly sensational. From the sentimental and gushing ("Hollywood's Dream Couple and Their Darling New Addition"), the titles moved to such things as "Who Fathered [so-and-so's] Baby?" It signaled a desperate attempt to hang onto readers, but one doomed to failure. The magical glitter that once characterized Hollywood had begun to wear off by the late fifties, but tawdriness would not replace it.

What millions of readers did turn to was a magazine called *Confidential*, along with pale imitators like *Dare, Exposed, Hush-Hush, Tip-Off, Uncensored,* and *Whisper*. A cheap scandal sheet around since 1951, *Confidential* reached its greatest circulation in 1955, with an estimated four-and-a-half million people reading it. After achieving this mark, it began to dwindle in popularity; in 1957, the Post Office Department indicted it for mailing obscene materials. Finally, to meet mounting debts, the owners sold the magazine in 1958. A much tamer version then came out, but it could never reclaim the huge readership the original *Confidential* had enjoyed just a few years earlier.[17]

The furor over *Confidential* and similar magazines did not go unnoticed by Hollywood. *Washington Story* (1952) involves a young woman reporter who works for a scandal-mongering tabloid. In a similar vein, *High Society* (1956) mirrors people's concern about confidentiality and the press. Outwardly a sophisticated comedy, *High Society* nonetheless allows for some pointed commentary about manners and privacy. Finally, a British import, *Your Past Is Showing* (1957; also titled *The Naked Truth*) humorously tells how some people solved their continuing problems with a *Confidential*-like magazine and its snoopy reporters.

Science-Fiction Magazines

With the onset of the Atomic Age, there existed fears of what the future might hold. Publishers capitalized on this anxiety with endless tales of radioactive monsters, mutations, and nuclear devastation. By 1953, some 35 different science-fiction magazines could be found on newsstands. Little more than updated versions of the old sex-violence-horror pulp magazines of the 1920s and 1930s, and printed on cheap paper and adorned with garish covers, they nonetheless did well, attracting a wide readership. Chief among them was *Galaxy*, debuting in 1950.

Many of the stories from these magazines, collected and reprinted in equally cheap paperback anthologies, led to original, novel-length works, prompting a small boom in science fiction. Of course, success in one medium leads to imitation in another, and so Hollywood produced innumerable sci-fi movies; network radio had series like *Dimension X* (1950–1951) and *X-Minus One* (1955–1958); and television began the first of its many ventures into the realm with early shows like *Out There* (1951–1952) and *Tales of Tomorrow* (1951–1953). In all, the nation was treated to a wide-ranging multimedia selection of science fiction, some of it good, some terrible, and most of it mediocre.

Other Specialty Magazines

Since teenagers had become identified as an important, affluent component of American society in their own right, a host of journals catered to them. Possibly the best known was *Seventeen*; its first issue appeared in 1944, but the magazine did not reach its stride until the 1950s, when it emerged as almost essential reading for young girls in junior and senior high schools. With the ages at which women married declining sharply during the late 1940s and early 1950s, savvy marketers began to use the pages of magazines like *Seventeen* to advertise not just teen fashions, but household items such as furniture and appliances. The period between high school and marriage grew short, and full-page spreads for stylish living room suites and electric stoves no longer seemed incongruous in a magazine once devoted to clothing and cosmetics. Competitors like *Young Miss* (1955; later retitled *YM Magazine*) followed *Seventeen*'s lead; the potential of the youth market was not to be ignored.

Males, young and old, could read *Golf Digest* (1950–), or indulge their fantasies about auto racing with *Road & Track* (1947–), *Hot Rod* (1948–), *Motor Trend* (1949–), and *Car and Driver* (1956–). *American Heritage* (1949–) and *Horizon* (1958–) appealed to anyone interested in history, and *Modern Maturity* (1958–) went out to millions of older Americans. Those needing spiritual uplift had *Guidepost* (1952–), whereas *Prevention* (1950–) focused on health care. By the end of the decade, over eight thousand periodicals were published in the United States, up from approximately six thousand in 1950. Most of these ventures, called "trade journals," had extremely limited circulations and readerships. Still, readers of every stripe could find some five hundred magazines of a more general type—or "consumer magazines." Whether a person wished to check on the evening's offerings in *TV Guide*, catch the latest archery tips in *Bowhunting World* (1952–), or read the record reviews in *Stereo Review* (1958–), there existed something for everyone.[18]

Some Failures

Along with the births of new magazines, the 1950s witnessed the deaths of a number of venerable titles. General-interest weeklies, once the mainstays of the business, led the list of the fallen. For instance, the *American Magazine*, which traced its lineage back to 1876, ceased publication in 1956; *Woman's Home Companion*, *Frank Leslie's Popular Monthly*, and *Liberty* also closed up shop at about the same time. They blamed their failures on a lack of advertising revenue, a most compelling reason. But other circumstances also contributed to the fall of these once-thriving journals. One example illustrates the problems faced by all.

After a 61-year run, *Collier's* magazine ceased publication in 1956. At the time of its demise, its circulation totaled almost four million, which sounds like a healthy number of readers. Like *American Magazine* and *Liberty*, *Collier's* was a general-interest periodical aimed at a diffuse, unspecified audience. No one could say with any precision exactly who read *Collier's*; marketing research that might provide that information was then in its infancy. By the 1950s, advertisers wanted to reach specific readers, and a large circulation figure offered no guarantee their target audiences constituted part of that number.

In the years prior to its closing, *Collier's* consistently lost money, and lots of it. In addition, operating costs, from postage to paper to staffing, continued to rise. The magazine refused to change its editorial policies, not realizing that this approach suggested to advertisers that *Collier's* readers were older and more conservative, not the active, youthful consumers that agencies desired. If they bought space in magazines, advertisers made it clear they would buy it in journals with clearly defined readerships. Thus newcomers like *Playboy* and *Sports Illustrated* could claim they went primarily to young, middle-class males and advertisers reacted accordingly, or *Time* and *Newsweek* might boast of the education and business backgrounds of their constituencies. Women's magazines, of course, already had a defined readership, although many attempted to refine that by appealing to specific groups of women. The exceptions seemed to be the broad-based general magazines. Even the most popular (i.e., largest circulation) of them all, the *Saturday Evening Post*, would fall in 1962, its failure brought about precisely because of the problems outlined above that began to manifest themselves in the 1950s.

Summary

The magazine industry underwent significant changes in focus and direction as advertisers looked to more specialized, identifiable audiences. Old favorites like *Collier's* and *The American* disappeared as a result, and several circulation leaders were threatened. Scandal magazines flourished, and the blatant sexuality of *Playboy* promised more changes in the future. Magazines in general, however, remained a strong popular medium.

NEWSPAPERS

The American newspaper enjoyed its greatest success and influence during the 1920s. The economic problems of the Great Depression, followed by World War II, plus the simultaneous rise of radio, dimmed that luster. As a result, the United States had 1,780 daily newspapers that ran about 55 million copies each day in 1950. By the end of the decade, the number had declined to 1,745 dailies, and total circulation, though up to 58 million, had risen only slightly. Since U.S. population increased significantly in that period, from 149 million to 178 million, a paltry three million rise in circulation meant that a smaller percentage of the total population read a daily paper. Some smaller papers enjoyed readership gains, but most major metropolitan dailies lost circulation between 1950 and 1960. One conclusion becomes inescapable: the traditional American newspaper was in trouble during the 1950s, and no one seemed to know exactly what to do about it.[19]

Consolidation and Chains

The consolidation of older papers with one another that had characterized the 1940s continued on into the 1950s. The economic pressures of successfully running a daily paper took their toll, and the era of the two- or three-newspaper city was drawing to a close; most communities found themselves with only one paper. In addition, the supremacy of the afternoon daily no longer held true; those papers that survived tended to be morning editions. Between 1945 and 1960, 350 daily newspapers went out of business, the majority of them evening papers. Some closed down entirely, and others merged or consolidated with what was once the competition. Advertising money, the lifeblood of the business, now flowed into morning editions that boasted page after page of ads.

Many papers surrendered their independent status and became parts of newspaper chains. Older names like Hearst and Scripps-Howard continued to own significant groups of papers, but their overall holdings dipped as newspapers merged or went out of business. Relatively new groups like Newhouse, Cox, Knight Newspapers, Ridder Publications, and Gannett acquired operations in many different locales. All the shifting within the business meant that by the 1950s chains controlled about half of national newspaper circulation, both daily and Sunday. Competition remained strong in those remaining cities with multiple papers, and chain ownership did not appear to bring about any sameness of product nor did it silence editors and columnists, as some had feared. A chain did, however, bring financial resources not always available to independent papers.

Economic Woes

Newspapers commanded 37 percent of all U.S. ad revenues in 1950, but advertisers sought new outlets, particularly in the growing medium of television. By 1960, the newspapers' share of the advertising pie, both local and national, had shrunk to 31 percent, clear evidence of the slow but steady erosion within the once imperial industry, and a situation that accelerated in subsequent years. Six percentage points may not seem like too much, but it marked the first downward shift in newspaper advertising since the Depression. At the same time, TV's share of the advertising pot rose from 3 percent in 1950 to about 30 percent in 1960, a tremendous increase. Other media, radio and magazines in particular, also witnessed drops in advertising as television continued its relentless growth.

In addition to the loss of important advertising revenue, labor unrest brought about several devastating newspaper strikes. In 1953, a prolonged walkout over wages crippled journals in New York City. Detroit and Cleveland papers suffered strikes in 1955. After hard-fought negotiations failed, New York newspapermen again walked out in the fall of 1956. The city did without newspapers for 11 days before the two sides reached a compromise. These instances illustrate but a few of the crippling union-management clashes that swept through the country in the fifties, paralyzing a number of city papers. At the end of each big disruption, the settlement invariably hit management hard, especially in the area of circulation. During these recurring strikes, readers discovered they could do without a daily paper, often turning to television as a substitute. When a strike was resolved, not all former readers returned; lower circulation meant lower ad rates, and that meant decreased revenue. Beleaguered owners frequently ended up raising prices, a move that drove away more readers.

Although gross revenues rose during the 1950s, expenditures climbed at an even faster rate, outweighing any increases in profits. As owners bought new technology to cut costs, workers feared for their jobs, and any savings usually disappeared in a new and bitter round of labor negotiations. As the number of personnel required to put out a modern newspaper dropped sharply, edgy labor unions exacted a stiff price in wages and benefits. Modernization and automation brought with them a host of "featherbedding" clauses in union contracts that allowed unneeded workers to stay on in obsolete jobs. In the worst cases, several papers went out of business, furthering the decline of the American newspaper.[20]

Publishers did put into play some innovative ideas during the decade in an effort to retain readers and advertisers. The most obvious change involved the increased use of color in the printing process. Both editorial and ad copy featured more color layouts. But this technological progress came at considerable cost. Aging printing equipment had to be replaced, and traditional lead type became a thing of the past. The composing room, slow to adapt new methods until mid-century, evolved from a noisy redoubt of hot metal into a smooth-running operation relying on fewer and fewer people. But most analysts considered it money well spent as newspapers strove to compete more effectively with other media.

As to newspaper content, various syndicates continued to offer horoscopes, health, bridge, cooking, home decorating, opinion columns, comics, and just about anything else that might sell. Over two hundred syndicates offered in excess of two thousand different features. Some five hundred columns alone were available, plus five hundred comics, panels, and cartoons. [The comics, since they constitute a mass medium in and of themselves, are covered in greater detail in chapter 12, "Visual Arts."]

Newspapers and the Cold War

The Cold War dominated the front pages every day. The doings of the House Un-American Activities Committee (HUAC), such as the investigations into Communist infiltration of Hollywood, received coverage. Readers no doubt thought that Reds hid under every bed during the near-hysteria of the McCarthy era. The senator from Wisconsin always had a tidbit or two for reporters, and all that he said—true or not—was dutifully recorded.

Editorial cartoonist Herbert Block, better known as "Herblock," was among the first to challenge the stridency of the anti-Communist campaign being waged by Senator McCarthy. In stinging cartoons that commenced in 1950, Herblock created both the word and the idea of "McCarthyism"—unfounded allegations designed to create fear, a kind of bullying attitude toward any opposing attitudes.

The Korean War likewise gained extensive coverage, and strict censorship hobbled efforts to report an accurate picture of the hostilities. General Douglas MacArthur, the commander of allied forces, kept a tight lid on all news, including the threat of courts-martial for reporters who broke his rules. Thus nothing negative, including specific words like "retreat," saw print. The public could read about the war, but what they received distorted the facts.[21]

Reporters

The image of the newspaper reporter, usually portrayed as exciting, with one "big story" following another, has long been a part of popular culture. Seldom examined is the tedium of researching, taking notes, tracking down leads, and actually writing an article. Thus the public's perception of newspaper life and the reality of the profession can be at odds. American movies tended to reinforce the stereotype, but *It Happens Every Thursday* (1953) provides a refreshing departure from this norm. The story of a couple putting out a small-town weekly, the comedy avoids most of the clichés surrounding the majority of films about journalists.

More conventional, but a powerful picture nevertheless, is *The Big Carnival* (1951). Kirk Douglas plays a reporter determined to use a story for personal gain. The plot comes from the real-life media frenzy that surrounded the 1925 entombment of Floyd Collins in a Kentucky cave. A grim movie, most viewers probably came away from it with the idea that reporters live cynical, self-serving lives.

The skeptical, sardonic newsman has been around for a long time, however, as has the crusading editor. Films like *Deadline—USA* (1952), *Kill Me Tomorrow* (1957), *Tijuana Story* (1957), and *Roots of Heaven* (1958) fall into the traditional mold. Adjectives like "hard-boiled" and "boozy" fit the characters in these stories, and so the media stereotypes lived on.

Radio likewise did little to dispel common perceptions about journalism. Oldest of the lot was *Big Town,* a crime-centered drama series that originally debuted in 1937 and endured until 1952. Throughout its history, *Big Town* told the story of a fictional urban daily, its battling editor, and his team of loyal reporters. NBC carried *Nightbeat* from 1950 until 1952, a straightforward crime series involving journalist Randy Stone who finds human-interest stories wherever he looks. *The Big Story* (NBC, 1947–1954) similarly presented weekly thrillers featuring reporters and their encounters with thieves and murderers. Not to be left out, CBS had *Casey, Crime Photographer* (1943–1950; 1954–1955), a series that starred a wise-cracking press photographer who usually ends up solving cases based on details he finds in his pictures. *Front Page Farrell* (1941–1954), a late-afternoon soap opera, took the unusual step of using a newspaper office for many of its tales. Despite numerous love entanglements, the show still managed to involve Farrell in some reporting and investigation also.

Television, still finding its way in the 1950s, looked to radio for many of its creative offerings. Both the aforementioned *Big Story* and *Big Town* made the transition to the small screen. *The Big Story* ran on NBC-TV from 1949 to 1957, at which time it went into syndication. CBS-TV offered *Big Town* from 1950 to 1956; NBC took it from 1954 until its demise in 1956. *Crime Photographer* marked television's incarnation of radio's *Casey, Crime Photographer.* The televised version ran on CBS only from 1951 to 1952. In all of these crossovers, the characters of the newspaper leads changed little if at all.

A television-only series was *Night Editor* (Dumont, 1954). One of TV's early 15-minute shows, *Night Editor* had little time to develop characterization of any kind, and usually consisted of a retelling of one of the stories taken from a fictive daily.

Advice Columnists

A feature that increased greatly in popularity was advice to the lovelorn. Although such columns were not new to American newspapers, two women who happened to be twins—"Ann Landers" (Esther Friedman) and "Abigail Van Buren" (Pauline Friedman)—increased the readership for such material significantly. Both enjoyed wide syndication, although their columns remained completely independent of one another. "Ann Landers" led the way, first appearing in the *Chicago Sun-Times* in 1955. Her sister followed a year later with "Dear Abby" in the *San Francisco Chronicle*.

The Friedman twins took a much more direct means of dispensing advice, eschewing the usually sappy messages their predecessors had followed. At times, they could even be critical of the letters they received, often replying in brief one- or two-word rejoinders that ended the discussion immediately. They provided a fresh approach to journalism aimed at the "woman's page," and readers responded positively, causing the columns to become popular features, read by women and men alike. In many ways, the two columnists served as barometers of American middle-class mores, a task they would perform for the remainder of the century. Their frank approach to sexual matters was ahead of its time, although their editorial positions in the 1950s might seem a bit dated to readers today.[22]

The dubious role of a newspaper advice columnist spilled over into the movies. A cheap "B" picture titled *Lonely Hearts Bandits* came out in 1950. More of a murder mystery than an examination of the profession, it nonetheless explores the role. A better film dealing with the same theme is *Lonelyhearts* (1958). Loosely based on Nathaniel West's 1933 novel, *Miss Lonelyhearts*, the film suggests that newspaper advice to the lovelorn has to be handled carefully, because such columnists seldom are trained counselors. The cautionary movies, however, apparently had no effect whatsoever on the rising careers of Ann and Abby.

Summary

The American newspaper, an important part of daily life, suffered diminishing influence during the 1950s. People found themselves fascinated with television, and the new medium was becoming a primary source of news. Rising expenses, labor disputes, declining profits, and a smaller percentage of the population reading the papers with any regularity further contributed to journalism's woes.

The 1950s

9

Music

The fifties opened with American popular music in the doldrums. The big bands had disappeared, and smaller groups and vocalists suffered hard economic times. Ferment characterized the business, but listeners generally were treated to banal songs of little merit. Recording and playback technologies changed, but as far as popular selections went, disc jockeys, already a well-established radio institution by the 1950s, controlled most programming. Not until the mid-fifties would pop music again emerge as a major force in American culture, powered by rock 'n' roll and its young fans.

POPULAR HITS AND TOP 40

At the onset of the 1950s, the public annually purchased about 189 million records, a respectable figure. But as the decade progressed, the numbers rose: 277 million by 1955, and an astounding 600 million by 1960. The face of American popular music had altered, a change brought about by rock 'n' roll; the typical record-buyers of the late 1940s and early 1950s were in their early 20s, but by the close of the decade teenagers bought 70 percent of all records.[1]

The content found in most mainstream pop songs of the early fifties can be exemplified by two number one compositions: "Cry" (1951) and "How Much Is That Doggie in the Window?" (1953). Singer and teenage heartthrob Johnnie Ray recorded "Cry," a slow, bathetic lament about lost love. His producers, sensing a possible hit, included on the "B" side—or "flip side"—of the record another song about tears titled "The Little White Cloud That Cried"; it climbed to number two on the charts. Patti Page, better known on the radio as "That Singing Rage, Miss Patti Page!" cut "How Much Is That Doggie in the Window?" two years later. Its title to the contrary, the song has little to do with pets and a lot to do with love. The lyrics involve a person traveling away from her sweetheart and wanting to get him a puppy as a companion and watchdog. Inserted throughout the tune are barks and "arfs," in case anyone missed some of the words.

Both songs illustrate the vapid sentimentality that characterized much popular music of the first half of the decade. Record producers envisioned a monolithic audience ready to accept their product without question. The overwhelming success of swing music during the thirties and forties had left the companies convinced that all Americans enjoyed the same thing. As a result, the pop sector lacked imagination and continued to direct recordings at no particular segment of the audience, adrift in a sea of mediocrity. In reality, composers and musicians struggled with many new approaches to their craft, but their efforts tended not to register with a corporate mentality satisfied with the status quo.

Similarly, American radio dispensed only the most noncontroversial music throughout the broadcast day. Drama and variety shows, displaced by television, had virtually disappeared from network schedules by the end of the decade, and stations at first seemed content to play the "Top 40" hits. Unscientific at best, these lists included all manner of music, from Western Swing through avant-garde jazz, but tended to be characterized by bland songs aimed at an unseen mass audience. Some of the Top 40 selections resulted from the sales of records and sheet music, others from the playlists of stations around the nation, while still others were doubtless created at the whim of disc jockeys and fans. Whatever the sources, Top 40 Radio (also called "middle of the road," "hit radio," "adult contemporary," and so on) came to define broadcasting for much of the listening audience.[2]

MEDIA CROSSOVER

There existed distinctive patterns of musical transfer from one medium to another. For example, the background music to the TV detective show *Peter Gunn* (1958–1961) received almost as much popular acclaim as the series itself. A swinging band led by Henry Mancini tried—quite successfully, in the eyes of audiences—to capture the ambience of smoky nightclubs and lurking danger. For many, the music epitomized "cool," or "hip"—important qualities if one wanted to be "with it." [Translation: the music sounded timely and up-to-date, especially for persons who did not wish to appear culturally illiterate. See chapter 2, "World of Youth," for more on 1950s slang.] An RCA Victor album of soundtrack songs from *Peter Gunn* sold extremely well and made Mancini an in-demand composer, arranger, and conductor. From *77 Sunset Strip* (1958–1964) came the silly novelty number, "Kookie, Kookie, Lend Me Your Comb" (1959). "Kookie" was actor Edd Byrnes, and the comb referred to his obsessive habit of running his comb through his luxuriant locks. It survived as a brief hit and further testified to the influence of television.

Broadway's *Guys and Dolls* (1950; film, 1955) and *The Pajama Game* (1954; film, 1957) represent but part of a bumper crop of 1950s musical comedies that fostered best-selling recordings of their scores. With the advent of the long-playing album, all the music from a play or its movie version could be included on one recording. Then, as the scores became better known, individual numbers could be released as singles, either taken from the score/soundtrack, or recorded individually by various artists. In this way, people became familiar with many theatrical songs even without attending the play.

Because millions of people did, however, attend the movies every week, often a single song from a particular film might enjoy hit status. Adding airplay could assure an audience far in excess of that which saw the picture. In 1952, Hollywood released a Western titled *High Noon*. The movie became a big hit, and a song from the soundtrack soared to the top of the charts. "Do Not Forsake Me, Oh My Darling" featured country singer Tex Ritter, and its sad, rambling story attracted listeners and sales. The title music for *The Man with the Golden Arm* (1955) likewise had many fans. The film, a controversial story about drug addiction, never became a box-office blockbuster, but the jazz elements in Elmer Bernstein's score made the soundtrack album a hit in its own right. Innumerable other songs from films achieved varying measures of fame throughout the decade: "Secret Love" (*Calamity Jane*, 1953), "The High and the Mighty" (*The High and the Mighty*, 1954), "Something's Gotta Give" (*Daddy Long Legs*, 1954), "Unchained Melody" (*Unchained*, 1954), "The Party's Over" (*Bells Are Ringing*, 1956), "April Love" (*April Love*, 1957), and "Tammy" (*Tammy and the Bachelor*, 1957) are but a sampling.[3]

CHANGING TECHNOLOGY

To facilitate locating radio stations, preset buttons for car receivers appeared on dashboards in 1952. This handy device already existed in home sets. The transistor radio, first marketed in 1954 and adapted for cars in 1956, made music more portable. Stereo recording of music commenced in 1954; by 1958, stereophonic records had become available to the public. These innovations demonstrated the importance of radios and recordings in making the hits of the day readily available to listeners.

Disc jockeys and program managers emphasized playing only the most current and popular songs, so that audiences frequently heard the same numbers over and over, even if they chose to change stations. A fast pace characterized radio programming of the day; it provided the maximum amount of music and advertising. Identifying the station became as important as its selections, because listeners tended to return to specific stations if they thought they could catch their favorite music. The DJs repeatedly proclaimed call letters and frequencies in order to get listeners to return. The Top 40 formula attracted a broad audience, and over one thousand such stations could be heard across the country at the end of the fifties.

RECORD SPEEDS AND HIGH FIDELITY

Until the end of the 1940s, the 78-rpm recording completely dominated the market. The records themselves tended to be heavy and breakable; the relatively high speed meant faster wear and increased surface noise. Most of the records measured 10 or 12 inches in diameter, which meant about three to five minutes playing time per side. It can fairly be said that the 78 had many years earlier dictated the length of the standard pop song, a case where technology influenced the content and format of a popular medium. But change was coming to the industry.

Columbia Records had, in 1947, introduced the long-playing microgroove recording that turned at 33 $\frac{1}{3}$ rpm. This slower speed allowed for much longer recording and playback times, something needed in the area of classical music or other genres requiring extended playing time. As a result, these new albums contained numerous songs, or tracks. The "33" or "LP" (for long playing) enjoyed huge success, but did not replace single-play recordings, the mainstay of the popular music business.

In the early spring of 1949, RCA Victor introduced its 45-rpm singles, seven-inch records (two songs; one per side) with a large, one-and-a-half-inch center hole. Manufactured of lightweight vinyl instead of the more brittle shellac that characterized the larger, heavier 78s then available, their slower speed meant clearer, less-scratchy sound and greater durability. And, like 78s, they cost little: $0.79 for a single.

RCA wisely marketed a single-speed 45-rpm player early in the fifties. Compact, portable, and virtually unbreakable, it featured a fat, one-and-a-half-inch spindle that accommodated the new discs. Buyers did not have to cope with "spiders," small inserts that fitted into the large center holes on 45s so they could be played on the smaller spindles found on conventional turntables. An instant hit with teenagers everywhere, 45-rpm records and players took possession of the singles market, a fact reflected in steadily rising sales for the decade, accounting for 98 percent of all single sales by 1959.

With 78s, 45s, and 33s all on the market, consumer confusion resulted. The sales of 33 $\frac{1}{3}$ albums soared throughout the fifties, but it would take

Here a young couple relaxes while listening to the latest hits on a small 45-rpm record player. The Radio Corporation of America (RCA) pioneered in the introduction and marketing of the "45." Cheaper and more portable than the old, easily broken 78-rpm discs, they quickly established themselves as the standard format for popular singles of the day. Source: Library of Congress.

time for record buyers to adjust to the new technologies of record reproduction for single discs. Traditions die hard, however; most manufacturers, even those marketing the new 45s, kept pressing 78s until almost the end of the 1950s. For many years thereafter, makers of record players had to make their units adjustable: three speeds—33 ⅓ rpm, 45 rpm, and 78 rpm—and two needles—one playback needle for the older 78s people still had in their collections, and another one for the newer microgrooved 45s and 33s they acquired.[4]

Another facet of the music business involved high fidelity, or "hi-fi." So named because it dealt with the effective and accurate reproduction of sound, the marketing and sale of units designed to achieve the best possible playback of records and radio rose to boom proportions during the decade. A host of companies, ranging from giants like RCA, Columbia, and Magnavox, to tiny shops that turned out exquisite custom units, shared the stage in raising and touting the sound standards emanating from their machines. In time, a person no longer referred to a phonograph as such; now the talk revolved around a hi-fi, or a "system." An important force in the growing market for superior sound reproduction came from the growing line of do-it-yourself kits sold by various manufacturers.

Heath Kits and Knight Kits, among others, competed for those audiophiles who wanted to construct their own high-performance components instead of buying something off the shelf at a department store.

All the statistics about wattage, decibels, and bass and treble levels focused on monaural sound; no matter how many speakers a system possessed, they reproduced the same instrumentation, the same vocalization, and so on. Then in 1958, the Decca and Capitol record companies introduced stereo recordings to the mass market. Although slow in gaining acceptance, the concept of stereo sound (sound broken into left and right channels, with separate controls for each) presaged the next step in high-fidelity engineering. It also meant entirely new record players, amplifiers, cartridges, and speakers, with the result that the business of sound reproduction soared dramatically at the end of the decade, even though it had prospered throughout the 1950s.

SINGERS

Both male and female singers dominated the popular market during the early fifties. Among the men, the choices ran the gamut from relative old-timers like Bing Crosby ("True Love," 1956) and Frank Sinatra (*Songs for Swingin' Lovers* album, 1956) to fresh-faced newcomers like Eddie Fisher ("Oh! My Pa-Pa," 1953) and Johnny Mathis ("Wonderful! Wonderful!" 1957), to the operatic arias of tenor Mario Lanza ("Be My Love," 1951). The women more than held their own: Teresa Brewer ("Let Me Go, Lover" 1954), Doris Day ("Que Sera, Sera," 1956), Connie Francis ("Who's Sorry Now?" 1958), Peggy Lee ("Fever," 1958), Patti Page ("The Tennessee Waltz," 1950), and Jo Stafford ("Shrimp Boats," 1951) could match any of their male counterparts in the competition for hits and sales.

Vocal groups, usually trios or quartets, also had their moments on the Top 40 charts. The Four Aces recorded "Heart and Soul" in 1952, the Hilltoppers reached hit status with "P.S., I Love You" in 1953, the same year the Ames Brothers cut "You, You, You." The Four Lads enjoyed a novelty hit with "Istanbul (Is Not Constantinople)" in 1953, and the following year the Crew Cuts harmonized the nonsense lyrics of "Sh-Boom." On the distaff side, the Andrews Sisters continued a long string of successes with "I Can Dream, Can't I?" in 1950. The McGuire Sisters made the charts in 1954 with "Goodnight, Sweetheart, Goodnight," the same year that the Chordettes crooned about "Mr. Sandman," and the Fontaine Sisters warbled "Hearts of Stone" the next year.

MOOD MUSIC

In addition to all the vocalists, instrumental mood music also became immensely popular during the early 1950s. Characterized by lush versions of old standards, usually with massed strings, slow tempos, and an absence of vocalizing, the producers and arrangers aimed to create a restful, at times romantic mood for background effect. Two English aggregations, the Mantovani Strings and the Frank Chacksfield Orchestra, had strong U.S. sales for their albums, and American groups like the 101 Strings and Andre Kostelanetz and His Orchestra likewise did well. As more and more consumers purchased albums instead of singles, these attractively packaged sets found a public anxious to put something soothing on the high-fidelity turntable. In no time, the field soon became crowded with music for every conceivable mood.

THE BIG BANDS

The fifties witnessed the decline of the big bands, those large aggregations that seemed so invincible during the thirties and forties. Many orchestras simply disappeared; others broke up into quintets and sextets in an attempt to remain active, and a hardy few hung on, hoping for a renaissance that never materialized. One band that did gain some popular recognition during the decade was Stan Kenton and his "Innovations in Modern Music Orchestra." For the most part, however, the big-band era fizzled out in the 1950s, replaced by small groups and a growing emphasis on vocal music.

JAZZ

Constant experimentation and exploration marked the decade. The music clearly had a popular following, but the audience divided into various and competing preferences. Labels for "schools" of jazz abounded, such as Dixieland, cool, bebop, funk, progressive, and West Coast. Disc jockey Al "Jazzbo" Collins hosted a popular jazz show from New York's WNEW called *The Purple Grotto*. He alerted his sizable audience to new trends and artists, and his personable style, spiced with the argot of bop and swing, epitomized the jazz life to many an impressionable listener. Likewise, Jean Shepherd entertained the Midwest with his mixture of jazz, informed comments about artists and recordings, and lengthy monologues on just about anything.

Tommy Smalls, better known as "Dr. Jive," also drew impressive audiences for his radio shows, plus he owned a nightclub, Smalls Paradise, in Harlem that was a favorite with rhythm and blues bands. His influence was such that even Ed Sullivan, the host of television's *Toast of the Town*, had him organize a segment that showcased the talents of many black entertainers who would otherwise not get such national coverage.[5]

Despite all the experimentation in jazz throughout the fifties, the overwhelming majority of fans preferred mainstream music with a danceable rhythm and obvious melody. Lambert, Hendricks, and Ross (Dave Lambert, Jon Hendricks, and Annie Ross), an enterprising group that attempted something a little different, took well-known jazz instrumentals and set words to them. Their lyrics consisted of vocal versions of tenor sax solos, trumpet lines, ensemble riffs, and so on; they made no attempt to create an imaginary "singer." Their debut album, *Sing a Song of Basie* (1958) took the instrumental numbers popularized by the Count Basie Orchestra during the Swing Era and set words to the various parts usually assigned to brass and reeds. To the surprise of many, the album sold well and led the innovative trio to expand its repertoire.

The growing popularity of jazz for a broad audience, albeit one divided into many niches, convinced producer George Wein to stage an outdoor festival at staid Newport, Rhode Island, during the summer of 1954. He featured musicians from all schools and it attracted a sell-out crowd. The Newport Jazz Festival went on to become an annual event

COUNTRY AND WESTERN

Although it lived on the fringes of true popular culture throughout the 1950s, country music did find a growing audience, both rural and urban. For the most part, the larger radio stations ignored this kind of music; when it did gain precious airtime, it usually occurred on small, low-power stations located primarily in the Southeast, Midwest, and Southwest. In the more densely populated upper half of the nation it received little exposure. But the demographics that would eventually favor country tunes were changing. During World War II, a great many rural Americans had made the move to large cities to take jobs in the burgeoning defense industries; they brought with them a rich heritage of music that most of their new urban neighbors knew little about. As the postwar years progressed, increasing numbers of independent radio stations began to play this music as part of their daily broadcasting. Once dismissed as "hillbilly music," country began to insinuate itself into the consciousness of many listeners.

Hank Williams reigned as the king of country music, or "King of the Hillbillies" as his promoters called him. The first musician in this genre to reach the true big-time, he had a string of hits that virtually defined country and western for years to come and introduced millions of urban Americans to the music. "I'm So Lonesome I Could Cry" (1950) and "Your Cheatin' Heart" (1952), with their stories of torment and suffering, inspired the later music of a generation of performers. Williams himself died in 1953 when he was just 29, having lived the life he portrayed in his music.

For its queen, country music had Patsy Cline during the 1950s. After playing dance halls and roadhouses throughout the South, Cline got her break when she appeared on the popular television series, *Arthur Godfrey's Talent Scouts* in 1957. She became an overnight sensation, and her theme song, "Walkin' After Midnight," soared to the top of both the country and the popular charts. Her success helped pave the way for both women and country artists in general to cross over into the more lucrative pop field and find success.

Two brothers, Don and Phil Everly, combined their talents and produced a string of country-tinged hits beginning with "Bye, Bye Love" and "Wake Up, Little Susie" in 1957. They followed those successes with "All I Have to Do Is Dream" and "Bird Dog" in 1958. With a strong beat and a nasal twang, they expanded the parameters of popular music, leading to the amalgamation of country music, rock 'n' roll, and traditional song formulas, a mix usually called "pop rock."

FOLK MUSIC

Like country and western, folk music usually dwelt at the edges of popular American music. During the later 1950s, however, folk songs enjoyed growing public acceptance. Established groups like the Weavers had prepared audiences for such traditional music early on with "Goodnight Irene" (1950). Their rendition proved so successful that a number of pop singers—Frank Sinatra and Jo Stafford among them—cut their own versions. "Goodnight Irene" also showed up on the country charts with interpretations by Ernest Tubb and Red Foley, and even in an offbeat rhythm and blues rendition by Paul Gayton. But "Goodnight Irene" proved the exception; as a rule, most folk-inspired songs garnered few sales, most of those generated by a small, devoted audience.

In 1958, however, a crew-cut, buttoned-down group of young men called The Kingston Trio began to inch up the pop charts with hits like "Tom Dooley" (1958) and "M.T.A." (1959). In many ways, they served as the advance guard of the folk music boom that would sweep the nation in the early 1960s. The trio resurrected old American melodies, as well as writing their own compositions, and added a bit of contemporary gloss to their arrangements, making them popular with a wide range of audiences. Their "Scotch and Soda" (1958) and "Sloop John B" (1958), demonstrated that folk songs could be melodic and fun, steering clear of the partisan "relevance," the strong political or social overtones, that marked much of the music by musicians who would follow them.

But all the foregoing—the Top 40, familiar, comfortable love songs, novelty numbers, mood music, big bands, jazz, country and western, traditional folk, and the like—is but prelude. When talking about the popular musical forces of the 1950s, one format stands out above all others: rock 'n' roll.

ROCK 'N' ROLL

No one really knew it at the time, but 1953 marked a turning point in American popular culture. A small combo broke onto the music scene with a raucous number called "Crazy Man Crazy." They followed it with their hit version of "Shake, Rattle, and Roll" in 1954; this tune had originated with Big Joe Turner, a black bluesman little known to white audiences at the time. The hit, the one millions of young people bought and knew, was performed by Bill Haley and His Comets, and their arrangement, along with the earlier "Crazy Man Crazy," electrified record buyers, most of whom had never heard music quite like this. The group added to their success with "Rock Around the Clock" (1955), another up-tempo number that helped make "rock" a part of the national lexicon. "Rock Around the Clock" also played on the soundtrack of *Blackboard Jungle*, a violent 1955 film about juvenile delinquency that equates rock music with antisocial behavior. [For more on the connections between rock 'n' roll and the movies, see chapter 10, "Performing Arts."]

Sensing a groundswell of youthful approval and with a canny eye to ratings, Cleveland disc jockey Alan Freed decided to push rock 'n' roll on his popular radio series, *The Moon Dog Show.* His growing audience enjoyed this musical form and the ratings shot up. In fact, Freed would later claim that he created the term "rock 'n' roll," although many would say the phrase had long existed among veteran rhythm and blues players as a euphemism for sex. In all fairness, Freed did do much to popularize the term, even changing his show's name to *The Moon Dog House Rock 'n' Roll Party.* And no one can deny that his station, WJW, soon became the top-rated one in the region. Freed emerged as a leading dance and record promoter as well as a powerful disc jockey. He moved to New York City's WINS in 1956 where he inaugurated a late-night show that introduced still more listeners to rhythm and blues and rock 'n' roll. The program gained immediate success, a message not lost on other station directors; the rock format quickly became established on both national and local radio.[6]

Two years later, however, Freed found himself fired by WINS because of trouble at a rock concert. Although Freed had no direct involvement with the incident, popular deejays—especially those who featured rock 'n' roll on their programs—were promptly the victims of a wave of adult paranoia about the inherent evils of the music. It had gotten too popular too fast. Parents, school administrators, zealous ministers and priests, and general upholders of civic virtue combined to attack rock 'n' roll in the waning years of the decade. A small number of disc jockeys, singers, and groups paid the price of public retaliation against their very popularity, but overall the critics had little impact on the music, on sales, or on American teenagers. Rock 'n' roll continued to be the biggest-selling format in American pop.

Radio record spinners like Freed, William B. Williams (who took over Freed's top spot in New York City), George "Hound Dog" Lorenz, Bill Randle, and Dick Biondi became arbiters of taste and success; their on-air comments, along with those records and artists they featured, could help mightily in determining what songs would and would not be hits. This kind of power led to corruption. At decade's end, a number of disc jockeys got caught up in the so-called payola scandals, the term coined to describe the unethical acceptance of payments to play particular songs on the air. No one viewed the practice as illegal, provided the money was reported as income, but the moral implications soon brought about restrictions. A federal investigation that commenced in 1959 exposed a dark underside to the booming music business that resulted in indictments for Freed, along with a host of lesser lights. For the fans, however, payola had virtually no importance. "Rock 'n' Roll Is Here to Stay" sang Danny and the Juniors in 1958, and they were right. Despite all the charges and countercharges, rock 'n' roll emerged as an important component in television and movies, and it ruled much AM radio. [See chapter 10, "Performing Arts," for more on music and radio programming.][7]

As to the music itself, nothing terribly original distinguished the work of Bill Haley and his group; black bands had been playing similar music since the 1940s, but the majority white audience knew little about them. Radio stations, most of which were white-owned, had been effectively segregating music for years. "Race records," recordings aimed at a predominately black clientele, differentiated between white and black bands. Because of such practices, rhythm and blues, the name applied to much of this music, went unheard and unappreciated by the majority of listeners.

And yet, despite segregation, unfair marketing, and biased programming, American popular music found itself heading in multiple directions at mid-decade. Never again could people reach a consensus about overwhelming favorites; there would henceforth be rock hits, pop hits, swing hits, jazz hits, romantic hits, and so on. The 1950s outwardly may have presented an image of cultural conformity, but behind the image there raged important discussions about the many-faceted music business.

By the later 1950s, the hybridization of rhythm and blues and rock 'n' roll led to hits like "Maybelline" (Chuck Berry, 1955), "Blueberry Hill" (Fats Domino, 1956), "Searchin'" (the Coasters, 1957), "Chantilly Lace" (the Big Bopper, 1958), and "Kansas City" (Wilbert Harrison, 1959). Significantly, all these artists are black; their success portended a major racial breakthrough in popular American music. Although most black musicians continued to labor in the shadow of their white counterparts, many black artists finally blossomed into recognizable stars in their own right. The era of white performers dominating the popular charts drew to a close.

In light of this change, some white rock 'n' rollers attempted to incorporate a more "authentic" rhythm and blues element into their music. For example, in 1957 Jerry Lee Lewis struck a responsive chord with youthful audiences with his "Whole Lotta Shakin' Goin' On" and quickly followed that with "Great Balls of Fire." Together, his two records sold millions of copies. His on-stage antics also helped him to get continuing press coverage, a needed element in the never-ending quest for success. But publicity was a two-edged sword: the lurid details of his personal life caused problems for his professional career.[8]

For many white artists, an easy approach to audience acceptance involved performing "covers" of songs popularized by black performers. For example, in 1956 singer Georgia Gibbs had a hit with "Dance with Me, Henry." But two years earlier Hank Ballard and the Midnighters had made the rhythm and blues charts with a number titled "Work with Me, Annie." Ballard's song, from its title onward, was filled with sexual innuendo. Gibbs's interpretation contained no suggestiveness—it even bore the subtitle of "Wallflower"; instead, it proved a moderate-tempo number with a good beat for dancing.

Similar examples can be advanced: Ricky Nelson's "I'm Walkin'" (1957) grew out of the original by Fats Domino (also 1957); the McGuire Sisters' "Sincerely" (1955) came from an original by the Moonglows (1954); and the aforementioned "Shake, Rattle and Roll" (1954) by Bill Haley and His Comets was first recorded by Joe Turner, also in 1954. The number of such covers precludes any definitive listing, but it becomes obvious that the practice was widespread. Thus did rock 'n' roll, despite its shady past and sexual undertones, reach a large white audience.[9]

The use of white artists to cover black performers represented a continuing fear among record producers: somehow black artists could not attract a large (i.e., profitable) white audience. They would be proved wrong, but it took much of the decade to convince them. One of the singular accomplishments of 1950s music, however, involves the eventual success of integrating black performers into the previously all-white mainstream. In many ways, this blending of musicians and compositions served as a preview of the civil rights triumphs of the late fifties and early sixties. Popular American music moved far ahead of social change, and it helped open many doors previously closed to minority artists.

Teenagers deserve much of the credit for this integration of black and white musical forms. In their record purchases, concert attendance, and other measurable preferences, they displayed a remarkable lack of bias when it came to music—especially rock 'n' roll.[10]

Teenage slang, always a sure means of separating teens from adults unsure of the nuances of new meanings for old words, took on distinct black overtones. The jargon spoken by musicians, especially black jazz musicians—words like "cool," "hip," "crazy," and so forth—was quickly picked up by teens everywhere. When Bill Haley and His Comets cut "Crazy Man Crazy" in 1953, the lyrics exclaim that the music is "gone, gone," and adolescents already knew exactly what he meant—the music is outstanding; it is truly inspired. Or, as teens might have put it at the time, it is "far out" and really "cool." [For more on teenage slang of the fifties, see chapter 2, "World of Youth."]

As is the way with adolescents, the more adults condemned rock 'n' roll, the more teens gravitated to it. With spendable cash in their pockets, American youth began to buy rock 'n' roll products in earnest. Record sales soared, concerts featuring any bands even vaguely connected to this new music sold out, and the movie industry geared up to make a glut of films featuring rock artists. A heady time for all, and no one personified the era better than a young man from Tupelo, Mississippi.

ELVIS PRESLEY

Elvis Presley's career had begun quietly enough. In 1953, he made a private recording of a song called "My Happiness." Nobody particularly noticed it, but Presley persevered. In 1954, he cut a series of tracks for tiny Sun Records in Memphis, Tennessee. His version of "That's All Right, Mama" caught the ears of those whom he had previously failed to impress, especially Sam Phillips, the owner of the label.

Phillips had created Sun Records in 1952. He championed many of the best black blues artists of the day, since the segregated nature of the music business prevented them from getting contracts with the major recording companies. But Phillips, a realist, knew that in order to be successful, he also had to find white artists for his struggling independent label. He looked for white singers who could approximate what black vocalists had been doing for years because he wanted to introduce the larger white audience to real rhythm and blues. Cold economic logic told him that using white performers would make the job that much easier. His solution brought forth a hybrid music called "rockabilly."

Rockabilly blends white country ("hillbilly") music with black rhythm and blues. A dominant rhythm section, coupled with an uninhibited vocalist, creates a mix that possesses a lively beat and urges listeners onto the dance floor. Phillips helped foster the early careers of Johnny Cash, Jerry Lee Lewis, Roy Orbison, Carl Perkins, and, of course, Elvis Presley. Unfortunately for Phillips, the success of these new artists meant they soon left Sun Records and headed for greener, more profitable pastures. He would never be a wealthy part of the fabulous rise of rock 'n' roll, but Sam Phillips would always be an integral part.

For Elvis Presley, those early Sun recordings led to a spot on the stage of the Grand Ole Opry radio broadcast later in the year. The positive response to that event led to regular appearances on the *Louisiana Hayride*

A 1956 portrait of Elvis Presley, just as he approached superstardom. Mixing blues, hillbilly, and a lot of rock 'n' roll, Presley emerged as the dominant musical talent of the decade. He struck many as controversial, but that did not stop millions of people, young and old, from buying his records and selling out his concerts. Source: Library of Congress.

Show. His star rapidly rising, Presley's career was taken over by a man named "Colonel" Tom Parker, an astute manager if ever there was one. In fact, Parker deprived Sam Philips of his star singer. In November of 1955, Parker had engineered an RCA Victor recording contract for Presley that would result in an unprecedented string of hits in 1956: "Heartbreak Hotel" (the single sold eight million copies in six months), "Blue Suede Shoes" (Presley's version far outsold Carl Perkins's 1955 Sun recording of the same song), "Hound Dog," "I Want You, I Need You, I Love You," and "Love Me Tender," making him the hottest new star in popular music.

His Victor album called, simply, *Elvis Presley* (1956), broke all existing sales records; from January 1956 until March 1958 and his induction into the Army, Elvis Presley had fourteen consecutive million-seller singles, an amazing achievement. Although no one could say for sure how to classify Elvis—rockabilly? hillbilly? country and western? rock 'n' roll?—the fact remained that he was the best thing to happen to popular music in years. The king of crossover, most of Presley's hits could be simultaneously assigned to the mainstream, country, rhythm and blues, and rock 'n' roll charts. His appeal was so great that virtually no other entertainer could match him on individual hits. A second Victor album, *Elvis* (1957), likewise soared to the top, making him one of the few major entertainers immediately identifiable by first name only.[11]

In 1956, Parker successfully negotiated a movie contract for Presley. His first release was to be called *The Reno Brothers*, but the inclusion of the ballad "Love Me Tender" convinced the producers to capitalize on Presley's soaring popularity as a singer. The movie was re-titled *Love Me Tender* and it cashed in at the box office. Its success led to *Loving You* and *Jailhouse Rock* in 1957, both also titled after songs included in the films. A fourth film, *King Creole*, came out in 1958.

Presley's skyrocketing career was not limited to records and movies. His television appearances on *The Ed Sullivan Show* have become the stuff of legend. Parker worked long and hard to get Presley on the top-ranked variety show in the fall of 1956. Given the young star's blossoming reputation, he had already appeared on several other programs by that time. But Sullivan ruled the ratings, and Parker knew that a few minutes on his show would introduce Presley to his largest audience ever. Time proved him right; over three-quarters of the American viewing audience tuned in to see this phenomenon. An instant hit, he appeared three times. The gyrations of "Elvis the Pelvis" had upset enough viewers that CBS took no chances: by his third visit, cameramen had been instructed to shoot him from the waist up. But even the upper half of Presley attracted viewers and the show drew a record audience.[12]

Elvis Presley projected a controversial image that troubled many Americans. In truth, Elvis was something of a dandy. He loved clothes, and his wardrobe bulged with hundreds of different outfits. From his rocker black slacks and pink jackets to his superstar satins and gold lamés, Presley delighted in costume. And it went beyond mere attire; his sideburns and brilliantined hair bothered some, and others decried his dancing as lascivious and degrading. But no one denied that his success, along with the acceptance of rock 'n' roll into American culture, announced the arrival of a new, probably unbridgeable, generation gap, along with a revolution in sexual mores. Although Presley would continue to be a superstar until his death in 1977, for the second half of the 1950s his name was synonymous with rock 'n' roll and the discovery of a new musical form.

Riding the crest of an unparalleled success, Presley entered the Army in March of 1958. The greasy hair came off and he disappeared into active duty. Upon his return from service in 1960, Presley would immediately reclaim his spot as one of America's top entertainers. His elevation into an icon of popular entertainment lay before him, but the raucous magic he had engendered in mid-decade had disappeared.

PAT BOONE

Despite the steamroller success of Elvis Presley, other singers managed to hold their own during the later fifties. Singer Harry Belafonte had back-to-back surprise hits with "Jamaica Farewell" in 1956 and "Banana Boat Song" ("Day-O!") in 1957; their success spurred a brief public clamor for calypso music. Crooners like Nat "King" Cole ("Ballerina," 1957), Perry Como ("Dream Along with Me," 1956), Johnny Mathis ("Chances Are," 1957), and Andy Williams ("Canadian Sunset," 1956) epitomized the clean-cut vocalist performing syrupy ballads that offended and threatened no one.

A young vocalist named Pat Boone was about the only male singer to challenge Presley with any regularity in the popularity sweepstakes. In 1957, he struck double gold with "Love Letters in the Sand" and "April Love." American teens were torn: the slow, sincere lyrics enunciated by Boone, or the suggestive, dangerous course plotted by Presley ("All Shook Up" and "Jailhouse Rock"). In typical adolescent fashion they had it both ways. Boone and Presley alternated with their respective hits.

Determined to reach as broad an audience as possible, Boone turned to covers of black hits. In 1955, Fats Domino, a reasonably successful black singer, had recorded "Ain't That a Shame." It climbed the charts, but only so far. Then Boone cut a much less "soulful" version of the song that same year and it promptly reached number one. Little Richard, a colorful rhythm and blues performer, enjoyed a big hit with "Tutti Frutti" in early 1956. But Boone scored an even bigger hit on the same song; in fact, his 1956 cover of "Tutti Frutti" outsold Little Richard's original. That success, along with his earlier "Ain't That a Shame," showed a pattern in Boone's work: he could take raunchy rhythm and blues songs, sanitize them, and have pop hits. Later in 1956 he again took a Little Richard number, this time "Long Tall Sally," and made it acceptable to parents and—more importantly—radio play. For many record executives, Pat Boone singing Little Richard's songs just seemed safer and more proper than hearing Little Richard performing them himself.[13]

In keeping with his choirboy good looks, Boone wrote a best-selling book about teenage behavior. Titled *Twixt Twelve and Twenty*, the 1958 volume contained a collection of dos and don'ts for young people. It enjoyed healthy sales for much of the year, an unusual accomplishment for that kind of book and a nod to Boone's remarkable popularity. For the remainder of the decade, Boone's traditional crooning would constitute an important force in American music. More than veterans like Bing Crosby, Perry Como, or Frank Sinatra, Boone managed to appeal to young people.

TELEVISION AND POPULAR MUSIC

Two shows that chronicled the changes in American music were *Your Hit Parade* (NBC, 1950–1958; CBS, 1958–1959) and *American Bandstand* (Local, 1952–1957; ABC, 1957–1987; Syndicated, 1987–1989). Both attracted primarily adolescents and young adults, although many other age groups also enjoyed them.

An outgrowth of the enormously popular radio show (NBC, 1935–1937; CBS, 1936–1947; NBC, 1947–1953) of the same name, *Your Hit Parade* premiered on television in July of 1950, and soon outshone its radio counterpart. It would flourish for much of the decade, but rock 'n' roll finally did it in; the rather staid, traditional renditions of pop songs that characterized *Your Hit Parade* seemed somewhat passé in the age of Elvis Presley and Little Richard. Without fanfare, the show left television at the end of the 1959 season.

What *Your Hit Parade* had accomplished so successfully on radio—and in its early TV days—was to chart the sales and appeal of a weekly list of the ten top-rated popular songs. Starting backward, with number ten being performed first, the singers and orchestra worked their way down to number one, breathlessly announcing the title with just enough time remaining to perform it. This approach generated audience suspense, and people enjoyed second-guessing the cast, trying to see if "Goodnight, Irene" (1950), "Shrimp Boats" (1951), "Three Coins in the Fountain" (1954), or hundreds of other ephemeral titles would hold the coveted position for that particular week.

Until the mid-fifties, *Your Hit Parade* served as a fairly accurate barometer of America's mass musical tastes. Viewership, however, dropped in the later years of the decade. Lucky Strike cigarettes, the sponsor of the show from its radio beginnings—its proper title was *Your Lucky Strike Hit Parade*—stayed until the end, but the show seemed something of an anachronism well before its cancellation. When "Rock Around the Clock," "Heartbreak Hotel," and all the other rock hits became the favorites of a new generation of listeners, popular music began a troubled transition away from the idea that mainstream implied the vast majority of the population. Radio stations had become specialized, with jazz, classical, country, Top 40, rock, and a number of other varieties playing to niche audiences. The show's choice of a "Number One Hit" did not necessarily represent everyone's favorite.[14]

American Bandstand (1952–1989) proved one of the most popular and enduring TV shows of the era. From 1956 onward, the likable Dick Clark hosted the afternoon show, taking it to national prominence. New artists, new hits, and new dances were introduced on the series, and several generations of American teens avidly watched to learn all the latest about the pop music scene. To the right of Clark hangs an album cover featuring Bobby Darin, a tremendously successful singer from the period. Source: Library of Congress.

In the meantime, Dick Clark's *American Bandstand* made its national network debut in 1957. Prior to that time, it had been a local show in Philadelphia, premiering in 1952 with somewhat boring film clips of older pop stars performing their hits. This all occurred before the time of the music video of the 1980s and 1990s, and these films look primitive compared to the slick productions later taken for granted.

American Bandstand from its inception reflected an effort by one local television station—Philadelphia's WFIL-TV—to save some money and fill some otherwise empty hours. The networks could provide only so much programming, and then the local affiliates had the responsibility of filling in any leftover hours. And so local television stations took a cue from their radio counterparts. They turned to disc jockeys and recorded music as one format, particularly in the late afternoon after kids were out of school. The networks provided soap operas in the early afternoon, but programming remained the locals' responsibility heading toward dinner time. Records and a disc jockey came cheap; because the shows frequently were simulcast on both radio and TV, a station could stand to make a modest profit in both mediums.

The early *American Bandstand* featured no dancing teenagers until low ratings drove the producers to innovate. They invited the audience to perform on-camera and rate records for "danceability," while live singers lip-synched popular tunes. It looked amateurish and technical problems frequently arose, but viewers loved it. The best move, however, came with the introduction of a new host, Dick Clark, in July of 1956. Clark moved to the show from radio, but he quickly adapted to the new medium. In no time, Clark emerged as the youthful voice of rock 'n' roll, first in Philadelphia and then across the country after ABC added the show to its late afternoon lineup. Always spiffy in jacket and tie, and blessed with boyish good looks, he reassured nervous adults everywhere; he would go on to host *American Bandstand* until 1989.

In 1956, *American Bandstand* was different from much American television: it did not hesitate to televise blacks and whites together on the dance floor, a picture of diversity noticeably lacking on most home screens. Both ABC and the sponsors expressed nervousness about this breach of unspoken racial rules, but the mostly adolescent audience seemed oblivious, making *American Bandstand* a mainstay of afternoon television. Clark nevertheless had to be insistent at the beginning, a time when TV still depicted blacks in stereotypical roles or not at all. He also made white America much more aware of black music and its composers and performers. By not backing down to network censors and commercial worries, he helped make rock 'n' roll a dominant musical form, and opened the audience's eyes to social change.[15]

CLASSICAL MUSIC

Because of the interest in FM radio and high fidelity recordings, classical music enjoyed modest popular success in the 1950s. The improved aural quality of FM enhanced orchestral compositions, and the development of the long-playing phonograph record in 1947 allowed these stations to play selections in their entirety. Unlike AM radio, the inherent limitations of a three-minute song followed by a 60-second commercial did not drive FM programming. Fortunately, a number of FM stations enjoyed subsidies underwritten by universities and other groups, since a common perception existed among most radio producers that classical music could not draw large audiences. Since AM broadcasters relied on commercial support and usually lived on tight budgets, those lucky FM stations provided outlets for alternative musical programming.

Despite limited broadcasting, serious music in reality had a sizable listenership, something borne out in steady record sales throughout the decade. It might not be popular culture on the scale of rock 'n' roll, but a handful of American composers like Samuel Barber, Aaron Copland, Howard Hanson, William Schuman, and Virgil Thompson found modest success both on FM radio and through recordings.

A young composer and conductor named Leonard Bernstein came to be a primary spokesman for classical music to millions of Americans. His compositions, ranging from film scores (*On the Waterfront*, 1954) to operas (*Trouble in Tahiti*, 1952) to blockbuster Broadway plays (*Wonderful Town*, 1953, *West Side Story*, 1957), along with his leadership of the New York Philharmonic, made him a man about music, and his face became familiar to many. Using the medium of television, he undertook to discuss music with shows such as *What Is Jazz?* (1956), and introduced young people to the modern symphony orchestra. Bernstein's engaging mannerisms and openness to all musical forms helped the cause of serious music.

Just as Bernstein's star was rising, another major voice in American classical music allowed his to set. Arturo Toscanini, the tempestuous but popular conductor of the NBC Symphony Orchestra, retired in 1954 at the age of 87. For most Americans, Toscanini personified serious music; his recordings on the RCA Red Seal label outsold virtually any other classical offerings, and his weekly radio broadcasts went out to two hundred NBC affiliates during the early 1950s. His farewell performance in 1954 drew a huge radio audience and resulted in a standing ovation from those in attendance. Radio would never again have a personality to match Toscanini's, and classical music virtually disappeared from the AM dial.[16]

On Christmas Eve of 1951, Gian-Carlo Menotti, a young American composer, premiered an opera destined to become a seasonal classic: *Amahl and the Night Visitors*. Commissioned by NBC television, it proved melodious and accessible. Although most Americans generally look askance at anything vaguely operatic, *Amahl and the Night Visitors* quickly became established as a Christmas favorite and was performed live around the country and not just on television.

Another event that kept some attention focused on the classical side of music involved cultural exchanges conducted between the United States and Russia. Despite the saber rattling of the Cold War, many in government strongly encouraged continued dialog by exchanging artists. This meant that American orchestras and performers would periodically visit the Soviet Union and vice versa. Most of the time, that translated as symphony orchestras, string quartets, and individual classical soloists; seldom did jazz musicians or popular performers receive State Department invitations, although occasional exchanges did occur.

Major groups like Bernstein's New York Philharmonic or the Philadelphia Orchestra would find themselves en route to Moscow, and their Russian counterparts would be winging their way to New York City. It seemed a good way to establish and strengthen cultural ties between the two superpowers, and it also served as a kind of cultural blackmail: when a diplomatic breakdown occurred, artists would be forbidden to travel from one country to another. After the diplomats resolved their issues, the exchanges resumed. It might seem silly in retrospect, but at the time the exchanging—or withholding—of artists carried with it considerable prestige, so both governments made such cultural negotiations an important part of their political agenda.

SUMMARY

At the onset of the 1950s, white mainstream pop overshadowed all other formats, accounting for more than 50 percent of total record sales. Disc jockeys ruled the airwaves, although payola scandals in 1959 would detract from their credibility. With their immense influence, they helped to usher in rock 'n' roll. The music itself evolved from many sources, especially the black heritage in rhythm and blues. Rock 'n' roll brought cultural diversity to American popular music, and the hegemony of majority middle-class tastes was broken. This change signaled the true demassification of musical culture in the United States, a change that only accelerated as the decade drew to a close. The rock hits came along so quickly that radio stations began calling songs recorded just a year or so earlier "golden oldies," creating an instant nostalgia about this new music. New or golden, rock 'n' roll transformed American popular music, a true 1950s phenomenon.

10

Performing Arts

The ascendancy and triumph of television as the nation's most popular medium marked the 1950s. At the beginning of the decade, 9 percent of American households possessed at least one TV; by 1959, some 86 percent owned receivers, leaving movies and radio as the big losers. By 1953, plummeting attendance had caused a quarter of the nation's movie theaters to close. In the late 1940s, almost 85 million patrons attended the movies on a weekly basis; by the mid-fifties that number had been more than halved. Radio, for its part, went from a schedule filled with variety to a format essentially based on popular recordings, brief newscasts on the hour, and occasional sports. The legitimate theater had sporadic hits and constant struggles, and only a dedicated few watched serious dance—but America's young people had discovered rock 'n' roll, and some new and disturbing popular dance steps were being practiced by adolescents everywhere.

MOVIES

Technical Innovation and Novelty

The decade opened with box-office sales relatively strong; by 1952, weekly movie attendance had dropped from previous highs of over eighty million down to about forty-six million patrons. In response, Hollywood began experimenting with technical gimmicks that might lure people back into theaters. After all, television, the film industry's archrival, was limited to a tiny screen and a monochromatic picture. Many larger-budget films already enjoyed color and high-fidelity sound; what else might the technical-effects people accomplish?

One of the first attempts to get audiences back into theaters proved ill fated: 3-D (three-dimensional). The Natural Vision Corporation manufactured film stock that held double images and it promised great changes. Through the use of polarized lenses, those images could be reconfigured to give the illusion of depth. Although many felt skeptical about audiences agreeing to wear ill-fitting cardboard glasses with green and red lens of colored cellophane, the naysayers were proved wrong. Amid much fanfare, millions dutifully donned the glasses to watch *Bwana Devil* (1952), the first of several mediocre 3-D offerings. It was followed by such titles as *Man in the Dark* (1953), *It Came from Outer Space* (1953), *House of Wax* (1953), and *Creature from the Black Lagoon* (1954). The 3-D format might have fared better if the initial releases had been superior films, but Hollywood provided hastily made and poorly acted features. *Bwana Devil* based its claims to fame on pitched spears and flaming arrows that appear to be coming off the screen and into the laps of viewers. That low level of innovation initially made money, but audiences soon tired of the novelty, the cheap glasses, and the inferior pictures. The fad lasted for only a couple of years, and then Hollywood had to look elsewhere to compete with television.[1]

About the same time as 3-D's introduction, another innovation came along. For many years, the projected theatrical image maintained a ratio of 1.33:1, meaning that the screen measured 1.33 times wider than its height. Over time, this ratio had become the standard, and accounts for the familiar shape of most television screens. The movie industry, desperate to compete with television, began to tinker with screen dimensions and proportions in hopes of widening the image.

In 1952, the Cinerama Corporation released *This Is Cinerama!* The film begins innocuously enough: a black-and-white picture appears on a standard screen, and all seems normal, just like any other Hollywood feature. But the black-and-white becomes color, the screen swells, and suddenly the audience finds itself in the midst of a terrifying roller coaster ride as the huge screen wraps an arc of 146 degrees. The horizontal-vertical ratio had been changed to 2.55:1, with images now 2.55 times wider than they were tall. *This Is Cinerama!* enjoyed immediate popularity in the select cities where it first showed on a limited basis, and other theaters quickly lined up for wide-screen adaptations.

CinemaScope, a slightly altered form of Cinerama, made its debut in 1953. Cinerama employs a curved screen and three interlocked cameras shoot the film; three projectors then simultaneously show the movie on the curving screen. Clearly, this involves a complex system not readily embraced by small, neighborhood theaters. For CinemaScope, the screen retains its traditional flatness and only one camera and one projector are involved, an innovation any theater could adapt. The first feature movie in CinemaScope, *The Robe*, came out in 1953. The wider screen, with its panoramic vistas and illusion of depth, soon became the preferred way to show big-budget pictures, although innumerable cheap, small-screen "B" movies continued to be a staple at many studios. Variations such as SuperScope, VistaVision, SuperRama, Todd-A-O, and Technirama emerged from rival groups, while 3-D and Cinerama virtually disappeared. Silly novelties like "Smellorama," (odors in the theater), Sensurround (movements and vibrations felt by the sitting audience), and ShockoVision (faint electric shocks felt by the audience) quickly ran their course. The majority of Hollywood's quality productions, however, employed CinemaScope, the clear leader of the pack.

By 1955, almost all larger American theaters had been equipped to show films in wide-screen versions, although the proportions were later reduced to somewhere between 2.2:1 and 1.85:1 to allow additional magnetic tracks. The use of so-called "Panavision lenses" provided sharp definition and an overall lack of distortion. When the studios released their wide-screen movies to television, parts of the horizontal image disappeared, because the TV screen accommodated only traditional films. The device of "letterboxing" stands as a relatively recent development that permits CinemaScope movies of the 1950s to be seen in all their original glory on 1.33:1 television screens. A compromise that works, opaque bands mask portions of the top and bottom of the TV screen giving a 2.2:1 viewing area.[2]

The success of wide-screen movies in the 1950s meant that audiences were less inclined to watch traditional-width films. In response, the studios released some of their vast libraries of old movies to television. Because of various union agreements, most of the pictures initially shown on TV had been made prior to 1948. But, with the television industry paying top dollar to get popular movies, more recent films became available after the mid-fifties. In 1955, RKO released 740 features to C&C Television. The unions agreed to this transaction, and the following year over 2,500 more movies became available to TV. Despite their long-standing rivalry with the new medium, all the major Hollywood studios by 1958 shared their troves of pictures with television.[3]

Drive-Ins

The decade also witnessed the popularization of the drive-in theater. The idea of watching movies under the stars and in the comfort and privacy of an automobile had first blossomed in the early 1930s, but not until the 1950s did entrepreneurs push the concept. By 1956, over 7,000 drive-ins dotted the nation. Some consisted of a cleared rural field with wooden speaker posts and a crude snack bar, others boasted elaborate layouts with sculpted rows so cars parked at the proper angle for optimum viewing, and the new snack bars often offered as much variety as a traditional restaurant.

One reason for the drive-ins' success involved the creation of the new residential suburbs outside the traditional city limits. Cities still had plenty of neighborhood theaters in the fifties, but the growth of television caused their attendance to plummet. To acquire the urban space necessary to accommodate a drive-in would have cost a fortune. The suburbs, on the other hand, had almost no theaters, but they had plenty of open fields. For a modest investment, a drive-in could be quickly constructed. It proved the ideal marriage: the spacious suburbs and the drive-in theater.

People, possibly strangers to one another in far-flung subdivisions, could meet in the vast parking areas of a drive-in and form a new community, albeit an artificial one that would disband with the completion of the evening's films. They felt secure in their cars and the entertainment cost little. No one had to dress up, and a picnic hamper could provide ample food. Surveys revealed the audience for drive-ins tended to differ from that which attended theaters. Families could pile into the car and not worry about noisy babies or rambunctious youngsters. In fact, many drive-ins provided playgrounds for the kids and even supervised activity rooms. Electric car heaters provided a nice extra touch that meant the theaters could function in cold weather. As time went on, high-fidelity speakers replaced the tinny originals, and the screens got bigger and wider, ready to handle any projector configuration.

Teenagers liked drive-ins because they could be alone with their dates in a safe place. The better outdoor theaters hired a man to walk among the parked vehicles, making sure—with a sharp tap on a steamy window—that couples did not "go too far." Unfortunately, many drive-ins got the reputation of being "passion pits" that had no restrictions on behavior. All too often these less savory locations even played terrible movies, knowing their customers seldom came for the bill of fare. It was not unusual, by the late fifties, for such places to advertise all-night movies "dusk 'til dawn," and so the actions of a few sullied the reputation of drive-ins as a whole.[4]

The Youth Market

The 1950s marked the full realization of movie marketing for the burgeoning teenage population along with the production of films starring actors who could pass for adolescents. Actor Tony Curtis (b. 1925) was among the first to capitalize on this discovery. In *City Across the River* (1949), he epitomizes the tough, streetwise "hood" who thumbs his nose at adult authority. The plot does not compare to the imagery, but for millions of adolescent moviegoers, that was inconsequential. This film spoke directly to them, and did not patronize their attitudes. The movie's modest success encouraged other filmmakers to exploit similar themes.

For many adults, the on-screen persona being created by Marlon Brando (b. 1924) proved far more threatening than anything Tony Curtis might project. In 1954's *The Wild One*, he created a memorable role, playing a lawless biker who brings his motorcycle gang to an innocent, unsuspecting town. Mumbling and clad in boots, tight jeans, and a T-shirt, he terrorized not only the townspeople, but also much of the audience. Teenage boys, however, saw in this inarticulate hero a kind of amoral role model. Yet, in that same year, Brando won an Academy Award for Best Actor in *On the Waterfront*. His sensitive portrayal of a victimized boxer caught up in mobs and crime demonstrated he could handle almost any role, although doubtless many teens wanted him to reprise his biker part.

Brando and Curtis were good, but no one typified the disaffected, aloof teen character better than James Dean (1931–1955). Although he had major roles in only three movies—*Rebel without a Cause* (1955), *East of Eden* (1955), and *Giant* (1956)—Dean came to symbolize the alienation of youth. In both his films and in life, he represented the loner struggling against the forces of conformity. His untimely death in an automobile accident only served to elevate him to cult hero, a place he would occupy for years afterward.

If young people had their pantheon of heroes, they also had their own movies. Most famous, perhaps, *The Blackboard Jungle* (1955) purports to show how juvenile delinquency is rampant in American schools. Vic Morrow (1929–1982) plays a sullen teen who seems incapable of good behavior. Sidney Poitier (b. 1927), in his first major screen role, portrays one of Morrow's fellow gang members. Glenn Ford, as their teacher, tries to reach the boys and break up their gang. In the background, Bill Haley and His Comets pound out "Rock Around the Clock," creating an association between rock 'n' roll and delinquency, just as people frequently connected jazz with crime.

A host of youth-and-rock films followed the success of *Blackboard Jungle*. Right on its heels came *Teen-age Crime Wave* (1955). In 1956, *Don't Knock the Rock*; *Rock Around the Clock*; *Rock, Pretty Baby*; and *Rock, Rock, Rock!* graced theater marquees. *Teenage Doll* (1957), *Go, Johnny, Go!* (1958), *High School Confidential!* (1958), and *Teenage Bad Girl* (1959) mixed delinquency with drugs, making American high schools seem like hotbeds of crime and perversion.

Movies like *The Bad Seed* (1956), *Teenage Monster* (1957), *Teenage Caveman* (1958), and *Teenagers from Outer Space* (1959) cast teens in adolescent versions of science fiction. One, *Earth vs. the Spider* (1958), involves teenagers and a giant spider. In a virtual parody of the classic monster film, the spider, benign and asleep, awakes to the beat of rock 'n' roll.

As drive-ins established themselves on the suburban scene, their marquees hawked cheap horror movies aimed at teenaged audiences. Often, they advertised a "night of horror," with three and even four such films filling the bill. *I Was a Teenage Werewolf* (1957) became the biggest hit of them all. A piece of Hollywood silliness, it stars Michael Landon, later to make his name in television's *Bonanza* and *Little House on the Prairie*. *I Was a Teenage Werewolf* did not stand alone, however. Look-alikes (and even sound-alikes) abounded: *I Was a Teenage Frankenstein* (1957), *Invasion of the Saucer Men* (1957), *Teenage Zombies* (1958), and innumerable—and forgotten—others. Harmless fun, it seems doubtful anyone ever came away truly terrified.

Film Themes

Not all the movies of the 1950s involved teens or rock 'n' roll. The decade also contributed a long list of outstanding films on a multitude of subjects. They range from original dramas like *All About Eve* (1950), sophisticated comedies (*Some Like It Hot*, 1959), sweeping Westerns (*Shane*, 1953), epics of war (*The Bridge on the River Kwai*, 1957), imaginative science fiction (*Destination Moon*, 1950), to the most forgettable "B" pictures imaginable (*Zombies of Moratau*, 1957). Within all this variety there evolved three cinematic reflections of the decade: 1) a liberal bias that argued for sensitivity and tenderness, 2) a mainstream approach that attempted no ideological stance other than entertainment, and 3) a conservative leaning that capitalized on the ongoing anti-Communist rhetoric of the period along with the idea of conforming to the perceived needs of American society. Examples of the first group might include *A Place in the Sun* (1951) or *Paths of Glory* (1957). For the mainstream category, typical choices could be *Singin' in the Rain* (1952) and *Giant* (1956). *I Was a Communist for the FBI* (1951) and *Strategic Air Command* (1955) could represent the third category. Within those broad categories, however, lies much ambiguity; in the movies, nothing is as simple as it may seem. Like the decade itself, contradictions and conflicts abound as filmmakers strove to appeal to a shrinking audience.

The Cold War and the Movies

Uncertainty became a recurring motif in the films of the fifties: who is good, who is evil? Who can be trusted? A kind of cinematic extension of the Cold War, at times the movies spelled out any doubts in simplistic plots, as in *Big Jim McLain* (1952). John Wayne, who stars as an agent of the House Un-American Activities Committee, has no problem second-guessing as he hunts down subversives. Made during the height of the McCarthy investigations, *Big Jim McLain*, along with a number of similar films, played on the popular fear of Communist infiltration into the fabric of American life. It took energetic lawmen to root out this menace, although civil libertarians might wince at some of the methods employed.

In other pictures, however, audiences were sometimes left hanging. For instance, in *Invasion of the Body Snatchers* (1956), townspeople discover ominous pods in their idyllic community. Are these pods some alien life form, or might they really be Communists in disguise? Ostensibly a science-fiction film, *Invasion of the Body Snatchers* can easily be interpreted as an allegorical approach to spies and paranoia. No matter which answer one chooses, a clear message emerges: dangerous people and forces hide behind respectable facades and must be uncovered before they can harm society. One must always be on his or her guard; nothing is as it seems. There exist none of the moral certainties that so characterized the World War II years. The early 1950s in particular witnessed an outpouring of anti-Communist moviemaking. For example, *I Married a Communist* (a.k.a. *Woman on Pier 13*, 1950), *I Was a Communist for the FBI* (1951), *The Whip Hand* (1951), *My Son John* (1952), *Red Planet Mars* (1952), and *Walk East on Beacon* (1952) all purport to be patriotic denunciations of the Red Menace. Today, these films seem awkward and preachy, their naïve jingoism an echo of a bygone era.[5]

Not all the products of Hollywood took such a political stance. Occasionally, a studio would move against the tide, creating pictures that challenged some of the more chauvinist rhetoric of the day. For example, *Trial* (1955) and *Storm Center* (1956) directly address questions about censorship, fairness, and prevailing political ideology. The first, a tepid study of crooked politics and red-baiting, involves a Mexican boy accused of rape and how local leftists (possibly Communists) decide to make him a martyr to their cause. The movie tries, but cannot decide where it really stands. Perhaps, given the times, *Trial* could do no more. In *Storm Center*, a librarian falsely charged with disseminating Communist literature must defend her actions. Although filled with clichés, *Storm Center* does succeed in raising issues about individual freedoms at a time when too many anti-Communist groups recklessly trampled upon such rights.

A far superior film, but one in a vein similar to the two preceding movies, is *12 Angry Men* (1957). It presents a drama about a man upholding an unpopular cause, and focuses on a hung jury—eleven for a murder conviction, one not so sure. Despite great pressure, especially from several indignant jurors (the truly "angry" ones of the title), the holdout argues his position and gradually brings the others to his point of view. A microcosm of popular thinking during the fifties, the film does a superlative job of defending the individual's right to confront the majority, no matter how hopeless or extreme his or her position may be.

Somewhat unusual in that it was adapted from a television play, *12 Angry Men* first appeared on the CBS series *Studio One* in 1954. Reginald Rose scripted both the teleplay and the screenplay. The winner of many awards and an almost instantaneous television classic, it reversed the traditional procedure of movies being adapted to television. When it appeared on TV, the country was in the midst of the Army-McCarthy hearings, a tempestuous series of encounters between Senator Joseph McCarthy and a legal team representing the U.S. Army. During the lengthy debates, McCarthy revealed himself to be a bullying inquisitor, a man ready to destroy others in his obsessive quest for dubious information. In short, some of the more aggressive jurors and their arguments in the original 12 Angry Men resemble Joseph McCarthy and his tactics.

Other Cold War events had their moments on film. In June of 1950, North Korean troops flooded across the border into South Korea. The invasion immediately escalated into an encounter between the so-called "Free World" and the Communist Bloc. On a small stage in faraway Asia, the Cold War had become hot. Troops under the flag of the United Nations responded, and a full-scale war ensued. Hollywood likewise responded with a series of low-budget combat movies depicting Americans at war. Most of the Korean-era films are forgettable, although Pork Chop Hill (1959) stands as a notable exception. Directed by the esteemed Lewis Milestone and starring Gregory Peck, the picture addresses both the battle of the same name and some of its political implications. Likewise, director Sam Fuller managed to get The Steel Helmet and Fixed Bayonets (both 1951) released. Brutally realistic in their depictions of warfare, Fuller's pictures also paint a veneer of cynicism in their stories. Combat possesses no inherent nobility, and the reasons for being in Korea are, at best, cloudy.

Several films attempted to capitalize on the mistreatment of American prisoners of war during their confinement. One of the sad truths to emerge from the conflict involved the clumsy attempts by the North Koreans to brainwash captured soldiers. Prisoner of War (1954) earnestly tries to expose this situation, but it ends up more as an anti-Communist diatribe than a thoughtful examination of the situation. The Rack (1956), on the other hand, gives a good psychological portrait of such a soldier after his return home. The movie also served as an effective stepping-stone in the career of Paul Newman.

Most of the movies about the Korean conflict, however, fall into the category of traditional war pictures and are at best mediocre. Examples include Retreat, Hell! (1951), One Minute to Zero (1952), Battle Circus (1953), Combat Squad (1953), Sabre Jet (1953), Battle Hymn (1957), and Battle Flame (1959). Politics and the Cold War play little role in these potboilers, and the heroes tend to be cut from the mold of the 1950s: clean-cut organization men who will work efficiently within the system—Army, Navy, Air Force, or Marines—and save the day.

In fact, these movies celebrate the American armed forces more than they do the men and women who served in them. Men of the Fighting Lady (1954), Strategic Air Command (1955), and Bombers B-52 (1957) extol the nation's military might and suggest how foolish it would be for any enemy to challenge the United States. The characters that populate these propaganda pieces represent ordinary citizens, suburban types who enjoy cook-outs and the idea of functioning as parts of a team. Sugary, understanding wives and girlfriends complete the picture.

Only a few films took on the dark, unspoken side of the Cold War—the possibility that another Korea could grow into World War III and lead to the nuclear annihilation of all parties. Australian novelist Nevil Shute had penned a story titled *On the Beach* in 1957. An apocalyptic vision of the world after such a war, the novel tells of the survivors—the people of Australia and the crew and passengers on board an American submarine in the South Pacific. With most of the world already dead, a lethal cloud of radiation drifts toward this final refuge. Everyone will die from the fallout, and the book focuses on how they face this extreme situation. In 1959, the novel, already a cult favorite, came out as a big-budget Holly-wood hit, despite its dreary plot. Completely apolitical, *On the Beach* boasts an all-star cast (Gregory Peck, Ava Gardner, and Fred Astaire, among others) plus a mammoth advertising campaign that helped it become a success at the box office. Something of a first for the fifties, *On the Beach* came late in the decade and spawned no rash of imitators. The only other popular movies of the 1950s that dealt with the perils of the nuclear age fell into the realm of science fiction and will be discussed shortly.

Drama

When it came to straight dramatic storytelling and mass production, Hollywood in the 1950s had no equal, even though French, Italian, Swed-ish, and Japanese directors also produced artistic triumphs. For example, *The 400 Blows* (France, 1959), *La Strada* (Italy, 1954), *The Seventh Seal* (Sweden, 1957), and *Rashomon* (Japan, 1950) are generally considered cin-ema classics, but limited distribution and audience reluctance to watch "foreign films" made their popular impact almost nil during the decade. By and large, Americans watched American-made movies. [See "Foreign Films" later in this section for more on imports.]

If popular culture in many ways mirrors the larger ongoing culture of a society, then Hollywood's glossy, dramatic interpretation of the 1950s stresses the white, middle-class values familiar to the majority of Ameri-cans. Only a handful of films examines minority groups in a sympathetic way and generally did poorly at the box office, while the poor and down-trodden are relegated to crime movies.

In *Executive Suite* (1954), some of the basic tenets of 1950s-era corporate culture receive examination. Based on Cameron Hawley's best-selling 1952 novel of the same name, the movie posits the belief that, for a man, a suc-cessful career must come first—family and personal concerns of necessity are secondary. The idea of women in the upper echelons of business life remained foreign to most American filmmakers; women nurtured the bruised egos of their men when the competition got rough, but they seldom entered the fray themselves.

Author Sloan Wilson penned another popular novel of the period, *The Man in the Gray Flannel Suit* (1955). Made into a movie in 1956, its title became a metaphor for both male fashions and advertising executives. A slick story about the lives of New York ad men on Madison Avenue, both book and movie claim to depict contemporary manners and mores, smoothly glossing over any difficult questions that might arise. Like *Executive Suite*, the male characters must choose between family and career. A successful job, a secure place in the system, an understanding wife—these were the goals to be attained in 1950s America.

A more thoughtful examination of corporate culture can be found in *Patterns* (1956), the movie adaptation of a Rod Serling script first presented on the *Kraft Television Theatre* in 1955. An indictment of an environment that places success above morality, both the TV and film versions enjoyed considerable critical acclaim. Despite the accolades, *Patterns* lacked some of the star power and big-budget appeal of other, competing productions, and gained more admiration than it did ratings or box-office receipts. The popular mind preferred the image of the hard-driving, handsome executive free of any ethical burdens.

Not every successful drama portrayed a buttoned-down, flannel-suited businessman. *Marty* (1955), a completely unanticipated hit, was a low-budget production that made a star of actor Ernest Borgnine and proved that, occasionally, audiences could be more discerning than might be expected. Yet another transfer from television, *Marty* first appeared on *The Goodyear Playhouse* in 1953, with Rod Steiger in the lead role. Marty works as a butcher, not an ad man, and Paddy Chayefsky's script (he wrote both the teleplay and the screenplay) gives a moving portrayal of urban loneliness. A commercial success, *Marty* garnered four Academy Awards, including Best Picture and Best Actor.

Film Noir

It should not be thought that Hollywood expended most of its energies on glossy dramas that focused on wealth and power. Film noir, or "black film," emerged as a film style that has come to have international renown. Most critics agree that the period from 1940 to 1960 marks the time of the greatest noir productions. The 1950s therefore played a significant role during this style's heyday, and many of that era's films have come down to the present as classics of the type. Little exists in film noir that moviemakers had not attempted before, but the success with which the industry produced a long string of pictures employing certain techniques gave rise to the term. As the phrase suggests, dark, shadowy dramas distinguish the noir style, and cinematography becomes as important as plotting, a condition that assures black and white as the preferred medium.

No one director, no one cinematographer, not even a particular studio, stands out as being preeminent in the noir style. For the twenty years that mark its greatest popularity, film noir remained a staple product of the movie industry and enjoyed a wide audience. That audience brought expectations into the theater about the style; a successful noir film will satisfy them by using tried and familiar imagery. A neon sign flickering on a fog-enshrouded street, cigarette smoke backlighted by lamps or headlights, the interplay of extremes of light and dark, nighttime in the darkened city as a metaphor for danger—these are some of the hallmarks of the style. Such familiarity stands at the heart of much popular culture; the fulfillment of expectations brings people back to formulaic movies, fiction, television, and music.

Mysteries represent the best noir films of the fifties. Audiences already knew the image of the detective, cigarette dangling from his lips, trench coat pulled tight against a misty rain. Most pictures in this genre were low-budget affairs, employing actors who had not attained true star status; they relied on plot, dialogue, and mood instead of expensive sets and large casts. Although the decade saw a bumper crop of noir pictures, a few of the more enduring titles include *In a Lonely Place* (1950), *Night and the City* (1950), *Detective Story* (1951), *Strangers on a Train* (1951), *Sudden Fear* (1952), *The Big Heat* (1953), *Cry Vengeance* (1954), *The Big Combo* (1955), *Kiss Me Deadly* (1955), *Beyond a Reasonable Doubt* (1956), *A Killer Is Loose* (1956), *The Killing* (1956), *The Sweet Smell of Success* (1957), and *Touch of Evil* (1958).

A number of events sealed the doom of film noir. In an attempt to lure more patrons, movie screens grew larger and color became the preferred film stock. Television, with the intimacy of the small screen and with most productions still produced in black and white, quickly claimed much of the noir territory. By the end of the decade, the style had virtually disappeared from theaters. For twenty years, however, Hollywood served up a threatening, dark vision of the urban world, something quite at odds with the usual bright, cheery images that characterized most film productions.[6]

Musicals

Perhaps the cheeriest of all the movie images coming from the Hollywood studios in the 1950s were those projected in musicals. And no studio made them like Metro-Goldwyn-Mayer. Starting with a rambunctious *Annie Get Your Gun* in 1950 and wrapping up the decade with *Gigi* in 1958, MGM completely dominated the genre. Using top talent, and matching that with quality production values, the studio produced a series of movie musicals that have come to be considered classics.[7]

Many of Hollywood's musicals have been adaptations of previous Broadway offerings. This cultural crossover began almost with the beginning of sound movies and continued unabated into the 1950s. For example, *Annie Get Your Gun* had opened on Broadway in 1946; Ethel Merman, one of the great stars of the American stage, played Annie Oakley. When discussions of a movie version came up, Merman was not available and the coveted role fell to Judy Garland. But Garland, beloved by millions for her role in MGM's *The Wizard of Oz* (1939), had health problems, and thus Betty Hutton, a veteran dancer and singer, got the part. It proved a wise choice, and the commercial success of the filmed *Annie Get Your Gun* (1950) emboldened Hollywood to plunge ahead with numerous other musical offerings.

Show Boat, first seen on Broadway in 1927, initially made it to the screen in 1929, and again in 1936. But the definitive film version came out in 1951 in a lavish MGM production. Audiences flocked to movie theaters to see steamboats and the Old South, and to hear the lovely Jerome Kern and Oscar Hammerstein II score. Clearly, people approved of Hollywood's approach to the musical.

Continuing the practice of borrowing from Broadway, *Gentlemen Prefer Blondes* (1953) took a 1947 play and added to the mix two potent sex symbols of the era, actresses Marilyn Monroe and Jane Russell. The growing popularity of Monroe assured a strong box-office return and even spurred a lackluster sequel, *Gentlemen Marry Brunettes* (1955). This later effort, however, did not include Monroe, and fared only modestly.

Kiss Me Kate (1953) used William Shakespeare's *The Taming of the Shrew* as interpreted in Cole Porter's witty 1948 Broadway hit, and created a popular film version of the comedy. To ensure its success, MGM also released this musical in 3-D, but the short-lived novelty added nothing to the production; later cuts of the movie were released in a conventional format. *Brigadoon* (1954) introduced movie audiences to the writing and composing talents of Alan J. Lerner and Frederick Lowe, whose play of the same name ran on Broadway in 1947. In a bit of unusual casting, MGM convinced Marlon Brando to play Sky Masterson in 1955's *Guys and Dolls*, the studio's adaptation of the 1950 classic musical. With help from the strong score and some excellent costars, Brando manages to carry his part. By this time, musicals were such a major constituent of film production that actors clamored for roles in them.

A big hit on Broadway in 1943, Richard Rodgers and Oscar Hammerstein's *Oklahoma!* finally made it to movie theaters in 1955. The picture's commercial success led to still more stage-to-screen conversions of older plays such as *Anything Goes* (stage, 1934; film, 1956), *Pal Joey* (stage, 1940; film, 1957), and *Carousel* (stage, 1945; film, 1956). The studios maintained a strong relationship with Broadway; although relatively few people ever see a New York stage musical, millions can watch the film version. In addition, radio and television further popularize the music from these productions, often making the score more familiar than the play itself. [For additional information on movie and stage musicals, see "Theater" in this chapter.][8]

Of course, Hollywood did not base all its musical productions on Broadway counterparts. In the eyes of many, the greatest musicals of the 1950s were created specifically for the screen. Two in particular stand out: *An American in Paris* (1951) and *Singin' in the Rain* (1952), both from MGM, and featuring Gene Kelly, one of America's great dancers. Their popular success marks the rise of the movie musical during the decade. Given their cinematic production values—large, changing sets, varied camera angles, manipulation of time and space—they would be difficult, if not impossible, to replicate on even the most modern stage.

No matter how good the movie, by 1958, box-office receipts had declined and the bloom seemed to be wearing off the movie musical. As a kind of last gasp, *Gigi* (1958) established stardom for Leslie Caron, but Rodgers and Hammerstein's long-awaited *South Pacific* (1958) arrived to anemic reviews, because it lacked the original Broadway cast of Mary Martin and Ezio Pinza. Given the high production expenses for musicals, the studios pulled back. The decade-long rise of the Hollywood musical had come to an end, and fickle audiences turned their attention to other fare.[9]

Religious Spectacles

The movie industry did not invest all its resources in musicals. As competition from television grew more intense, studio executives employed a device available only to film: the ability to project large-scale action and spectacle onto the screen. An obvious attempt to woo viewers away from their TV sets and back into theaters, it worked, but only to a degree.

Producers early on turned to the religious epic. Boasting elaborate staging, these spectacles tended to be set in the early Christian era. This allowed for all the old, tried-and-true props of miracles in the desert, gladiators and chariots, mystics and believers, and fantastic costumes and sets. Historical and theological accuracy never seemed a concern. Among the more notable efforts are *Samson and Delilah* (1950), *Quo Vadis?* (1951), *David and Bathsheba* (1951), *The Robe* (1953—also the first CinemaScope production), *Demetrius and the Gladiators* (1954), *The Ten Commandments* (1956), *Solomon and Sheba* (1959), and the last religious saga of the decade, *Ben-Hur* (1959).

As long as audiences did not object to the obvious tinkering with the Bible, they could sit back and enjoy Charlton Heston hurling down thunderbolts as Moses in *The Ten Commandments*, or be enthralled as Charlton Heston (his acting style lent itself well to such pictures) races his chariot around the Roman Forum in *Ben-Hur*. Bombastic and utterly lacking in subtlety, the religious epics of the 1950s perhaps serve as reminders of a lost innocence. Their calls to a blind faith in an age of anxiety and ambiguity gave audiences a brief time-out from contemporary concerns; that it all consists of hokum and lots of special effects matters little. Unlike so many forgotten films from the era, the religious epics have developed a life of their own. At Christmas and Easter, network, cable, and satellite broadcasters run them over and over, and the ratings remain consistently high.

Science Fiction

With all the technological advances of the decade, along with new fears about nuclear weapons and their aftermath, it seemed inevitable that the 1950s would produce a number of science fiction films. Their overall quality varied wildly. In many instances, the monsters and aliens that populate these films are depicted as the results of well-meaning but poorly executed experiments. When things go wrong—and it became an article of faith in these movies that things would go wrong—science run amok earned the blame. With daily reports of atomic bomb tests, with the knowledge that the nation's enemies themselves possessed weapons of mass destruction unimaginable just a few years earlier, it's little wonder that popular culture echoed these anxieties.

At the opening of the decade, films like *Destination Moon* (1950) and *Rocketship X-M* (1950) utilized straightforward stories of space exploration. They reflected the growing certainty that space would be the next frontier, and carried no subtext about an out-of-control technology. Even *When Worlds Collide* (1951) relies on the hoary idea of planets on a collision course. Based on a 1932 story, man and his science had nothing to do with the impending disaster. But that same science can, and will, save mankind, as people race to build a rocket ship that will take a select few to a neighboring planet for colonization and a new start. The worlds do collide— spectacularly—but at least a handful survives, providing the audience a final glimmer of hope.

The War of the Worlds (1953), a dazzling version of the classic 1898 H.G. Wells story, although it cautions against an over-reliance on machines, resolves itself in an almost-religious way, with the Martians being destroyed by earthly germs, "the littlest things." Similarly, *The Next Voice You Hear* (1950) stands as a curious film that also looks to religion for its resolution. Intercepted TV broadcasts from Mars reveal that God rules the nearby planet. A mix of fantasy and propaganda—God counsels the overthrow of Communism—the picture casts technology to the side in its earnest attempt to impart both a spiritual and a political message.

But the films above stand as exceptions. Most of the cinematic science fiction of the fifties comes across as dark and pessimistic. In *The Day the Earth Stood Still* (1951), a flying saucer announces the arrival of a visitor from "somewhere else," presumably a much-advanced civilization. The visitor, accompanied by an impregnable robot named Gort, warns Earth that it must stop experimenting with atomic weapons and submit to more enlightened leadership. To refuse will mean destruction.

The idea that nuclear knowledge could have threatening consequences was not new in the fifties, but it took on an urgency as the decade progressed and weaponry became more deadly. The thought of mutual assured destruction (MAD), as the policy was known, only reinforced the anxieties of the time. *The Thing* (1951) led a series of films that played on that kind of foreboding. Scientists stationed at an Arctic outpost discover a nonhuman intruder among their group. The monster is seldom seen, and then only briefly, allowing audiences to imagine what they will. As much a horror picture as an exercise in science fiction, *The Thing* also fits in nicely with the anti-Communist rhetoric of the time. The story suggests that suspicious characters lurk everywhere; one risks everything to let down any guards.

If *The Thing* stands as a cautionary tale, then *Invaders from Mars* (1953), *Creature from the Black Lagoon* (1954), *Them!* (1954), *Tarantula* (1955), *It Came from Beneath the Sea* (1955), and *It Conquered the World* (1956) show what scientific carelessness can cause. Children see things but their parents will not believe them, mutated creatures rise up from muck or hatch from eggs nobody noticed, insects grow to incredible sizes, and finally horrible creatures hitch rides on space satellites and invade an unprepared Earth. The fact that Hollywood produced so many movies with similar themes suggests the remarkable popularity of these films during the 1950s.[10]

These pictures tended to be a mix of horror, bad acting, cheap special effects, and silly stories. The intended audience—usually teenagers packed into a car for an evening of drive-in entertainment—did not mind, and only a few of the films rose above their perceived audience. For instance, *Forbidden Planet* (1956) has come to be recognized as a minor science-fiction classic. Based loosely on Shakespeare's *The Tempest*, the story involves space explorers looking for a lost colony of adventurers, and ends up with a brave new world on a distant planet. Robby the Robot steals the show, an obedient, good-natured mechanical servant anxious to please his human masters.

The last years of the decade saw special effects displacing plot and character. Radiation from botched experiments causes unanticipated results in *The Incredible Shrinking Man* (1957), whereas a human brain implanted into a huge robot creates the opposite effect in *The Colossus of New York* (1958). *The Deadly Mantis* (1957) delivers just what its title promises: a huge mantis released from a centuries-old sleep. In *The Blob* (1958), a very young Steve McQueen battles a Jell-O-like creature; only he and other teens can save the earth. Haphazard treatments with wasp enzymes of course result in *The Wasp Woman* (1959). Regardless of storyline, all these films return to a theme of meddling with the natural order of things and the horrible results. The decade was not called the age of anxiety for nothing.

Westerns

From *The Great Train Robbery* in 1903 and the beginning of American movie history, the Western has always played a prominent part. Things were no different a half-century later; some of the best films of the fifties involve cowboys, Indians, shoot-'em-ups, and the whole mythic story of the West. On the other hand, many of the Westerns produced during the decade survive as little more than cheap "B" movies, quickly shot on the back lots of Hollywood studios and rushed into distribution. Either way, the Western occupies a significant part of the era's movie history, and demonstrates that, in popular culture, a successful formula will be utilized as long as audiences pay the price of admission and it turns a profit.

The 1950s began with the "B" Western already an established part of the film industry. Lesser-known studios like Monogram, Republic, and Allied Artists found such productions their very lifeblood, shooting endless short (sixty to ninety minutes) features, and often inserting stock footage from previous movies to hold down costs. They relied on an array of actors, both good and bad. For example, singing cowboy Gene Autry made some thirty forgettable low-budget Westerns during the decade, but diehard fans kept asking for more. Close behind Autry in this kind of sweepstakes came Randolph Scott, a versatile actor who had appeared in many different kinds of movies, but a man who wound down his career in the fifties by appearing in over two-dozen Westerns. His filmography lists such titles as *The Stranger Wore a Gun* (1953) and *Westbound* (1958), unrecognized pictures today, but ones that drew in audiences at the time.

A continuing list of other minor actors—Rory Calhoun, Wild Bill Elliott, George Montgomery, Wayne Morris, and, of course, Roy Rogers—shows both the perennial popularity of the Western and the sheer number of films released. Not until the inroads of television and the rise of the so-called "adult Western" in that medium did Hollywood's production of theatrical cowboy pictures go into a sharp decline. In reality, the studios shifted production over to television; the "B" Western found a new home on the small screen. [See below for more on television Westerns.][11]

Despite the demise of the cheap movie Western, the big-budget variety continued to be made consistently throughout the 1950s. With wide screens, Technicolor, and top stars, Hollywood could still turn out a product that drew crowds at the box office and was unavailable to television.

Some memorable titles, ranging from the claustrophobic *The Gunfighter* (1950) to the epic *Man of the West* (1958), entertained legions of fans.

Although a bit old for a Western hero, Gary Cooper rose to the occasion in *High Noon* (1952), a classic of the genre, and it gained him an Academy Award for Best Actor. In this movie, director Fred Zinnemann created a narrowly focused story about the conflicts surrounding an individual and the larger community. Cooper plays a beleaguered sheriff who must stand alone and resist the simplistic thinking of the crowd. Made at a time when "going along" and the concept of the compliant "organization man" were in vogue, the picture portrays a good character in a bad situation. In reality, many equally good people found their reputations and careers ruined by overly zealous investigative committees, and few individuals would stand with them against this kind of attack. *High Noon* sides with the lonely sheriff and his decision, although it did not result in any significant number of new pictures that sympathized with the underdog.

In *Shane* (1953), a lonely gunfighter, attempting to reform, must once again strap on the six-shooters and defend the honor of a frontier family. Alan Ladd gives a fine performance in the title role, and CinemaScope captures the vastness and emptiness of the Old West beautifully. But *Shane* speaks most directly to its audience in the re-creation of the Western myth—the settlers, the land barons, the outlaws, the lonely hero who must do what he has to do. The film demonstrates that certain stories, certain myths, have been etched on the national consciousness, and through popular entertainment such as movies, books, songs, and even advertising, those symbolically expressed values can sustain and strengthen the audience's understanding of them.

As a rule, the movie Western looks to the good side of American myth. Occasionally, however, a movie comes along that shows the dark underside of the story. In 1956, John Wayne, an actor long associated with the genre, collaborated with director John Ford, a man with whom he had made some of his best films. The result of that collaboration was *The Searchers*, a story that revolves around the dogged search for the whereabouts and fate of Wayne's niece, played by Natalie Wood. In a complex plot that covers years, Wayne's character emerges as an Indian-hater, a man obsessed by racial fears. Both Ford in his direction and Wayne in his performance emerge as problematical figures; the Indians are treated with sensitivity, a rarity in Westerns at that time, but the hatreds and single-mindedness of the quest reflect much about American society at the time. Relentless in his search, Wayne brooks no arguments that might turn him aside, and Ford does not portray him sympathetically. Instead, the director shows Wayne to be an extremist, an avenging angel in Western dress.

Because they claim to be based on history, Westerns at times support themes that would be forbidden in other movie genres. For example, racism appears not just in *The Searchers*, but in many 1950s Westerns. White supremacy overrides everything, and Indians assume the roles traditionally taken by blacks. Throughout the decade, Wayne burnished his image as a defender of staunch conservative values, a position that endeared him to many, but irritated others. It would become a persona that sometimes lapsed into caricature in his later years.

The Bravados (1958) serves as another picture that speaks to the times. It involves vigilantism, an unfortunate part of American history, one usually hushed up. But in this grim Western, the theme of vengeance gone awry becomes the focus. For the late 1950s, with its recent past of McCarthyism and general congressional witch-hunting, the idea of continuing to seek revenge when an opposite truth has become known must have made audiences uncomfortable. In the meantime, the main character sinks to the level of those he seeks. Not a typical Western, *The Bravados* suggests that changes are afoot. The old verities no longer seem quite so certain, and it clearly indicates that the standard horse opera had evolved into a more complex and provocative genre by decade's close.

Women's Movies

Hollywood has long produced films that appeal particularly to women. The accuracy of this perception may be open to question, but it has nonetheless served as a continuing marketing ploy. During the 1950s, dozens of pictures seemingly played on the feelings of women. Formulaic, the movies tend to feature strong women characters that must endure an emotional roller coaster as they resolve complex relationships. The male characters, usually presented as weak or downright weepy, rely on the strengths of a caring woman. But, in consideration of the times, even the strongest women defer to the men in the story.

An example would be *Magnificent Obsession* (1954). The title speaks volumes: this film does not deal with a normal love affair or some distant goal, but an obsession, something all consuming. Thus the adjectives "good," "wonderful," or "worthy" prove insufficient; this situation can only be described as "magnificent." Most of the so-called "women's movies" were only a step or two removed from the bathos that characterized radio and television soap opera of the period. Part of the collective studio thinking about these films dictated that the audience wanted wrenching emotional drama, often at the cost of plausible stories or convincing acting. A liberal amount of sex—usually more implied than depicted—also did not hurt the box-office receipts.

Magnificent Obsession focuses on a drunken playboy who kills a man and blinds the man's wife in an automobile accident. After much soul-searching, along with the stabilizing love of a good woman, he mends his ways, becomes a surgeon, and therefore can restore the widow's sight. Melodramatic in every frame, the film typifies this category of picture. It also made a star of Rock Hudson. And, as evidence of the durability of the genre, it had been filmed once before; in 1935 Robert Taylor played the same role and received the same star treatment.

Bigger at the box office even than *Magnificent Obsession* was *Peyton Place* (1957). Based on the steamy, best-selling 1956 novel by Grace Metalious, the movie promised lurid sex and lots of it. It also offered an all-star cast headed by Lana Turner, Arthur Kennedy, and Lloyd Nolan, along with young stars Terry Moore and Russ Tamblyn. The 20th Century-Fox studio spared no expense, either in production or marketing, riding the crest of the wave of success enjoyed by the book. It assured audiences that here was a "three handkerchief movie," meaning emotions ran high and the melodramatic plot would bring forth tears, a common assumption among those producing films "for women."

Peyton Place may not have satisfied everyone, but it nevertheless drew people to theaters. Peyton Place, a fictional small town in rural New Hampshire, serves as the focus for the story. All sorts of nasty things go on in this outwardly idyllic community, which provides a good commentary on 1950s mores. The vaunted sexual revolution had not yet occurred, and traditional morality still ruled the day. Metalious's frank presentation of behaviors that exceeded most norms caused a storm of controversy— and resulted in sales and admissions that probably exceeded most early estimates. The book, blessed with press freedom, contains much more explicit sex than the movie. What the novel details, the movie, given Code restrictions, must only hint at. Nonetheless, the movie does contain a great deal of melodramatic acting, as characters discover unpleasant truths about one another. The sex may be oblique, but the heavy breathing and histrionics of the cast seemed to titillate 1957 audiences, and called attention to a prurience usually repressed by American popular culture. [For more on the book version, see chapter 8, "Literature."]

Come Back, Little Sheba (1952) and *The Country Girl* (1954), two acclaimed films, strove to rise above their often-tawdry material. Thanks to strong performances by the female leads, they succeed. Shirley Booth and Grace Kelly both won Academy Awards, but the recognition by the Academy lends credence to the importance Hollywood placed on this kind of feature. Many other "women's pictures" graced marquees during the 1950s: *The Rose Tattoo* (1954), *Foxfire* (1955), *All that Heaven Allows* (1955), *Picnic* (1956), *An Affair to Remember* (1957), *Written on the Wind* (1957), and *Imitation of Life* (1959) represent some of the more memorable titles churned out by studios. Since these pictures enjoyed commercial success, it has to be assumed that men also purchased tickets. No gender breakdowns exist that might suggest only women attended these films or that men avoided them; like the leading soap operas on radio and television, the ratings and box-office numbers lead to the conclusion that both men and women constituted the audience for them.[12]

Foreign Films

Toward the end of the decade, European and Japanese filmmakers had begun to distribute increasing numbers of movies in the United States. Little neighborhood theaters, struggling for patrons, transformed themselves into "cinemas" or "art houses." With coffee and hot chocolate in the lobby and subtitles on the screen, these theaters found a small but enthusiastic following for the latest imported movies. Their success, albeit limited, slowly widened the audience and encouraged an occasional mainstream theater to book a foreign title or two. This small artistic wave did not solve the larger problem of overall declining attendance, but it brought some relief for those theaters willing to go the art-house route. For most of the 1950s, however, the impact of foreign films remained negligible and the mass audience stayed faithful to Hollywood's offerings.

In 1956, *And God Created Woman*, a French film by director Roger Vadim, shocked audiences with an opening sequence that showed a supine—and unclothed—Brigitte Bardot, the "woman" of the picture. Tame by contemporary standards, the import lined up the would-be censors on one side and the film-as-art supporters on the other. The censors lost and the movie made several million dollars in the United States. Its success encouraged quality pictures like *Wild Strawberries* (Sweden, 1957), *Throne of Blood* (Japan, 1957), *Black Orpheus* (Brazil, 1959), and *Hiroshima, Mon Amour* (France/Japan, 1959).

One foreign film from 1956 deserves mention in any discussion of popular culture: Japan's *Godzilla: King of the Monsters!* A cheaply made picture about a sleeping monster awakened by atomic blasts, it features clips of American actor Raymond Burr intercut with the Japanese story. Apparently the producers wanted to make the film more attractive to U.S. audiences, but his arbitrary inclusion proves needless, distracting, and at times hilarious. The fascination of *Godzilla* rests with the monster itself and the resultant action. A hulking beast crudely shot in miniature, stop-action sequences, Godzilla wreaks havoc on every model city he attacks. Stilted, awkward, amateurish—*Godzilla* quickly rose to cult status. Since 1956, over twenty sequels have been shot, but none matches the lumbering original.

Censorship

Hollywood chafed under the restrictions on language, imagery, and content imposed by the Production Code Administration, a group of industry censors that had been ruling what could and could not be seen and said in films since 1934. For example, characters could not swear, sex could only be hinted at, and nudity was banned. In order to be assured distribution, all commercial movies had to pass Code approval, thus allowing it to effectively control American movie content.

In 1953, a light comedy titled *The Moon Is Blue* (1953) defied the Hollywood Code. Directed by the esteemed Otto Preminger and adapted from a hit Broadway play, the film employs innuendo freely, and the forbidden words "virgin," "seduce," and "pregnant" are spoken. Denied a seal of approval, United Artists released it anyway, and the resultant publicity caused the feature to do well. Defenders of the film argued that movies have protection under the free speech clause of the Constitution. The defense proved successful, the first of several winning challenges to the outmoded code, and caused censors to loosen their grips significantly.

Two years later, in *The Man with the Golden Arm* (1955), Frank Sinatra plays a heroin addict. This movie went against code restrictions about depictions of drug use, but the studio defended its release and censors did nothing. With its authority weakened, and with continuing assaults on its rules, plus worries about declining attendance at theaters, the code underwent significant revision in 1956. The thought of liberalizing the code had long tantalized producers. They believed this move would allow Hollywood to put previously forbidden subjects on the screen, something television could not do because of its governance by the Federal Communications Commission. In short order, pregnancy and interracial marriage, along with miscegenation, abortion, and prostitution, could serve as legitimate movie topics provided directors handled them in a seemly manner. A victory for Hollywood and commercial films, such changes also mirrored a general relaxation in manners and mores across the nation.

Summary

Even with small victories, movie attendance continued its inexorable decline. By 1955, estimates placed weekly attendance at fifty million, and only about a third of movie theaters made a profit on box-office receipts alone. As a result, producers cut movie production and began to spend larger amounts on individual pictures. More spectacle and more stars, went the reasoning, equaled larger audiences. For hits, this philosophy worked, but it backfired when expensive pictures flopped. In the meantime, fewer and fewer "B" movies were made as studios cut their budgets.[13]

With the television networks devouring movies both old and relatively recent, and with more television shows being produced on film and using movie studio resources, the interrelationships between the film industry and television emerged as complementary instead of adversarial; the two old foes slowly came to the conclusion that their connections outweighed their differences.

RADIO

In the immediate postwar period (1946–1949), radio experienced extensive growth as new stations went on the air, but it also got hit, but not too hard, by the rapid rise of interest in television. As late as 1948, only one person in ten had even seen a television broadcast. Radio therefore tended to continue in its established, successful ways. After all, in 1950, 95 percent of American households had at least one radio, making for a well-entrenched medium, or so everyone thought. Then, with the beginning of the new decade, listenership plummeted. In response, the radio networks fought television's inroads by employing more stars in ever-larger, longer variety shows, but the move had little effect; the public could not get enough of the new medium. Faced with the inevitability of change, radio went about reinventing itself, returning to its roots of music and news. By the close of the 1950s, virtually no original programming could be heard on either network or locally independent stations; all had gone to a schedule of disc jockeys and recorded music, along with a sprinkling of sports and news.

Radio's Dilemma

In December of 1954, a small firm named Regency Electronics marketed the first miniature transistor radio. At $50, they cost a lot—a small table radio with superior sound could be had for half the price—but they sold well. Powered by small flashlight batteries, people were taken with the novelty of the item. In the long run, however, transistor radios did little to stanch the hemorrhaging of listeners to television. Nevertheless, new stations, long postponed by the Depression and World War II, came into being at a rapid rate in the late forties and early fifties. The number of AM (amplitude modulation) stations jumped from 930 in 1945 to more than 2,300 by 1952. FM (frequency modulation) experienced even more explosive growth, jumping from just 46 stations at the end of the war to over 600 broadcasters in 1952, although that growth would be tempered during the fifties by a host of problems (discussed below). In addition, several hundred would-be operators, just waiting for the opportunity to go on the air, had licenses pending in 1952 with the Federal Communications Commission (FCC).[14]

By 1959, and despite the fierce competition of television, 3,431 AM and 850 FM (688 commercial, 162 educational) stations could be found across the United States, for a total of 4,281 radio broadcasters. If the foregoing figures do not seem rosy enough, more than half of all U.S. automobiles had radios by the early 1950s, and the number kept rising. Yet, despite the growth in numbers of stations and receivers in the postwar years, significant changes occurred in ownership and programming. In 1945, over

90 percent of all stations shared a network affiliation—ABC, CBS, NBC, Mutual, or Keystone—that allowed them access to national stars and shows. By the early fifties, however, those affiliations had been slashed; only half of the nation's broadcasters continued to be associated with a network, a situation that would accelerate throughout the remainder of the decade. Even with this setback, the networks scheduled more programming during the 1953–1954 season than they ever had in all their previous history. Their efforts, however, proved a doomed holding action; affiliations continued to drop, and network programming dropped off sharply following 1954.[15]

A mere two years later the networks had ceased most original productions; they offered little more than news to their affiliates. Gone were the comedians, the mysteries, the variety revues, and all the other elaborate programming that so characterized immediate postwar American radio. During that same period, more and more TV stations came on the air, and they jumped on the affiliate bandwagon vacated by radio—the same ABC, CBS, and NBC networks. Television could claim more entertainers, more big names, and more variety, while radio helplessly watched its former stars move to the new medium. From a financial standpoint, this change devastated network radio. National advertisers moved their accounts to television, abandoning radio to smaller, less-profitable local accounts.

Although radio hardly disappeared as an important mass medium, it underwent two significant changes: 1) despite the loss of national accounts, total radio advertising revenue actually rose in the early 1950s. The creation of new AM stations and the expansion of regional and local radio advertising helped compensate for the decline in network revenues, with the precipitous losses being absorbed by the networks themselves; 2) because so many new stations came on the air in the fifties, each station's individual share of available ad dollars declined. A national medium evolved into a localized one; by the end of the decade, two-thirds of a typical station's income came from local advertisers.

FM Broadcasting

One area of radio held out great hope for broadcasters: FM. The 1950s were expected to be FM's glory decade, with people everywhere acquiring new receivers and listening to quality high-fidelity programming. Had television not happened along at the same time, the dream might have been realized. But people did not rush to buy FM radios and sponsors did not line up to underwrite FM programming. Instead, people rushed to buy new television receivers and sponsors lined up to buy time on television. In addition, a series of unwise decisions by the FCC during the late 1940s limited the FM spectrum available to radio broadcasters, further dampening enthusiasm for the creation of new stations.

During this time, strong, entrenched AM stations frequently owned a fledgling FM operation. As a result, the programs on both AM and FM were often the same, the FM version a duplicate of the AM schedule. Why buy an expensive new FM receiver, why sponsor a show, when the same programming could be heard on AM? Those FM stations that attempted independent programming, usually classical music, found they attracted small, dedicated audiences. In a nation where radio stations are privately owned and must operate in the black, advertisers displayed little interest in such limited listenership; only a handful of new FM stations came on the air for most of the 1950s. Many already-existing stations folded after the euphoria brought about by the big jump in numbers during the late forties wore off and reality set in. Between 1952 and 1959, FM showed a net gain of only fifty-one stations. A handful of subsidized educational stations, often run by colleges and universities, did come into being, but the anticipated boom in FM broadcasting had to wait until a later day to materialize.[16]

Stereo Broadcasting

Stereophonic broadcasting, an aural device, was widely discussed as a means of gaining listeners. Radio stations had been experimenting with stereo programming since 1952. Their approach usually involved broadcasting through dual channels, one on the AM frequency and the other over FM. Although this form of stereophonic transmission worked, it required separate AM and FM receivers that could be played independently of one another. A combination AM-FM receiver would not work because the two formats could not be played at the same time, plus 1950s sets had only one speaker, not the requisite two.

Because television sound is broadcast over the FM band, the experiments continued with occasional musical shows playing on one channel through a television set, while the other channel played over an AM radio. This gambit failed; the AM sound proved inferior to FM, plus listeners had to have a radio and TV on simultaneously. Not until the early sixties did stereophonic broadcasting through a single source become technologically feasible.

Radio Soap Operas

One of the staples of American radio programming had long been the soap opera. Melodramatic serial dramas that usually focused on the tormented love lives of their many characters, they gained their name in the early 1930s because of widespread sponsorship by various soap and detergent manufacturers. The "soaps" flourished on radio until the early fifties, and only floundered with the surging popularity of television.

As late as 1950, the networks devoted seventy hours a week to afternoon soap operas, or about thirty different serials a day, each running fifteen or thirty minutes in length. By the following year, however, the bottom began to fall out, and the decline of the genre commenced. It proved a slow death; radio executives convinced themselves that soap operas remained unique to the medium, and they stubbornly continued to produce the shows throughout the decade, even introducing new ones as old favorites died out.[17]

Table 10.1 shows the major soap operas that survived into the 1950s, and should give an idea of the importance this genre had in programming. Many of these shows originated in the 1930s and 1940s. Overall, NBC led the three major radio networks (NBC, CBS, ABC) in soap opera production.

At mid-decade, twenty-nine radio soap operas remained on the air (NBC with fourteen, CBS with fourteen, ABC with one), but by 1959 the number had shrunk to fourteen, with five on NBC and nine on CBS (ABC had dropped all soap operas programming in 1957). NBC canceled its productions in late 1959, leaving CBS the lone radio network still carrying "the soaps." In November of 1960, an era came to a quiet close when CBS simultaneously axed its handful of remaining shows.

During the difficult 1950s, radio soap operas strove to find successful plot devices that would keep listeners tuned to their receivers. They tried involving more and more of the characters with criminal elements. By 1952, over half of all the radio serials had crimes occurring along with efforts to solve them. Not that the love interest disappeared; a murder or a kidnapping just made it all more intriguing. Or so the producers hoped. As a device, it came too late for radio but served nevertheless as a lesson well learned; as the radio soaps made the transition to television, crime figured heavily in the story lines.

Variety Shows

The history of radio programming glows with nostalgic memories of *The Texaco Star Theater*, *The Fred Allen Show*, *The Jack Benny Show*, *The Bob Hope Show*, *Burns and Allen*, and dozens of other offerings filled with music, skits, and patter. The variety show grew out of vaudeville formats and found a receptive medium in radio. But then along came television and its visual element, and old-time vaudeville was rediscovered for this new medium. By the early 1950s, the major names had packed up and moved on to TV.

The Big Show, NBC's last-gasp attempt to retain the variety package on network radio, ran on Sunday evenings from the fall of 1950 until the spring of 1952. Top-name guests appeared regularly, and husky-voiced actress Tallulah Bankhead hosted the proceedings, ably assisted by a studio orchestra led by Meredith Willson (who would later gain renown for

Table 10.1
Radio Soap Operas of the 1950s

ABC	CBS	NBC
Against the Storm (1951–1952; originally NBC, 1939–1942)	*Aunt Jenny's True Life Stories* (1937–1956)	*The Affairs of Dr. Gentry* (1957–1958)
Joyce Jordan, M.D. (1951–1952; originally CBS, 1938–1945; NBC, 1945–1948, 1955)	*Backstage Wife* (1955–1959; originally NBC, 1936–1955)	*Aunt Mary* (1942–1951)
Lone Journey (1951–1952; originally NBC 1940–1943, 1946–1947)	*Big Sister* (1936–1952)	*David Harum* (1936–1947 and 1950–1951; CBS, 1947–1950)
The Story of Mary Marlin (1951–1952; originally NBC, 1935–1945)	*The Brighter Day* (1949–1956; originally NBC, 1948–1949)	*The Doctor's Wife* (1952–1956)
Valiant Lady (1951–1952; originally CBS, 1938; NBC, 1938–1942; CBS, 1942–1946)	*The Couple Next Door* (1937–1960)	*Front Page Farrell* (1942–1954)
When a Girl Marries (1951–1957; originally CBS, 1939–1941; NBC, 1941–1951)	*The Guiding Light* (1947–1956; originally NBC, 1937–1946)	*Just Plain Bill* (1936–1955; originally CBS, 1932–1936)
	Ma Perkins (1942–1960; originally NBC, 1933–1949; concurrent with NBC, 1942–1949)	*Life Can Be Beautiful* (1938–1954)
	Nona from Nowhere (1950–1951)	*The Light of the World* (1940–1950)
	Our Gal Sunday (1937–1959)	*Lora Lawton* (1943–1950)

Our Gal Sunday (1937–1959)

The Right to Happiness (1940–1941 an 1956–1960; originally NBC, 1939–1940; NBC, 1941–1956)

The Romance of Helen Trent (1933–1960)

Rosemary (1945–1955; originally NBC, 1944–1945)

The Second Mrs. Burton (1941–1960)

Wendy Warren (1947–1958)

Whispering Streets (1959–1960; originally ABC, 1953–1959)

*Young Dr. Malone (1940–1960; originally NBC, 1939–1940)

Lora Lawton (1943–1950)

Lorenzo Jones (1937–1955)

Marriage for Two (1949–1950)

*One Man's Family (1932–1959)

Pepper Young's Family (1932–1959)

*Portia Faces Life (1941–1951; originally CBS, 1940–1941)

Real Life Stories (1958–1959)

*Road of Life (1937–1954; concurrent with CBS, 1938–1942, 1945–1947, and 1952–1954; CBS, 1954–1958)

Stella Dallas (1938–1955)

This Is Nora Drake (1947–1959)

Today's Children (1933–1937, 1943–1950)

We Love and Learn (As the Twig Is Bent) (1949–1951)

Woman in My House (1951–1959)

Young Widder Brown (1938–1956)

Note: Listed alphabetically by network; those that went on to become television soap operas are marked by an asterisk (*).[18]

The Music Man in 1957). But Sunday evenings found former NBC star Jack Benny on CBS television at the same time. Despite its quality production, *The Big Show* was unable to land adequate sponsorship and demonstrated that radio would have to head in directions other than those already claimed by television in order to survive.

Another quasi-variety show was *Monitor* (NBC, 1955–1974). Packaged so affiliates could broadcast it in four-hour blocks, *Monitor* offered audiences a smorgasbord of comedy, drama, interviews, sports, and news throughout the weekend. A changing roster of hosts, ranging from *Today*'s Dave Garroway to comedians Bob and Ray, provided continuity during each of the blocks. *Monitor* survived for almost 20 years, a testament to imaginative programming and the willingness of NBC to stick with at least a semblance of network radio. But rising costs, an absence of sponsors, and the steady decline of local affiliates sealed *Monitor*'s doom.

Science Fiction

Despite declining advertising revenues and disappearing audiences, a momentary bright spot flickered for network programmers in the form of science fiction. During the 1950s, a spate of new shows attracted listeners, and they shared common themes of space exploration, invention, and fantasy. One of the first, and best, was *Dimension X*, an NBC production that premiered in 1950 and ran well into 1951. Capitalizing on the vogue for science-fiction movies, the show used imaginative sound effects instead of futuristic visual sets. *Dimension X* came too late for the golden days of network radio, but it filled a niche hitherto unexplored by the medium. In 1955, NBC scheduled *X-Minus One*, a virtual twin to *Dimension X*. It ran until 1958, adding new scripts and new fans to the genre.

Both *Dimension X* and *X-Minus One* borrowed from the popular science fiction pulp magazines of the day. Authors like Ray Bradbury, Robert Bloch, Robert Sheckley, and a host of others, all veterans of the pulps, contributed to both series. They provided a level of radio performance seldom heard during the faltering 1950s.

Not to be outdone, CBS scheduled a series titled *Escape* (1947–1954). Focusing more on adventure stories than straight science fiction, *Escape* nonetheless provided enthralled listeners (when they could find it; CBS was notorious for shifting the show around) with tales of survival and fantasy. It, too, relied on the pulp magazines for many of its writers, finding their detailed, descriptive writing styles well suited to the aural medium of radio. As good as it was, *Escape* could not establish a regular sponsor, and CBS struck it from its schedule in 1954.

Other contenders in the field appeared sporadically. CBS and ABC concurrently presented *Tales of Tomorrow* during the 1953 season. Similar in format and content to *Dimension X*, it never played on the air long enough to build an audience, plus sponsorship proved a problem. Mutual, a smaller radio network, briefly had *Two Thousand Plus* (1950–1952), another science fiction anthology show.

Two radio science fiction series aimed at younger audiences that had counterparts in television were *Space Patrol* (1950–1955) and *Tom Corbett, Space Cadet* (1952). Both products of ABC-Radio, the serials initially ran in the late afternoon, although *Space Patrol* shifted over to Saturday mornings in 1951. ABC-TV also produced *Space Patrol* for television from 1950 until 1955. *Tom Corbett, Space Cadet* enjoyed a considerably longer and more varied life on TV. The series began in 1950 on CBS, shifted to ABC in 1951, and then went to NBC for two years. DuMont, a small TV network of the time, picked it up for the 1953 and 1954 seasons, and the show returned to NBC in 1955 where it ended that summer. Despite all the network switching, the considerably longer TV career of *Tom Corbett, Space Cadet* illustrated the fact that television could provide both sponsors and audiences, something increasingly difficult for network radio to accomplish.

Top 40 Programming

While radio was losing all its old mainstays, a new concept in broadcasting began taking hold in the Midwest. In 1955, a station in Omaha, Nebraska, played only those songs identified in published lists as being the most popular in the country. Limited to hits listed from #1 to #40, once a song fell to #41 or lower, its replacement on the pop charts took over the vacancy. This Top 40 device proved successful with youthful audiences, and many smaller stations adopted the practice, although some of the larger urban markets proved resistant. They employed various formats of music and news, but not always with an emphasis on just the major hits. Top 40 programmers based their rationale around the perception that, by the mid-1950s, most popular music consisted of rock 'n' roll, and station directors assumed the audience would consist primarily of teenagers.

Surveys showed that indeed much of the adult radio audience had by this time drifted to television or recordings, leaving the youth market as primary listeners. Desperate for an assured audience, the Top 40 format thus proved irresistible to many stations. At the same time, this move provided the death knell for most network productions other than news or sports. Using colorful, talky disk jockeys, along with contests, giveaways, and other promotions, stations succeeded in attracting a large listener base and, more importantly, numerous sponsors. It might not be terribly imaginative programming, but Top 40 pumped new life into 1950s radio.

The unrelenting emphasis on Top 40 songs marked the final union between the recording industry and radio. Out of this came a scandal dubbed "payola"—the act of bribing disk jockeys to play certain songs on the air. [For more on disk jockeys and payola, see chapter 9, "Music."] In order to lessen criticism of their programming practices, many stations began to experiment with more varied formats in the late 1950s. "Oldies" (songs from the recent past), adult contemporary, religious, country and western, jazz, and middle of the road emerged as programming approaches evolving from the Top 40 concept. By the end of the decade, American AM radio had clearly decided that its future lay with recorded popular music. The local disk jockey reigned as king, and network affiliations lacked much importance. In less than a decade, the medium had completely transformed itself.[19]

Summary

At the beginning of the 1950s, radio underestimated the impact of television. The networks continued with much the same scheduling, only to see their stars, audiences, and sponsors lured away by the sweeping popularity of TV. Owners and producers knew that traditional programming could no longer support network radio, and a process of reorganization, rethinking, and experimentation commenced. Local stations shed their once-strong network affiliations, and broadcasters focused on a diet of popular music presented by disk jockeys.

TELEVISION

Regularly scheduled television broadcasts began in the United States in 1927, but so few people had access to this new technological marvel that not until the postwar years did American TV emerge as a mass medium. In 1946, wartime restrictions were lifted and receivers could again be manufactured. Sixteen stations were on the air in 1947, a number that jumped to 107 by 1951. As ownership of television sets swelled, people became increasingly visually literate, making decisions about who and what they liked and disliked on the basis of the images projected on the home screen. Hearing and reading, while still important, took a backseat to seeing. Image making emerged as a new popular art form; the proper image led to success, the wrong one to failure.

Early Broadcasting

Considerable time passed before television started to realize its potential as a new medium, and the 1950s constituted a learning period. In the beginning, much television drama relied on traditional theatrics—actors moving about on a small stage, all within the gaze of a fixed camera. Producers gave emphasis to creativity in playwriting and performance, and the medium's debts to legitimate theater and vaudeville were many. Improved technology freed up the TV camera, the same as in the pioneering days of moviemaking. By the early 1950s, television became much more cinematic and much less a static medium. It shook off its reliance on the stage and looked instead to Hollywood for its aesthetic inspiration.[20]

Postwar commercial television struggled, primarily from a lack of equipment and allied technical problems. Between 1948 and 1952, the Federal Communications Commission imposed a freeze on new stations as the industry sought to solve a myriad of shortcomings. Since over 350 stations had pending licenses, everyone awaited FCC permission to begin broadcasting. In time, most licenses gained approval and by the end of the fifties well over 500 TV stations (515 commercial, 44 educational) had gone on the air.[21]

Radio suffered the biggest losses in the changeover to television. Although more people than ever owned radios, the amount they listened and what they heard shifted radically. In essence, radio surrendered its traditional roles of news and variety entertainment; it became background sound with an emphasis on popular music.

Network television, with the successes and failures of radio as models, moved quickly in the early 1950s to provide as much variety as possible. The TV menu presented to viewers each evening rivaled anything radio had provided in its best days. Plus, of course, a picture accompanied the sound, something viewers clearly endorsed by making television their medium of choice.

VHF, UHF, and ETV

As television stations began to proliferate, the FCC in 1951 allowed many new stations to broadcast on the UHF (ultrahigh frequency) waveband, a move that opened up the potential for more than a thousand additional stations across the country. Designed to supplement the VHF (very high frequency) band where all broadcasters had previously been assigned, UHF broadcast channels 14–89. VHF carried channels 2–13 (channel 1 was reserved for emergencies and service broadcasting). The FCC stipulated that channels 14–69 would carry commercial stations, reserving 70–89 for special broadcasting. This well-meaning move attempted to open up competition to many more stations, but it overlooked the fact that most existing sets could pick up only VHF signals.

To get around the inability of existing television sets to receive UHF signals, a number of devices came on the market that promised to overcome the problem. These gadgets attached to a set's existing antenna terminals and supposedly expanded its range. They provided inferior picture quality, however, and few people rushed out to buy them. Not until ten years later, in 1961, did the FCC decree that all new receivers had to have the ability to pick up UHF as well as VHF broadcasting. As a result, very few UHF stations could make a commercial go of it in the fifties, since sponsors were loath to support channels that only a few could receive. Between 1952 and 1959, 165 UHF stations went on the air, but only 75 remained active at the end of the period. At the same time, VHF prospered, increasing from 108 stations in 1952 to 440 in 1959. The parallels between the problems faced by UHF television and FM radio cannot be ignored; in both cases, emerging technology and lack of commercial support conspired to hold back the progress of these new media.[22]

The FCC also ruled in 1951 that some television channels had to be reserved for educational programming, or ETV (educational television). In 1953, the first ETV station began broadcasting, and was soon followed by a number of others. Out of this grew National Education Television (NET), a loose grouping of stations dedicated to creating programs that would be valuable for children and adults. Instructional TV frequently went on the air early in the morning (5:30–6:00 AM) to allow working people to take courses. By 1959, 45 NET stations had come on the air. Because most of them got assigned to the UHF band, they lacked any commercial support and without subsidies, their survival proved problematical. Not until after the 1950s would educational TV gain a real foothold in the overall television spectrum, finally evolving into the more familiar PBS, or Public Broadcasting Service, in 1967.[23]

Television Impacts

During the transition from radio to television, roughly 1948 to 1952, many cities had no television reception. Social scientists curious about the impacts of television saw a unique opportunity: how did a television city differ from a non-television one? Their research disclosed that movie attendance dropped sharply in those areas receiving a signal, whereas those without TV reception showed no commensurate drop. In a similar fashion, people did not go out to sporting events or restaurants as frequently when they could watch TV at home. Even libraries reported lowered circulation in cities with access to television. By the mid-1950s, however, virtually the entire country could receive at least one channel, and any remaining pockets of isolation were quickly identified and efforts made to reach them. Television had become, in just a few short years, the primary carrier of both entertainment and information. In fact, by 1960, 13 percent of American households had more than one TV set, a sure sign of the medium's success.[24]

Despite the illusion of being "free," television proved an expensive investment for consumers. In 1952, a typical set cost about $250 plus installation. A rooftop antenna, a necessity in most places if the owner wanted to get reasonable reception, took additional dollars. Such a lowly necessity became a status symbol in this decade of consumerism. The more elaborate, the more complicated its outward appearance, the better it must be. And, of course, the reception inside must be superior also. Cheap "rabbit ears," so called because they consisted of two unsightly prongs that sat atop a receiver and boosted the incoming signal, could be seen in many homes. Actually, a metal coat hanger would do almost as well as commercial rabbit ears, and a bit of aluminum foil taped to the tips revealed many a do-it-yourselfer's secret for a clear picture.

The early sets themselves were not much more sophisticated than the antennas that picked up the local stations. In 1950, a TV buyer got, in return for an outlay of several hundred dollars, a black-and-white receiver that had an 11- or a 12-inch screen, although a lucky shopper might find a 14-inch one. But mass production soon brought the high prices down, the screens grew larger, and the overall quality rose. By the middle of the decade, the same amount of money—$250 to $350—would buy a vastly improved 21-inch set.

In 1955, General Electric introduced the first truly portable TV set. Until then, receivers were large, bulky boxes, often handsomely constructed with wood cabinets that resembled fine furniture, and they could easily weigh over one hundred pounds. The new GE model had a 14-inch screen and weighed only 26 pounds. A sturdy handle ran the length of the casing for convenient carrying. No longer disguised as part of a living room suite, the portable TV found a ready audience. By 1956, virtually every manufacturer offered portable models, and they assumed their place as "second sets." Television had gone from being a novelty to a mass medium in which second and even third sets became commonplace in American homes.

Color Television

If the VHF-UHF muddle did not confuse viewers enough, the issue of color telecasting also arose in the fifties. In a race with rival NBC, CBS had come up with the technology to broadcast in color at the beginning of the decade, but the network's rush to be first overlooked major problems. Sets could receive only black-and-white signals; they lacked the equipment to pick up the color signal broadcast by CBS. Nevertheless, officials arranged a trial broadcast in 1951, and it appeared CBS would emerge as the leader in color television. The first color receivers compatible with the CBS system appeared in 1953 and cost $1,000 or more. Despite their color compatibility, and their ability to reproduce black-and-white signals also, the networks broadcast virtually nothing in color, making the purchase a dubious one.

At the time of these color experiments, Americans were purchasing new black-and-white sets at a record pace. By 1953, over twenty million families owned receivers, virtually all of them incompatible with CBS's proposed system. Rather than have so many people buy new, expensive color sets, the FCC approved rival NBC's color technology as the national standard. The NBC system, while inferior in overall quality to CBS's, boasted of its compatibility with existing receivers. Viewers could watch color broadcasts in black and white, something the CBS system would not allow. People would not have to scrap their present units in order to enjoy the full network schedule. Economy won out over technology, with the result that consumers had to accept a second-rate color image, but they could satisfy themselves they had saved a few dollars and the nuisance of a second set.

By 1954, both NBC and CBS commenced limited color telecasting using the NBC system. ABC, short on cash and perennially in third place among the three networks, did not begin color broadcasts until 1958. The whole controversy turned into a major victory for NBC, and made them the industry leader for the remainder of the decade. In 1957, NBC's famed "color peacock" was born, and its colorful tail feathers served as an icon for the network. By that time, a fairly good color set could be purchased for around $600 and the networks worked at presenting more and more of their lineup in "living color." Most shows and series remained black-and-white, but color broadcasting nonetheless expanded, and by 1957, the networks transmitted about five hundred hours of color annually—still less than two hours a day. They called these color shows "specials": one- or two-hour productions independent of any ongoing series.[25]

But people wanted color, even with a black-and-white receiver, and sly merchandisers rushed to provide it. For just a couple of dollars, a set of three colored decals might do, with green at the bottom, pinkish red in the middle, and blue at the top. When stuck directly to a TV screen, viewers had "grass," "flesh tones," and "sky." Of course, if the picture being broadcast did not quite meet that arrangement, patience was advised. Eventually something would approximate the decals.

Another questionable gadget for disguising black-and-white images involved a rotating disc placed in front of the TV screen. It consisted of pie-shaped wedges of red, green, and blue-colored cellophane. The disc slowly revolved in front of the TV set and provided a surreal illusion of color to those peering through the cellophane.

The DuMont Television Network

Any history of American commercial television usually revolves around the three primary networks, ABC, CBS, and NBC. But another network existed in the early days of the medium, the Dumont system, or "Fourth Network." Allen B. DuMont, an electronics engineer, created a company to manufacture black-and-white TV sets under his name. During the early 1940s, DuMont receivers filled a respected niche in the small but grow-

In the early days of the television industry, DuMont
played a leading role. (Shown is a ca. 1952 DuMont
receiver.) By 1954, however, sales seriously lagged and
the company network lacked both the audiences and
shows; in 1955 DuMont ceased operations. J. Fred
Muggs, a chimpanzee who shared the small screen
with Dave Garroway, the host of NBC's morning show,
Today (1952–present; Muggs appeared from 1953 until
1957), leans against the receiver. Muggs became an
instant celebrity in his own right, and the above
stuffed animal represents the many merchandising tie-
ins that existed between television and marketers.

ing market, and their sales success prompted the company to go into the
business of broadcasting. Starting with WABD in New York City in 1944,
DuMont added several more stations and linked them into a small network in 1946.[26]

The fledgling DuMont system, the only television network not built on a prior radio background, lacked both financial resources and a roster of experienced performers. In addition, DuMont manufactured black-and-white sets and had little interest in color. Despite these liabilities, some honestly thought the DuMont Network might make a go of it. But most metropolitan areas, or markets, had fewer than four stations in the fifties, and so tiny DuMont (and frequently newcomer ABC) found itself excluded.

Advertising agencies, well aware that DuMont could command few viewers, compounded the problem by not buying time on DuMont shows. In retrospect, DuMont had some good offerings. One of the best was *Cavalcade of Stars* (1950–1952), a variety and comedy show featuring the talents of Jackie Gleason. Premiering in 1950, *Cavalcade of Stars* used the proven format of brief comedy sketches. Because of Gleason's natural affinity for television, the show did well, so well that it caught the eye of giant rival CBS. When his DuMont contract expired in 1952, Gleason promptly signed on with CBS to do *The Jackie Gleason Show* (see below). With no big names on its roster, the DuMont network was reduced to producing only 21 hours of television a week—three hours each evening—and it folded in 1955.[27]

TV Ratings

While the FCC attempted to impose order in the color debates, the Big Three networks wanted to know who watched what programs. The idea of tracking audiences and their preferences originated with radio. Since the 1930s, broadcasters had employed the services of ratings organizations. Thus, in 1950, the firm of A.C. Nielsen landed contracts with the TV networks to collect data about the viewing public. They used the Nielsen Television Index, a meter attached to a TV set that monitored when a particular channel was on and for how long. Nielsen could demonstrate which channels a sample audience preferred. The sample consisted of 1,200 families across the United States that had agreed to have the machine installed in their homes.

The meter, crude by later standards, could not prove if anyone actually watched, only that the set had been tuned to a specific channel. Nevertheless, the results impressed broadcasters. When selling time to advertisers, television executives deemed it important to present this information with authority. The network with the best ratings (i.e., the most sets tuned to that network) could therefore charge the highest fees for advertising time in that slot. This kind of competition commenced in the earliest days of commercial television, a practice that some critics say sacrificed quality for popularity.[28]

Television Programming

American television, the most popular mass medium ever, reflected contemporary culture, but it presented a distorted picture of that culture. For example, during the 1950s, there existed no television shows directed at black Americans. People who preferred an alternative lifestyle would find nothing on network offerings. Older Americans likewise found themselves rendered invisible or at best the butts of crude humor. For most of the decade, the daily and nightly schedules called for shows about middle-class white characters, a narrow, one-dimensional picture of modern society.

Slightly more than a third of the 1950s TV schedule was devoted to the wide category of "drama." This included crime and detective shows, dramatic series, original teleplays, and Westerns. Depending on the season, another quarter to a third of all programming presented music, comedy, and variety shows, although toward the end of the decade, that percentage dropped. Quiz shows, long a staple of the television day, occupied roughly 15 percent of the schedule. Children's programming accounted for just less than ten percent. News and information (which includes weather, sports, interviews, and the like) usually garnered seven percent. Finally, about five percent of the TV schedule, classified as "miscellaneous," included programs like movies, specials of various kinds, and some cultural offerings.[29]

Live, Tape, and Film

Unlike most television today, live broadcasting characterized the pioneer period of the medium. Instead of using film or videotape, over three-quarters of all productions were broadcast directly from a studio, or "live." As a result, most of the visual record of the early formative years (1947–1951) of commercial television has been lost forever. Since few shows could afford the costs of elaborate film production, they sometimes synchronized a regular movie camera with the flickering, on-screen television image. The resultant film, called a kinescope, served as an inferior copy of the original production. So poor was the reproduction quality that few kinescopes were made; except for some rare but grainy pieces of film, priceless performances will never again be seen.

In 1951, magnetic videotape came on the market. It proved vastly superior to kinescopes, but early videotapes hardly equal later ones. It took several more years of constant refinement to achieve quality reproduction. As the technology improved, most production shifted over to the new format, one that allowed editing of the final image. By the end of the decade, less than 30 percent of all television remained live. Purists might argue that TV lost spontaneity with the advent of videotape, but most audiences enjoyed watching smooth, polished productions without glitches.

Packaged Television

As American television strove to find technical and aesthetic standards for itself, the networks and sponsors shared in developing and producing much prime-time programming. Although this level of control sometimes led to abuses [see chapter 3, "Advertising"], it also meant American television frequently displayed more diversity and variety than would later be the case. For example, *Omnibus* (CBS, 1952–1956; ABC, 1956–1957; NBC, 1957–1959) was perceived as a "highbrow" show that appealed to audiences with education and money. For most network executives, the show's demographics were too limiting; they wanted greater mass appeal. For some sponsors, however, the show served as an ideal vehicle. As long as sponsors had control of *Omnibus*, this limited, niche audience fit their marketing strategies. As a result, *Omnibus* enjoyed a long run, even though it switched from network to network. It never achieved great ratings, but pleased those sponsors willing to support it.

With time and the growing sophistication of marketing strategies for television, companies known as packagers took on the job of developing new program ideas, supplanting both networks and sponsors. These firms would bring an idea for a show to the network or sponsor. The packager would create a pilot, or a sample program, assembling writers, actors, and any technical facilities that might be required. The packager would next oversee the actual production of the show in question. Using this process, packagers produced almost two-thirds of network programming by the end of the decade. Sponsors and advertising agencies bought time, not the production itself, and thus had much less say about any aspect of those shows they financed.

For the packagers, since they often owned the shows they produced, syndication emerged as a profitable sideline. Once a show had run its course and no longer appeared in the regular schedules, the packager could rent it to any station for a fee. As a result, popular 1950s series like *Bonanza, Gilligan's Island*, and *I Love Lucy* never really disappeared; in syndication they could seemingly go on forever, creating handsome residual profits for those parties that retained financial interests in them.

The rise of packaged TV responded to a real need; network television devoured material at a dizzying rate. The second half of the fifties saw the networks airing almost fifty new shows each and every season. Only about twenty or so of these new entries made it to a second season; many were canceled after just a few episodes. Neither the networks nor the sponsors could turn out new material at such a rate, and so the packagers stepped in to relieve the pressure.

Another way to satisfy television's insatiable demand for shows involved lengthening them. The early fifties had 15-minute and half-hour productions, a carryover from radio, but 1955–1959 saw the hour show move into dominance. By the end of the decade, hour-and-a-half and two-hour productions were not at all unusual. The industry frequently called anything over an hour a "special," or even a "spectacular," assuming that more time equaled more excitement, more color, more stars, more viewer enjoyment, and higher ratings.

Variety and Comedy Shows

Commercial television early on established itself as a vehicle for comedy. Building on the visual slapstick traditions of vaudeville, audiences laughed at the antics of a host of talented clowns who used the small screen to their advantage. At the beginning of the decade, NBC demonstrated its confidence in television profitability by granting comedian Milton Berle a 30-year, multimillion-dollar contract. Already a veteran of the last days of vaudeville, Berle took to television naturally, and his *Texaco Star Theater* (1948–1953) quickly became a favorite among those with receivers. His astronomical salary was indicative of things to come; the networks were prepared to spend whatever it took to become the dominant medium.

The Texaco Star Theater reached its zenith in the early fifties, and Berle was dubbed "Mr. Television," a tribute to his enormous popularity. By virtue of being one of the first comedy/variety shows, it established many of the standards for subsequent TV comedy. In many ways, *The Texaco Star Theater* served as an updated version of an old vaudeville revue. Berle's visual comedy appealed to audiences because of his lack of restraint. Pies in the face and banana peels punctuated the show, and they worked well in the early, formative days of the medium. In time, however, "Uncle Miltie's" manic approach to comedy wore thin as audiences looked for something a bit more sophisticated. His ratings dropped, and in 1956, NBC canceled both his show and his aforementioned contract. Although he continued to work steadily with the network, this pioneer never again achieved the success he had first enjoyed.

At the same time NBC introduced *The Texaco Star Theater*, rival CBS launched a variety show called *Toast of the Town* (1948–1971). Working on an initial budget of only a few hundred dollars, the show's host, syndicated newspaper columnist Ed Sullivan, brought together a collection of performers that might remind audiences of the days when vaudeville was king. The formula worked, despite the obvious unease Sullivan exhibited under the unblinking eye of the television cameras. *Toast of the Town* (renamed *The Ed Sullivan Show* in 1955) became an early TV hit and reigned supreme among variety shows for the next twenty-three years. Sullivan himself remained stiff and ill at ease throughout its celebrated run—the target of endless co-medians and mimics—perhaps a part of the show's success.

Throughout the fifties, *The Ed Sullivan Show* meant show-business variety, a traditional revue. From trained animal acts to current superstars to European opera personalities, his hour-long program featured them all. Any entertainers desiring national exposure had, at some point in their careers, to appear on the *Sullivan* show. In 1956, Elvis Presley made the first of several appearances on the top-ranked program. Although not a newcomer to TV, his *Sullivan* performances made Middle America aware of both him and his music. The reaction was electric; Presley's on-screen gyrations triggered sensational record sales and denunciations from many a pulpit. But the reaction also demonstrated how deeply television had penetrated American lives by 1956. Sullivan may have seemed stilted and inarticulate on-camera, but he was the premiere star-maker in the coun-try; he possessed an uncanny sense about audiences and artists, and he had the clout to get anyone he wanted on his show.[30]

The aforementioned *Cavalcade of Stars* (1949–1952), another entry in the catalog of TV variety shows, starred comedian Jackie Gleason. He created a number of comic characters, the best known of whom is Ralph Kramden, the main figure in a running skit within the show titled "The Honey-mooners." It proved so popular that CBS lured him away from DuMont, and the resultant *Jackie Gleason Show* (1952–1957) is remembered as one of the most imaginative offerings ever on television.

Although *The Jackie Gleason Show* prospered, Gleason himself was not happy with it. In 1955 he dropped the program and focused all his atten-tion on *The Honeymooners* (CBS, thirty-nine half-hour episodes, 1955–1956). He made it into one of the all-time great situation comedies. After its CBS run, *The Honeymooners* went into syndication and has remained on the small screen ever since.

Some other comedy/variety shows worthy of note included *Your Show of Shows* (NBC, 1950–1954), *The Colgate Comedy Hour* (NBC, 1950–1955), *The Jack Benny Program* (CBS, 1950–1964; NBC, 1964–1965), and *The Garry Moore Show* (CBS, afternoons, 1950–1958; evenings, 1958–1964). By the late 1950s, the big, multitalented variety show went into decline. Since much of their content revolves around topical jokes and popular music and their guests consist of those personalities currently in the headlines, it can be said that comedy/variety often relies on the ephemeral. This quality makes them difficult to syndicate or put into reruns.

Situation Comedies, or "Sitcoms"

An outgrowth of radio comedy, the sitcom endured fewer changes than any other format in TV. As television productions grew ever more expen-sive, the sitcom remained the only genre that resisted the tendency to make shows longer in length. With more time, more stars appeared, along with more singing and dancing, but more importantly, more commercials could be run. Ratings might rise, and that meant greater charges to sponsors. Fighting that philosophy, and perhaps working on the theory that narrative humor cannot be sustained for an hour, most comedies held to the familiar half-hour format.

One sitcom in particular towered over the field for the 1950s: *I Love Lucy* (1951–1957). This all-time favorite premiered on CBS in October of 1951, and because of its success, became the weekly comedy show by which all others were judged. By 1952, *I Love Lucy* ranked as the most popular show on television, a coveted position it would hold through much of its six-year run.

The series features Lucille Ball, along with her real-life husband Desi Arnaz, and costars William Frawley and Vivian Vance. Everyone involved is very talented, but people watched to see Lucy herself; she dominates the show. Ball came to television from a mediocre movie career, appearing in over eighty mostly "B" pictures, often uncredited. Active also in radio, she costarred with Richard Denning in *My Favorite Husband* (CBS, 1948–1951). An evening network comedy, Ball played Liz Cooper, a flighty character that served as a clear forerunner to the Lucy TV persona.

Few realized it at the time, but *I Love Lucy* proved instrumental in the death of live television. Until then, most situation comedies and other TV fare were televised live, with no retakes when mistakes occurred and no editing. One of the first shows to use film, both Ball and Arnaz believed they would have greater control of the production process in that format. *I Love Lucy* had a studio audience, and no one seemed to mind that the show combined live television and traditional movie techniques, a practice that eventually spread to other programs. The comedy ran through the 1957 season and, given its popularity, soon thereafter went into ceaseless network and syndicated reruns, thanks to being preserved on film. A knowledgeable businesswoman, Ball insisted on residuals—set fees for repeated airings—something few others did in those early days of television. Because *I Love Lucy* remained in constant syndication, Ball and Arnaz became wealthy in a short period of time.[31]

A reason for the continuing popularity of many 1950s sitcoms rests in the way they portray American values. For many, the sanitized view of family life they provide has evolved into a kind of collective nostalgia for a way of life (white, middle-class, suburban) that never accurately represented America. The fifties, through the imagery of television situation comedies of the period, represent for many the best of times, but that rose-colored sentiment conveniently overlooks any problems the country might have been facing. The irony in this approach is that those who criticize media today as "too violent" or "too negative," and long for a return to the past, often base their view of that past on a media-created image that never existed in the first place.

Certainly *I Love Lucy* presents a picture of strong middle-class aspirations and familial bonds, a recurring theme found in much of the television fare of the day. In the stories, Lucy has little to do except concoct her schemes while husband Desi holds down a regular job. The humor comes from the portrait of Lucy—harebrained, forgetful, cute, but harmless. Hardly a flattering picture, but the humor keeps it from becoming a mean-spirited stereotype. This characterization of women receives reinforcement in other sitcoms. In *The Burns and Allen Show* (CBS, 1950–1958), Gracie Allen transferred, to the 1950s, a character she had successfully developed in radio comedy in the 1930s. The real-life wife of George Burns, her comedic "Gracie" is, like Lucy, a scatterbrained woman who constantly befuddles her more conventional husband. Both Lucille Ball and Gracie Allen are such brilliant comedians that the artifice works and no one took any offense. At times, however, what played as innocuous then seems sexist and demeaning today.

The well-named *Father Knows Best* (radio: NBC, 1949–1953; television: CBS, 1954–1955; NBC, 1955–1958; CBS, 1958–1962; ABC, 1962–1963) looks to the other half of marriage in presenting a patient, wise, warmhearted, and wonderful husband/father. All the good points of Desi Arnaz and George Burns are brought together in Robert Young's convincing portrayal of Jim Anderson, a man who calmly oversees his family and provides the solid rock they can all lean on. Their home fits a suburbanized ideal, and Jane Wyatt, as his sweet and lovely wife, serves as the antithesis of the Ball/Allen characters. Always smartly dressed, including heels and a crisp, spotless apron, this woman exists for her family, and leaves wage earning and decision making to her spouse. *Father Knows Best* can often be cloying in its sweetness, but it reinforces the second-class citizenship imposed on sitcom women and, by extension, women in general.

Another show that first found its niche on radio was *The Adventures of Ozzie and Harriet* (radio: CBS, 1944–1948; NBC, 1948–1949; ABC, 1949–1954; television: ABC, 1952–1966). A success on radio, it went to greater fame as the longest-running sitcom ever. Ozzie Nelson plays himself in the husband/father role, and his wife Harriet (Hilliard) Nelson enacts her real-life role of spouse and mother. The couple's two sons, David and Rickie (later, Rick), play themselves over the 22-year span of the show, and audiences watched them grow. But roles remain clear: Ozzie, despite a bumble or two, remains at the head of the table, and Harriet is the immaculate wife, always at home for any of her men. In fact, even Ozzie appears to hold no job, but instead seems a stay-at-home dad, dispensing paternal wisdom and guiding his sons through childhood and adolescence.

The image of good parenting and perfect homes continued with *Make Room for Daddy* (ABC, 1953–1957), a series that evolved into *The Danny Thomas Show* (CBS, 1957–1964), and *My Little Margie* (CBS, 1952–1953;

NBC, 1953–1955), renamed *The Gale Storm Show* (CBS, 1956–1959; ABC, 1959–1962). The focus shifted to the offspring of these happy matches in the popular *Leave It to Beaver* (CBS, 1957–1958; ABC, 1958–1963). Husbands, wives, or children, it made no difference for the idyllic families portrayed in these domestic comedies—they looked at the decade through the rosiest of glasses, and painted a lasting picture that some nostalgia buffs persist in viewing as the correct and accurate one for the period.[32]

Music and Television

Music of all kinds provided a backdrop for most commercial TV productions. For example, Perry Como, a popular 1950s crooner, had success both with recordings and television. He headlined *The Chesterfield Supper Club* (NBC, 1948–1950; CBS, 1950–1955), a fifteen-minute mix of music and patter that grew into *The Perry Como Show* (NBC, 1955–1963), a big-budget, hour-long music and variety series that endeared him to millions of viewers. Similarly, singer Dinah Shore parlayed her vocal talents into the long-running *Dinah Shore Show* (NBC, 1951–1962). Like Perry Como's *Supper Club*, her series ran only fifteen minutes until 1957, when it grew into an hour-long variety package. Faithfully sponsored by Chevrolet throughout the decade, her theme song, "See the U.S.A. (in Your Chevrolet)," was known far and wide and doubtless contributed to Chevrolet's strong sales position during those years.

A mediocre pianist with a gift for flamboyant showmanship first appeared on home screens in 1951. Born Wladziu Valentino Liberace, he preferred using only his last name. And, as Liberace, he became an instant hit. By 1952 he had been picked up by NBC for a summer series, and from there he moved into syndication. Innumerable stations ran his show, and he returned to the network scene with ABC for the 1958–1959 season.

Liberace's show featured a trademark candelabrum that rested atop his grand piano as he played, and he costumed himself in an ever-changing, outlandish wardrobe made from gold lamé, sequins, and anything else he thought might catch the audience's eye. His enormous success surprised everyone, but his mix of kitsch and homogenized light classics captivated viewers ready for something new and different.

Another new musical series that made no pretense of presenting "great" compositions was *The Lawrence Welk Show* (ABC, 1955–1971). Hosted by a folksy bandleader who featured polkas, waltzes, and "Champagne Music" (popular favorites played in a "bubbly" manner), it found a large and appreciative audience among older Americans looking for an escape from a constant diet of Top 40 pop. At one point during the 1950s, Welk had three different shows on ABC, but they all featured his innocuous blend of musical styles. The success enjoyed by his orchestra pointed up the lack of programming for adults outside the usual 21–40 demographics.

Just as American television ignored racial issues during the fifties, so did it ignore large segments of its audience.

Classical music found a home on *The Voice of Firestone* (NBC, 1949–1954; ABC, 1954–1963), one of the few TV shows willing to feature it. Hosted by the erudite John Daly and backed by Howard Barlow and his orchestra, it gamely presented the classics each and every week. The show actually dated back to 1928 and the pioneer days of radio. It ran on the NBC radio network until 1954, and ABC then carried it from 1954 until 1957. Although *The Voice of Firestone* enjoyed strong TV ratings, both NBC and ABC thought it important to have a "prestige show" in their lineup. The fact that it appeared on commercial television, however, does not make *The Voice of Firestone* popular culture; it would take a mass audience, along with a repertoire appealing to that audience, for a show like *The Voice of Firestone* to cross over from essentially high culture to the broader realm of popular entertainment.

Television Drama

For many, the early fifties represent the "Golden Age" of American television. During the period 1950–1955, countless dramatic shows proliferated across the TV dial, and many people fondly remember them as fine examples of writing for this new medium. As a rule, the audience watched intense, one- and two-hour live, original dramas. The stories exploited the camera's ability to create gripping characters without benefit of sweeping scenery or special effects. In time, this intimate, small-scale format would change more than any other aspect of television. During the 1950s, the networks moved many of their operations from New York City to Los Angeles. Filmed performances supplanted live ones, and the "anthology" concept of individual and original dramas came briefly into vogue. These stories bore no relation to preceding or succeeding ones, and eventually were replaced by continuing series with familiar characters and settings that carried over from week to week. By the later 1950s, most of the transition had occurred, closing a unique era in American television history.[33]

In the industry's early days, fewer people watched television. With advertising charges based on audience size (the larger the audience, the higher the rate), television's small viewership made it a cheaper medium than radio. Thus directors could take chances with offbeat or controversial topics and sponsors would back them without too much financial risk. Writers and directors enjoyed a brief period of working freely with casts and crews and not being held back by formulaic conventions. All that would change, of course, as the formulas came into place and the money involved skyrocketed, but the early fifties witnessed a remarkable outpouring of fresh and unusual drama enacted on the small screen.

Not many of these dramatic productions have survived, although a few have been saved on grainy kinescopes. So the vast majority of these pioneering dramas are lost to posterity, a part of television that can be read about, but never again seen. More than two-dozen anthology shows played on network television in the early fifties, and those listed in Table 10.2 remain among the best-remembered.

Because so many anthology dramas appeared on television, their quality was bound to be uneven. The "Golden Age" applies only to a minority of these shows. Any nostalgia for *Studio One* or *Armstrong Circle Theatre* relies on memories of a handful of stellar productions, not for the entire series. For every "Our Town" (*Producer's Showcase*, 1955, with Paul Newman and Frank Sinatra), "No Time for Sergeants" (*U.S. Steel Hour*, 1955, with Andy Griffith), or "The Miracle Worker" (*Playhouse 90*, with Patty McCormick and Teresa Wright), plenty of absolutely forgettable dramas also came on the air.

In a significant reversal of tradition, some of the best of the new television dramas later made the transition to the movie screen. Distinguished teleplays like Paddy Chayefsky's *Marty* (TV, 1953; movie, 1955), Reginald Rose's *12 Angry Men* (TV, 1954; movie, 1957; remade as television movie in 1997), Rod Serling's *Patterns* (TV, 1955; movie, 1956) and *Requiem for a Heavyweight* (TV, 1956; movie, 1962) can be counted among a number of such productions. Some critics would argue that the originals surpassed their cinematic versions. They base their conclusions on the fact that these close-up, intimate dramas had been designed for the 12- to 21-inch home screen, not for a vast screen in an auditorium seating hundreds.

Television Soap Operas

Any extension of television drama would have to include soap operas. Recognizing both the popularity and profitability of radio "soaps," television producers early on decided to create their own serials. With the appearance of more and more TV soap operas during the afternoon hours of the broadcasting day, one of the last bastions of network radio fell. After many years on the air, the radio survivors gradually were canceled (see "Radio" above) and television gained this lucrative daily field to itself. A partial listing of 1950s television soap operas appears in Table 10.3.

A remarkable thing about soap operas is how many have been attempted. In 1954 alone, the networks launched thirteen new serials, and as the titles show, only three survived beyond that opening season. But the industry remained undeterred; every year new soap operas appeared, with just a few enjoying any success. CBS wears the crown for the longest-running serials; six stayed on the air for twenty years or more: *As the World Turns*, *Edge of Night*, *Guiding Light*, *Love of Life*, *Search for Tomorrow*, and *The Secret Storm*. Such longevity continues to be almost unheard of in the competitive world of commercial television, a world that considers most new prime-time offerings lucky to last their first season.

Table 10.2
Television Anthology Dramas of the 1950s

ABC	CBS	NBC
Pepsi-Cola Playhouse (1953–1955)	Ford Theater (1948–1951; NBC, 1952–1956; ABC, 1956–1957)	The Alcoa Theatre (1955–1960)
		Armstrong Circle Theater (1950–1957; CBS, 1957–1963)
	Four Star Playhouse (1952–1956)	Fireside Theatre (1949–1955)
	The General Electric Theater (1953–1961)	Hallmark Hall of Fame (1951–present)
	Playhouse 90 (1956–1961)	The Kaiser Aluminum Hour (1956–1957)
	Schlitz Playhouse of Stars (1951–1955)	Kraft Television Theatre (1947–1958; also on ABC, 1953–1955)
	Studio One (1948–1958)	
		Lux Video Theatre (1951–1957)
	U.S. Steel Hour (1953–1963)	Philco Television Playhouse (1948–1955)
		Producers' Showcase (1954–1957)
		Robert Montgomery Presents (a.k.a. The Lucky Strike Theater; 1950–1957)

Note: Listed alphabetically by network.[34]

Table 10.3
Television Soap Operas of the 1950s

CBS	NBC
As the World Turns (1956–present)	*The Bennetts* (1953–1954)
*The Brighter Day (1954–1962)	*Concerning Miss Marlowe* (1954–1955)
The Edge of Night (1956–1975; ABC, 1975–1984)	*A Date with Life* (1955–1956)
The First Hundred Years (1950–1952)	*Fairmeadows, U.S.A.* (1951–1952)
For Better or Worse (1959–1960)	*First Love* (1954–1955)
*The Guiding Light (1952–present)	*Follow Your Heart* (1953–1954)
Hotel Cosmopolitan (1957–1958)	*From These Roots* (1958–1961)
Love of Life (1951–1980)	*Golden Windows* (1954–1955)
*Portia Faces Life (1954–1955)	*The Greatest Gift* (1954–1955)
*Road of Life (1954–1955)	*Hawkins Falls, Pop. 6200* (1950–1955)
Search for Tomorrow (1951–1982; NBC, 1982–1986)	*The House in the Garden* (1952–1954; part of *The Kate Smith Hour*)
The Secret Storm (1954–1974)	*The House on High Street* (1959–1960)
The Seeking Heart (1954)	**Kitty Foyle* (1958)
*Valiant Lady (1953–1957)	*Miss Susan* (1951)
Woman with a Past (1954)	*Modern Romances* (1954–1958)
	*One Man's Family (1949–1952, 1954–1955)
	Three Steps to Heaven (1953–1954)
	A Time to Live (1954)
	Today Is Ours (1958)
	The Way of the World (1955)
	*Young Doctor Malone (1958–1963)

Note: Listed alphabetically and by network; ABC ran no soap operas during the 1950s. An asterisk (*) indicates the show also had a radio version.

The afternoon soap operas tempted audiences with daily commentaries on the manners and mores of contemporary America, with the emphases being on mores. Working on small, confined sets, the TV cameras relied on intimate close-ups of the characters, thereby exaggerating their emotional responses to ongoing events. The plots moved at a molasses-like pace in order that viewers could miss an episode or two and not lose any continuity, a device taken directly from their radio counterparts. The black-and-white world of the soaps—both technically and morally speaking—reflected a period searching for some absolutes. Their stories punished adultery, seldom presented divorce as an option, condemned pregnancy outside marriage, cursed illegitimacy, and tended to portray all men as emotionally weak and all good women as strong and resourceful. But femmes fatales lurked everywhere, and only the most solid families could resist their temptations. In short, producers created a product aimed, rightly or wrongly, at an audience composed mainly of women.

The TV networks liked the low staging costs of the serials, and their dominance of afternoon programming guaranteed high ratings, which in turn meant sponsorship never arose as a problem. When soap operas first made the move from radio, they retained the old fifteen-minute length. But production pressures, along with the need to air more commercials, led most TV soaps to go to a half-hour format in the mid-fifties.[35]

Westerns

In the second half of the 1950s, Westerns began to appear nightly on the nation's growing number of television sets. Long a favorite of the movies, many felt that the expansiveness of the Western would not translate well to the small screen. The prognosticators, however, were proved wrong. The stampede began modestly with *Hopalong Cassidy* (NBC, 1949–1951; syndication thereafter), an aging cowboy who led the way in the spring of 1948. Shortly thereafter, radio's long-running *Lone Ranger* began to share time with a television counterpart (radio, 1933–1954; ABC-TV, 1949–1957). Traditional shoot-'em-ups like *The Roy Rogers Show* (NBC, 1951–1957), *Wild Bill Hickok* (syndicated, 1951–1958), *The Cisco Kid* (syndicated, 1950–1955), and *Death Valley Days* (syndicated, 1952–1970) also found audiences. Their success led to new series, designed more with the small screen in mind. Walt Disney's *Frontierland* (a spin-off of his *Disneyland*, ABC, 1954–1961) produced a brief series on Davy Crockett during 1954–1955. The success of all four episodes, usually considered more children's shows than serious Western fare, gained the networks' attention.

From 1955 on, the industry produced some 50 different television Western series. These new shows may not have been cinematic epics like *Shane* (1953), *Gunfight at the OK Corral* (1957), or *The Big Country* (1958), but their tight, character-focused plotting found millions of at-home viewers. First and foremost among this innovative genre was *Gunsmoke* (CBS, 1955–1975), a deftly plotted series that became the archetypal television Western. *Gunsmoke* had begun on CBS Radio in 1952. The gravel-voiced William Conrad played the lead character, Marshall Matt Dillon, a stern lawman ensconced in Dodge City, Kansas. One of the few radio successes of the 1950s, it ran until 1961. James Arness played Dillon in the TV version, and his selection proved perfect typecasting. Tall and rugged-looking, Arness embodied John Wayne, Gary Cooper, Henry Fonda, Randolph Scott, and a host of other actors often associated with Westerns. (Wayne was actually offered the role but turned it down and suggested Arness.) Each episode involves intense character studies instead of sprawling action scenes. It befalls the marshal to resolve conflicts, which means lots of talk and limited physical activity. Occasionally, the producers incorporated stock footage of the Kansas prairies, but most of the action consists of interior shots or on the carefully bounded main street of the Dodge City set.

The show became a hit, displacing *I Love Lucy* and dominating the ratings throughout the late 1950s. *Gunsmoke* remained on the air until 1975, making it one of the longest-lived series of any kind in prime time. That it resembled a dramatic series in cowboy dress more than it did a traditional Western seemed not to bother the millions of fans who watched it each week.

As an indicator of their rapid growth, in the 1955–1956 season, six Westerns graced the TV schedule. By the 1957–1958 season, eighteen Westerns could be found, and by the 1959–1960 season, audiences could choose from thirty shows. The stories featured strong male leads who suffered identity crises, resisted discrimination, and generally fought the good fight against dishonesty and persecution. The old standbys of rustlers, stagecoach robbers, and gold thieves—not to mention cowboys and Indians—had virtually disappeared as subjects. In the 1950s, introspection and pop psychology replaced action and the old myths for this new breed of drama.

The networks happily adopted the term "adult Western" to identify their hot new offerings. In no time at all, their rosters had grown to include titles like those listed in Table 10.4.

Table 10.4
"Adult Westerns" of the 1950s

ABC	CBS	NBC
Cheyenne (1955–1963)	*Gunsmoke* (1955–1975)	*Bat Masterson* (1958–1961)
Colt .45 (1957–1962)	*Have Gun, Will Travel* (1957–1963)	*Bonanza* (1959–1973)
The Lawman (1958–1962)	*Rawhide* (1959–1966)	*The Californians* (1957–1959)
Maverick (1957–1962)	*Tales of the Texas Rangers* (1955–1957)	*Laramie* (1959–1963)
The Rebel (1959–1961)	*Wanted: Dead or Alive* (1958–1961)	*The Restless Gun* (1957–1959)
The Rifleman (1958–1963)		*Tales of Wells Fargo* (1957–1962)
Sugarfoot (1957–1960)		*Wagon Train* (1957–1962; ABC, 1962–1965)
Tombstone Territory (1957–1959)		

Note: Listed alphabetically by network.

The emphases placed on character and psychological motivation differentiated this new breed of Western from the traditional movie version. The sweeping scenery so characteristic of a movie Western is lost on the small screen. A wagon train going across a desert appears as specks on a gray sea. Because virtually all television production utilized black and white during the 1950s, directors could not avail themselves of the luxury of color. Indians on the warpath, cavalry charges, stampedes, isolated forts, and all the other icons associated with the genre had to be replaced with new methods of storytelling.

Taking their cue from the many dramatic shows already running on television, producers employed close-ups and many interior shots. They filmed most of the shows on studio back lots, and budget constraints meant few large-scale sets. In addition, relentless weekly scheduling demanded a constant supply of new stories. So the television Western evolved into an intimate dramatic form that owed as much to traditional theater as it did to the movies.[36]

Television Quiz Shows

Led by *The $64,000 Question* (CBS, 1955–1958) and a handful of other big-money productions, television quiz shows attracted an unusually receptive audience. Along with beating radio down in all categories, television clearly had no hesitation in stealing creative ideas from its onetime competitor. Working on the premise that success begets success, *The $64,000 Question* grew out of a successful radio quiz called *Take It or Leave It* that had run on CBS from 1940 to 1947. At that time, NBC took over the show, renaming it *The $64 Question*, a reference to its top prize. Contestants started at $1 and kept doubling their money ($1-$2-$4-$8-$16-$32-$64) through a sequence of seven questions. It ran on radio until 1952 and contributed a phrase, "the sixty-four dollar question," to the language.

Producers, however, apparently found $64 beneath contempt in the heady new world of television. Big jackpots would draw big audiences, and both did grow until 1958, when the bottom fell out of public trust. Before the day of reckoning, however, contestants became overnight celebrities on these extravagant shows. Columnist and psychologist Joyce Brothers won $64,000 on *The $64,000 Question* late in 1955, but scholarly Columbia College professor Charles Van Doren won $129,000 on *Twenty-One* the next season. That was just the beginning. A ten-year-old, Robert Strom, amassed a record $242,600 on *The $64,000 Challenge* in 1958, but Teddy Nadler shortly surpassed him, becoming the biggest winner of them all, with a total of $252,000 on the same show.

The sky seemed the limit, but later in 1958 a scandal arose that marred all the fun and excitement. A grand jury investigation revealed that many contestants had been supplied hints or outright answers for shows like *Dotto*, *Twenty-One*, and *The $64,000 Challenge*. Overnight, audience faith

American television discovered huge audiences for contrived quiz shows. Ratings shot up when a network could place a high-paying quiz in any evening time slot. As a result, new, more expensive giveaways crowded the nightly schedules until 1958 with the realization that contestants had been supplied answers; with that, the bottom fell out, and the quiz show virtually disappeared from TV. This photo shows a winner being congratulated after answering a question correctly on *The $64,000 Question*. The strange structure is an "isolation booth"—something designed to keep participants from receiving any outside assistance, but actually par of show-business hokum. Source: Library of Congress.

in the shows evaporated. During congressional hearings conducted in 1958 and 1959, Van Doren, the darling of the audiences, admitted receiving assistance, and his testimony helped axe any remaining series. By the end of 1958, the network quiz shows involving huge sums of money had become a thing of the past.

Prior to the scandal, quiz shows proliferated on all three networks. When a popular contestant, such as Brothers or Van Doren, seemed on the verge of winning big money, ratings ran high, often eclipsing such power-houses as *I Love Lucy* or one of the increasingly popular adult Westerns. The shows proved cheap to produce, sponsors liked their simplicity, and no one seemed to grow tired of them. Some of the better-known network quiz shows are listed in Table 10.5.

Although the boom for big-money quiz shows fizzled out, a number of more innocuous variations survived. For instance, *The G.E. College Bowl* premiered in 1959 on CBS amid all the scandal, and *What's My Line?* (CBS, 1950–1967), a long-running series, quietly endured. With no prizes, the rewards were more cerebral. The humorous patter of panelists Dorothy Kilgallen, Arlene Francis, Bennett Cerf, along with a weekly visiting pan-elist and moderator John Daly, constituted the proceedings. A devoted audience faithfully followed the witty conversation as the group at-tempted to identify unusual professions or trades pursued by a succes-sion of guests. *What's My Line?* demonstrated that commercial television did not have to rely on spectacle or give away small fortunes to attract good ratings.

Another unique quiz show was *You Bet Your Life* (NBC, 1950–1961), a carry-over from radio (ABC, 1947–1949; CBS, 1949–1950; NBC, 1950–1956) hosted by the irreverent comedian Groucho Marx. Moderator George Fenneman served as the perfect foil to Groucho and his barbs. Through-out both its radio and television incarnations, *You Bet Your Life* awarded modest cash prizes as contestants took their chances with Groucho and a series of easy questions. In fact, no one ever departed the stage without at least something. When all else failed, Groucho would ask, "Who was buried in Grant's Tomb?" In that way, perhaps *You Bet Your Life* was "fixed," but no one ever thought to investigate the show, either on radio or television.[37]

Crime Shows

Faced with the overwhelming success of Westerns and quiz shows, the old reliable crime, police, and private-eye shows virtually disappeared from the nightly schedules for much of the decade. Jack Webb's *Dragnet* (NBC, 1951–1959; movie version in 1954) and Erle Stanley Gardner's *Perry Mason* (CBS, 1957–1966) proved to be exceptions. *Dragnet*, a police proce-dural, was unique: it had a radio twin that debuted on NBC in 1949 and lasted until 1957. Thus the two—radio and TV broadcasts—ran simulta-neously and featured virtually the same casts. *Perry Mason* starred actor Raymond Burr as a lawyer who behaves more like a private detective. It, too, enjoyed a radio run on CBS from 1943 until 1955. No overlap existed

Table 10.5
Television Quiz Shows of the 1950s

ABC	CBS	NBC
*Break the Bank (1948–1949 and 1954–1956; NBC, 1949–1952; CBS, 1952–1953; NBC, 1953)	*Beat the Clock (1950–1958; ABC, 1958–1961)	The Big Surprise (a.k.a. The $100,000 Big Surprise; 1955–1957)
Treasure Hunt (1956–1957; NBC, 1957–1959)	Dotto (CBS [daytime] and NBC [nighttime], 1958)	Break the $250,000 Bank (1956–1957)
	High Finance (1956)	Masquerade Party (1952,1957,1958–1959, and 1960; CBS, 1953–1954; ABC, 1954–1956; CBS, 1958; CBS, 1959–1960)
	*I've Got a Secret (1952–1967)	The Price Is Right (1956–1963; ABC, 1963–1965; CBS, 1972–present)
	Pantomime Quiz (1949–1951, 1952–1953, 1954 and 1955–1957; NBC, 1952; DuMont, 1953–1954; ABC, 1955; ABC, 1958–1959)	*Queen for a Day (1956–1960)
	The $64,000 Challenge (1956–1958)	*The Quiz Kids (1949–1952; CBS, 1953–1956)
	*The $64,000 Question (1955–1958)	Tic Tac Dough (1956–1959)
	To Tell the Truth (1956–1968)	Twenty-One (1956–1958)
	*Truth or Consequences (1950–1951; NBC, 1952–1965)	*Twenty Questions (1949; ABC, 1950–1951; DuMont, 1951–1954; ABC, 1954–1955)
		*Two for the Money (1952–1953; CBS, 1953–1957)
		*Who Said That? (1948–1954; ABC, 1955)

Note: Listed alphabetically by network. An asterisk (*) indicates the show was also broadcast in a radio version.

between the two media, since actor John Larkin portrayed the radio Mason during the 1950s. A perennial favorite, *Perry Mason* remained a weekly television offering well into the 1960s, whereupon it enjoyed a second life in a long series of made-for-TV movies that lasted until 1993.

In 1958, in the midst of the quiz-show debacle, ABC premiered two new crime series, *Naked City* (1958–1963) and *77 Sunset Strip* (1958–1964), moves that reinvigorated the genre. The latter featured actor Edd "Kookie" Byrnes in a recurring role, and adolescents everywhere loved his hip character. He even parlayed his popularity into a minor hit record in 1959, "Kookie, Kookie (Lend Me Your Comb)," an up-tempo comment on his wavy, brilliantined hair.

Over at NBC, *Peter Gunn* (1958–1960; ABC, 1960–1961) marked the arrival of another new TV detective. Featuring a smart, jazzy score by composer/arranger Henry Mancini, the music proved as popular as the show. Not to be outdone, ABC introduced *The Untouchables* in 1959, a crime series that brought the life and legend of G-Man Eliot Ness to the small screen, along with the familiar voice of columnist Walter Winchell as narrator. *The Untouchables* ran until 1963, and enjoys the dubious honor of ranking among the most violent series ever made for network TV.

All of these new shows served up contemporary, detective-oriented fare, and each found large, receptive audiences. It might be the adult Western decade, but a roster of new crime shows would shortly challenge the old order.[38]

News

The 1950s saw news and information emerge as important components of the television broadcast day. In 1948, CBS had introduced *Douglas Edwards with the News*, a show Edwards would anchor until 1962. The next year, NBC premiered *The Camel News Caravan*, a similar news show hosted by John Cameron Swayze. He remained at that spot until 1956, when the team of Chet Huntley and David Brinkley took over the slot with *The Huntley-Brinkley Report*, a program that continued for the next 14 years. Both audiences and critics had praised the effectiveness of the duo at the 1956 political conventions, and NBC decided to replace the rather bland Swayze. It proved a wise decision; for the remainder of the decade, *The Huntley-Brinkley Report* grew in popularity, finally overtaking perennial front-runner CBS during the 1959–1960 season.

Not until 1952 did ABC inaugurate a widely seen evening news broadcast, *All-Star News.* An hour-long production (the CBS and NBC counterparts ran 15 minutes), ABC replaced it in early 1953 with *ABC News*, a more conventional quarter-hour offering hosted by John Daly. With its late start, and with fewer affiliates, ABC never captured as large an audience as that enjoyed by the other networks.

These early network newscasts played like glorified radio broadcasts, and all the anchors came from previous radio backgrounds. At first, the newscasters read scripts directly into the camera. Very few film clips were employed, and videotape had not yet become available. Most visuals consisted of still photographs projected onto the screen.

A show that predated the regular network newscasts was NBC's *Meet the Press*, a lively discussion of current events that premiered in November of 1947. Still going strong at this writing, *Meet the Press* certainly ranks as the oldest news program on network television. Instead of attempting an overview of the week's stories, *Meet the Press* invites top journalists and guests to discuss issues, a format that usually allows reporters to grill the guests. Endlessly imitated since its inception, *Meet the Press* has enlarged the horizons of television news coverage.

In the early 1950s, the most renowned newscaster on television was Edward R. Murrow for CBS. Murrow had made a name for himself in World War II with dramatic radio broadcasts from London and Europe during the dark days of the conflict. Upon his return to the United States, he and his CBS colleagues put together a powerful news team that more than outdistanced the competition.

Edward R. Murrow emerged as the dean of radio and television newsmen during the decade. As host of *Hear It Now* (radio, 1950–1951) and *See It Now* (television, 1951–1955), Murrow projected an air of probity on his broadcasts, and his exposure of Senator Joseph McCarthy as an unprincipled bully brought about the downfall of the Wisconsin politician.
Source: Library of Congress.

Murrow found the challenges of early television to be to his liking, and he created two innovative shows, *See It Now* (CBS, 1951–1958) and *Person to Person* (CBS, 1953–1961). *See It Now* was an adaptation of a program he had created for CBS radio titled *Hear It Now* (1950–1951), which in turn he had taken from a series of phonograph recordings made for Columbia Records called *I Can Hear It Now*. The success of these endeavors led to weekly television broadcasts featuring in-depth research into current events. Public affairs programs, *See It Now* focused on reporting and *Person to Person* consisted of wide-ranging interviews with people in the news.

See It Now inspired many later investigative shows. CBS, although immensely proud of the series, also saw it as a liability. It had low ratings, meaning people might admire it, but they did not watch it. A prime-time offering, *See It Now* did not draw as many viewers as competing comedy and quiz shows. In 1955, CBS cut its weekly broadcasts, replacing them with six to eight specials a season. Finally, in 1958, CBS canceled the series outright, a loss to television and to news coverage in general. Embittered over what he perceived as the sacrifice of good reporting for commercial gain, Murrow himself appeared less and less on television for the remainder of the decade and left commercial TV in 1961.

Although a term did not exist for it then, a blending of straight news with drama, controversy, and celebrity gradually supplanted traditional reporting. At the same time, many TV reporters became as famous as their subjects. Eventually, this mix would be called "infotainment" (information + entertainment), a neologism that carries some negative connotations today, but seemed appropriate for these pioneers attempting to stretch the limits of news gathering.[39]

In 1952, both the Republican and Democratic national conventions were televised; for the first time, Americans witnessed the whole presidential nominating process. Compared to more recent convention coverage, the 1952 events seemed awkward affairs, if for no other reason than the difficulties encountered by reporters as they lugged around bulky equipment and had to put up with second-rate sound. A learning process, the networks proved quick studies. The technical proficiencies of reporters and their crews had made quantum leaps by the 1956 national conventions.

In the meantime, President Eisenhower in 1955 allowed TV cameras to tape his press conferences. Eisenhower's staff had editing privileges, but the footage presented the public with an image of its president at work. He also permitted radio microphones, along with the same editing provisos. For many Americans, the television tapes reinforced Eisenhower's persona as a kind of paternal leader, the first inkling of TV's image-making capabilities.

As the public grew accustomed to getting news from television—instead of from newspapers, magazines, or radio—the perception of how to interpret the steady stream of information went through a significant shift. People saw TV as immediate journalism, news of and on the hour. It might not be reflective, but it provided a stream of images that changed almost constantly.

Sports

In the early days of television, the heavy cameras and associated equipment made any kind of mobility difficult. As a result, sports telecasting consisted of those activities where a stationary camera could be set up and easily follow the action. This helps to explain the popularity of wrestling, boxing, and even the roller derby in the early 1950s. The ring and the track provided limited spaces the camera could cover without problems. Although earlier attempts had been made to televise baseball, football, basketball, and tennis, the constant movement and the large areas required by these sports created problems for camera crews.

Television technology, however, evolved quickly in the fifties, and soon cameras became smaller and more portable. Because of the newness of TV, and the belief that it would hurt attendance, many teams resisted the medium. They had come to terms with radio, plus they tended to receive substantial payments from stations for the privilege of broadcasting. It would take time before the networks worked out similar television contracts to everyone's satisfaction. But once TV gained a foothold in sports, radio's position weakened commensurately. Soon, only local radio stations carried sports, and they usually broadcast their small, home teams, not the big games or professional sports that television was taking over.

As many had feared, attendance at major sporting events took a plunge with TV's growing coverage. Many communities blacked out broadcasts of games played locally in an effort to lure people back to the stadiums and arenas. But with so much being offered on the television schedule, attendance continued its drop. During the decade, minor-league baseball suffered a 60 percent decline in patrons; boxing saw an even greater loss of fans at live events. Everyone agreed that television hurt overall sports attendance, particularly for small teams and local clubs, but no one offered a solution.[40]

Between 1950 and 1959, the amounts of money paid for telecasting rights skyrocketed as teams and leagues demanded ever-larger payments from the networks. At the same time, Americans demonstrated an insatiable demand for televised sports, so the networks found and paid the asking prices, and the decade ended with TV poised to make greater inroads into organized athletics.

Children's Programming

From the beginnings of commercial television, children have been recognized as a vast potential audience. The visual aspects of the medium made it instantly appealing to youngsters, and producers tried to capitalize on that attribute. *Kukla, Fran and Ollie* (NBC, 1948–1954; ABC, 1954–1957), *The Soupy Sales Show* (ABC, 1955–1960), *Mr. I. Magination* (CBS, 1949–1952), *Paul Winchell and Jerry Mahoney* (NBC, 1950–1956; ABC, 1957–1961), and a host of other children's shows attempted quality programming aimed at younger audiences. Sponsors loved the dedication of these youthful viewers, making most series profitable. The issue of commercials and their impacts on young, impressionable minds was only just emerging. It would later become a hot topic of debate after most of the 1950s children's shows existed as pleasant memories of an earlier, more innocent time.[41]

NBC's *Howdy Doody* (1947–1960) became one of the most successful of the early children's shows. Although it had first aired at the end of 1947, *Howdy Doody* did not catch on until the early 1950s when the number of stations and set ownership increased. The show featured a cowboy marionette and the zany citizens of Doodyville, including Buffalo Bob and Clarabell the Clown, and captured the hearts of American youngsters. *Howdy Doody* avoided the satire and occasional cynicism of later children's programming, projecting instead a naïveté that charmed parents and enthralled their offspring.

In 1955, in response to the success of *Howdy Doody*, CBS launched a morning children's show called *Captain Kangaroo* (1955–1984). Featuring Bob Keeshan (who had formerly played Clarabell on *Howdy Doody*) as a kind and amiable man who happened to have a collection of equally gentle friends, the long-running series spoke directly to children and never patronized them. Low-key from beginning to end, *Captain Kangaroo* became a morning ritual in many American homes with youngsters.

ABC struggled against the wealth of NBC and CBS throughout the decade. It could never seem to land the stars or adapt to the latest programming trends, placing it in a perennial number three position among the Big Three networks. Finally, in 1954, the network signed a contract with Walt Disney Productions to present some of their "family programming," a decision that resulted in the evening *Disneyland* (1954–1961; title changed to *Walt Disney Presents*, 1958–1959, and then *Walt Disney's World*, 1959–1961). The deal to produce *Disneyland* included an afternoon offering titled *The Mickey Mouse Club*. The overwhelming popularity of these shows made ABC much more of a competitor for the remainder of the decade.

As coincidence would have it, ABC began running *The Mickey Mouse Club* on October 3, 1955, the same day that *Captain Kangaroo* premiered on CBS. But *Captain Kangaroo* ran in the morning, whereas *The Mickey Mouse Club* aired in the afternoon, so Disney's show competed more directly for the *Howdy Doody* audience. In fact, *The Mickey Mouse Club* proved so successful that *Howdy Doody* moved to Saturday mornings the follow-

A daily television treat for children was *Captain Kangaroo* (1955–
1984). A precursor to Public Broadcasting's *Sesame Street*, Bob
Keeshan played the gentle host of the show throughout its run.
Called "Kangaroo" because of the spacious pockets on his
jacket, Keeshan eschewed violence or any other images
that might be disturbing to young viewers.
Source: Library of Congress.

ing year. With children's TV programming commanding the late-afternoon
time slot, the last of radio's old-time adventure serials finally ceased production. Another radio tradition surrendered to the relentless pressures
of television competition.

The content of *The Mickey Mouse Club* consisted of items borrowed from
the Disney Studio's vast vaults, such as cartoons and documentaries. The
Mouseketeers, a group of child performers who sang and danced their
way through each afternoon's show, enchanted legions of devoted
viewers. *The Mickey Mouse Club* actually carried over from similar clubs
founded during the 1930s. But this time, the club activities were promoted
on television for all to see, especially the enthusiasm of the Mouseketeers,
all wearing their little black beanies with mouse ears, ritually chanting
"M-I-C-K-E-Y M-O-U-S-E." Adults remained conspicuously absent from
most productions, adding to the charm and popularity of the series,
although it ran only until 1959.

Experimentation

In a different realm, NBC's Sylvester "Pat" Weaver brought a popular programming genius to TV—he created *Today* and shared with others in the development of *The Tonight Show*. Unique for their use of short, unconnected pieces, both *Today* and *The Tonight Show* initiated a new kind of television format. Weaver also became identified with many NBC "Specials," another pioneering effort for television. That same streak of conceptual genius evidenced itself on NBC Radio with the popular *Monitor* [see "Radio" above].

Today made its debut in January of 1952 with host Dave Garroway, a role he would retain until 1961. An early-morning mix of news, weather, features, and interviews, the network attempted to capture a new segment of the audience. Until then, commercial television had more or less ignored the morning hours. *Today* got off to a shaky start, experiencing difficulties in picking up sponsors and affiliates, but growing numbers of viewers began turning on their TVs when they arose. When a chimpanzee named J. Fred Muggs joined the cast in 1953, children also began to watch, and the ratings soared; the affable chimp remained a regular until 1957. Patching in local news and weather in each half hour gave the show regional appeal, and *Today* emerged as an American institution and consistent moneymaker for NBC. It has become one of the longest-running shows in the history of television, and its popularity dealt another blow to radio, which until then felt assured of the morning audience.

The history of *The Tonight Show* is not nearly as simple as that of *Today*. NBC had experimented with late-night programming with *Broadway Open House* during the 1950–1951 season, following that with *Seven at Eleven* and *The Left Over Revue*. None of its efforts attracted big audiences, but NBC persevered. Finally, *The Tonight Show* took form as a local New York City telecast in 1953; it joined the national network in 1954 with the versatile Steve Allen as host. The ninety-minute show, a kind of late-night comedy version of the early-morning *Today*, gained a significant audience almost immediately. Allen moved on to other projects in 1957, but comedian Ernie Kovacs took the reins of *Tonight* two evenings a week from October 1956 until January 1957. Then came *Tonight! America After Dark* from January until July of 1957, a dismal failure. Finally, Allen's permanent replacement, Jack Paar, came on board that summer. He seemed perfect for the show and would remain ensconced there until 1962. Ratings soared, and Paar's slightly acerbic style and offbeat guest lists succeeded in keeping millions of viewers up late at night.[42]

Summary

In the early 1950s, TV wanted big audiences; it needed numbers to establish itself as the country's primary mass medium. By so doing, it tended to write off old people, ethnic and racial groups, and the economically disadvantaged in order to maximize its appeal to a white, middle-class demographic. But, because of the size and diversity of its programming, television can appeal to everybody—some of the time, if not all of the time. TV, by virtue of its intimate nature, comes across as intensely individual and personal, causing people to identify with the images the screen provides. In fact, some would argue that TV images seem "more real" than reality itself. As television strove to define itself in the 1950s, people sensed the potency of this new medium; the end of the decade saw it firmly established in the living rooms of more than three-quarters of American families. TV had supplanted movies and radio, and it clearly served as the primary carrier of popular culture.

THEATER

Although much theatrical activity took place on the local and regional levels throughout the 1950s, New York City's Broadway remained the home for most major productions. True, New York theater prospered and offered top-notch plays of all kinds during the decade, but only a limited part of the potential national audience saw plays with their original casts and sets. For most people, seeing a hit play with big-name performers meant seeing the movie adaptation. Fortunately, the film industry did just that, quickly translating Broadway's best into a string of movies. They might vary in overall quality, but they at least allowed people to see "theater" on the screen. Theater therefore functioned as a form of popular culture once removed.

Musicals

The biggest theatrical box-office grosses came from musicals, most of which soon came out in movie versions. A partial listing of the many musicals that entertained Broadway audiences during the 1950s appears in Table 10.6.

Many of these musicals have become perennial favorites for local and regional theater productions, and many high school and college drama groups have attempted them as well. *Guys and Dolls*, *The King and I*, and *The Music Man* can claim countless amateur productions, and *My Fair Lady* and *West Side Story* have become true American classics. In addition, these musicals have crossed the line from being plays seen by an essentially white, middle-class audience that lived in or near New York City to plays known by all, from rural to suburban to urban, all races, all economic classes. They have become part of the collective culture of the nation and certainly qualify as products of popular culture.

Table 10.6
Broadway Musicals of the 1950s and Their Film Adaptations

Frank Loesser's *Guys and Dolls* (1950; film, 1955)

Irving Berlin's *Call Me Madam* (1950; film, 1953)

Richard Rodgers and Oscar Hammerstein's *The King and I* (1951; film, 1956)

Alan Jay Lerner and Frederick Loewe's *Paint Your Wagon* (1951; film, 1969)

Aleksandr Borodin's [adapted] *Kismet* (1953; film, 1955)

Cole Porter's *Can-Can* (1953; film, 1960)

Richard Adler and Jerry Ross's *The Pajama Game* (1954; film, 1957)

Richard Adler and Jerry Ross's *Damn Yankees* (1955; film, 1958)

Jule Styne's *Bells Are Ringing* (1956; film, 1960)

Alan Jay Lerner and Frederick Loewe's *My Fair Lady* (1956; film, 1964)

Frank Loesser's *The Most Happy Fella* (1956)

Gene de Paul and Johnny Mercer's *Li'l Abner* (1956; film, 1959)

Leonard Bernstein's *West Side Story* (1957; film, 1961)

Meredith Willson's *The Music Man* (1957; film, 1962)

Richard Rodgers and Oscar Hammerstein's *Flower Drum Song* (1958; film, 1961)

Jule Styne and Stephen Sondheim's *Gypsy* (1959; film, 1962)

Richard Rodgers and Oscar Hammerstein's *The Sound of Music* (1959; film, 1965).

Note: Listed chronologically with composers, followed by film release dates.

Through extensive and well-promoted media interplay, public awareness of Broadway and its top-drawing productions achieved high visibility
during the 1950s. The addition of names like Rodgers and Hammerstein,
Cole Porter, Irving Berlin, and Lerner and Lowe assured box-office success. As soon as rights could be secured, Hollywood brought out glossy
film versions of musicals that had even a modicum of popularity [see
"Movies" above for more on this subject]. In the meantime, record companies released original cast albums, usually with extensive liner notes,
because public interest demanded them. Vocalists and musical groups,
especially in the realm of jazz, created interpretative albums of specific
musicals, further increasing the listenership for the scores. This flurry of
recording activity carried over into radio. Disc jockeys pushed individual
songs, and many a composition achieved hit status, both in its original
form and in its many adapted versions. Across the land, people
hummed—or maybe even attempted a vocal rendition of "Maria" (*West
Side Story*), "On the Street Where You Live" (*My Fair Lady*), "Seventy-Six
Trombones" (*The Music Man*), or dozens of other songs that have come
down to the present as standards.

"Serious" Plays

Despite their outstanding box-office record, musicals were not the only performances offered to playgoers during the fifties. T.S. Eliot's *The Cocktail Party* (1950) introduced British actor Alec Guinness, destined to make a popular name for himself in films like *The Bridge on the River Kwai* (1957); unfortunately, few saw him in Eliot's play. Arthur Miller's *The Crucible* (1953), Samuel Beckett's *Waiting for Godot* (1956), and John Osborne's *Look Back in Anger* (1957) likewise received raves from critics but did not reach truly national audiences.

For example, Miller's *The Crucible*, ostensibly about the Salem witch trials, conceals a thinly veiled attack on another kind of witch-hunt, McCarthyism and the methods of the House Un-American Activities Committee. For its limited Broadway audience, it proved an immediate hit, suggesting that theatergoers grasped Miller's underlying symbolism and wanted to find a popular vehicle prepared to carry the message. But it would take years before Hollywood would touch the play, 1996 to be exact, and regional theater groups, although not quite so timid, mounted few productions of the drama.

Taking a cue from its 1957 television success, Broadway staged William Gibson's powerful *The Miracle Worker* in 1959, starring Anne Bancroft and Patty Duke in the story of the life of Helen Keller. It provided vibrant theater, but only when Bancroft and Duke re-created their stage roles in a 1962 movie did the true mass audience experience this drama. No matter how good the play or how strong the performers, until the transfer to film or television occurred, it would be difficult to call American theater in the 1950s true popular culture.

Summary

The high-powered Broadway musical stands as the one form of American theater that easily lent itself to popular culture. Because of their natural affinity to Hollywood, musicals emerged as the most successful of all dramatic formats during the decade.

DANCE

Thanks in large part to exposure by television, some elements of modern dance at last captured a significant audience during the 1950s. Many TV variety shows featured individual dancers or dance troupes as part of their presentations, and more often than not the choreography included routines that could be called more modern than traditional.

If the Abstract Expressionists had made New York the center for painting during the fifties, then a talented group of television choreographers made the same city the dance capital during the decade. In addition, the popularity of musicals, both on stage and on film, allowed for occasional forays into modern dance. Gene Kelly, a popular star in many movie musicals, was himself an outstanding dancer and choreographer. His roles in the hugely successful *An American in Paris* (1951) and *Singin' in the Rain* (1952) gave him the artistic freedom to direct and star in *Invitation to the Dance* (1956). The picture did not do well at the box office, reinforcing studio fears about anything that might go over the audience's head, but it nevertheless provided an inventive approach to modern dance. In a technological and editing tour de force, Kelly even performs with characters taken from the popular Hanna-Barbera cartoons of the period, a nice crossover from one format to another.

On a more popular front, people attempted to master the mambo, along with other Latin-influenced dances such as the rumba and the merengue. In 1954, "Mambo Italiano," "Papa Loves Mambo," and "They Were Doing the Mambo" all became musical hits. The Cuban cha-cha and the West Indian calypso also attracted dance fans and spawned a number of best-selling records. Bandleaders Perez Prado and Tito Puente arose as two of the leading exponents of the cha-cha, and Harry Belafonte and his vocals popularized calypso.

Old-fashioned square dancing reappeared as the anything-Early American fad spread into leisure activities. *The Arthur Murray Party* (all networks, various dates, 1950–1960) offered more formal instruction. Hosted by Arthur and Kathryn Murray, two successful and popular dance instructors, the show consisted of a mix of teaching, exhibition, and salesmanship for their studios. Despite its blatant commercialism, the series introduced older viewers to ballroom dancing, along with many newer novelty steps.

More in keeping with the changing times, Dick Clark's Philadelphia-based *American Bandstand* (ABC, 1957–1987) ran on afternoon network television. Teen-oriented, the show quickly showed national audiences what Philadelphians already knew: young people had developed a complex body of dances to accompany rock 'n' roll. Some were shocked at what they saw, deeming it obscene, but more found the dancing a healthy way to let off youthful high spirits. Plus, the show allowed teens—and probably a healthy number of adults—from all over the country to learn the latest dance steps.

For example, in 1957 trumpeter Ray Anthony enjoyed a big hit with a record titled "The Bunny Hop." An instrumental, it featured a frivolous dance in which people line up, grasp the person in front of them, and hop around the floor in rhythm to the music. The teenage dancers on *American Bandstand* popularized the Bunny Hop on national television, making it a short-lived dance craze. [For more on Clark and *American Bandstand*, see chapter 9, "Music."]

Summary

As the 1950s drew to a close, it became clear that youth-oriented dancing had come to dominate popular taste. Rock 'n' roll, rhythm and blues, or just plain up-tempo pop were what Americans saw on television or in the movies, and those dance styles eclipsed any competition. A revolution had occurred, and popular dance would never be the same again.

11

Travel and Recreation

Henry Ford may have introduced the mass production of motorized vehicles with his Model T Ford in 1908, but the true flowering of the American automobile—cars for everyone, the car as a major component of popular culture—did not take place until the 1950s. At the conclusion of World War II in 1945, the average American car was five or more years old, and many struggled on their last legs. The Great Depression of the 1930s and the scarcities imposed by the war had combined to create a population anxious to purchase automobiles in record numbers. Everyone waited for Detroit to retool, to move from defense production back to consumer goods.

AUTOMOBILES AND AMERICAN LIFE

The prosperity of the 1950s created a boom for automakers the likes of which had never before been seen. By 1955, the number of cars on the road doubled from 1945. A showroom-fresh, big, powerful American automobile symbolized success; throughout the decade, dealers sold over seven million cars and trucks each year. By 1958, about 70 percent of all American families owned an automobile, up almost 20 percentage points from the beginning of the decade. Most people bought new models, and three-quarters or more of them had radios. The end of the fifties saw some 50 million cars on America's roads, or one automobile for every 3.58 persons.[1]

The move of the middle class to the suburbs was coupled with a desire for new cars. Almost overnight a new category of worker emerged: the automobile commuter. Around large cities like Boston, New York, and Chicago, commuting by railroad had long been in place, fostering the image of employees patiently awaiting a train to take them to their jobs.

In much of the country, however, the thought of being far from one's job still struck many as a novel idea. Even with rapid suburban growth, there came few attempts to connect outlying areas to passenger rail lines or bus systems. The Greyhound Company introduced its Scenicruiser bus in 1954. Conceived by the famous designer Raymond Loewy, its upper level provided an unrivaled view of the road and passing scenery, but it arrived on the market too late. By that time, mass transit no longer held a high place in anyone's list of priorities. This abandonment of commercial transportation left employees with only one choice: driving to work.

But if Dad took the family car to his job, what would Mom do about grocery shopping, schools, and clubs? The answer lay in the rise of the two-car family, his and hers. Unanticipated problems created by the growth of the suburbs and the increased number of automobiles involved the disappearance of neighborhood amenities and the unavailability of public transportation. Supermarkets located in a shopping center often miles from one's home displaced the corner grocery store. As school districts consolidated, the neighborhood school became a fond memory. Access to an automobile was deemed a necessity, and over ten percent of all families possessed more than one car by the end of the decade. Parking emerged as an urban problem that grew out of suburban living. Each morning, millions of commuters descended on American cities, parked their cars, put in an eight-hour day, and then returned to the suburbs. Cities contemplated building huge parking lots, and yet their downtown businesses saw little commerce. Shoppers flocked to the new, outlying malls springing up almost as fast as the housing developments they were built to serve. The 1950s marked the Age of the Automobile and all its concurrent problems.

Superhighways

The postwar years witnessed a surge in highway building. By 1950, most roads in the United States proved woefully inadequate to handle all the new cars that people eagerly bought. There existed many a wonderful route for a Sunday drive, but a winding country lane proved ill suited to the spiraling demands of the time. The picturesque parkways of the 1930s, designed for recreational driving, no longer met transportation needs. But the freeways and expressways of the 1950s, dedicated to speed, of getting from one place to another, moved millions quickly and efficiently. The prosperity of the 1950s allowed such construction to begin in earnest.

In the late thirties and early forties, the Bureau of Public Roads had come up with ambitious plans for a 30,000-mile interregional highway system. The war halted any enactment of these ideas, but they were not forgotten; officials simply put them on hold. After the war, the 1950 opening of an eastern extension of the Pennsylvania Turnpike, "America's Dream Road," along with a western addition in 1951, marked the beginning of a momentous chapter in the modernization of American roads.

In 1950, construction commenced on the New Jersey Turnpike, a multi-lane toll road that owns the dubious honor of being the most heavily traveled highway in America. The Korean War drove up costs, caused shortages, and slowed construction, but despite these complications and some uncompleted portions, its dedication took place in November of 1951, with a final link opening in early 1952. In order to save money, engineers on the project paid little heed to aesthetics, saying such efforts were superfluous and distracting. The New Jersey Turnpike therefore offered drivers virtually no visual embellishment, but stood instead as a triumph of function over form, a true machine in the Garden State, and it led the way for a new kind of automotive culture. Turnpike driving, in New Jersey or anywhere else, involves anonymous rest stops, service areas, and sustained high-speed driving.[2]

At the same time the New Jersey Turnpike sliced its way through cities, towns, and countryside, the Garden State Parkway, hardly a traditional parkway, inched down the state also. Begun in 1946, but not completed until 1956, it complemented its sister Turnpike. Other states likewise had plans for new highways, multilane expressways that enjoyed limited access and permitted no intersecting streets, no railroad crossings, and no stoplights.

New York began constructing its ambitious Thruway in 1946, but tight finances made it slow going until 1950. By 1955, the Thruway had its first

The 1950s truly stand as the Golden Age of the American Automobile. It seemed everyone had a car, and the antiquated prewar highway system was ill equipped to handle the millions of vehicles flooding the roads. Many states embarked on large-scale road-building projects, and the New York State Thruway, with its ultra-modern tollbooths (above), was but one of them. In 1956, seeing the need for nationwide highway improvement, the federal government embarked on the multi-billion dollar Interstate Highway System. Source: Library of Congress, photo by Jim Hansen.

service areas and reached completion in 1960. Similarly, West Virginia (1954), Ohio (1955), Indiana (1956), Kansas (1956), Massachusetts (1957), Oklahoma (1957), Connecticut (1958), and several other states and localities plunged ahead with massive highway plans in the 1950s. When opened, the Indiana-Ohio-Pennsylvania-New Jersey connections provided an almost nonstop 840-mile express route between New York City and Chicago. Financed largely by the states themselves and through the imposition of tolls, all this ambitious building slowed precipitously in 1956 when the federal government unveiled its own plans for highways.[3]

The Interstate Highway System

In 1954, the Federal-Aid Highway Act laid the groundwork for a massive system of modern roads, but set aside insufficient monies. An expanded version of the legislation came out in 1956 called the Interstate Highway Act. It provided $25 billion for construction fees, 90 percent of which would be federal funding, the money coming from gasoline and road use taxes. This gargantuan plan mandated the development of some 41,000 miles of new highways. An agreeable Congress enthusiastically received the Act and then increased federal highway aid by almost another $2 billion in 1958.

The project got underway and soon moved into high gear. As the new ribbons of concrete crept across the countryside, builders faced one of two possibilities when they approached population centers: they could slice right through the cities or they could bypass them. Those communities that were bisected usually in time recovered from the disruption, although it took years and the ugly slash of highway could seldom be disguised. Those towns that were bypassed by the system watched helplessly as downtown commerce collapsed and once-flourishing business districts turned into ghost towns. All the action took place "out by the highway."

Interchanges on the growing interstates emerged as new economic centers, with motels, gas stations, and restaurants appearing almost overnight. Oases to thirsty, tired motorists, these shiny clusters of commerce reversed what trolleys and buses had attempted to accomplish years earlier. Instead of taking people into the heart of a city, the new interstates took them out, to malls, shopping complexes, and acres of free parking.

Many communities reinvented themselves by creating vast malls and industrial parks outside the traditional city center. If people flocked to the suburbs, why not provide urban amenities and jobs there also? In a transformation that continues to play itself out today, businesses of all kinds began to move some or all of their operations to these new towns that grew on the fringes of older population centers. For the 1950s, however, the vast majority of traditional jobs remained in the cities. The advent of the interstates constituted a demographic shift of almost unimaginable proportions, and much of it occurred in the late 1950s.

Automobiles of the 1950s

The beginning of the decade found about forty-nine million motor vehicles registered in the United States. By 1959, the number had climbed to almost seventy-four million vehicles, a jump of more than one-third in ten years. During that same period, the cost of an automobile likewise rose about 33 percent, from an average $1,270 to $1,822, but the cars underwent significant improvements throughout that time.[4]

With postwar prosperity and unprecedented demand for new automobiles, unfamiliar names like Muntz and Crosley briefly made their appearance and attracted the curious, but few actually sold. Most smaller companies failed during the fifties, a decade of consolidation that saw the Big Three—General Motors, Ford, and Chrysler—tighten its grip on the American consumer.

Throughout the 1950s, GM dominated everyone else, claiming 40 percent or more of the total market. Ford came in second, with about a quarter of the pie, followed by Chrysler, with approximately 15 percent. Smaller, independent domestic companies, along with a slow but rising tide of imports, divided up the remaider. But it was slim pickings for the competition; in 1955, 1956, and 1959, the Big Three's combined market share averaged 94 percent.[5]

Industry Innovations

Despite the disappearance of the smaller auto companies during the decade or shortly thereafter, the 1950s remain one of the most remarkable periods in American motoring history. Those ten years saw the introduction of the hardtop, a pillarless four-door automobile that blended a sedan with a convertible. The hardtop quickly became the most popular body style of the era; it brought the outdoors into the car's interior. Its design complemented similar attempts in home construction, where carports and patios, along with glass sliding doors, blurred the boundaries between the house and the yard. For both homes and automobiles, advertisers touted the freedom and expansiveness allowed by modern design. It made no difference if someone tooled down a multilane highway or grilled on a patio; the image of openness and space prevailed.

At the onset of the 1950s, most American cars had six-cylinder motors, and these power plants seemed to satisfy people's needs. But through clever marketing, the public became convinced that bigger engines would provide greater acceleration, speed, and torque for the larger cars pouring out of Detroit. This attitude prompted increased sales of large, chrome-bedecked automobiles that necessitated big, fuel-guzzling engines. By the end of the decade, more than 80 percent of new American cars had eight-cylinder motors, or V-8s as they were commonly called.[6]

In 1953, General Motors introduced the Chevrolet Corvette, a fiberglass-bodied sports car designed to compete with the influx of foreign sports

Table 11.1
American-Made Automobiles, 1950–1959[7]

Popular Name	Parent Company	Production Years
Buick—also called Century, LeSabre, Riviera, Roadmaster, Skylark, Special, others	General Motors	Buicks were manufactured throughout the decade.
Cadillac—also called Coupe de Ville, Eldorado, Fleetwood, others	General Motors	Cadillacs were manufactured throughout the decade.
Checker—also called Specials, Superbas	Checker Motors	Designed and built as taxis, Checkers first became available to the public in 1959.
Chevrolet—also called Bel Air, Delray, Impala, Nomad, Styleline, others; in addition, Chevrolet marketed a sports car called a Corvette	General Motors	Chevrolets were manufactured throughout the decade; the Corvette sports car was introduced in 1953.
Chrysler—also called New Yorker, Newport, 300, Town and Country, Windsor, others	Chrysler Corporation	Chryslers were manufactured throughout the decade.
Continental—also called Mark II, Mark III, Mark IV	Ford Motor Company	Continentals were manufactured 1956–1958; after that date, they were marketed as Lincoln Continentals.
Crosley—also called Hotshots, Super Sports	Crosley Appliances	A midget car, Crosley ceased production in 1952.
DeSoto—also called Adventurer, Custom, Firedome, Fireflite, Firesweep, others	Chrysler Corporation	DeSotos were manufactured throughout the decade.
Dodge—also called Coronet, Royal Lancer, Sierra, Wayfarer, others	Chrysler Corporation	Dodges were manufactured throughout the decade.
Edsel—also called Citation, Corsair, Ranger	Ford Motor Company	The Edsel was introduced in 1958; production ceased in 1960.

Ford—also called Country Squire, Crestliner, Fairlane, Galaxie, Skyliner, Tudor, Victoria, others; in addition, Ford marketed a sports car called a Thunderbird	Ford Motor Company	Fords were manufactured throughout the decade; the Thunderbird sports car was introduced in 1955.
Frazer—also called Manhattan, Standard	Kaiser-Frazer Corporation	The Frazer was in production only from 1946 to 1951.
Henry J—also called Corsair, Vagabond; another version, called the "Allstate," was marketed through Sears, Roebuck	Kaiser-Frazer Corporation	One of the first compact cars, the Henry J was in production from 1951 to 1954; the Allstate was sold from 1952 to 1953.
Hudson—also called Italia, Hornet, Super Jet, Wasp, others	Hudson Motors (merged into American Motors Corporation in 1954)	Hudson ceased production in 1957.
Imperial—also called Crown Southampton, Custom, Newport	Chrysler Corporation	A luxury Chrysler, Imperials gained autonomy in 1955 and remained so for the decade.
Kaiser—also called Dragon, Manhattan, Special, Traveler; in addition, Kaiser marketed a sports car called a Darrin	Kaiser-Frazer Corporation	The Kaiser was in production only from 1949 to 1955; the Darrin sports car was marketed only in 1954.
Lincoln—also called Capri, Cosmopolitan, Premiere, Continental Mark IV	Ford Motor Company	Lincolns were manufactured throughout the decade; in 1959, the formerly autonomous Continentals took on the Lincoln name.
Mercury—also called Medalist, Montclair, Monterey, Park Lane, Turnpike Cruiser, others	Ford Motor Company	Mercurys were manufactured throughout the decade.
Muntz—also called Jet	Muntz Motors	Muntzes were manufactured from 1950 to 1954.

continued

Table 11.1 *Continued*

Popular Name	Parent Company	Production Years
Nash—also called Airflyte, Ambassador, Metropolitan, Rambler, Statesman; in addition, Nash marketed a sports car called a Nash-Healey	Nash-Kelvinator (merged into American Motors Corporation in 1954)	Nashes were manufactured until 1957; the Rambler brand became autonomous in 1955; the Nash-Healey sports car was marketed from 1951 to 1955.
Oldsmobile—also called Dynamic 88, Fiesta, Futuramic, Golden Rocket, Holiday, Starfire, Super 88, others	General Motors	Oldsmobiles were manufactured throughout the decade.
Packard—also called Clipper, Custom Eight, The Four Hundred, Mayfair, Pacific, 250, others	Packard Motors (merged into Studebaker-Packard in 1954)	Packards remained in production until 1958.
Plymouth—also called Belvedere, Cranbrook, Fury, Savoy, Special, Suburban, others	Chrysler Corporation	Plymouths were manufactured throughout the decade.
Pontiac—also called Bonneville, Catalina, Chieftain, Safari, Star Chief, Streamliner, others	General Motors	Pontiacs were manufactured throughout the decade.
Pontiac—also called Bonneville, Catalina, Chieftain, Safari, Star Chief, Streamliner, others	General Motors	Pontiacs were manufactured throughout the decade.
Studebaker—also called Commander, Champion, Conestoga, Golden Hawk, Hawk, Lark, President, Scotsman, Sky Hawk, Starliner, others	Studebaker Corporation (merged into Studebaker-Packard in 1954)	Studebakers were manufactured throughout the decade.
Willys—also called Aero-Ace, Aero-Eagle, Aero-Wing, Bermuda, Jeep, Jeepster, others	Willys-Overland (merged with Kaiser-Frazer in 1954 to form Kaiser-Willys Sales Corporation)	Willys cars were manufactured until 1955; the Jeep (considered a truck, not a car) continued production throughout the decade.

cars then entering the market in significant numbers. The Corvette cost approximately $3,200—expensive then—but modest sales encouraged the company to promote the car. Two years later, the Ford Motor Company introduced its Thunderbird, another two-seat sports car created to share in that growing market. The T-Bird became an immediate favorite with the public and sales quickly surpassed those of the Corvette. For reasons best explained in the secrecy of corporate boardrooms, Ford in 1958 changed its Thunderbird into a four-seat model, and any aura of a true sports car disappeared. General Motors, on the other hand, continued with its line of two-seat Corvettes, giving them a virtual monopoly for American-made sports cars and creating, in the process, a mystique about the car, an aura that clever advertising reinforced throughout the decade.[8]

Hot on the heels of its success with the Thunderbird, Ford in 1957, amid great fanfare, introduced the Edsel. It entered salesrooms as the first completely new American brand in years. With a price in excess of $5,000, the Edsel aimed for the upscale buyer. But Ford failed in the area of market research, relying instead on its engineering department, and its design turned off potential purchasers. Sluggish sales finally forced the automaker to drop the Edsel in the fall of 1959. This ill-fated attempt to bring out a new car cost Ford $250 million, making it the costliest automotive failure in history, and causing the term "Edsel" to be synonymous with any great business disaster.

Foreign Competition

Blinded by its own success, Detroit ignored foreign imports, calling them "cheap" and "crowded," and claiming the American public would ultimately reject them once any novelty wore off. U.S. automakers displayed a nearsighted complacency about consumers, thinking Americans would naturally "buy American," and at first they seemed correct in their dismissal of foreign competition. A trickle of imports in the early 1950s hardly warranted concern, since domestic companies counted their sales in the millions. But foreign manufacturers persisted, and by 1957 had captured ten percent of the market, or over 600,000 cars sold for the year. At this same time, another warning sounded for Detroit because, for the first time ever, the United States imported more automobiles than it exported.

To illustrate: Volkswagen sold only 330 of its Beetles in 1950. By 1955, the trickle had grown to a stream, when about 30,000 of the ungainly "Bugs" were imported. At the close of the decade, the company sold over 150,000 Volkswagen sedans, and potential buyers had to get on a waiting list for the next available vehicle. In addition, the German manufacturer also marketed the Volkswagen camper van, or Westphalia, then one of the few mass-produced vehicles designed for touring and camping. The Westphalia proved an immediate success, capitalizing on a wave of auto

Although it held little of the U.S. auto market in the 1950s, Germany's Volkswagen "Beetle" hinted at things to come. Clever advertising, combined with good engineering and fuel economy, caused Volkswagen to make its first significant inroads in 1955. In like manner, England, France, Italy, and Japan hungrily eyed the huge U.S. market, introducing models of their own at decade's end. By 1959, foreign automakers had claimed about ten percent of total sales, a figure destined to rise at Detroit's expense. Source: Library of Congress.

tourism that flourished throughout the 1950s. With nothing comparable on the market, Volkswagen enjoyed a monopoly.

Volkswagen reinforced its already significant foothold among U.S. consumers by capitalizing on a humorous, self-effacing ad campaign crafted by the American firm of Doyle, Dane, Bernbach, Inc., that commenced in the fall of 1959. The ads, appearing in various print media, consisted of a succession of single black-and-white photographs that included a Beetle but seldom under glamorous circumstances, and some pithy copy touting the reliability or uniqueness of the car. They resonated with people, both for their deadpan humor and their honesty, and served as a welcome break from the monotony of most automobile advertising. As the 1950s came to an end, Volkswagen, already the front-runner among imports, seemed poised to become a major competitor in the American automobile market.[9]

Detroit made no effort to design and manufacture competitive U.S. models until late in the decade. Finally, the Big Three reacted. In 1959, Ford introduced its Falcon, Chevrolet followed suit with its unique Corvair, and

Plymouth promoted its Valiant. The first mass-market compact cars manufactured in the United States, they served as a belated acknowledgment of foreign competition. At the same time, many other American-made behemoths only grew larger and more gadget-laden. Chrome bullets poked out from complex chrome grilles, salesmen touted electric door locks and powered mirrors, and air-conditioning became more commonplace.

Automotive Design

Until the 1950s, most American automobiles possessed a utilitarian look. Form truly followed function, and even some of the most elegant cars of the 1920s and 1930s retained a pragmatic appearance. With the postwar era, however, a new vision beguiled the industry. Style overtook safety and practicality. Influenced by Hollywood, fashion, science fiction, technology, military aircraft, and unfettered imaginations, Detroit took off on a design flight unlike anything encountered before.

Breathless advertising promoted cars that suggested streamlined rockets and swept wing jets. Names like (Buick) LeSabre; (Ford) Thunderbird and Galaxie; (Hudson) Jet and Super Jet; and (Oldsmobile) Rocket 88 and 98 even spoke of aerodynamics and speed. In addition, the dashboard and its instrumentation often resembled something found in an aircraft cockpit, further reinforcement of the car-plane symbolism. By the mid-1950s, the analogies between automobiles and airplanes became impossible to ignore.

During this period of excess, automotive designers discovered the fin. A completely nonfunctional appendage that grew out of the rear fender, it became the symbol of the 1950s American automobile. With each yearly model change, fins grew larger and more prominent. By the middle of the decade, they soared into the air, they lengthened the body, and everybody wanted them. Detroit, eager to please the customer, knew that consumers could be a notoriously fickle group. As quickly as fins had emerged as a style statement, the desire for longer and taller fins evaporated with the close of the decade, and buyers moved on to the next design fad. But the long, long 1959 Cadillac Coupe de Ville will always be remembered for resembling nothing so much as a jet aircraft poised for takeoff.

Harley J. Earl

The person given most of the credit for fins was Harley J. Earl of General Motors. He joined the company in the mid-1920s and helped popularize the concept of annual design at the giant automaker. Starting with a team of fifty people, the group eventually swelled to over 1,000 by the 1950s. Earl brought styling on a grand scale to automobile manufacturing. Although his crew could do little during World War II amid all the restrictions on consumer products, after 1945 GM granted him much greater latitude. He pushed for planned obsolescence in design and stated he wanted cars that looked longer and lower.

Earl consciously employed symbolism in auto design. In addition to tail fins, he pioneered the wrap-around windshield and the free use of sculptural chrome. Earl liked the look of a World War II fighter plane officially called the P-38, but better known as the Lockheed Lightning. He admired its streamlining, particularly its unusual twin tail booms, and hints of that assembly crept into the 1948 Cadillac in the form of slightly exaggerated rear taillights. By the 1950s, manufacturers other than General Motors had also raised and flared the rear fenders of their products, and thanks to Harley Earl the race for bigger, more flamboyant, more outlandish fins was on.[10]

Movies, Music, and Automobiles

The presence of automobiles in virtually any contemporary movie objectified the concept that the car belonged in all aspects of American culture, that it represented American culture. Both subliminally and overtly, automobiles dominated their film scenes, whether in a mystery, a musical, or a comedy. Larger than life up on the screen, cars offered escape, pursuit, sanctuary, a sense of style, affluence, and—most importantly—a reason for consumption. In many ways, the movies of the 1950s also served as dramatic commercials for the auto industry, showcasing the necessity of individual transportation in contemporary America.

Although few commercial movies came out about cars per se, a handful did focus on aspects of motoring. For instance, racing found a niche in *Drive a Crooked Road* (1954) and *The Devil's Hairpin* (1957). Films that dealt with youth and the hot-rodding fad of the 1950s proved more popular; titles like *Hot Rod Girl* (1956), *Hot Rod Rumble* (1957), *Hot Rod Gang* (1958), and *Joy Ride* (1958) drew large audiences to theaters and drive-ins.

In 1951, Jackie Brenston and the Kings of Rhythm scored a minor musical hit, "Rocket 88," a song that celebrated Oldsmobile's latest model and also the pleasures of cruisin' around town in a new car. Brenston's success inspired a host of other car-and-music numbers like "V-Ford Blues" (1951), "Cadillac Daddy" (1952), "Drivin' Slow" (1952), and "Maybelline" (1955), and some groups, like the Cadillacs and the El Dorados, took popular automobile names as their own. [For more on teen culture and cars, see chapter 2, "World of Youth."]

Trailers, Mobile Homes, Station Wagons, Campers, and Recreational Vehicles

The marked improvement of highways and the booming vacation market of the 1950s led to the popularity of recreational vehicles of all kinds. Manufacturers responded by producing transportation to fit every taste and pocketbook. Immediately following World War II, Americans took to the road in record numbers. For many, a converted bus served as their mobile vacation residence. But a bus conversion required time and handyman skills, although the do-it-yourself craze of the era supported such endeavors. Entrepreneurs, eager to accommodate this small but growing market, came out with all sorts of gadgets to make such touring more pleasurable. Everything, from small, portable stoves and refrigerators to nylon window screens and mesh "patios" could be purchased, and elaborately furnished vehicles often resulted. Those who could afford one, however, might prefer to purchase a ready-made motor home, and several small firms commenced limited production of prefabricated models. For example, Nash, an old-line automobile company, advertised reclining seats in its Airflyte sedans that converted to full-size beds, aiming their marketing at hunters and other outdoor sportsmen.

Detroit was not oblivious to the attractions of motor homes, and the postwar station wagon reflected the need for more than mere transportation. Throughout the 1950s, station wagons grew in size, and dealers promoted their dual use as capacious vacation vehicles that allowed for sleeping in the large cargo areas. The concept caught on, and sales soared, with one out of every eight American cars a station wagon in 1956. Americans appreciated their roominess and ease of handling. They also gave evidence of prosperity; parked on blacktopped suburban driveways, station wagons announced to all that their owners had achieved material success. The utility of hauling groceries and kids during the week, attractive all-steel bodies, and the ability to pack the family's gear and still have room left over for crowded sleeping on vacation trips made them sure sellers for affluent consumers.[11]

Pickup trucks likewise enjoyed some popularity for vacationing. A camper body could be attached to the truck bed that allowed protected storage and possibly sleeping arrangements. Throughout the decade, a number of small manufacturers produced a variety of aluminum bodies for this purpose. The campers possessed a disadvantage in that the driver and other front-seat passengers lacked direct access to the unit, and this discouraged would-be buyers. In addition, during the 1950s, many perceived the pickup as a utilitarian truck, not a potential recreational vehicle. Sales remained sluggish and did not take off until the 1960s when attitudes shifted, making the lowly pickup fashionable transportation.

Travel and the Growth of Tourism

From 1951 onward, either in her fifteen-minute music show on television, *The Dinah Shore Show* (1951–1957), or her hour-long variety offering that replaced it, *The Dinah Shore Chevy Show* (1957–1962), singer Dinah Shore invited her viewers to "See the U.S.A. in your Chevrolet." That advertising theme song crept into the popular mind, the invitation seemingly irresistible.

With all the emphasis on the acquisition of new cars, auto travel doubled in the United States between 1950 and 1960. Recreational travel led the way; wherever they went and whatever they did, Americans equipped themselves for travel as never before. Leisure clothing, luggage, convenience foods, camping and boating supplies, sporting goods, and souvenirs enjoyed rapid increases in sales.

For the first time most American employers offered workers with at least one year of service paid vacations, a situation that led to more and longer trips. The number of paid holidays also increased during the 1950s, and the baby boom of the immediate postwar years created a new, young population of families eager to travel. For many, particularly those with children in school, summer meant one thing: a journey by automobile. Over 80 percent of such travel was undertaken by car, compared to 13 percent by train, and the miniscule remainder by air or ship. On average, these auto trips ran from one week to two weeks on the road, with stopovers at motels, hotels, and the homes of friends and relatives. Some camping also took place, but on a limited scale. Almost half of all families engaged in vacation touring during the 1950s, and their journeys tended to be about six hundred miles in length. Education and economic status played a role in travel. Those in the middle class possessing high school and college degrees proved more prone to travel; the greater a family's affluence, the farther they chose to go.[12]

Most American tourists during the 1950s traveled to locations within the continental United States. Any border crossing usually meant Canada; not until air travel began to boom in the 1960s did foreign destinations gain impressive numbers of visitors. In addition, more than half those Americans traveling by car tended to return to the same place annually. Travel may have been popular during the 1950s, but it lacked adventure for most participants.

Many tourists chose to journey to one or more of the many national parks and monuments scattered across the country. The National Park Service found itself coping with thousands of additional visitors each year, a job made difficult by antiquated and inadequate facilities. Tourism at parks and monuments more than doubled during the decade, going from nineteen million visitors in 1950 to over thirty-eight million in 1959. Most of these tourists arrived by automobile, a fact that necessitated additional parking and camping slots. In response, 1956 saw the inauguration of Mission 66, a decade-long effort that attempted to upgrade and modernize the park system by 1966, the fiftieth anniversary of its founding.[13]

As road building moved into high gear across the United States, more and more tourist facilities were erected alongside these new highways. Motels, restaurants, service stations, and assorted attractions rose at an accelerated pace, making travel easier and more reassuring than it had ever been. That a certain facelessness—an anonymity—also became part of this highway culture did nothing to dampen the spirits of those on the road; virtually any place was now accessible by automobile, and entrepreneurs made familiarity and predictability part of American travel culture.

Motels, Hotels, and Drive-In Businesses

To accommodate this horde of motorists, American lodging underwent significant changes. The venerable motor hotel, or "motel," evolved from rather pedestrian clusters of little buildings, or "cabins," to elaborate architectural designs that called themselves "motor inns." In addition, the field proved ripe for quality lodging, a concept that required money and

In this 1953 picture, happy tourists have pulled into a cozy California "motor hotel." That term would soon shorten to "motel," and new establishments began to appear across the landscape as more Americans took to the road. Small, independent units dominated for the first years of the decade, but with the opening success of Holiday Inn in 1954, large national chains commenced to overtake the lodging industry, a situation that remains unchanged today. Source: Library of Congress.

brought in corporate financing. Names like Best Western, Howard Johnson's, Ramada, Travelodge, among many others, soon eclipsed the older mom-and-pop operations. Franchising dominated the market, and the small, independent motel owner faced overwhelming competition. Available motel rooms in the suburbs and countryside multiplied, but in cities across the land, the number of traditional hotel rooms plunged as worried owners cut back on operations in the face of this competition.[14]

Kemmons Wilson, a Tennessee architect and builder, led the motel charge. He opened the first Holiday Inn in Memphis in 1954. It had 120 rooms, far more than other motels of the day. In addition, the venture offered air-conditioning, in-room telephones, free ice, and a host of other features new to the industry. Wilson, dissatisfied with the inferior lodging then available to travelers and tourists, saw his new Holiday Inn become an immediate, popular success. He continued building; by the end of the decade more than two hundred Holiday Inns graced the American landscape—plus numerous new competitors eager to cash in on the heretofore unrealized potential of the U.S. tourism market. Whereas about 30,000 motels had been scattered around the United States in 1950, by 1960 that figure had mushroomed to 60,000 and showed no signs of slowing.[15]

The 1950s also witnessed the blossoming of the drive-in, from theaters to markets to restaurants to banks. Many businesses rebuilt existing structures to accommodate automobiles. Once-stodgy banks now welcomed customers with drive-up windows. Numerous restaurant and fast-food chains evolved by catering to vehicular traffic, not walk-ins. The movie business, buffeted by the competition of television during the 1950s, enjoyed a brief rejuvenation with the meteoric rise in popularity of the drive-in theater. [For more details on drive-in theaters, see chapter 10, "Performing Arts."]

Amusement Parks

As millions of adults and their children embarked on vacations, entrepreneurs everywhere attempted to entice them with endless attractions. The 1950s chronicle a long line of seedy parks and zoos, "unimaginable wonders" and "unbelievable sights," tourist traps, and outright frauds—all of it advertised with endless cheap signs that dotted the highways. Not until the advent of Walt Disney's concept of family entertainment did there occur a marked change in roadside attractions.

In 1954, the Walt Disney Company began construction of a large recreational facility in Anaheim, California. It opened as Disneyland in July 1955. Taking its name and much of its funding from the popular ABC television series, the park proved successful from its inception. By the end of 1957, Disneyland had recorded its ten-millionth visitor, surely a record for such a short period of time. Instead of the traditional roller coasters and

Ferris wheels that typified most parks, Disneyland used American history, the company's own cartoon characters, and other innovative approaches to differentiate it from the competition. Walt Disney himself meticulously oversaw each and every step in the development of the park. He had a vision, and he stuck to it. Profitable within months after opening, Disneyland attracted young and old, eagerly lined up, waiting to get in.[16]

Miniature Golf

First introduced in the late 1920s, and a brief fad during the Depression years, miniature golf had faded from public attention by the time of World War II. But with millions of cars on the roads, and with more leisure time than ever before, Americans rediscovered miniature golf during the booming 1950s. Instead of being located in towns and cities, however, the new courses tended to be sited along commercial strips in suburban areas.

Often, these reincarnations of older, simpler courses now served as lures to get motorists to pull off the busy highway. Many miniature golf operations followed in the path of the originals—home-built affairs with crude hazards and rough detailing. But when coupled with motels, drive-in theaters, or as part of large suburban shopping centers, they displayed a growing sophistication in design, with numerous small manufacturers offering complete, ready-made units from tees to hazards to cups. The more polished layouts featured fancy, carpeted "fairways," more complex hazards, and fluorescent lighting for night play. By the end of the decade, miniature golf had been reestablished as a favorite roadside pastime.[17]

Rail Travel

The decline of American rail service continued unabated into the 1950s. Total track mileage fell below what had existed at the turn of the century as rail companies slashed service and facilities. In 1950, the railroads still transported over three-quarters of distant passenger traffic; the airlines carried about 24 percent. But, in a rapid turnaround, by 1960 the airlines had captured almost two-thirds of this traffic; the railroads had only about 39 percent. Clearly, Americans preferred the speed and convenience of air travel to the slower trains.[18]

Faced with sharply rising costs and declining revenues, the nation's major railroads argued that they had no choice but to cut back. For example, during the 1950s, for every dollar taken in on dining cars, the railroads spent $1.44. Fighting back, they experimented with "Vistadome" observation cars and "Slumbercoaches" in the mid-1950s as a way of luring passengers, but the innovations had only limited success. Many lines spent large sums of money on passenger amenities, but the costs always exceeded any gains in revenue. In addition, the railroads faced skyrocketing labor expenses and recalcitrant unions that fought modernization with antiquated "featherbedding" rules. Frequently, labor costs absorbed more than 40 percent of the revenue on a typical run. In contrast, the airlines at the time could cover greater distances more quickly and labor accounted for only about 15 percent of all costs.

The speed of jet planes, the convenience of automobiles, and the difficulty of getting trains to specific destinations all contributed to the railroads' decline. In addition, tax laws drawn up during the heyday of rail travel favored road and airport construction, but ignored the needs of rail service. In order to keep up with this kind of competition, American railroads faced the onerous problems of obsolete equipment and the tremendous expense of modernizing. As a result, they chose to do nothing. Rather than upgrade their stock, they attempted to divest themselves of passenger service, arguing it cost too much to maintain. After considerable indecision, Congress and the Interstate Commerce Commission began to allow many lines to discontinue passenger service. As a result, by late in the decade only about half of the available tracks carried passengers, and in many small and medium-sized cities long accustomed to regular rail service, passenger trains existed only as a memory. For all practical purposes, American railroads abdicated their passenger responsibilities during the 1950s.

If the railroads saw any future at all in passenger service, it existed with commuters situated around the nation's larger cities. More and more families moved to the burgeoning suburbs, but most jobs remained in the cities. The challenge of transporting millions of commuters from home to job and back again might have been a bonanza for the railroads in those areas, but it seldom happened. A negative public perception about rail travel, brought about by years of neglect, led instead to the construction of endless superhighways and expressways to funnel people in and out of the cities, an approach that ignored the potential of rail travel.[19]

Air Travel

Prosperity meant that Americans strove to enlarge their travel horizons. The number of Americans who traveled abroad more than doubled between 1950 and 1959, with almost two million tourists heading across the seas. With only a couple of weeks at their disposal, they wanted to reach their destinations quickly, and that translated into air travel—the speedier the better.

The commercial airlines competed fiercely with each other to offer faster, longer flights. At the beginning of the decade, Lockheed's Super Constellation, an airliner powered by four piston engines, gained wide acclaim as the last word in air service. Fast and quiet, it offered comfortable seating, long range, and reliability. By 1953, TWA became the first airline to provide nonstop service between New York and California. In 1957, Pan American Airways offered nonstop flights over the profitable North Atlantic route, flying passengers from New York to London. In each of these examples, rival lines quickly caught up, and no one airline held an advantage for more than a few months.

In October of 1958, BOAC (British Overseas Airways Corporation) led the transition into jet travel by unveiling the de Havilland Comet passenger jet. It flew nonstop between London and New York in just over six hours, or about half the flight time of propeller-driven craft. Douglas and Boeing, the two largest U.S. airplane manufacturers, were not far behind; that same month they began marketing their own models, especially Boeing's 707, destined to become one of the most successful and popular jets of all time. Soon domestic carriers offered jets to several overseas cities and suddenly the world had grown smaller.[20]

As airplanes accommodated more and more passengers, the airlines began offering different grades of seating. They modeled this move on what railroads had long practiced: coach and first class. First class provided the traveler a slightly larger seat and more amenities, but coach offered a lower fare. People reacted positively to this change, and air travel surged. Between 1950 and 1960, passenger boardings more than doubled—from about seventeen million to almost forty million—and much of this came at the expense of the beleaguered railroads. In 1955, for the first time, the number of air passengers surpassed those riding trains.[21]

This rise in air traffic brought unanticipated demands on airports, and the fifties witnessed a rush to build or modernize facilities to keep up with demand. A kind of irony accompanied the expansion of airports: as these splendid new structures arose, the once-great rail terminals fell into disrepair and disuse. The government reacted to the growth of air travel by creating the Federal Aviation Administration (FAA) in 1958; it oversaw air safety, a much-needed authority following several disastrous crashes during the decade.

Ship Travel

On its maiden voyage in July of 1952, the S.S. *United States*, a brand-new American luxury liner, established a transatlantic speed record of 3 days, 10 hours, 40 minutes (United States to England), or 35.6 knots/hour, a mark that remains unbroken. On the westward return, the *United States* took only 3 days, 12 hours, 12 minutes (England to United States). As fate would have it, these accomplishments coincided with the rapid growth of North Atlantic air travel, where the same crossing took but hours. The *United States*, new as it was, would be decommissioned in 1969, its brief seventeen-year life a futile attempt to make sea travel an attractive tourist alternative. The era of the great ocean liners had drawn to a close.

SUMMARY

The American love affair with the automobile reached its height in the prosperous 1950s. People purchased new cars in record numbers, they moved to the suburbs and drove to work in the cities, they traveled more, and they demanded all the latest in style and equipment from their vehicles. In response, American culture adapted to this romance: the suburban shopping center emerged as a hub for both commerce and entertainment, as sparkling motels, drive-ins, and restaurants grew alongside the new highways networking the country. Traditional modes of travel, especially rail and ship, suffered precipitous declines. For most people, the automobile reigned supreme, and they readily accepted its rule.

The 1950s

12

Visual Arts

With the advent of the postwar era, it seemed that many artists turned their backs on realism and representation, that a fevered improvisation held more significance than a carefully rendered study. Elitist critics assured audiences that true art expressed raw emotion and that traditional painting had become hopelessly passé. Most American museums, conservative by nature, nonetheless relied on more traditional art to attract patrons. In response, avant-garde artists and critics attacked the system in manifestos accusing museums of provinciality, but for most Americans realism ruled the day. In other visual arts, newspaper comic strips continued to attract an impressive audience, but lapses of taste in comic books threatened an otherwise flourishing industry.

PAINTING

Popularizing Art

By the early 1950s, more Americans attended college than ever before; as a result, a commensurate rise in demand for "art" took place. In galleries and "art shoppes" across the country, the sales of original paintings increased markedly, and department stores and other nontraditional shopping outlets saw a soaring demand for prints and lithographs. Museums large and small experienced growth, and exhibitions of every kind welcomed young patrons eager for "culture."

With the exception of a few larger cities, most museums focused on well-known artists or classic periods in art, like the Renaissance or the "Old Masters" of the eighteenth and nineteenth centuries. Exhibitions displayed little contemporary work because curators feared public rejection or lack of funding. Even in the late fifties, the majority of major shows continued to revolve around traditional, representational art.

Established realistic artists like Edward Hopper (1982–1967), Georgia O'Keeffe (1887–1986), Ben Shahn (1898–1969), and Charles Sheeler (1883–1965), continued to produce work of considerable merit. A younger painter, Andrew Wyeth (b. 1917) increased his already significant audience throughout the decade. His meticulously detailed watercolors made him one of the most popular painters of the period.

Commercial television, rapidly becoming the most popular carrier of mass culture, occasionally attempted to add some luster to its usual lineup of sitcoms, detective shows, dramas, and sports by sponsoring a program dedicated to "Art"—be it classical music, ballet, serious drama, painting, sculpture, or any of the other so-called "high arts." And, because television is a visual medium, painting proved an obvious choice for these prestige presentations. Shows like *Omnibus* (1952–1959), *Camera 3* (1956–1979), and *Person to Person* (1953–1960) provided periodic outlets for discussions of contemporary painting, a subject not much broached in mass media.

Such productions, however, usually simplified artistic expression, a patronizing approach that attempted to both demystify art and make it understandable to the public. This came about because of the networks' ambivalence about anything modern or different. Outside of New York City, those artists working in the most modern, or avant-garde, styles could seldom gain an audience, whereas tried-and-true realists like Norman Rockwell and Grandma Moses were trotted before the cameras and received enthusiastic acclaim. In some popular magazines, a few of the more experimental painters might find their work discussed or reproduced, but often with a sardonic tone.

Norman Rockwell

A prolific artist and illustrator, Norman Rockwell (1894–1978) has served, for generations of Americans, as the epitome of a good, hardworking painter. A superb technician and stylist, Rockwell's talents also embraced a storyteller's vivid imagination. Essentially realistic narratives, most of his thousands of pictures reveal a bit of story that viewers find easy to follow. His greatest successes can be seen on the covers of the *Saturday Evening Post*, the primary carrier of his work. Rockwell painted 322 cover illustrations for the popular magazine, a series that commenced in 1916 when he was only 22 and went on until 1963, and he executed 42 of them during the 1950s. The *Post* boasted high circulation, so four million people, on average, saw each cover, allowing him the largest audience ever enjoyed by an artist before or since.[1]

A true classical painter who worked in the European tradition of bourgeois storytelling, Rockwell chose to focus on the passing American scene.

He displayed a penchant for folksy settings, casting them in a warm, sentimental, glow. Viewers can identify with a Rockwell narrative and make sense of the story. With this approach, and capitalizing on his technical skills, he set the standards for American illustration from the 1920s through the 1950s.

Most of those illustrators who followed in Rockwell's footsteps have been forgotten, as have many of the "serious" artists presumed to be superior to him. But Norman Rockwell's artwork survives, as well known now as during the fifties. His has been the lasting art, successfully blurring the line between high and low culture by focusing on popular culture. His work appeals to a large, diverse mass of people, and his public acceptance has ensconced him as the most beloved—and possibly the most influential—American artist of all time.

Grandma Moses

Other artists, besides Rockwell, employed a sentimentalized past as a primary focus. These include Queena Stovall (1887–1980) and Anna Mary Robertson Moses (1860–1961), better known to the public as "Grandma Moses." Of the two self-taught primitive painters, Moses gained greater popular renown and came to widespread attention during the 1940s. Already into her eighties and hardly a skilled technician, she at first employed common house paint, cheap brushes, and worked on any flat surfaces she could find. Gradually, however, she refined her techniques and began to employ artists' oils. More importantly, Moses possessed a keen business sense; in her own, plainspoken way, she understood audiences and promotion.[2]

She painted her recollections of rural America during the late nineteenth and early twentieth centuries. The details of farming—tiny cows and pigs, along with immaculate little houses, barns, and lots of people going about their everyday chores—fill her compositions. Her vision and technique may have been naïve, and she consistently portrayed an America that never truly existed, but one nonetheless reconstructed in collective memory. It struck a responsive chord with urbanized and suburbanized viewers, and soon sophisticated metropolitan galleries clamored for her paintings.

By the 1950s, people everywhere recognized the work of Grandma Moses. For audiences turned off by abstraction and other modern movements, she served as the perfect antidote. Her intricately detailed pictures of a bucolic past held great appeal in an age threatened with nuclear annihilation. In addition, her simple compositions told would-be artists that they, too, could paint. It all tied in nicely with the do-it-yourself craze that swept the country during the decade. President Harry Truman, more of an amateur piano player than painter, publicly lauded Moses, and at the same time denigrated "modern art."

Anna Mary Robertson Moses (1860–1961), better
known as Grandma Moses, is here seen in a posed
portrait, with rocking chair and "Grandma Moses
Wallpaper" serving as an appropriate background.
She touched a responsive chord among Americans
and rose to extraordinary fame and popularity in the
1950s; she reminded people of simpler times—"the
good old days." With anything Early American then
in vogue, her seemingly simple studies of
nineteenth-century farm life, complete with people,
machinery, architecture, and flora and fauna, found
a ready audience. She served as a link to the past,
albeit a carefully controlled and rendered past.
Source: Library of Congress.

The last years of Grandma Moses's life proved productive ones; she
turned out an estimated 1,500 paintings between 1938 and 1961. Her work
could be found reproduced on ceramics, tea towels, greeting cards, and a
host of other products. Through the merchandising of "Grandma Moses,"
she served as the subject of a TV documentary in 1955. Despite all the
hoopla and clever marketing, Moses seldom traveled, relying instead on
memory and photographs, along with the view from her home in Hoosick
Falls, New York. Moses died in 1961 at 101 years of age; by then a national
icon, she remained an active artist until a few months before her death.

Although she never achieved the popularity of her
contemporary, Grandma Moses, Queena Stovall (1887–1980)
nonetheless enjoyed a strong following among collectors
of paintings of American folklife. Widely exhibited in
galleries, her paintings sold briskly and have been
reproduced as prints. Her detailed evocations of rural life
in Virginia, as in *Toting Water* (above, 1951), are drawn
from memory or experience and often feature black
families, and established her as an important artist of the
time. Source: The Daura Gallery, Lynchburg College.

Abstract Expressionism

In retrospect, Abstract Expressionism can be seen as one of the defin-
ing movements in modern art. Sometimes referred to as "The New York
School," it signaled the shift of contemporary art from Paris to New York
City, that Paris had at last been replaced as the art capital of the world.
Unlike most movements in so-called "high," or elite, culture, Abstract
Expressionism received considerable press coverage. This stands as an
unusual situation, because traditional popular media usually shows little
interest in high culture. Despite the publicity, this emotional, expression-
istic approach to painting had precious little public appreciation during
the 1950s. None of the leading painters in the field could be considered
household names; the average person remained oblivious to almost all of
them, preferring instead the safety of tradition and convention.[3]

Paintings featuring jagged slashes of color and energetic brushstrokes with no identifiable images characterized the style, one that was personal in emotion, but monumental and public in scale. Over time, Abstract Expressionism affected every aspect of visual art, from advertising to fashion to traditional painting, but by itself the movement could hardly be considered a significant part of popular culture. Ripples from Abstract Expressionism permeated the nation's visual sensibility, so that wallpaper, fabrics, costume jewelry, graphics, illustration, and iconography reflected it in a variety of ways.

Artist Jackson Pollock (1912–1956), thanks to his colorful personality and unique method of dribbling and splattering paints directly onto a canvas, became the subject of much of the attention focused on this new generation of artists. Dubbed "Jack the Dripper" in mass magazines, he seemed to symbolize the creative genius as only slightly removed from madness. The media treated Pollock in a patronizing, disdainful tone instead of a laudatory one, and made little attempt to analyze or explain his controversial work. Most of his fellow artists did not receive even this level of recognition; Abstract Expressionism—often dismissively referred to as "modern art" when mentioned at all—became the butt of cheap shots by cartoonists and humorists. For most Americans, however, it was all undecipherable squiggles and blotches of paint, devoid of meaning—an unpopular art worth neither time nor attention. Even with the flurry of media interest, the general public remained blissfully unaware of these changes in the art world, with the result that the gulf between the average person and serious artistic expression grew ever wider.[4]

Paint-By-Number

In a decade marked by interest in hobbies and "do-it-yourself," a growing number of would-be artists tried painting. They would be assisted by the entrepreneurial Palmer Paint Company, a Detroit-based firm. As Palmer Paint watched the rising sales for original art and reproductions, several company employees hit upon the clever idea of do-it-yourself paintings that could be undertaken by anyone. Out of this came "Paint-by-Number." Palmer introduced its new products in 1951, and used the trade name Craft Master. Although they did not invent the concept—several other firms had similar products on the market by the late 1940s—the Palmer kits caught the public fancy. A boxed Paint-by-Number kit included up to 90 tiny capsules of premixed oil paint, two brushes, and a carefully printed canvas that showed a composition broken down into its constituent parts. Prices ranged from a dollar for a 12-color kit to a princely $8.95 for a panoramic, 90-color Super Craft Master. The canvases looked like nothing so much as tracings of original works. Minuscule outlined and numbered units separated details into light and dark, providing most of the colors and shadings found in the original. By matching the numbers to those on each vial of paint, and then applying the paint to the predetermined areas, a semblance of the original work would begin to emerge.[5]

Abhorred by critics and loved by the public, Paint-by-Number proved dull, tedious work, and it allowed for little or no improvisation. But the completed painting could usually be identified as a reasonable copy of the original–or at least so thought millions of would-be, bleary-eyed Rockwells and Rembrandts, bent over their canvases, carefully applying vermilion to all the shapes marked "24," and burnt sienna to those numbered "47." In many ways a popular response to the incomprehensibility of much modern art, the Paint-by-Number subjects provided traditional, recognizable realism, and proud artists who had labored over the numbered diagrams could claim the finished product was an original of sorts.

Craft Master saw demand for its products peak in 1954, with over twelve million units sold. Rivals like Craftint, Master Artists Materials, and Picture Craft rushed out imitations, but sales leveled out in the mid-fifties, when more than thirty-five firms competed for would-be painters. For much of the decade, however, Paint-by-Number kits, along with all the competition, remained steady sellers. In the meantime, critics of popular culture everywhere found "By-the-Numbers" a handy whipping boy for the perceived dilution of culture occurring during the fifties. For many, the fad represented a cheapening of traditional art, an unwonted intrusion by amateurs into the sacrosanct world of high art; for those eagerly purchasing the latest Craft Master kit, however, it gave them an outlet for creative urges once closed because of lack of education, training, or even skill.

SCULPTURE

General

Americans have never been especially keen about sculpture. The strong pioneer woman out by the state capital steps, baby cradled in her arms, facing the dangers of the frontier would be acceptable, as would the heroic leader, astride his horse, saber in the air, on the courthouse lawn. The primary criteria applied to most public sculpture have been that it be recognizable and understandable. Those governing bodies or committees chosen to select civic statues and monuments have tended to reject abstract forms or controversial subject matter. But some of that traditionalism began to break down in the 1950s, albeit slowly and reluctantly.

Alexander Calder

Among the handful of sculptors to achieve some renown during the 1950s, Alexander Calder (1898–1976) is best remembered for his "mobiles"—large, hanging arrangements of abstract organic shapes that turn and shimmer in the slightest breeze. They appear to defy gravity as they float above the spectator's head, and their bright colors catch the eye. People enjoyed looking at them, and their modern, nonrepresentational appearance did not detract from this pleasure. Calder mobiles graced several new buildings, bringing about an unconscious acceptance of more abstract sculpture. He also constructed a number of "stabiles"—large, motionless metal pieces that resembled his mobiles, but remained stationary on the ground. Calder fortunately won numerous commissions for his modernistic constructions, and the public tended to respond favorably to his work.[6]

Louise Nevelson

A lover of the "found object," Louise Nevelson (1899–1988) worked primarily in wood, employing turnings; stock items such as newel posts and moldings; and strays and discards obtained from demolition sites, junkyards, and lumber mills. She would stack this mix of odds and ends in various boxes until they created a freestanding wall. As a rule, she then painted the three-dimensional construction in a uniform flat black, white, or gold, giving the final result a surreal quality. Onlookers have to consider the assembly almost like a painting and view it as one would a stage, and the recognizable references to the building blocks of modern life attracted many people. Like Alexander Calder, Nevelson worked with abstraction, and also on a level that did not repel the audience.[7]

Other Sculpture

Calder's and Nevelson's work found an audience, albeit a small, selective one. On the other hand, the huge *Atomium*, the signature sculpture of the 1958 Brussels World Fair, was seen by millions, either at the fair site or endlessly reproduced on souvenirs. Those millions included a disproportionate number of traveling Americans, and they carried a vision of this combination of sculpture and architecture back to the United States. Built on the designs of Belgian engineer/architect Andre Waterkeyn, the structure represents an atom from an iron crystal, but magnified some 165 billion times. Over three hundred feet high, complete with the requisite restaurant and viewing area, it has become an icon, representing both the fair and a faith in the technological future. Its atomic motif suggests both hope for the future (the peaceful uses of nuclear energy) and the inherent threat of experimentation (nuclear annihilation).

Although the *Atomium* can be called neither "realistic" nor "American," it nonetheless achieved striking recognition and popularity in this country; its protons and electrons have been endlessly reproduced in advertising graphics and decorative items, its architecture flourished in modernistic strip malls, restaurants, and coffee shops, and its shiny streamlining reappeared in countless kitchen appliances.

One of the odder sculptural works of the twentieth century was begun in 1921 and reached completion in 1955. Simon Rodia's (1879–1965) Watts Towers, a soaring assemblage of structural steel, concrete, and found materials that the artist put together in his modest yard in the Watts section of Los Angeles, attracted little fanfare. But the Watts Towers stand as true vernacular art, an idiosyncratic composition that employs the detritus of everyday American life, from bottle caps to junked car parts, and speaks to the American ethic of consumption. Located in a somewhat rundown neighborhood, the towers have never attracted huge, overwhelming crowds, but they remain an iconoclastic comment on art, culture, and consumerism, and illustrate the truest kind of popular art.

PHOTOGRAPHY
Amateur Photography

By the 1950s, Americans everywhere were familiar with documentary photography. Every week, a new copy of *Life* or *Look* magazine arrived in their mailboxes, each filled with photographs chronicling events throughout the world. More importantly, such periodicals gave the public images of how the nation lived—what it consumed, what it liked and disliked, and what it found important. These magazines presented, in visual form, essays about American culture aimed at a vast audience. In addition, book-length collections of photographs, ranging from the hardships of the Great Depression to the horrors of World War II and the Korean War, graced people's coffee tables, and inexpensive cameras and film had long since made amateur photography accessible to all.

Home photography boomed in the 1950s. In the years following World War II, the giant Eastman-Kodak Corporation virtually monopolized the sales of small cameras and projectors. The mass importation of competitive German and Japanese cameras did not move into high gear until the later 1950s and early 1960s. As a result, Kodak Brownies and Hawkeyes dominated the market for small, inexpensive cameras. In addition, the Brownie eight-millimeter movie camera, introduced in 1951, allowed anyone to shoot home movies inexpensively.

About the only area of amateur photography not under Kodak's thumb involved instant pictures. In 1947, the first Polaroid cameras went on sale. The early models carried hefty price tags and proved sophisticated devices. Gradually prices came down, along with the cameras' complexity; by 1954, a Polaroid "Highlander" could be bought for $60 and consumers found it simple to use. Instant photography remained a niche market, but a popular one, and Polaroid had no competition throughout the decade.

The Family of Man

In 1955, when New York's Museum of Modern Art mounted a huge photography show titled *The Family of Man*, the curators confidently anticipated that viewers would be familiar with the medium. Organized by the respected photographer Edward Steichen (1879–1972), the exhibit consisted of over five hundred images that attempted to show, as its title states, the connectedness—the *family*—that is mankind. The museum displayed the work of 273 photographers from 68 different countries, the final choices culled from an initial, wide-ranging survey of over six million pictures. The majority came from the voluminous files of *Life* magazine, and staffers reduced the millions to 10,000 images, then to 1,000, and finally to the 503 photographs that constitute the exhibition. Steichen and his colleagues chose well; the show's success immediately dispelled any worries about its appeal: no grouping of black-and-white photographs, before or since, has ever attracted such a large audience.[8]

It has been estimated that by the end of the twentieth century well over nine million people had seen *The Family of Man*, either by attending the exhibition or by purchasing the best-selling book of the same name that reproduced the photographs. The book, however, cannot be equated with the show. The exhibition, laid out thematically and sequentially, moved viewers from room to room. The photographs themselves varied greatly in size and presentation. The book, on the other hand, exists as a record of the photographs, but reproduces them in roughly the same size on its pages, outside the contexts of the exhibition.

Many critics attacked the show as playing on cheap emotion, that it came across too sentimentally and lacked intellectual rigor, but therein rested its appeal. Steichen and his colleagues correctly assumed that people would react emotionally, not intellectually, to the imagery. Their theme built on the concept of the family overcoming the perils of the modern, industrialized world, making the exhibition particularly appropriate for the family-centered fifties. A popular term in the 1950s was "togetherness," and the hundreds of photographs linked common events—birth, eating, sleeping, love, death—into universal experiences. These pictures did not fall into the category of "art photographs" designed for the enjoyment of the connoisseur; instead, they provided snapshots of the human condition. For the United States, *The Family of Man* attracted primarily a middle-class, mass audience. It displayed the American ideal of "the pursuit of happiness" in clear images. So well did it reflect then-current national values that the United States Information Agency took the show on a seven-year worldwide tour, visiting over sixty countries.

COMIC STRIPS AND COMIC BOOKS

Comic Strips

By the 1950s, comic strips constituted a standard feature in virtually every American newspaper (over the years, the *Wall Street Journal* and the *New York Times* have been the major holdouts). Some people refer, nostalgically, to the 1920s and 1930s as the golden age of the comics, but the 1950s certainly possessed more than its fair share of memorable strips and artists. Many of the old pioneers still turned out quality material and continued to appear daily on the comic pages, but a number of new artists and writers nonetheless broke into this highly competitive business in the years following World War II. The decade turned out to be one of transition, as strips became more comical and less serious, as action and adventure gave way to more humor and family-oriented themes. Even with change, the comics retained their popularity and influence throughout the 1950s.[9]

As a rule, the younger cartoonists preferred a simpler visual style, rejecting much of the detail that characterized so much prewar comic art. Uncluttered frames and less shading became the hallmarks of much postwar drawing. Although many tried their hand at newspaper comics in the fifties, only a few rose to become popular favorites. Among that select group were the following:[10]

Charles Schulz

A struggling young cartoonist named Charles Schulz (1922–2000) in 1947 finally sold a daily strip to a St. Paul newspaper. He called his series *Li'l Folks* and attracted modest attention. Three years later, Schulz expanded the concepts he had been working with in *Li'l Folks* and United Features Syndicate picked up the revised strip. Renamed *Peanuts*, eight newspapers initially ran it. Within a year other papers subscribed to this unique comic that featured a round-headed boy named Charlie Brown and his circle of friends. *Peanuts* grew rapidly during the 1950s, establishing itself as a leading contender in a tight market; by the end of the decade, the strip appeared in over four hundred dailies. *Peanuts* emerged as one of the most popular of the many new postwar series that came along during the late forties and on into the fifties.

Schulz recognized the money to be made in merchandising: *Peanuts* lunch pails, posters, books, and other paraphernalia proliferated. The books alone, simple compendiums of the newspaper strips, did extremely well, selling in the hundreds of thousands. In a bow to the strip's popularity, in 1959 the Coasters recorded a new song, "Charlie Brown," that celebrated in a rock 'n' roll way the series' lead character.

Hank Ketcham

The fifties marked the baby boom, and numerous comic strips acknowledged the importance Americans placed on children. In 1951, Hank Ketcham's (b. 1920) *Dennis the Menace* made its debut. Like *Peanuts*, it quickly gained readers and popularity, distinguishing itself by being a single-panel cartoon, instead of the more traditional strip consisting of three or four separate frames. Deceptively simple in its drawing, Ketcham's flowing lines and effective use of silhouettes make an eye-catching panel. Dennis himself is an incorrigible—but loveable—five-year-old who delights readers with his constant mischief. He pretends innocence, however, and reflects the old American adage that "boys will be boys." Margaret, the primary girl appearing in the cartoon, is smart but prissy, and her presence reinforces some gender stereotypes, although this kind of criticism would have been almost nonexistent during the 1950s. By the end of the decade, *Dennis* ran in more than six hundred daily papers, and seven bound collections had been issued.

Mort Walker

Although World War II was over, military life still concerned many. The Cold War raged throughout the fifties, and the Korean conflict (1950–1953) cost America thousands of lives in casualties. Young men had to register for the draft, and each month trainloads of new recruits entered basic training. Small wonder, then, that a comic strip about citizen soldiers would find a receptive audience. *Beetle Bailey*, created by Mort Walker (b. 1923), met that need.

In the late 1940s, Walker had attempted an early cartoon series that dealt with a hapless young collegian called Spider. Facing stiff competition from other strips about adolescents, Walker in 1950 renamed Spider "Beetle." But no syndicates wanted college humor, so in 1951 Beetle found himself inducted into the Army, just as American involvement in the Korean War rose to its height. An immediate success after the change, *Beetle Bailey* climbed into the top ranks of comics. The humorous trials of Beetle, Sergeant Snorkel, Killer, General Halftrack, and a host of other recognizable characters soon had the strip syndicated in over seven hundred papers. Real wars and violence never play a role in the misadventures at Camp Swampy, but the entanglements with Army bureaucracy and the endless goofing off struck a responsive chord for millions of readers, many of them veterans.

Walt Kelly

Another crowded area in the daily comics involved animals. With Mickey Mouse, Bugs Bunny, and Felix the Cat attracting young readers, few papers expressed much interest in yet another talking dog, cat, or whatever. But cartoonist Walt Kelly (1913–1973) persisted. After a couple of abortive starts, including a stint doing comic books, he managed to introduce a lyrical newspaper strip called *Pogo* in 1949. Destined to enchant legions of devoted readers, *Pogo* seems, superficially, to be a continuing group of fables set in the Okeefenokee Swamp of Georgia. Given its locale, animals make up the cast—Pogo a possum, his friend Albert an alligator, Porky a porcupine, Seminole Sam a fox, Beauregard a bloodhound, and so on. He endows each character not only with a personality but also often with distinctive lettering in the speech balloons, and some speak in their own dialects.

If *Beetle Bailey* chronicles life in the Army, and *Peanuts* and *Dennis the Menace* the childhood years, *Pogo* tries for something much greater: a running commentary on the human condition. It sounds grandiose, but in true fabliaux tradition, the brief stories succeed in what they attempt. Greed, anger, envy, laziness—all the usual foibles have their day in poetic retellings read by young and old. Current events even receive some play, most memorably a 1952 episode that involves the notorious Senator Joseph McCarthy. Anything topical rarely provides fodder for the comics, but McCarthy—appropriately depicted as a jackal and named "Simple J. Malarkey"—receives his comeuppance from Kelly. To see something as contentious as the Army-McCarthy hearings on a newspaper comics page was unusual indeed.

Pogo won the hearts of its readers; they quickly supported a merchandising blitz featuring their favorite swamp figures. A series of *Pogo* books, incorporating reprinted material along with original work, became perennial best-sellers. The phrase, "I Go Pogo," insinuated itself into the language after the diminutive possum ran for political office. With over five hundred papers subscribing to the strip, *Pogo* stands as an unexpected success story in the rough-and-tumble world of comics.

Comic Books

In the years following World War II, a comic-book boom occurred; newsstands featured some 650 different titles, and by the early 1950s annual sales had climbed to one billion copies. Controversy, however, accompanied the industry's swelling numbers. The superheroes of World War II (Captain America, Blackhawk, Superman, Captain Marvel, et al.) seemed dated by the end of the forties, although a few of them did fight Commies, Reds, and any other enemy sympathizers during the Korean conflict. Teenage comic characters (Buzzy, Andy Hardy, Katy Keene, Suzie, Henry Aldrich, etc.) also appeared out of step with the times, especially with rock 'n' roll entering the picture. About the only consistency in the business revolved around children's comics—harmless tales of animals like Mighty Mouse, Woody Woodpecker, and Peter Rabbit, along with the whole Disney menagerie—steady sellers that underwent little change.[11]

Throughout the late forties and early fifties, publishers, in an attempt to lure more males to their product, freely used cheesecake, or attractive women in skimpy attire. "Jungle comics" proved especially popular in the early fifties, most of which featured half-dressed, statuesque women as their stars. Sheena, Queen of the Jungle, led the pack, but had competition from Lorna the Jungle Girl, Jann of the Jungle, Judy of the Jungle, Jungle Jo, and numerous others wearing leopard skins and little else. For their female readers, publishers borrowed from the popular confession magazines of the day and created *Secret Romances*, *Sweethearts*, *Young Love*, *Young Romance*, and a host of similar titles. Like radio soap operas and their pulp counterparts, these comics stressed domesticity, along with torn emotions, broken hearts, jealousy, and some heavy breathing and innuendo, but virtually no sex.

Still concerned about content and audiences, the industry experimented with crime and horror comics in the late forties. Stories about criminals had been a staple for some time, especially in the popular *Crime Does Not Pay* comic books. Horror, on the other hand, involved relatively new territory. The warm reception accorded *Adventure Into the Unknown* in late 1948 led to several imitators the following year. By 1950, publishers judged the experiment a success and jumped onto the crime and horror bandwagon. Their jump would have unexpected consequences.

William M. Gaines

In 1947, William M. Gaines inherited his father's company, Educational Comics (or EC on their cover logo). The firm published children's materials, and Gaines thought it hopelessly behind in the changing world of comic books. He tried several other approaches, such as Westerns and science fiction, and finally developed a new line of horror comics in 1950. Gaines still used the old logo, although he did change the meaning of the initials to mean "Entertaining Comics." Titles like *The Haunt of Fear*, *Shock SuspenStories*, *Tales from the Crypt*, and *The Vault of Horror* immediately found an adolescent/young adult market. Controversy dogged this new EC line, however, because the stories contained explicit drawings that critics thought exceeded all bounds of good taste.

Publishers ignored most of the criticism, and a flood of horror and fantasy comics appeared on newsstands, along with a number of violent crime comics. *Astonishing*, *Chamber of Chills*, *Crime Exposed*, *Crime Suspense Stories*, *Gangsters and Gun Molls*, *Terrifying Tales*, *Uncanny Tales*, *Weird Worlds*, and *Witches Tales* could be counted among the titles of these new sensations. Sales soared and the chorus of disapproval rose in volume.

Despite threats of censorship within the industry, Gaines remained undaunted; in 1952 he launched a new comic destined to become a classic: *Mad*. A kind of combination horror comic and satirical takeoff on movies, radio, celebrities, and the like, it mixed gore with hilarious spoofs of much ongoing popular culture. His target market of primarily adolescent boys reacted positively, but his timing was poor. In 1953, Congress began an investigation into the whole comic-book industry (discussed below), and distributors were wary of anything like *Mad*. As a result, Gaines altered *Mad*'s format in the summer of 1955. He eliminated color, printed on a higher-quality paper, raised the price, and called the "new" *Mad* a magazine. Now newsstands could carry *Mad* somewhere other than in the comic racks, solving the problem. In addition, the new, revised version of *Mad* focused almost exclusively on satire, making it a favorite of high school and college students. From that time onward, the magazine earned a profit and stirred little controversy—except occasionally from those who served as the butts of its sometimes-barbed humor.[12]

Censorship

While Gaines tinkered with *Mad*, rival publishers were stepping over most boundaries of good taste in their horror and crime comics. In 1954, psychiatrist Fredric Wertham published *Seduction of the Innocent*. Subtitled *The Influence of Comic Books on Today's Youth*, the book set off a groundswell of debate, much of it focusing on juvenile delinquency. Wertham, already prominent in the media as a social critic, claims in his book that reading comics leads to antisocial behavior, although he offers no supporting research. He comes down particularly hard on crime and horror comics, saying they provide virtual blueprints for criminal acts. Both superheroes and other favorites are blasted; Wertham maintains that the level of sex and violence in most comics overwhelms young, susceptible readers; exposure to such reading will lead to juvenile crime. A handful of carefully cropped illustrations purports to support his thesis, even suggesting that comic books contain hidden pornographic drawings. *Seduction of the Innocent*, as sensational as anything to be found in the comics, led to serious repercussions.[13]

That same year, a congressional committee led by Senator Estes Kefauver began investigating the causes of juvenile delinquency and added comic books to its list of subjects. Dr. Wertham, his book already a controversial best-seller, was asked by the committee to lead the attack on the industry. In the fall of 1954, twenty-six publishers of comic books responded by collaborating in the formation of the Comics Code Authority, an industry self-regulatory body. The Authority came up with "a seal of approval," an emblem that had to prominently adorn the covers of most new comic books found on newsstands in the United States. Many whole-salers refused to stock comics that lacked the seal, and so the industry quickly fell into line. Gaines dropped his horror series, as did many oth-ers, and colorless mediocrity seemed the safest route for the time. The bland content of the new approved titles bore little resemblance to the freewheeling stories of just a few months earlier.

By 1955, only about three hundred comic titles remained on newsstands, about half of what had been available five years earlier. Overall sales had fallen sharply, a trend that would continue for the remainder of the decade. Despite the industry's efforts, the public no longer saw comic books as harmless entertainments. But, while senators and psychologists searched for hidden meanings in comic books, television—another visual medium—was busy establishing itself in American homes. It presented itself as an electronic successor to the comic book for millions of kids and did more to hasten the industry's decline than any congressional hearings or muckraking books.

The latter half of the 1950s therefore found the comic-book industry treading water. Innocuous children's comics fared well, and science fic-tion, provided it avoided anything too frightening, had a following. Crime comics virtually disappeared from the racks, and horror and fantasy were toned down into blandness. A few superheroes—Superman, Batman, Wonder Woman—held on during these dark times, but not until the 1960s would the industry recoup and thrill a new generation of readers.[14]

The Comics on Film, Radio, and Television

Hollywood, along with radio and television, looked out for subjects that would attract audiences; early on, these entertainment media capitalized on the continuing popularity of newspaper strips and comic books. Both movies and radio enjoyed a considerable head start, but as TV overtook its old rivals, it quickly closed any gap that might have existed.

Chic Young's *Blondie*, dating from 1930 and one of the most durable newspaper strips ever, had the distinction of being the subject of twenty-eight feature films between 1938 and 1950, with two produced in 1950 alone. In addition, it appeared as an occasional comic book and played on radio from 1944 until 1950; it moved to television for a short-lived NBC series in 1957. Several actresses played Blondie in these incarnations, but Arthur Lake owned the character of Dagwood Bumstead, playing the role in the movies, on radio, and on television.

Similarly, *Superman* showed up in various media offerings. First a comic book back in 1938, then a daily strip that started in 1939 and ran until 1966, Superman was well established as a superhero in the public mind by the 1950s. And, given the Man of Steel's popularity, a radio serial chronicled his adventures from 1940 to 1951. Hollywood, slow to capitalize on the character, did release a couple of cartoons and two serials, one in 1948 and the other in 1950. Released as a feature-length film, *Superman and the Mole Men* (1951) served as the pilot for a television series starring George Reeves as both Clark Kent and the caped hero. The low-budget TV version ran in syndication from 1951 to 1957, eventually encompassing 104 episodes.[15]

A number of other newspaper strips enjoyed television production in the fifties: *Buck Rogers in the 25th Century* (1950–1951), *Dick Tracy* (1950–1951), *Joe Palooka* (1954), *Jungle Jim* (1955), *Mandrake the Magician* (1954), *Red Ryder* (1956), *Steve Canyon* (1958–1959), and *Terry and the Pirates* (1952). In addition, industry syndicators recycled over 250 of the classic *Popeye the Sailor* cartoons, making Saturday morning ritual viewing for youngsters around the country.

The *Sheena, Queen of the Jungle* comic books also made it to television in a 1955, syndicated version. By and large, however, the controversies surrounding the industry in the 1950s kept TV producers away from shows based on comic books. Instead, in the cleaned-up atmosphere of comic publishing, writers and illustrators took to borrowing from television and movies. *Davy Crockett*, *Gunsmoke*, *Howdy Doody*, *I Love Lucy*, and dozens of other popular TV shows had their comic-book versions, as did a number of big-name movies. Even a brief 3-D (for three-dimensional) fad flourished following the release of *Bwana Devil* in 1953. Readers however soon tired of reading comic books that required special red and green glasses, plus the stories proved not much better than their mediocre film counterparts. [See chapter 10, "Performing Arts," for more on the 3-D craze.]

Summary

A decade that embraced Paint-by-Number, the 1950s also introduced a dubious public to Abstract Expressionism. With time, a few of the newer, more abstract, artists did gain some recognition, but popular taste remained true to realistic, representational tradition. The success of *The Family of Man* invigorated photography, as did the strong sales of small cameras. A group of new cartoonists added life to newspaper comics, but comic books suffered restrictions after investigations led to the formation of the Comics Code Authority.

Cost of Products
in the 1950s

In order to figure the costs of goods and services during the fifties, several important adjustments have to be made either to the era's prices or to contemporary ones. Dollars then do not equal dollars now. Adjusted for inflation and averaged over the decade, the 1950s dollar is, in 2004, worth approximately $6.71. Conversely, a present-day dollar would be worth about 15 cents if spent during the fifties.

As an example of how conversion works, steak, the first item in the listing below, can serve as an illustration. In the fifties it averaged 94 cents a pound. Today, using a value of $1.00 (1950s) = $6.71 (2004), that pound of steak would cost (.94 × 6.71) about $6.31 a pound. Gasoline, also below, can do likewise: in the 1950s it could be had for around 20 to 25 cents a gallon. Again, using $1.00 = $6.71, 1950s gasoline today would cost $1.34 to $1.67 per gallon (.20 or .25 × 6.71). Similar calculations can be made for any of the other products and services listed below.[1]

Unless otherwise noted, all the figures given are approximations and averages for the decade, not precise, unchanging numbers. Prices tended to be lower during the first years of the decade, but inflation drove them steadily upward as time progressed.

FOOD

Steak, 94 cents/pound
Eggs, 72 cents/dozen
Milk, 21 cents/quart
Bread, 14 cents/loaf
Coffee, 55 cents/pound

CLOTHING

Men's oxford cloth shirt, $4–$5

Blue jeans, $3.75

Summer-weight sport coat, $15–$20

SHELTER AND FURNISHINGS

Median price for a single-family house (1950), $10,050

Typical bedroom suite, $50

Refrigerator, approximately $200

Electric stove, about $100

Bed sheets, 50 cents—$1.00 each

Bath towels, $1.50

PERSONAL ITEMS

Pocket Paper-Mate ballpoint pen, $1.69

Typical mid-grade wristwatch, $25

Hi-fi tape recorder, $49.95

After climbing steadily, yearly college tuition averaged $1,300 by the late 1950s

Three-minute, long-distance telephone call, $2.50

TRANSPORTATION

Round-trip air, New York to California, $88

Round-trip air, New York to Paris, $475

Rental car, $6/day plus 8 cents/mile

Street cars and buses, 10 cents a ride

Taxis, 25 cents first half-mile, 10 cents each half-mile thereafter

At the end of the decade, a mid-grade American sedan cost about $2,800

At the same time, imported compact cars sold for around $1,500

MEDICAL COSTS

Aspirin (30 tablets), 30 cents

Tooth extraction, $5.50

ENTERTAINMENT AND LEISURE

Portable typewriter, $37.50

A 12-inch TV cost about $400 in 1952; by the end of the decade it had fallen to $150 (with a larger screen)

A 12-inch long-playing record normally cost $3.98

An "English Bike" (one with gears, narrow tires, hand brakes, etc.) cost around $50

First-run movie tickets cost anywhere from $1to $2 (more in large cities)

Notes

CHAPTER 1: EVERYDAY AMERICA

1. See Clifford Edward Clark, Jr., *The American Home: 1800–1960* (Chapel Hill: University of North Carolina Press, 1986), 206, and Richard Layman, ed., *American Decades: 1950–1959* (Detroit, MI: Gale Research, 1994), 85.

2. For more on this aspect of American culture, see W.T. Lhamon, Jr., *Deliberate Speed: The Origins of Cultural Style in the American 1950s* (Washington, DC: Smithsonian Institution Press, 1990), 16, and Phil Patton, *Open Road: A Celebration of the American Highway* (New York: Simon & Schuster, 1986), 188.

3. J. Ronald Oakley, *God's Country: America in the Fifties* (New York: Dembner Books, 1986), 228.

4. Oakley, *God's Country*, 231.

5. James S. Olson, *Historical Dictionary of the 1950s* (Westport, CT: Greenwood Press, 2000), 66–67.

6. Joseph L. Seldin, *The Golden Fleece: Selling the Good Life to Americans* (New York: Macmillan, 1963), 42–54.

7. Theodore Caplow, Louis Hicks, and Ben J. Wattenberg, *The First Measured Century: An Illustrated Guide to Trends in America, 1900–2000* (Washington, DC: The AEI Press, 2001), 68–69, 78–79, 84–85.

8. Bill Osgerby, *Playboys in Paradise: Masculinity, Youth and Leisure-Style in Modern America* (New York: Berg, 2001), 63–76.

9. An overview of the civil rights crisis can be found in James T. Patterson, *Grand Expectations: The United States, 1945–1974* (New York: Oxford University Press, 1996), 375–406.

10. Oakley, *God's Country*, 298–99.

11. Eugenia Kaledin, *Daily Life in the United States, 1940–1959: Shifting Worlds* (Westport, CT: Greenwood Press, 2000), 91–115.

12. Paul Boyer, *By the Bomb's Early Light: American Thought and Culture at the Dawn of the Atomic Age* (New York: Pantheon Books, 1985), 303–33.

13. *TIME-LIFE* Editors, *The American Dream: The 50s* (Alexandria, VA: Time-Life Books, 1998), 82–85.

14. For more on the McCarthy era, see Patterson, *Grand Expectations*, 165–205.

15. Douglas T. Miller and Marion Nowak, *The Fifties: The Way We Really Were* (Garden City, NY: Doubleday, 1960), 314–21.

16. Layman, *American Decades*, 237–42, 247–48.

17. See Oakley, *God's Country*, 136–37, and Layman, *American Decades*, 195–210.

18. A discussion of the culture debates can be found in Dwight Macdonald, *Against the American Grain* (New York: Vintage Books, 1965), especially the lead article, "Masscult and Midcult," 1–75.

CHAPTER 2: WORLD OF YOUTH

1. Douglas T. Miller and Marion Nowak, *The Fifties: The Way We Really Were* (Garden City, NY: Doubleday, 1960), 269–90.

2. J. Ronald Oakley, *God's Country: America in the Fifties* (New York: Dembner Books, 1986), 280–88.

3. Thomas Doherty, *Teenagers and Teenpix: The Juvenilization of American Movies in the 1950s* (Boston: Unwin Hyman, 1988), 54–61.

4. For more on Gilbert, see Quentin J. Schultze, et al., *Dancing in the Dark: Youth, Popular Culture, and the Electronic Media* (Grand Rapids, MI, 1991), 76–83.

5. William Y. Elliott, *Television's Impact on American Culture* (East Lansing: Michigan State University Press, 1956), 182–86, 192–97.

6. A source for dances of the 1950s is StreetSwing.com. Available: http://www.streetswing.com/histmain/d5index.htm. (Accessed April 2, 2003).

7. For more on teenagers and cars, see Michael L. Berger, *The Automobile in American History and Culture: A Reference Guide* (Westport, CT: Greenwood Press, 2001), 151–55.

8. A narrative about this subculture is Tom Wolfe, *The Kandy*Kolored Tangerine*Flake Streamline Baby* (New York: Farrar, Straus & Giroux, 1963), 76–107.

9. Statistical data about the decade can be found in Theodore Caplow, Louis Hicks, and Ben J. Wattenberg, *The First Measured Century: An Illustrated Guide to Trends in America, 1900–2000* (Washington, DC: The AEI Press, 2001). Marriage data on 68–69.

10. Caplow, Hicks, and Wattenberg, *The First Measured Century*, 70–73, 86–87.

11. Peter Biskind, *Seeing Is Believing: How Hollywood Taught Us to Stop Worrying and Love the Fifties* (New York: Pantheon Books, 1983), 197–227.

12. Elliott, *Television's Impact on American Culture*, 173, 271–72.

13. Oakley, *God's Country*, 342–54.

14. Miller and Nowak, *The Fifties: The Way We Really Were*, 147–81.

15. Additional 1950s slang can be found in Howard Junker, "As We Used to Say in the '50s: A Short Course in Tribal Linguistics," *Esquire* (June 1983): 179–81.

CHAPTER 3: ADVERTISING

1. A collection of reprints of 1950s advertisements can be found in Jim Heimann, ed., *50s: All-American Ads* (New York: Taschen, 2001).

2. Donald C. Godfrey and Frederic A. Leigh, eds., *Historical Dictionary of American Radio* (Westport, CT: Greenwood Press, 1998), 4–9.

3. An anthology of old radio commercials can be found on Golden Age Radio, *101 Old Radio Commercials* (Plymouth, MN: Metacom, n.d.), compact disc.

4. Two Internet sources for old television commercials are The Internet Archive (Available: http://www.archive.org/movies/movies.php. [Accessed May 30, 2003]) and USA TV ADS (Available: http://www.usatvads.com. [Accessed May 30, 2003]).

5. Paul Rutherford, *The New Icons?: The Art of Television Advertising* (Toronto, Canada: University of Toronto Press, 1994), 10–14.

6. Lawrence R. Samuel, *Brought to You By: Postwar Television Advertising and the American Dream* (Austin: University of Texas Press, 2001), 46–50, 122–28.

7. Stephen Fox, *The Mirror Makers: A History of American Advertising and Its Creators* (New York: William Morrow, 1984), 172–73.

8. For more such examples, see Samuel, *Brought to You By*, 79–84.

9. Joseph L. Seldin, *The Golden Fleece: Selling the Good Life to Americans* (New York: Macmillan, 1963), 227–54.

10. Daniel Delis Hill, *Advertising to the American Woman, 1900–1999* (Columbus: Ohio State University Press, 2002), vii–xi.

11. Jim Hall, *Mighty Minutes: An Illustrated History of Television's Best Commercials* (New York: Harmony Books, 1984), 38–68.

12. Hill, *Advertising to the American Woman*, 215.

13. Hall, *Mighty Minutes*, 193–211.

14. Karal Ann Marling, *As Seen on TV: The Visual Culture of Everyday Life in the 1950s* (Cambridge: Harvard University Press, 1994), 202–40.

15. Samuel, *Brought to You By*, 34–37.

16. Jane Webb Smith, *Smoke Signals: Cigarettes, Advertising, and the American Way of Life* (Chapel Hill: University of North Carolina Press, 1990), 30–31.

17. Eric Clark, *The Want Makers: Inside the World of Advertising* (New York: Penguin Books, 1988), 233–258.

18. Mary Cross, ed., *A Century of American Icons: 100 Products and Slogans from the 20th-Century Consumer Culture* (Westport, CT: Greenwood Press, 2002), 116–17.

19. Fox, *The Mirror Makers*, 225–39.

20. Gerry Schremp, *Kitchen Culture: Fifty Years of Food Fads* (New York: Pharos Books, 1991), 55–56.

21. *God's Country* (New York: Dembner Books, 1986), 131–37.

CHAPTER 4: ARCHITECTURE AND DESIGN

1. Both Arthur J. Pulos, *The American Design Adventure, 1940–1975* (Cambridge, MA: MIT Press, 1988), 50–107, and Lester Walker, *American Shelter* (Woodstock, NY: The Overlook Press, 1996), 238–53, 258–63, are useful sources on innovative architecture of the 1950s, including prefabricated dwellings.

2. Clifford Edward Clark, Jr., *The American Home: 1800–1960* (Chapel Hill: University of North Carolina Press, 1986), 193–216.

3. Virginia McAlester and Lee McAlester, *A Field Guide to American Houses* (New York: Alfred A. Knopf, 1984), 475–83.

4. The trailer phenomenon is covered in Allan D. Wallis, *Wheel Estate: The Rise and Decline of Mobile Homes* (New York: Oxford University Press, 1991) and Andrew Hurley, *Diners, Bowling Alleys, and Trailer Parks: Chasing the American Dream in Postwar Consumer Culture* (New York: Basic Books, 2001), 195–272.

5. Dolores Hayden, *Redesigning the American Dream: The Future of Housing, Work, and Family Life* (New York: W.W. Norton, 1984), 1–38, and Theodore Caplow, Louis Hicks, and Ben J. Wattenberg, *The First Measured Century: An Illustrated Guide to Trends in America, 1900–2000* (Washington, DC: The AEI Press, 2001), 94–97.

6. Kenneth T. Jackson, *The Crabgrass Frontier: The Suburbanization of America* (New York: Oxford University Press, 1985), 234–45.

7. Gwendolyn Wright, *Building the Dream: A Social History of Housing in America* (New York: Pantheon Books, 1981), 240–61.

8. Lifestyles in these new communities are covered in Herbert J. Gans, *The Levittowners: Ways of Life and Politics in a New Suburban Community* (New York: Columbia University Press, 1982); information on landscaping can be found in Virginia Scott Jenkins, *The Lawn: A History of an American Obsession* (Washington, DC: Smithsonian Institution Press, 1994), 96–115.

9. John Keats, *The Crack in the Picture Window* (Cambridge, MA: Riverside Press, 1956).

10. Elaine Tyler May, *Homeward Bound: American Families in the Cold War Era* (New York: Basic Books, 1988), 103–13, and Willard Bascom, "Scientific Blueprint for Atomic Survival," *Life*, 42:11 (March 15, 1957), 146–62.

11. Christopher Finch, *Highways to Heaven: The AUTO Biography of America* (New York: HarperCollins, 1992), 225–47.

12. This unique area of architecture is covered in Alan Hess, *Googie: Fifties Coffee Shop Architecture* (San Francisco: Chronicle Books, 1986).

13. John A. Jakle, Keith A. Sculle, and Jefferson S. Rogers, *The Motel in America* (Baltimore, MD: The Johns Hopkins University Press, 1996), 262–85.

14. Hess, *Googie*, 96–107.

15. Alison J. Clarke, *Tupperware: The Promise of Plastic in 1950s America* (Washington, DC: Smithsonian Institution Press, 1999) covers the Tupperware phenomenon.

16. An overview of changing domestic design can be found in Arthur J. Pulos, *The American Design Adventure, 1940–1975* (Cambridge, MA: MIT Press, 1988), 110–61.

17. For a photographic overview of 1950s design, see Kathryn Hiesinger, *Design Since 1945* (Philadelphia: Philadelphia Museum of Art, 1983), 43–201, and Lisa Phillips, *High Styles: Twentieth-Century American Design* (New York: Whitney Museum of American Art, 1985), 128–157.

18. Cara Greenberg, in *Mid-Century Modern: Furniture of the 1950s* (New York: Harmony Books, 1984), examines mass-produced furniture and synthetics.

CHAPTER 5: FASHION

1. Lynn Schnurnberger, *Let There Be Clothes: 40,000 Years of Fashion* (New York: Workman Publishing, 1991), 373.

2. Frank W. Hoffmann and William G. Bailey, *Fashion & Merchandising Fads* (New York: The Haworth Press, 1994), 35.

3. Kate Mulvey and Melissa Richards, *Decades of Beauty: The Changing Image of Women, 1890s–1990s* (New York: Checkmark Books, 1998), 117–34.

4. Georgina Howell, *In Vogue: 75 Years of Style* (London: Conde Nast Books, 1991), 136–45.

5. Mulvey and Richards, *Decades of Beauty*, 127–29.

6. Jane Dorner, *Fashion in the Forties and Fifties* (New Rochelle, NY: Arlington House, 1975), 79–101.

7. Ernestine Carter, *The Changing World of Fashion: 1900 to the Present* (New York: G.P. Putnam's Sons, 1977), 71.

8. Ellen Melinkoff, *What We Wore: An Offbeat Social History of Women's Clothing, 1950 to 1980* (New York: Quill, 1984), 30.

CHAPTER 6: FOOD AND DRINK

1. Sherrie A. Innes, *Dinner Roles: American Women and Culinary Culture* (Iowa City: University of Iowa Press, 2001), 142–47.

2. Both Karal Ann Marling, *As Seen on TV: The Visual Culture of Everyday Life in the 1950s* (Cambridge, MA: Harvard University Press, 1994), 203–40, and Gerry Schremp, *Kitchen Culture: Fifty Years of Food Fads* (New York: Pharos Books, 1991), 39–43, provide information on 1950s cookbooks.

3. Rom J. Markin, *The Supermarket: An Analysis of Growth, Development, and Change* (Pullman: Washington State University Press, 1963), 1–3, 43–52.

4. "Topher's Cereal Character Guide." Available: http://www.lavasurfer.com/cereal-guide.html. (Accessed May 16, 2003).

5. National Association of Margarine Manufacturers. "History of Margarine." Available: http://www.margarine.org. (Accessed May 16, 2003).

6. Joseph L. Seldin, *The Golden Fleece: Selling the Good Life to Americans* (New York: Macmillan, 1963), 51.

7. Kenneth Morris, Marc Robinson, and Richard Kroll, eds., *American Dreams: One-Hundred Years of Business Ideas and Innovation from "The Wall Street Journal"* (New York: Light Bulb Press, 1990), 136.

8. Alison J. Clarke, *Tupperware: The Promise of Plastic in 1950s America* (Washington, DC: Smithsonian Institution Press, 1999), 34–128.

9. Charles Panati, *Extraordinary Origins of Everyday Things* (New York: Harper & Row, 1987), 105–07.

10. The story of Ray Kroc and McDonald's can be found in John F. Love, *McDonald's: Behind the Arches* (New York: Bantam Books, 1986).

11. Christopher Finch, *Highways to Heaven: The AUTO Biography of America* (New York: HarperCollins, 1992), 237–38.

12. Jane Stern and Michael Stern, *American Gourmet* (New York: HarperCollins, 1991), 97–131.

13. Harvey Levenstein, *Paradox of Plenty: A Social History of Eating in Modern America* (New York: Oxford University Press, 1993), 125–27.

14. Two books about American drinking habits are Barnaby Conrad, III, *The Martini: An Illustrated History of an American Classic* (San Francisco: Chronicle Books, 1995), and Joseph Lanza, *The Cocktail: The Influence of Spirits on the American Psyche* (New York: St. Martin's Press, 1995).

15. Chris H. Beyer, *Coca-Cola Girls: An Advertising Art History* (Portland, OR: Collectors Press, 2000), 216–69.

16. Mark Pendergrast, *For God, Country and Coca-Cola* (New York: Charles Scribner's Sons, 1993), 237–76, has much on the "cola wars."

CHAPTER 7: LEISURE ACTIVITIES

1. For information on pranks, as well as other fads, see Charles Panati, *Panati's Parade of Fads, Follies, and Manias* (New York: HarperCollins, 1991), 266–68.

2. For information on chlorophyll as a food additive, as well as other fads, see Paul Sann, *Fads, Follies and Delusions of the American People* (New York: Crown Publishers, 1967), 133–35.

3. Charles Panati, *Extraordinary Origins of Everyday Things* (New York: Harper & Row, 1987), 372–73.

4. For information on Scrabble and other games, see Andrew Marum and Frank Parise, *Follies and Foibles: A View of 20th Century Fads* (New York: Facts on File, 1984), 82, 86.

5. Panati, *Panati's Parade of Fads, Follies, and Manias*, 251–52.

6. Sann, *Fads, Follies and Delusions of the American People*, 27–30.

7. For more on Hasbro Toys, visit their Web site. Available: http://www.Hasbro.com. (Accessed March 3, 2003).

8. History of Boy's Clothing. Available: http://www.histclo.hispeed.com/style/head/cap/. (Accessed May 22, 2003).

9. For a good overview of powered toys, see Richard O'Brien, *The Story of American Toys: From the Puritans to the Present* (New York: Abbeville Press, 1990), 164–85.

10. Japanese imports are covered in Teruhisa Kitahara, *Yesterday's Toys: Robots, Spaceships, and Monsters*, vol. 3 (San Francisco: Chronicle Books, 1989).

11. William H. Young, "Barbie," in *Encyclopedia of American Studies*, vol. 1, ed. George T. Kurian, et al. (New York: Grolier Educational, 2001), 216–17.

12. Steven M. Gelber, in *Hobbies: Leisure and the Culture of Work in America* (New York: Columbia University Press, 1999), provides information on the subject.

13. For a discussion of this phenomenon, see Carolyn M. Goldstein, *Do It Yourself: Home Improvement in 20th-Century America* (New York: Princeton Architectural Press, 1998).

14. Both William L. Bird, Jr., *Paint by Number: The How-To Craze that Swept the Nation* (Princeton, NJ: Princeton Architectural Press, 2001), and Dan Robbins, *Whatever Happened to Paint by Numbers? A Humorous Personal Account* (Delavan, WI: Possum Hill Press, 1998) cover this phenomenon.

15. A discussion of the cultural significance of bowling can be found in Andrew Hurley, *Diners, Bowling Alleys, and Trailer Parks: Chasing the American Dream in Postwar Consumer Culture* (New York: Basic Books, 2001), 107–93.

16. More on Native Dancer can be found online. Available: http://www.fortunecity.com/marina/commodity/nativedancer.html. (Accessed May 20, 2003).

17. Joseph L. Seldin, *The Golden Fleece: Selling the Good Life to Americans* (New York: Macmillan, 1963), 54.

CHAPTER 8: LITERATURE

1. An overview of the paperback revolution can be found in Richard Lupoff, *The Great American Paperback: An Illustrated Tribute to Legends of the Book* (Portland, OR: Collectors Press, 2001).

2. Another source of information on paperbacks is Piet Schreuders, *Paperbacks, U.S.A.: A Graphic History, 1939–1959* (San Diego: Blue Dolphin Enterprises, 1981).

3. James S. Olson, *Historical Dictionary of the 1950s* (Westport, CT: Greenwood Press, 2000), 245.

4. For a biography of Graham, see William Martin, *A Prophet with Honor: The Billy Graham Story* (New York: William Morrow, 1991).

5. For an introduction to writers of the period, including Salinger, see Jonathan Baumbach, *The Landscape of Nightmare: Studies in the Contemporary American Novel* (New York: New York University Press, 1965).

6. Richard Layman, ed., *American Decades: 1950–1959* (Detroit, MI: Gale Research, 1994), 46.

7. Emily Toth, *Inside Peyton Place: The Life of Grace Metalious* (New York: Doubleday, 1981).

8. Alfred Appel, Jr., ed., in Vladimir Nabokov, *The Annotated "Lolita"* (New York: McGraw-Hill Book Company, 1970), ix–lxxvi.

9. Holly George-Warren's collection, *The "Rolling Stone" Book of the Beats: The Beat Generation and American Culture* (New York: Hyperion, 1999), provides a starting point for studying these writers.

10. Thomas Newhouse, *The Beat Generation and the Popular Novel in the United States, 1945–1970* (Jefferson, NC: McFarland, 2000), 49–71.

11. For more on the Great Books Program, visit The Great Books Foundation Web site. Available: http://www.greatbooks.org/about/index.shtml. (Accessed April 22, 2003).

12. See Lynn Z. Bloom, *Doctor Spock: Biography of a Conservative Radical* (Indianapolis: Bobbs-Merrill, 1972), and Jessica Weiss, *To Have and to Hold: Marriage, the Baby Boom & Social Change* (Chicago: University of Chicago Press, 2000), 92.

13. Paul Sann, *Fads, Follies and Delusions of the American People* (New York: Crown Publishers, 1967), 123–25.

14. Much of the statistical information in this section comes from Edwin Emery, *The Press and America: An Interpretative History of Journalism* (Englewood Cliffs, NJ: Prentice-Hall, 1962), 651–87.

15. Theodore Peterson, in his *Magazines in the Twentieth Century* (Urbana: University of Illinois Press, 1964), provides sketches of the periodicals discussed in this section.

16. Jay S. Harris, ed., *"TV Guide": The First 25 Years* (New York: Simon & Schuster, 1978).

17. Peterson, *Magazines in the Twentieth Century*, 379–82.

18. Most of the failures and successes among magazines of the 1950s are listed in Amy Janello and Brennon Jones, *The American Magazine* (New York: Harry N. Abrams, 1991).

19. Emery, *The Press and America*, 670–87.

20. A standard history of newspapers is Frank Luther Mott, *American Journalism, A History: 1690–1960*, 3rd edition (New York: Macmillan, 1962), 803–57.

21. Louis Solomon, *America Goes to Press: The Story of Newspapers from Colonial Times to the Present* (New York: Crowell-Collier Press, 1970), 104–23.

22. See Jan Pottker and Bob Speziale, *Dear Ann, Dear Abby: The Unauthorized Biography of Ann Landers and Abigail Van Buren* (New York: Dodd, Mead & Company, 1987).

CHAPTER 9: MUSIC

1. J. Ronald Oakley, *God's Country: America in the Fifties* (New York: Dembner Books, 1986), 280.

2. Carl Belz, *The Story of Rock*, 2nd ed. (New York: Oxford University Press, 1972), 45ff.

3. Roy M. Prendergast, *A Neglected Art: A Critical Study of Music in Films*, 2nd ed. (New York: New York University Press, 1992), 98–174.

4. Russell Sanjek, *Pennies from Heaven: The American Popular Music Business in the Twentieth Century* (New York: Da Capo Press, 1988), 333–66.

5. Wes Smith, *Pied Pipers of Rock 'n' Roll: Radio Deejays of the 50s and 60s* (Marietta, GA: Longstreet Press, 1989), 160ff.

6. Another study of the American disc jockey is Arnold Passman, *The Deejays* (New York: Macmillan, 1971).

7. Sanjek, *Pennies from Heaven*, 439–90.

8. Myra Lewis and Murray Silver, *Great Balls of Fire: The Uncensored Story of Jerry Lee Lewis* (New York: William Morrow, 1982).

9. Donald Clarke, *The Rise and Fall of Popular Music* (New York: St. Martin's Press, 1995), 365–401.

10. Richard Welch, "The Making of the American Dream: Rock 'n' Roll and Social Change," *History Today*, 40 (February 1990): 32–39.

11. Among the many biographies is Peter Guralnick, *Last Train to Memphis: The Rise of Elvis Presley* (Boston: Little, Brown, 1994).

12. A good study of the Presley phenomenon is Greil Marcus, *Mystery Train: Images of America in Rock 'n' Roll Music* (New York: E.P. Dutton, 1975).

13. See Arnold Shaw, *The Rockin' 50s* (New York: Hawthorn Books, 1974), 122–29, and Joe Smith, *Off the Record: An Oral History of Popular Music* (New York: Warner Books, 1988), 109–10.

14. For the radio version, see John Dunning, *On the Air: The Encyclopedia of Old-Time Radio* (New York: Oxford University Press, 1998), 738–40; for television, see Alex McNeil, *Total Television: The Comprehensive Guide to Programming from 1948 to the Present*, 4th ed. (New York: Penguin Books, 1996), 936.

15. For more on *American Bandstand*, visit The Museum of Broadcast Communications Web site. Available: http://www.museum.tv/archives/etv/A/htmlA/americanband/americanband.htm. (Accessed May 30, 2003).

16. Dunning, *On the Air*, 177–78.

CHAPTER 10: PERFORMING ARTS

1. Hal Morgan and Dan Symmes, *Amazing 3-D* (Boston: Little, Brown, 1982), 7–105.

2. For more on the technical aspects of film and various projection systems, see James Monaco, *How to Read a Film* (New York: Oxford University Press, 1981), especially chapter 2, "Image and Sound," 86–91.

3. William Boddy, *Fifties Television: The Industry and Its Critics* (Urbana: University of Illinois Press, 1990), 138.

4. Kenneth Hey, "Car and Films in American Culture, 1929–1959" in *The Automobile and American Culture*, David L. Lewis and Laurence Goldstein, eds. (Ann Arbor: University of Michigan Press, 1983), 193–205.

5. An overview of this subject is Nora Sayre, *Running Time: Films of the Cold War* (New York: Dial Press, 1982), particularly 3–29.

6. Both James Naremore, *More Than Night: Film Noir and Its Contexts* (Berkeley: University of California Press, 1998) and Alain Silver and Elizabeth Ward, *Film Noir: An Encyclopedia of the American Style* (Woodstock, NY: Overlook Press, 1992) provide introductions to this style.

7. John Douglas Eames, in *The MGM Story: The Complete History of Fifty Roaring Years* (New York: Crown, 1975), 232–97, covers the giant studio during the 1950s.

8. An overview of the stage and film is Amy Henderson and Dwight Blocker Bowers, *Red, Hot & Blue: A Smithsonian Salute to the American Musical* (Washington, DC: Smithsonian Institution Press, 1996).

9. MGM/UA has released three videos (VHS format) that cover movie musicals. They are *That's Entertainment!*, dir. Jack Haley, Jr. (1974), *That's Entertainment! Part II*, dir. Gene Kelly (1976), and *That's Dancing!*, dir. Jack Haley, Jr. (1985).

10. John Baxter, *Science Fiction in the Cinema* (New York: A.S. Barnes, 1970), 102–69.

11. George N. Fenin and William K. Everson, *The Western: from Silents to Cinerama* (New York: Orion Press, 1962), 264–317, 331–41.

12. James Harvey, *Movie Love in the Fifties* (New York: Alfred A. Knopf, 2001), 311–29.

13. Boddy, *Fifties Television*, 132–49.

14. Christopher Sterling and John M. Kittross provide a history of postwar American radio in *Stay Tuned: A Concise History of American Broadcasting* (Belmont, CA: Wadsworth Publishing, 1990), 246–315.

15. Frank Luther Mott, *American Journalism, A History: 1690–1960*, 3rd edition (New York: Macmillan, 1962), 822–28.

16. Sterling and Kittross, *Stay Tuned*, 253–55, 277–90.

17. Raymond William Stedman, *The Serials: Suspense and Drama by Installment* (Norman: University of Oklahoma Press, 1971), 380–480.

18. There exist numerous listings of American radio programming through the decades. One of the most thorough is John Dunning's *On the Air: The Encyclopedia of Old-Time Radio* (New York: Oxford University Press, 1998); it has served as the source for the titles and dates in table 10.1.

19. Erik Barnouw, *A History of Broadcasting in the United States. Vol. 2: The Golden Web* (New York: Oxford University Press, 1968), 216–303.

20. A discussion of the aesthetics of television can be found in Karal Ann Marling's *As Seen on TV: The Visual Culture of Everyday Life in the 1950s* (Cambridge, MA: Harvard University Press, 1994), 165–201.

21. As was the case with radio (above), Sterling and Kittross's *Stay Tuned*, 290–300 is also a good source on television history.

22. Sterling and Kittross, 324–28.

23. Erik Barnouw, *Tube of Plenty: The Evolution of American Television* (New York: Oxford University Press, 1982), 140–48.

24. Lawrence W. Lichty and Malachi C. Topping, *American Broadcasting: A Source Book on the History of Radio and Television* (New York: Hastings House, 1975), 522.

25. Irving Settel and William Laas, *A Pictorial History of Television* (New York: Grosset & Dunlap, 1969), 59–60.

26. Harry Castleman and Walter J Podrazik, *Watching TV: Four Decades of American Television* (New York: McGraw-Hill, 1982), 11–14, 104–8.

27. Boddy, *Fifties Television*, 49–57.

28. A discussion of all the rating systems can be found in Karen S. Buzzard, *Chains of Gold: Marketing the Ratings and Rating the Markets* (Metuchen, NJ: Scarecrow Press, 1990).

29. A number of statistical and chronological studies of TV programming can be found in most libraries. One is Alex McNeil's *Total Television: The Comprehensive Guide to Programming from 1948 to the Present*, 4th edition (New York: Penguin Books, 1996).

30. *Variety* Books, *The "Variety" History of Show Business* (New York: Harry N. Abrams, 1993), 97–99.

31. A good source on *I Love Lucy* and other popular sitcoms is Gerard Jones, *Honey, I'm Home. Sitcoms: Selling the American Dream* (New York: Grove Weidenfeld, 1992), 3–133.

32. Lynn Spigel, in *Make Room for TV: Television and the Family Ideal in Postwar America* (Chicago: University of Chicago Press, 1992), discusses the domestic sitcom at length.

33. For more on this television genre, see Larry James Gianokos, *Television Drama Series Programming: A Comprehensive Chronicle, 1947–1959* (Metuchen, NJ: Scarecrow Press, 1980).

34. This listing and all subsequent ones in this section, as well as the parenthesized dates in the text, come from McNeil, *Total Television*.

35. For more on this television genre, see Muriel G. Cantor and Suzanne Pingree, *The Soap Opera* (Beverly Hills, CA: Sage Publications, 1983), 47–95.

36. For more on this television genre, see J. Fred MacDonald, *Who Shot the Sheriff? The Rise and Fall of the Television Western* (New York: Praeger, 1987).

37. For more on the scandals and quiz shows in general, see Kent Anderson, *Television Fraud: The History and Implications of the Quiz Show Scandals* (Westport, CT: Greenwood Press, 1979).

38. For more on this television genre, see Robert Larka, *Television's Private Eye: An Examination of Twenty Years of Programming of a Particular Genre, 1949–1969* (New York: Arno, 1979).

39. For more on television coverage of news, see Edward J. Epstein, *News from Nowhere: Television and the News* (New York: Random House, 1973), 133–236.

40. The interrelationships between sports and television are covered in Benjamin G. Rader, *In Its Own Image: How Television Has Transformed Sports* (New York: Free Press, 1984), 7–46.

41. McNeil, *Total Television*, 843–46, 850–57.

42. Castleman and Podrazik, *Watching TV*, 31–32, 39, 103, 138.

CHAPTER 11: TRAVEL AND RECREATION

1. Joseph L. Seldin, *The Golden Fleece: Selling the Good Life to Americans* (New York: Macmillan, 1963), 48–49.

2. Information on the New Jersey Turnpike and other 1950s highways can be found in Angus Kress Gillespie and Michael Aaron Rockland, *Looking for America on the New Jersey Turnpike* (New Brunswick, NJ: Rutgers University Press, 1989).

3. John B. Rae, *The Road and the Car in American Life* (Cambridge, MA: MIT Press, 1971), 170–94.

4. For information on the automobile culture of the decade, see David Halberstam, *The Fifties* (New York: Villard Books, 1993), 487–95.

5. The business side of the industry is discussed in James M. Rubenstein, *Making and Selling Cars: Innovation and Change in the U.S. Automotive Industry* (Baltimore, MD: The Johns Hopkins University Press, 2001), 185–215.

6. Yasutoshi Ikuta, *Cruise-O-Matic: Automobile Advertising of the 1950s* (San Francisco: Chronicle Books, 1987), 19.

7. Much of the information for this chart was adapted from *Consumer Guide* Editors, *Automobiles of the '50s* (Lincolnwood, IL: Publications International, 1999), 4–96.

8. *Automobile Quarterly* Editors, *Corvette! Thirty Years of Great Advertising* (Princeton, NJ: Princeton Publishing, 1983), 6–57.

9. The Volkswagen story is detailed in Frank Rowsome, Jr., *Think Small: The Story of Those Volkswagen Ads* (Brattleboro, VT: Stephen Greene Press, 1970).

10. Earl's influence is chronicled in Stephen Bayley, *Harley Earl and the Dream Machine* (New York: Alfred A. Knopf, 1983), 47–110.

11. A good study of these vehicles is Roger B. White, *Home on the Road: The Motor Home in America* (Washington, DC: Smithsonian Institution Press, 2000), 83–162.

12. John A. Jakle, *The Tourist: Travel in Twentieth-Century North America* (Lincoln: University of Nebraska Press, 1985), 185–89.

13. J. Ronald Oakley, *God's Country: America in the Fifties* (New York: Dembner Books, 1986), 259.

14. John Margolies, *Home Away from Home: Motels in America* (Boston: Little, Brown, 1995), 90.

15. Wilson's account is given in Kemmons Wilson, *The Holiday Inn Story* (New York: The Newcomen Society, 1968).

16. The rise of contemporary amusement parks is detailed in Judith A. Adams, *The American Amusement Park Industry: A History of Technology and Thrills* (Boston: Twayne Publishers, 1991), 87–104.

17. Chester H. Liebs, *Main Street to Miracle Mile: American Roadside Architecture* (Baltimore, MD: The Johns Hopkins University Press, 1985), 136–51.

18. Oakley, *God's Country*, 396.

19. John F. Stover, *The Life and Decline of the American Railroad* (New York: Oxford University Press, 1970), 192–271.

20. *American Heritage* Editors, *The "American Heritage" History of Flight* (New York: Simon & Schuster, 1962), 375.

21. Richard Layman, ed., *American Decades: 1950–1959* (Detroit, MI: Gale Research, 1994), 87.

CHAPTER 12: VISUAL ARTS

1. More on Rockwell's work can be found in Thomas S. Buechner, *Norman Rockwell: Artist and Illustrator* (New York: Harry N. Abrams, 1970), and Maureen Hart Hennessey and Anne Knutson, *Norman Rockwell: Pictures for the American People* (New York: Harry N. Abrams, 1999).

2. Two good studies of Grandma Moses are Jane Kallir's *Grandma Moses: The Artist Behind the Myth* (New York: Clarkson N. Potter, 1982) and in Karal Ann Marling's *As Seen on TV: The Visual Culture of Everyday Life in the 1950s* (Cambridge, MA: Harvard University Press, 1994), 75–80.

3. Much has been written about abstract expressionism; one starting place is Thomas Crow, *Modern Art in the Common Culture* (New Haven, CT: Yale University Press, 1996), 1–48. In addition, critic Clement Greenberg's seminal essay, "Avant-Garde and Kitsch," can be found in his *Art and Culture* (Boston: Beacon Press, 1961), 3–21.

4. Irving Sandler, *The New York School: The Painters and Sculptors of the Fifties* (New York: Harper & Row [Icon], 1978), 1–28.

5. Two histories of this phenomenon are William L. Bird, Jr., *Paint by Number: The How-To Craze That Swept the Nation* (Princeton, NJ: Princeton Architectural Press, 2001) and Dan Robbins, *Whatever Happened to Paint by Numbers? A Humorous Personal Account* (Delavan, WI: Possum Hill Press, 1998).

6. For more on Calder, see Joan M. Marter, *Alexander Calder* (New York: Cambridge University Press, 1991).

7. For more on Nevelson, see Arnold B. Glimcher, *Louise Nevelson* (New York: Praeger, 1972).

8. An overview of the show can be found in Eric J. Sandeen, *Picturing an Exhibition: "The Family of Man" and 1950s America* (Albuquerque: University of New Mexico Press, 1995).

9. Discussions of many popular newspaper strips can be found in Maurice Horn's *100 Years of American Newspaper Comics* (New York: Gramercy Books, 1996), and his *The World Encyclopedia of Comics* (New York: Chelsea House Publishers, 1976).

10. The new cartoonists of the 1950s are treated in Stephen Becker, *Comic Art in America* (New York: Simon & Schuster, 1959), 262–87, 351–57, and Jerry Robinson, *The Comics: An Illustrated History of Comic Strip Art* (New York: G.P. Putnam's Sons, 1974), 185–236.

11. Two histories of comic books are Michael Barrier and Martin Williams, eds., *A Smithsonian Book of Comic-Book Comics* (Washington, DC: Smithsonian Institution Press, 1981) and Ron Goulart, *Over 50 Years of American Comic Books* (Lincolnwood, IL: Mallard Press, 1991).

12. For more on Gaines and his connections to the comic-book industry, see Frank Jacobs, *The Mad World of William M. Gaines* (Secaucus, NJ: Lyle Stuart, 1972).

13. William W. Savage, Jr., *Comic Books and America, 1945–1954* (Norman: University of Oklahoma Press, 1990), 95–103.

14. Bradford W. Wright, *Comic Book Nation: The Transformation of Youth Culture in America* (Baltimore, MD: The Johns Hopkins University Press, 2001), 154–225.

15. Alex McNeil, *Total Television: The Comprehensive Guide to Programming from 1948 to the Present*, 4th edition (New York: Penguin Books, 1996), 803–5.

COST OF PRODUCTS IN THE 1950s

1. A source for information on costs and prices is Scott Derks, ed., *The Value of a Dollar: Prices and Incomes in the United States, 1860–1999* (Lakeville, CT: Grey House Publishing, 1999).

Further Reading

Adams, Judith A. *The American Amusement Park Industry: A History of Technology and Thrills*. Boston: Twayne Publishers, 1991.

Advertising Age Editors. *How It Was in Advertising: 1776–1976*. Chicago: Crain Books, 1976.

Allen, Frederick. *Secret Formula*. New York: HarperCollins, 1994.

Allen, Frederick Lewis. *The Big Change*. New York: Bantam Books, 1952.

Allen, G. Freeman. *Railways: Past, Present, and Future*. New York: William Morrow and Company, 1982.

Allen, Henry. *What It Felt Like: Living in the American Century*. New York: Pantheon Books, 2000.

Altschuler, Glenn C., and David I. Grossvogel. *Changing Channels: America in "TV Guide."* Urbana: University of Illinois Press, 1992.

Ambrose, Stephen E. *Eisenhower: The President*. New York: Simon & Schuster, 1984.

American Bandstand. Available: http://www.museum.tv/archives/etv/A/americanband/americanband.htm. (Accessed May 30, 2003).

American Heritage Editors. *The American Heritage History of Flight*. New York: Simon & Schuster, 1962.

Anderson, Kent. *Television Fraud: The History and Implications of the Quiz Show Scandals*. Westport, CT: Greenwood Press, 1979.

Antfarm [Chip Lord]. *Automerica: A Trip Down U.S. Highways from World War II to the Future*. New York: E.P. Dutton, 1976.

Artman, John, and Gary Grimm. *The 1950s: Remembering and Reminiscing*. Carthage, IL: Gary Grimm & Associates, 2000.

Ashley, Bob. *The Study of Popular Fiction: A Source Book*. Philadelphia: University of Pennsylvania Press, 1989.

Associated Press Sports Staff. *A Century of Sports*. New York: The Associated Press, 1971.

Atwan, Robert, Donald McQuade, and John L. Wright. *Edsels, Luckies, and Frigidaires: Advertising the American Way*. New York: Dell [Delta], 1979.

Austin, James C., ed. *Popular Literature in America*. Bowling Green, OH: Popular Press, 1972.

Austin, Joe, and Michael Nevin Willard, eds. *Generations of Youth: Youth Cultures and History in Twentieth-Century America*. New York: New York University Press, 1998.

Automobile Manufacturers Association, Inc. *Automobiles of America*. Detroit, MI: Wayne State University Press, 1968.

Automobile Quarterly Editors. *Corvette! Thirty Years of Great Advertising*. Princeton, NJ: Princeton Publishing, 1983.

Baeder, John. *Gas, Food, and Lodging*. New York: Abbeville Press, 1982.

Bailey, Beth L. *From Front Porch to Back Seat*. Baltimore, MD: Johns Hopkins University Press, 1988.

Bailey, Robert Lee. *An Examination of Prime Time Network Television Special Programs, 1948–1966*. New York: Arno, 1979.

Baker, R.S., and P.L. Van Osdol. *The World on Wheels*. Boston: Allyn & Bacon, 1972.

Ballard, Bettina. *In My Fashion*. New York: David McKay, 1960.

Baritz, Loren. *The Good Life: The Meaning of Success for the American Middle Class*. New York: Alfred A. Knopf, 1989.

Barnouw, Erik. *A History of Broadcasting in the United States. Vol. 2: The Golden Web*. New York: Oxford University Press, 1968.

———. *A History of Broadcasting in the United States. Vol. 3: The Image Empire*. New York: Oxford University Press, 1970.

———. *Tube of Plenty: The Evolution of American Television*. New York: Oxford University Press, 1982.

Barr, Andrew. *Drink: A Social History of America*. New York: Carroll & Graf, 1999.

Barrier, Michael, and Martin Williams, eds. *A Smithsonian Book of Comic-Book Comics*. Washington, DC: Smithsonian Institution Press, 1981.

Barson, Michael, and Steven Heller. *Red Scared! The Commie Menace in Propaganda and Popular Culture*. San Francisco: Chronicle Books, 2001.

Bascom, Willard. "Scientific Blueprint for Atomic Survival." *Life*, 42:11 (March 15, 1957): 146–62. Basinger, Jeanine. *A Woman's View: How Hollywood Spoke to Women, 1930–1960*. New York: Alfred A. Knopf, 1993.

Batterberry, Michael, and Ariane Batterberry. *Mirror Mirror: A Social History of Fashion*. New York: Holt, Rinehart and Winston, 1977.

Baumbach, Jonathan. *The Landscape of Nightmare: Studies in the Contemporary American Novel*. New York: New York University Press, 1965.

Baxandall, Rosalyn, and Elizabeth Ewen. *Picture Windows: How the Suburbs Happened*. New York: Basic Books, 2000.

Baxter, John. *Science Fiction in the Cinema*. New York: A.S. Barnes, 1970.

Bayley, Stephen. *Harley Earl and the Dream Machine*. New York: Alfred A. Knopf, 1983.

———. *In Good Shape: Style in Industrial Products, 1900 to 1960*. New York: Van Nostrand Reinhold, 1979.

Becker, Stephen. *Comic Art in America*. New York: Simon & Schuster, 1959.

Belz, Carl. *The Story of Rock*. 2nd ed. New York: Oxford University Press, 1972.

Benton, Mike. *The Comic Book in America: An Illustrated History*. Dallas: Taylor Publishing, 1989.

Berger, Michael L. *The Automobile in American History and Culture: A Reference Guide.* Westport, CT: Greenwood Press, 2001.

Beyer, Chris H. *Coca-Cola Girls: An Advertising Art History.* Portland, OR: Collectors Press, 2000.

Bigelow, Marybelle S. *Fashion in History: Western Dress, Prehistoric to Present.* Minneapolis, MN: Burgess Publishing, 1979.

Bilstein, Roger E. *Flight in America: From the Wrights to the Astronauts.* Baltimore, MD: Johns Hopkins University Press, 1984.

Binyon, T.J. *"Murder Will Out": The Detective in Fiction.* New York: Oxford University Press, 1989.

Bird, William L., Jr. *Paint by Number: The How-To Craze that Swept the Nation.* Princeton, NJ: Princeton Architectural Press, 2001.

Biskind, Peter. *Seeing Is Believing: How Hollywood Taught Us to Stop Worrying and Love the Fifties.* New York: Pantheon Books, 1983.

Blackbeard, Bill, and Martin Williams. *The Smithsonian Collection of Newspaper Comics.* Washington, DC: Smithsonian Institution Press, 1977.

Bliss, Edward, Jr. *In Search of Light: The Broadcasts of Edward R. Murrow, 1938–1961.* New York: Alfred A. Knopf, 1967.

Block, Geoffrey. *Enchanted Evenings: The Broadway Musical from "Showboat" to Sondheim.* New York: Oxford University Press, 2000.

Bloom, Lynn Z. *Doctor Spock: Biography of a Conservative Radical.* Indianapolis, IN: Bobbs-Merrill, 1972.

Blum, Daniel. *A Pictorial History of the American Theatre, 1860–1970.* New York: Crown 1969.

Boddy, William. *Fifties Television: The Industry and Its Critics.* Urbana: University of Illinois Press, 1990.

Bode, Carl. *The Half-World of American Culture: A Miscellany.* Carbondale: Southern Illinois University Press, 1965.

Bonn, Thomas L. *Under Cover: An Illustrated History of American Mass Market Paperbacks.* New York: Penguin Books, 1982.

Bordman, Gerald. *American Theatre: A Chronicle of Comedy & Drama, 1930–1969.* New York: Oxford University Press, 1996.

Boyer, Paul. *By the Bomb's Early Light: American Thought and Culture at the Dawn of the Atomic Age.* New York: Pantheon Books, 1985.

Breines, Winni. *Young, White, and Miserable: Growing Up Female in the Fifties.* Boston: Beacon Press, 1992.

Brenner, Joel Glenn. *The Emperors of Chocolate: Inside the Secret World of Hershey and Mars.* New York: Random House, 1999.

Breward, Christopher. *The Culture of Fashion: A New History of Fashionable Dress.* Manchester, England: Manchester University Press, 1995.

Bridwell, E. Nelson, ed. *"Superman": From the Thirties to the Seventies.* New York: Bonanza Books, 1971.

Brinkley, Douglas. *"American Heritage" History of the United States.* New York: Viking, 1998.

Broekel, Ray. *The Great American Candy Bar Book.* Boston: Houghton Mifflin, 1982.

Brooks, Tim. *The Complete Directory to Prime Time TV Stars: 1946–Present.* New York: Ballantine Books, 1987.

Brooks, Tim, and Earle Marsh. *The Complete Directory to Prime Time Network TV Shows, 1946—Present.* New York: Ballantine Books, 1988.

Brown, Bob, and Eleanor Parker. *Culinary Americana: 1860–1960.* New York: Roving Eye Press, 1961.

Brown, Curtis F. *Star-Spangled Kitsch.* New York: Universe Books, 1975.

Brown, Les. *Les Brown's Encyclopedia of Television.* 2nd ed. New York: Zoetrope, 1982.

Buechner, Thomas S. *Norman Rockwell: Artist and Illustrator.* New York: Harry N. Abrams, 1970.

Buzzard, Karen S. *Chains of Gold: Marketing the Ratings and Rating the Markets.* Metuchen, NJ: Scarecrow Press, 1990.

Byrnes, Garrett Davis. *Fashion in Newspapers.* New York: Columbia University Press, 1951.

Cameron, Kenneth M. *America on Film: Hollywood and American History.* New York: Continuum Publishing, 1997.

Campbell, Robert. *The Golden Years of Broadcasting: A Celebration of the First 50 Years of Radio and TV on NBC.* New York: Charles Scribner's Sons, 1972.

Cantor, Muriel G., and Suzanne Pingree. *The Soap Opera.* Beverly Hills, CA: Sage, 1983.

Caplow, Theodore, Louis Hicks, and Ben J. Wattenberg. *The First Measured Century: An Illustrated Guide to Trends in America, 1900–2000.* Washington, DC: AEI Press, 2001.

Capp, Al. *The Best of Li'l Abner.* New York: Holt, Rinehart and Winston, 1978.

Carney, George O., ed. *Fast Food, Stock Cars & Rock-n-Roll: Place and Space in American Pop Culture.* Lanham, MD: Rowman & Littlefield, 1995.

Carruth, Gordon, editor. *The Encyclopedia of American Facts and Dates.* New York: Thomas Y. Crowell, 1959.

Carter, Ernestine. *The Changing World of Fashion: 1900 to the Present.* New York: G.P. Putnam's Sons, 1977.

Carter, Paul A. *Another Part of the Fifties.* New York: Columbia University Press, 1983.

Castleman, Harry, and Walter J. Podrazik. *Watching TV: Four Decades of American Television.* New York: McGraw-Hill, 1982.

Chenoweth, Lawrence. *The American Dream of Success: The Search for the Self in the Twentieth Century.* North Scituate, MA: Duxbury Press, 1974.

Churchill, Allen. *Remember When.* New York: Golden Press, 1967.

Clancy, Deirdre. *Costume Since 1945: Couture, Street Style, and Anti-Fashion.* New York: Drama Publishers, 1996.

Clarens, Carlos. *Crime Movies: From Griffith to the Godfather and Beyond.* New York: W.W. Norton, 1980.

——. *An Illustrated History of the Horror Film.* New York: Capricorn Books, 1967.

Clark, Clifford Edward, Jr. *The American Home: 1800–1960.* Chapel Hill: University of North Carolina Press, 1986.

Clark, Eric. *The Want Makers: Inside the World of Advertising.* New York: Penguin Books, 1988.

Clarke, Alison J. *Tupperware: The Promise of Plastic in 1950s America.* Washington, DC: Smithsonian Institution Press, 1999.

Clarke, Donald. *The Rise and Fall of Popular Music.* New York: St. Martin's Press, 1995.

Cleary, David Powers. *Great American Brands.* New York: Fairchild Publications, 1981.

Cline, William C. *In the Nick of Time: Motion Picture Sound Serials.* Jefferson, NC: McFarland, 1984.

Cochran, David. *America Noir: Underground Writers and Filmmakers of the Postwar Era.* Washington, DC: Smithsonian Institution Press, 2000.

Coffey, Frank, and Joseph Layden. *America on Wheels: The First 100 Years, 1896–1996.* Los Angeles: General Publishing Group, 1998.

Coffin, Tristam Potter. *The Old Ball Game: Baseball in Folklore and Fiction.* New York: Herder and Herder, 1971.

Cogley, John. *Report on Blacklisting I: The Movies.* New York: Fund for the Republic, 1956.

———. *Report on Blacklisting II: Radio-Television.* New York: Fund for the Republic, 1956.

Cohen, Stanley. *The Game They Played.* New York: Farrar, Straus & Giroux, 1977.

Cohn, Jan. *The Palace or the Poorhouse: The American House as a Cultural Symbol.* East Lansing: Michigan State University Press, 1979.

Cohn, Nik. *Awopbopaloobop Alopbamboom: The Golden Age of Rock.* New York: Da Capo Press, 1969.

Coleman, James S. *The Adolescent Society.* New York: Free Press, 1961.

Collins, Max Allan. *The History of Mystery.* Portland, OR: Collectors Press, 2001.

Colmer, Michael. *Pinball: An Illustrated History.* London: Pierrot Publishing, 1976.

Commercial Archives. Available: http://www.moviearchive.org. (Accessed May 30, 2003).

Conrad, Barnaby, III. *The Martini: An Illustrated History of an American Classic.* San Francisco: Chronicle Books, 1995.

Consumer Guide Editors. *Automobiles of the '50s.* Lincolnwood, IL: Publications International, 1999.

Cook, Bruce. *The Beat Generation.* New York: Charles Scribner's Sons, 1971.

Coontz, Stephanie. *The Way We Never Were: American Families and the Nostalgia Trap.* New York: Basic Books, 1992.

Cooper, B. Lee, and Wayne S. Haney. *Rock Music in American Popular Culture II: More Rock 'n' Roll Resources.* New York: Harrington Park Press, 1997.

Corn, Joseph J., and Brian Horrigan. *Yesterday's Tomorrows: Past Visions of the American Future.* New York: Summit Books, 1984.

Cotten, Lee. *All Shook Up: Elvis, Day-By-Day, 1954–1977.* Ann Arbor, MI: Pierian Press, 1985.

———. *Shake Rattle &Roll: The Golden Age of American Rock 'n' Roll, Vol. 1: 1952–1955.* Ann Arbor, MI: Pierian Press, 1989.

Couperie, Pierre, and Maurice C. Horn. *A History of the Comic Strip.* New York: Crown, 1968.

Cowan, Ruth Schwartz. *More Work for Mother.* New York: Basic Books, 1983.

Craven, Wayne. *American Art: History and Culture.* New York: Harry N. Abrams, 1994.

Crocker, Betty. *Betty Crocker's Picture Cookbook.* New York: McGraw-Hill, 1950.

Cross, Mary, ed. *A Century of American Icons: 100 Products and Slogans from the 20th-Century Consumer Culture.* Westport, CT: Greenwood Press, 2002.

Crow, Thomas. *Modern Art in the Common Culture.* New Haven, CT: Yale University Press, 1996.

Crumpacker, Bunny. *The Old-Time Brand-Name Cookbook.* New York: Smithmark, 1998.

———. *The Old-Time Brand-Name Desserts.* New York: Abradale Press, 1999.

Csida, Joseph, and June Bundy Csida. *American Entertainment: A Unique History of Popular Show Business.* New York: Watson-Guptil, 1978.

Cullen, Jim. *The Art of Democracy: A Concise History of Popular Culture in the United States.* New York: Monthly Review Press, 1996.

Dalton, David. *James Dean: The Mutant King.* New York: St. Martin's Press, 1983.

Daniels, Les. *Comix: A History of Comic Books in America.* New York: Bonanza Books, 1971.

Delamater, Jerome. *Dance in the Hollywood Musical.* Ann Arbor, MI: UMI Research Press, 1981.

Delong, Thomas A. *Radio Stars.* Jefferson, NC: McFarland, 1996.

Denison, Edward F. *Trends in American Economic Growth, 1929–1982.* Washington, DC: The Brookings Institution, 1985.

Derks, Scott, ed. *The Value of a Dollar: Prices and Incomes in the United States, 1860–1999.* Lakeville, CT: Grey House Publishing, 1999.

———. *Working Americans, 1880–1999: Vol. I: The Working Class.* Lakeville, CT: Grey House Publishing, 2000.

———. *Working Americans, 1880–1999: Vol. II: The Middle Class.* Lakeville, CT: Grey House Publishing, 2001.

Dettelbach, Cynthia Golumb. *In the Driver's Seat: The Automobile in American Literature and Popular Culture.* Westport, CT: Greenwood Press, 1976.

Dickson, Paul. *The Worth Book of Softball: A Celebration of America's True National Pastime.* New York: Facts on File, Inc., 1994.

Diggins, John Patrick. *The Proud Decades.* New York: W.W. Norton, 1988.

Dodds, John W. *Everyday Life in Twentieth Century America.* New York: G.P. Putnam's Sons, 1965.

Doherty, Thomas. *Teenagers and Teenpix: The Juvenilization of American Movies in the 1950s.* Boston: Unwin Hyman, 1988. Dorner, Jane. *Fashion in the Forties and Fifties.* New York: Arlington House, 1975.

Doss, Erika, ed. *Looking at "Life" Magazine.* Washington, DC: Smithsonian Institution Press, 2001.

Douglas, George H. *All Aboard! The Railroad in American Life.* New York: Paragon House, 1992.

Dreishpoon, Douglas, and Alan Trachtenberg. *The Tumultuous Fifties: A View from the "New York Times" Archives.* New Haven, CT: Yale University Press, 2001.

Drexler, Arthur, and Greta Daniel. *Introduction to Twentieth Century Design from the Collection of the Museum of Modern Art.* New York: Museum of Modern Art, 1959.

Duany, Andres, Elizabeth Plater-Zyberk, and Jeff Speck. *Suburban Nation: The Rise of Sprawl and the Decline of the American Dream.* New York: North Point Press, 2000.

Duden, Jane. *1950s.* New York: Crestwood House, 1989.

Dulles, Foster Rhea. *A History of Recreation: America Learns to Play.* Englewood Cliffs, NJ: Prentice-Hall, 1965.

Dunning, John. *On the Air: The Encyclopedia of Old-Time Radio.* New York: Oxford University Press, 1998.

———. *Tune in Yesterday: The Ultimate Encyclopedia of Old-Time Radio, 1925–1976.* Englewood Cliffs, NJ: Prentice-Hall, 1976.

Durgnat, Raymond. *The Crazy Mirror: Hollywood Comedy and the American Image.* New York: Dell, 1969.

Eames, John Douglas. *The MGM Story: The Complete History of Fifty Roaring Years.* New York: Crown, 1975.

Eberly, Philip K. *Music in the Air: America's Changing Tastes in Popular Music, 1920–1980.* New York: Hastings House, 1982.

Edmunds, Lowell. *The Silver Bullet: The Martini in American Civilization.* Westport, CT: Greenwood Press, 1981.

Ehrenreich, Barbara. *The Hearts of Men: American Dreams and the Flight from Commitment.* New York: Anchor Press/Doubleday, 1983.

Eisler, Benita. *Private Lives: Men and Women of the Fifties.* New York: Franklin Watts, 1986.

Eliot, Marc. *Rockonomics: The Money Behind the Music.* New York: Watts, 1989.

Elliott, William Y. *Television's Impact on American Culture.* East Lansing: Michigan State University Press, 1956.

Ellis, C. Hamilton. *The Lore of the Train.* New York: Grosset & Dunlap, 1971.

Emery, Edwin. *The Press and America: An Interpretative History of Journalism.* Englewood Cliffs, NJ: Prentice-Hall, 1962.

Engelhardt, Tom. *The End of Victory Culture: Cold War America and the Disillusioning of a Generation.* New York: Basic Books, 1995.

Ennis, Philip H. *The Seventh Stream: The Emergence of Rocknroll in American Popular Music.* Hanover, MA: Wesleyan University Press, 1992.

Epstein, Beryl William. *Young Faces in Fashion.* Philadelphia: J.B. Lippincott, 1956.

Epstein, Edward J. *News from Nowhere: Television and the News.* New York: Random House, 1973.

Ermoyan, Arpi. *Famous American Illustrators.* New York: Society of Illustrators, 1997.

Escott, Colin, with Martin Hawkins. *Good Rockin' Tonight: Sun Records and the Birth of Rock 'n' Roll.* New York: St. Martin's Press, 1991.

Ettinger, Roseann. *Fifties Forever! Popular Fashions for Men, Women, Boys & Girls.* Atglen, PA: Schiffer Publishing, 1998.

Everett, Linda. *Retro Barbeque: Tasty Recipes for the Grillin' Guy.* Portland, OR: Collectors Press, 2002.

Ewen, David. *All the Years of American Popular Music.* Englewood Cliffs, NJ: Prentice-Hall, 1977.

Ewen, Stuart. *Captains of Consciousness: Advertising and the Social Roots of the Consumer Culture.* New York: McGraw-Hill, 1976.

Ewen, Stuart, and Elizabeth Ewen. *Channels of Desire: Mass Images and the Shaping of American Consciousness.* New York: McGraw-Hill, 1982.

Ewing, Elizabeth. *History of Twentieth Century Fashion.* London: B.T. Batsford, 1974.

Fates, Gil. *What's My Line? The Inside Story of TV's Most Famous Panel Show.* Englewood Cliffs, NJ: Prentice-Hall, 1978.

Faulk, John Henry. *Fear on Trial.* New York: Simon & Schuster, 1964.

Faulkner, Thomas, ed. *Studies in Design and Popular Culture of the Twentieth Century.* Newcastle-Upon-Tyne, England: Newcastle-Upon-Tyne Polytechnic Press, 1976.

Feather, Leonard. *The New Edition of the Encyclopedia of Jazz.* New York: Bonanza Books, 1962.

Feather, Leonard, and Ira Gitler. *The Biographical Encyclopedia of Jazz.* New York: Oxford University Press, 1999.

Fehrman, Cherie, and Kenneth Fehrman. *Postwar Interior Design: 1945–1960.* New York: Reinhold, 1987.

Feldman, Gene, and Max Gartenberg, eds. *The Beat Generation and the Angry Young Men.* New York: Citadel Press, 1958.

Fenin, George N., and William K. Everson. *The Western: from Silents to Cinerama.* New York: Orion Press, 1962.

Fielding, Raymond. *The American Newsreel, 1911–1967.* Norman: University of Oklahoma Press, 1972.

Finch, Christopher. *The Art of Walt Disney: From Mickey Mouse to the Magic Kingdoms.* New York: Harry N. Abrams, 1975.

———. *Highways to Heaven: The AUTO Biography of America.* New York: Harper-Collins, 1992.

———. *Norman Rockwell's America.* New York: Harry N. Abrams, 1975.

Fine, Benjamin. *1,000,000 Delinquents.* Cleveland, OH: World Publishing, 1955.

Fishwick, Marshall, and J. Meredith Neil, eds. *Popular Architecture.* Bowling Green, OH: Popular Press, 1974.

Flesch, Rudolf. *Why Johnny Can't Read and What You Can Do About It.* New York: Harper & Row, 1955.

Flexner, Stuart Berg. *Listening to America.* New York: Simon & Schuster, 1982.

Flink, James J. *The Car Culture.* Cambridge: MIT Press, 1975.

Flusser, Alan. *Clothes and the Man: The Principles of Fine Men's Dress.* New York: Villard Books, 1989.

Foley, Karen Sue. *Television and the Red Menace.* New York: Praeger, 1985.

Foley, Mary Mix. *The American House.* New York: Harper & Row, 1980.

Ford, James L.C. *Magazines for Millions: The Story of Specialized Publications.* Carbondale: Southern Illinois University Press, 1969.

Foreman, Joel, ed. *The Other Fifties: Interrogating Midcentury American Icons.* Urbana: University of Illinois Press, 1997.

Forty, Adrian. *Objects of Desire: Design and Society since 1750.* New York: Thames & Hudson, 1986.

Fowles, Jib. *Advertising and Popular Culture.* Thousand Oaks, CA: Sage, 1996.

Fox, Stephen. *The Mirror Makers: A History of American Advertising and Its Creators.* New York: William Morrow, 1984.

Fraser, Antonia. *A History of Toys.* New York: Delacorte Press, 1966.

Fraser, James. *The American Billboard: 100 Years.* New York: Harry N. Abrams, 1991.

Freeman, Larry, ed. *Yesterday's Games.* Watkins Glen, NY: Century House, 1970.

Friedwald, Will. *Jazz Singing: America's Great Voices.* New York: Da Capo Press, 1996.

Galbraith, John Kenneth. *The Affluent Society.* Boston: Houghton-Mifflin, 1958.

Gans, Herbert J. *The Levittowners: Ways of Life and Politics in a New Suburban Community.* New York: Columbia University Press, 1982.

Gehring, Wes D., ed. *Handbook of American Film Genres.* Westport, CT: Greenwood Press, 1988.

Gelber, Steven M. *Hobbies: Leisure and the Culture of Work in America.* New York: Columbia University Press, 1999.

George-Warren, Holly. *The "Rolling Stone" Book of the Beats: The Beat Generation and American Culture.* New York: Hyperion, 1999.

Gianokos, Larry James. *Television Drama Series Programming: A Comprehensive Chronicle, 1947—1959.* Metuchen, NJ: Scarecrow Press, 1980.

Gilbert, James. *Another Chance: Postwar America, 1945–1968.* Philadelphia: Temple University Press, 1981.

Gillespie, Angus Kress, and Michael Aaron Rockland. *Looking for America on the New Jersey Turnpike.* New Brunswick, NJ: Rutgers University Press, 1989.

Gillett, Charlie. *The Sound of the City: The Rise of Rock and Roll.* New York: Pantheon Books, 1983.

Gitelson, Joshua. "Populox: The Suburban Cuisine of the 1950s." *Journal of American Culture* 15: 3 (Fall 1992): 73–78.

Gleason, Ralph J., ed. *Jam Session: An Anthology of Jazz.* New York: G.P. Putnam's Sons, 1958.

Glimcher, Arnold B. *Louise Nevelson.* New York: Praeger, 1972.

Godfrey, Donald C., and Frederic A. Leigh, eds. *Historical Dictionary of American Radio.* Westport, CT: Greenwood Press, 1998.

Golden Age Radio. *101 Old Radio Commercials.* Plymouth, MN: Metacom, n.d. Compact disc.

Goldstein, Carolyn M. *Do It Yourself: Home Improvement in 20th Century America.* New York: Princeton Architectural Press, 1998.

Goldstein, Fred, and Stan Goldstein. *Primetime Television: A Pictorial History from Milton Berle to "Falcon Crest."* New York: Crown, 1983.

Goodrich, Lloyd. *Three Centuries of American Art.* New York: Frederick A. Praeger, 1966.

Goodrum, Charles, and Helen Dalrymple. *Advertising in America: The First 200 Years.* New York: Harry N. Abrams, 1990.

Gordon, Lois, and Alan Gordon. *American Chronicle: Six Decades in American Life, 1920–1980.* New York: Atheneum, 1987.

Gottlieb, William P. *The Golden Age of Jazz.* New York: Simon & Schuster, 1979.

Goulart, Ron. *Cheap Thrills: An Informal History of the Pulp Magazines.* New York: Arlington House, 1972.

———. *Over 50 Years of American Comic Books.* Lincolnwood, IL: Mallard Press, 1991.

Goulart, Ron, ed. *The Encyclopedia of American Comics.* New York: Facts On File, 1990.

Gourse, Leslie. *Louis' Children: American Jazz Singers.* New York: Quill, 1984.

Gow, Gordon. *Suspense in the Cinema.* New York: A.S. Barnes, 1968.

Great Books Program. Available: http://www.greatbooks.org/about/index/shtml. (Accessed April 22, 2003).

Green, Harvey. *Fit for America: Health, Fitness, Sport, and American Society.* New York: Pantheon Books, 1986.

Green, Stanley. *Encyclopaedia of the Musical Film.* New York: Oxford University Press, 1981.

Greenberg, Cara. *Mid-Century Modern: Furniture of the 1950s.* New York: Harmony Books, 1984.

Greenberg, Clement. *Art and Culture.* Boston: Beacon Press, 1961.

Greenfield, Jeff. *Television: The First Fifty Years.* New York: Harry N. Abrams, 1977.

Greenfield, Thomas Allen. *Radio: A Reference Guide.* Westport, CT: Greenwood Press, 1989.

Griffith, Richard, and Arthur Mayer. *The Movies.* New York: Simon & Schuster, 1970.

Grimes, William. *Straight Up or on the Rocks: A Cultural History of American Drink.* New York: Simon & Schuster, 1993.

Gruber, Frank. *The Pulp Jungle.* Los Angeles: Sherbourne Press, 1967.

Guralnick, Peter. *Last Train to Memphis: The Rise of Elvis Presley.* Boston: Little, Brown, 1994.

Gutman, Richard S.J. *The American Diner: Then and Now.* New York: HarperCollins (Harper Perennial), 1993.

Guttman, Allen. *The Olympics: A History of the Modern Games.* Urbana: University of Illinois Press, 1992.

———. *A Whole New Ball Game: An Interpretation of American Sports.* Chapel Hill: University of North Carolina Press, 1988.

Hackett, Alice Payne. *60 Years of Best Sellers, 1895–1955.* New York: R.R. Bowker, 1955.

Haddon, Robert H. *Pavilions of Plenty: Exhibiting American Culture Abroad in the 1950s.* Washington, DC: Smithsonian Institution Press, 1997.

Halberstam, David. *The Fifties.* New York: Villard Books, 1993.

Hall, Jim. *Mighty Minutes: An Illustrated History of Television's Best Commercials.* New York: Harmony Books, 1984.

Halle, David. *Inside Culture: Art & Class in the American Home.* Chicago: University of Chicago Press, 1993.

Halpern, John. *New York/New York: An Architectural Portfolio.* New York: E.P. Dutton, 1978.

Hamilton, Ian. *In Search of J.D. Salinger.* New York: Random House, 1988.

Hamm, Charles. *Yesterdays: Popular Song in America.* New York: W.W. Norton, 1979.

Handlin, David P. *American Architecture.* New York: Thames and Hudson, 1985.

Harris, Jay S., ed. *"TV Guide": The First 25 Years.* New York: Simon & Schuster, 1978.

Harris, Neil. *Cultural Excursions: Marketing Appetites and Cultural Tastes in Modern America.* Chicago: University of Chicago Press, 1990.

Hart, Jeffrey Peter. *When the Going Was Good! American Life in the Fifties.* New York: Crown, 1982.

Harvey, Brett. *The Fifties: A Women's Oral History.* New York: HarperCollins, 1993.

Harvey, James. *Movie Love in the Fifties.* New York: Alfred A. Knopf, 2001.

Harvey, Robert C. *The Art of the Comic Book: An Aesthetic History.* Jackson: University Press of Mississippi, 1996.

———. *The Art of the Funnies: An Aesthetic History.* Jackson: University Press of Mississippi, 1994.

———. *Children of the Yellow Kid: The Evolution of the American Comic Strip.* Seattle, WA: Frye Art Museum, 1998.

Hasbro Toys. Available: http://www.hasbro.com. (Accessed March 3, 2003).

Haspiel, James. *Marilyn: The Ultimate Look at the Legend.* New York: Henry Holt, 1991.

Hayden, Dolores. *Redesigning the American Dream: The Future of Housing, Work, and Family Life.* New York: W.W. Norton, 1984.

Heide, Robert, and John Gilman. *Dime-Store Dream Parade: Popular Culture, 1925–1955. New York:* E.P. Dutton, 1979.

Heidenry, John. *Theirs Was the Kingdom: Lila and DeWitt Wallace and the Story of the "Reader's Digest".* New York: W.W. Norton, 1993.

Heimann, Jim, ed. *50s: All-American Ads.* New York: Taschen, 2001.

———. *California Crazy and Beyond: Roadside Vernacular Architecture.* San Francisco: Chronicle Books, 2001.

Heimann, Jim, and Rip Georges. *California Crazy: Roadside Vernacular Architecture.* San Francisco : Chronicle Books, 1980.

Heller, Nancy, and Julia Williams. *Painters of the American Scene.* New York: Galahad Books, 1976.

Henderson, Amy, and Dwight Blocker Bowers. *Red, Hot & Blue: A Smithsonian Salute to the American Musical.* Washington, DC: Smithsonian Institution Press, 1996.

Henderson, Mary C. *Broadway Ballyhoo.* New York: Harry N. Abrams, 1989.

———. *Theater in America: 200 Years of Plays, Players, and Productions.* New York: Harry N. Abrams, 1986.

Henderson, Sally, and Robert Landau. *Billboard Art.* San Francisco: Chronicle Books, 1981.

Hennessey, Maureen Hart, and Anne Knutson. *Norman Rockwell: Pictures for the American People.* New York: Harry N. Abrams, 1999.

Hentoff, Nat, and Albert McCarthy, eds. *Jazz.* New York: Grove Press, 1959.

Hentoff, Nat, and Nat Shapiro, eds. *The Jazz Makers.* New York: Grove press, 1957.

Hess, Alan. *Googie: Fifties Coffee Shop Architecture.* San Francisco: Chronicle Books, 1986.

Hiesinger, Kathryn. *Design Since 1945.* Philadelphia: Philadelphia Museum of Art, 1983.

Higby, Mary Jane. *Tune In Tomorrow.* New York: Cowles Education Corporation, 1968.

Higgs, Robert J. *Sport: A Reference Guide.* Westport, CT: Greenwood Press, 1982.

Higham, Charles. *The Art of the American Film, 1900–1971.* Garden City, New York: Anchor Press, 1973.

Hill, Daniel Delis. *Advertising to the American Woman, 1900–1999.* Columbus: Ohio State University Press, 2002.

Hilliard, Robert L., and Michael C. Keith. *The Broadcast Century: A Biography of American Broadcasting.* Boston: Focal Press, 1992.

Hillier, Bevis. *Austerity Binge: The Decorative Arts of the Forties and Fifties.* London: Cassell & Collier Macmillan, 1975.

———. *The Style of the Century: 1900–1980.* New York: E.P. Dutton, 1983.

Hilmes, Michele. *Radio Voices: American Broadcasting, 1922–1952.* Minneapolis: University of Minnesota Press, 1997.

Hine, Thomas. *Populuxe*. New York: Alfred A. Knopf, 1986.

———. *The Rise and Fall of the American Teenager*. New York: Avon Books [Bard], 1999.

Hirshhorn, Paul, and Steven Izenour. *White Towers*. Cambridge: MIT Press, 1979.

"History of Boy's Clothing." Available: http://www.histclo.hispeed.com/style/head/cap/. (Accessed May 22, 2003).

Hobbs, Robert Carleton, and Gail Levin. *Abstract Expressionism: The Formative Years*. New York: Whitney Museum of American Art, 1978.

Hoffmann, Frank W., and William G. Bailey. *Fashion & Merchandising Fads*. New York: The Haworth Press, 1994.

———. *Sports & Recreation Fads*. New York: Haworth Press, 1991.

Hooker, Richard J. *Food and Drink in America: A History*. Indianapolis, IN: Bobbs-Merrill, 1981.

Horn, Maurice. *Women in the Comics*. New York: Chelsea House Publishers, 1977.

Horn, Maurice, ed. *100 Years of American Newspaper Comics*. New York: Gramercy Books, 1996.

———. *The World Encyclopedia of Comics*. New York: Chelsea House Publishers, 1976.

Horn, Richard. *Fifties Style, Then and Now*. New York: Beech Tree, 1985.

Hornung, Clarence P., and Fridolf Johnson. *200 Years of American Graphic Art*. New York: George Braziller, 1976.

Horwitz, Elinor Lander. *The Bird, the Banner, and Uncle Sam*. Philadelphia: J.B. Lippincott, 1976.

Houston, Penelope. *The Contemporary Cinema, 1945–1963*. Baltimore, MD: Penguin Books, 1963.

Howell, Georgina. *In Vogue: 75 Years of Style*. London: Conde Nast Books, 1991.

Hughes, Robert. *American Visions: The Epic History of Art in America*. New York: Alfred A. Knopf, 1997.

Hunter, Christine. *Ranches, Rowhouses & Railroad Flats. American Homes: How They Shape Our Landscapes and Neighborhoods*. New York: W. W. Norton, 1999.

Hurley, Andrew. *Diners, Bowling Alleys, and Trailer Parks: Chasing the American Dream in Postwar Consumer Culture*. New York: Basic Books, 2001.

Huss, Roy, and T.J. Huss. *Focus on the Horror Film*. Englewood Cliffs, NJ: Prentice-Hall, 1972.

Ierley, Merritt. *Open House*. New York: Henry Holt, 1999.

Ikuta, Yasutoshi. *Cruise-O-Matic: Automobile Advertising of the 1950s*. San Francisco: Chronicle Books, 1987

Inge, M. Thomas. *Comics As Culture*. Jackson: University Press of Mississippi, 1990.

Inge, M. Thomas, ed. *Concise Histories of American Popular Culture*, 3 vols. Westport, CT: Greenwood Press, 1982.

———. *Handbook of American Popular Culture*, 3 vols. Westport, CT: Greenwood Press, 1981.

Innes, Sherrie A. *Dinner Roles: American Women and Culinary Culture*. Iowa City: University of Iowa Press, 2001.

Jackson, Carlton. *Hounds of the Road: A History of the Greyhound Bus Company*. Bowling Green, OH: Popular Press, 1984.

Jackson, John A. *American Bandstand: Dick Clark and the Making of a Rock 'n' Roll Empire.* New York: Oxford University Press, 1997.

Jackson, John Brinckerhoff. *Landscape in Sight: Looking at America.* New Haven, CT: Yale University Press, 1997.

Jackson, Kathy Merlock. *Images of Children in American Film.* Metuchen, NJ: Scarecrow Press, 1986.

Jackson, Kenneth T. *The Crabgrass Frontier: The Suburbanization of America.* New York: Oxford University Press, 1985.

Jackson, Lesley. *The New Look: Design in the Fifties.* London: Thames & Hudson, 1991.

Jacobs, Frank. *The Mad World of William M. Gaines.* Secaucus, NJ: Lyle Stuart, 1972.

Jakle, John A. *The Tourist: Travel in Twentieth-Century North America.* Lincoln: University of Nebraska Press, 1985.

Jakle, John A., and Keith A Sculle. *The Gas Station in America.* Baltimore, MD: Johns Hopkins University Press, 1994.

Jakle, John A., Keith A. Sculle, and Jefferson S. Rogers. *The Motel in America.* Baltimore, MD: Johns Hopkins University Press, 1996.

Jandl, H. Ward. *Yesterday's Houses of Tomorrow: Innovative American Homes, 1850–1950.* Washington, DC: Preservation Press, 1991.

Janello, Amy, and Brennon Jones. *The American Magazine.* New York: Harry N. Abrams, 1991.

Jenkins, Virginia Scott. *The Lawn: A History of an American Obsession.* Washington, DC: Smithsonian Institution Press, 1994.

Jennings, Jan, ed. *Roadside America: The Automobile in Design and Culture.* Ames: Iowa State University Press, 1990.

Johnson, Paul. *Modern Times: From the Twenties to the Nineties.* New York: HarperCollins, 1991.

Jonas, Susan, and Marilyn Nissenson. *Going, Going, Gone: Vanishing Americana.* San Francisco: Chronicle Books, 1994.

Jones, Gerald. *Honey, I'm Home. Sitcoms: Selling the American Dream.* New York: Grove Weidenfeld, 1992.

Jones, Landon V. *Great Expectations: America and the Baby Boom Generation.* New York: Coward, McCann & Geoghegan, 1980.

Jones, R.L. *Great American Stuff.* Nashville, TN: Cumberland House, 1997.

Jowett, Garth. *Film: The Democratic Art.* Boston: Little, Brown, 1976.

Junker, Howard. "As We Used to Say in the '50s: A Short Course in Tribal Linguistics." *Esquire,* June 1983: 179–79.

Kaledin, Eugenia. *Daily Life in the United States, 1940–1959: Shifting Worlds.* Westport, CT: Greenwood Press, 2000.

Kallir, Jane. *Grandma Moses: The Artist Behind the Myth.* New York: Clarkson N. Potter, 1982.

Kammen, Michael. *American Culture, American Tastes: Social Change and the 20th Century.* New York: Alfred A. Knopf, 2000.

Kanfer, Stefan. *Journal of the Plague Years.* New York: Atheneum, 1973.

Kaplan, Donald, and Alan Bellink. *Classic Diners of the Northeast.* Boston: Faber & Faber, 1980.

Kaye, Marvin. *A Toy Is Born.* New York: Stein and Day, 1973.

Keats, John. *The Crack in the Picture Window*. Cambridge, MA: Riverside Press, 1956.

———. *The Insolent Chariots*. Philadelphia: J.P. Lippincott, 1958.

Keepnews, Orrin, and Bill Grauer, Jr. *A Pictorial History of Jazz*, 2nd edition. New York: Crown, 1966.

Kern-Foxworth, Marilyn. *Aunt Jemima, Uncle Ben, and Rastus: Blacks in Advertising, Yesterday, Today, and Tomorrow*. Westport, CT: Greenwood Press, 1994.

Kidwell, Brush, and Valerie Steele, eds. *Men and Women: Dressing the Part*. Washington, DC: Smithsonian Institution Press, 1989.

Kidwell, Claudia B., and Margaret C. Christman. *Suiting Everyone: The Democratization of Clothing in America*. Washington, DC: Smithsonian Institution Press, 1974.

Kinsey, Alfred C., and The Institute for Sex Research. *Sexual Behavior in the Human Female*. Philadelphia: Saunders, 1953.

Kirchner, Bill, ed. *The Oxford Companion to Jazz*. New York: Oxford University Press, 2000.

Kitahara, Teruhisa. *Yesterday's Toys: Celluloid Dolls, Clowns, and Animals*. Vol. 1. San Francisco: Chronicle Books, 1989. 3 vols.

———. *Yesterday's Toys: Planes, Trains, Boats, and Cars*. Vol. 2. San Francisco: Chronicle Books, 1989. 3 vols.

———. *Yesterday's Toys: Robots, Spaceships, and Monsters*. Vol. 3. San Francisco: Chronicle Books, 1989. 3 vols.

Klapp, Orrin E. *Heroes, Villains, and Fools: The Changing American Character*. Englewood Cliffs, NJ: Prentice-Hall, 1961.

Knight, Arthur. *The Liveliest Art*. New York: New American Library [Mentor], 1957.

Kostof, Spiro. *America by Design*. New York: Oxford University Press, 1987.

Kouwenhoven, John A. *The Beer Can by the Highway*. New York: Doubleday, 1961.

Kowinski, William. *The Malling of America: An Inside Look at the Great Consumer Paradise*. New York: William Morrow, 1985.

Kozol, Wendy. *Life's America: Family and Nation in Postwar Photojournalism*. Philadelphia: Temple University Press, 1994.

Kraus, Richard. *Recreation and Leisure in Modern Society*. Englewood Cliffs, NJ: Prentice-Hall, 1971.

Kroc, Ray. *Grinding It Out: The Making of McDonald's*. Chicago: Regnery, 1977.

Kuznick, Peter J., and James Gilbert, eds. *Rethinking Cold War Culture*. Washington, DC: Smithsonian Institution Press, 2001.

Laforse, Martin W., and James A. Drake. *Popular Culture and American Life*. Chicago: Nelson-Hall, 1981.

Lahue, Kalton C. *Continued Next Week: A History of the Moving Picture Serial*. Norman: University of Oklahoma Press, 1964.

Lamont, Helen Otis, ed. *A Diamond of Years: The Best of "The Woman's Home Companion."* New York: Doubleday, 1961.

Landau, Robert, and James Phillippi. *Airstream*. Salt Lake City, UT: Peregrine Smith Books, 1984.

Lanza, Joseph. *The Cocktail: The Influence of Spirits on the American Psyche*. New York: St. Martin's Press, 1995.

Larka, Robert. *Television's Private Eye: An Examination of Twenty Years of Programming of a Particular Genre, 1949–1969.* New York: Arno, 1979.

Larrabee, Eric, and Rolf Meyersohn, eds. *Mass Leisure.* Glencoe, IL: Free Press, 1958.

Layman, Richard, ed. *American Decades: 1950–1959.* Detroit, MI: Gale Research, 1994.

Lears, Jackson. *Fables of Abundance: A Cultural History of Advertising in America.* New York: Basic Books, 1994.

Lender, Mark Edward, and James Kirby Martin. *Drinking in America: A History.* New York: Free Press, 1987.

Leonard, Neil. *Jazz and the White American: The Acceptance of a New Art Form.* Chicago: University of Chicago Press, 1962.

Leonard, Thomas C. *News for All: America's Coming-of-Age with the Press.* New York: Oxford University Press, 1995.

Leslie, Fiona. *Designs for 20th-Century Interiors.* London: V & A Publications, 2000.

Lesser, Robert. *A Celebration of Comic Art and Memorabilia.* New York: Hawthorn Books, 1975.

Lester, Paul Martin, ed. *Images that Injure: Pictorial Stereotypes in the Media.* Westport, CT: Praeger, 1996.

Leuchtenburg, William E. *A Troubled Feast: American Society Since 1945.* Boston: Little, Brown, 1979.

Levenstein, Harvey. *Paradox of Plenty: A Social History of Eating in Modern America.* New York: Oxford University Press, 1993.

Levin, Martin, ed. *Hollywood and the Great Fan Magazines.* New York: Arbor House, 1970.

Levinson, David, and Karen Christensen, eds. *Encyclopedia of World Sport.* New York: Oxford University Press, 1996.

Lewine, Harris. *Good-Bye to All That.* New York: McGraw-Hill, 1970.

Lewis, David L., and Laurence Goldstein, eds. *The Automobile and American Culture.* Ann Arbor: University of Michigan Press, 1983.

Lewis, Lucinda. *Roadside America: The Automobile and the American Dream.* New York: Harry N. Abrams, 2000.

Lewis, Myra, and Murray Silver. *Great Balls of Fire: The Uncensored Story of Jerry Lee Lewis.* New York: William Morrow, 1982.

Lewis, Peter. *The Fifties.* New York: J.B. Lippincott, 1958.

Ley, Sandra. *Fashion for Everyone: The Story of Ready-to-Wear, 1870's–1970's.* New York: Charles Scribner's Sons, 1975.

Lhamon, W.T., Jr. *Deliberate Speed: The Origins of Cultural Style in the American 1950s.* Washington, DC: Smithsonian Institution Press, 1990.

Lichty, Lawrence W., and Malachi C. Topping. *American Broadcasting: A Source Book on the History of Radio and Television.* New York: Hastings House, 1975.

Liebman, Nina. *Living Room Lectures: The Fifties Family in Film & Television.* Austin: University of Texas Press, 1995.

Liebs, Chester H. *Main Street to Miracle Mile: American Roadside Architecture.* Baltimore, MD: Johns Hopkins University Press, 1985.

Liesner, Thelma. *Economic Statistics, 1900–1983.* New York: Facts on File, 1985.

Life Editors. *Life: The Second Decade, 1946–1955.* Boston: Little, Brown, 1984.

Lifshey, Earl. *The Housewares Story*. Chicago: National Housewares Manufacturers Association, 1973.

Linton, Calvin D., ed. *The American Almanac*. New York: Thomas Nelson, 1977.

Lippa, Mario, and David Newton. *The World of Small Ads*. Secaucus, NJ: Chartwell Books, 1979.

Longley, Marjorie, Louis Silverstein, and Samuel A. Tower. *America's Taste: 1851–1959*. New York: Simon & Schuster, 1960.

Love, Brian. *Play the Game*. Los Angeles: Reed Books, 1978.

Love, John F. *McDonald's: Behind the Arches*. New York: Bantam Books, 1986.

Lovegren, Sylvia. *Fashionable Food: Seven Decades of Food Fads*. New York: Macmillan, 1995.

Low, David. *The Fearful Fifties: A History of the Decade*. New York: Simon & Schuster, 1960.

Lowenthal, Leo. *Literature, Popular Culture, and Society*. Englewood Cliffs, NJ: Prentice-Hall, 1961.

Lucie-Smith, Edward. *American Realism*. New York: Harry N. Abrams, 1994.

———. *Visual Arts in the Twentieth Century*. New York: Harry N. Abrams, 1996.

Lupoff, Dick, and Don Thompson, eds. *All in Color for a Dime*. New York: Arlington House, 1970.

Lupoff, Richard. *The Great American Paperback: An Illustrated Tribute to Legends of the Book*. Portland, OR: Collectors Press, 2001.

Lupton, Ellen. *Mechanical Brides: Women and Machines from Home to Office*. Princeton, NJ: Princeton Architectural Press, 1993.

Lydon, Michael. *Rock Folk: Portraits from the Rock 'n' Roll Pantheon*. New York: Dell [Delta], 1971.

Lynes, Russell. *The Domesticated Americans*. New York: Harper & Row, 1963.

———. *The Lively Audience*. New York: Harper & Row, 1985.

———. *The Tastemakers*. New York: Harper & Brothers, 1954.

Lynn, C. Stephen. *Sonic: 40 Years of Success, 1953–1993*. New York: The Newcomen Society, 1993.

Macdonald, Dwight. *Against the American Grain*. New York: Vintage Books, 1965.

MacDonald, J. Fred. *Don't Touch That Dial! Radio Programming in American Life, 1920–1960*. Chicago: Nelson-Hall, 1979.

———. *Who Shot the Sheriff? The Rise and Fall of the Television Western*. New York: Praeger, 1987.

Maddocks, Melvin. *The Great Liners*. Alexandria, VA: Time-Life Books, 1978.

Mailer, Norman. *Advertisements for Myself*. New York: G.P. Putnam's Sons, 1959.

Maltby, Richard. *Passing Parade: A History of Popular Culture in the Twentieth Century*. New York: Oxford University Press, 1989.

Maltin, Leonard. *The Great American Broadcast: A Celebration of Radio's Golden Age*. New York: Dutton, 1997.

Manchester, William. *The Glory and the Dream: A Narrative History of America, 1932–1972*. 2 vols. Boston: Little, Brown, 1974.

Mandel, Richard D. *Sport: A Cultural History*. New York: Columbia University Press, 1984.

Manring, M.M. *Slave in a Box: The Strange Career of Aunt Jemima*. Charlottesville: University Press of Virginia, 1998.

Marcus, Greil. *Mystery Train: Images of America in Rock 'n' Roll Music.* New York: E.P. Dutton, 1975.

Margolies, John. *Home Away from Home: Motels in America.* Boston: Little, Brown, 1995.

———. *Pump and Circumstance: Glory Days of the Gas Station.* Boston: Little, Brown, 1993.

Margolies, John, and Emily Gwathmey. *Ticket to Paradise: American Movie Theaters and How We Had Fun.* Boston: Little, Brown, 1991.

Mariani, John F. *The Dictionary of American Food and Drink.* New York: Ticknor & Fields, 1983.

Markin, Rom J. *The Supermarket: An Analysis of Growth, Development, and Change.* Pullman, WA: Washington State University Press, 1963.

Marling, Karal Ann. *As Seen on TV: The Visual Culture of Everyday Life in the 1950s.* Cambridge, MA: Harvard University Press, 1994.

———. *The Colossus of Roads: Myth and Symbol along the American Highway.* Minneapolis: University of Minnesota Press, 1984.

Marquette, Arthur F. *Brands, Trademarks and Goodwill.* New York: McGraw-Hill, 1967.

Marschall, Richard. *America's Great Comic-Strip Artists.* New York: Stewart, Tabori & Chang, 1997.

Marter, Joan M. *Alexander Calder.* New York: Cambridge University Press, 1991.

Martin, Richard. *American Ingenuity: Sportswear, 1930s–1970s.* New York: The Metropolitan Museum of Art, 1998.

Martin, William. *A Prophet with Honor: The Billy Graham Story.* New York: William Morrow, 1991.

Marum, Andrew, and Frank Parise. *Follies and Foibles: A View of 20th Century Fads.* New York: Facts on File, 1984.

Marzulla, Elena, ed. *Pictorial Treasury of U.S. Stamps.* Omaha, NE: Collectors Institute, 1974.

Mathy, Francois. *American Realism: A Pictorial Survey from the Early Eighteenth Century to the 1970's.* New York: Skira, 1978.

Mattfeld, Julius. *"Variety" Music Cavalcade.* Englewood Cliffs, NJ: Prentice-Hall, 1962.

Matthew-Walker, Robert. *Broadway to Hollywood: The Musical and the Cinema.* London: Sanctuary Publishing, 1996.

May, Elaine Tyler. *Homeward Bound: American Families in the Cold War Era.* New York: Basic Books, 1988.

Mazo, Joseph H. *Prime Movers: The Makers of Modern Dance in America.* New York: William Morrow, 1977.

McAlester, Virginia, and Lee McAlester. *A Field Guide to American Houses.* New York: Alfred A. Knopf, 1984.

McArdle, Kenneth, ed. *A Cavalcade of Collier's.* New York: Barnes & Noble, 1959.

McArthur, Colin. *Underworld U.S.A.* New York: Viking Press, 1972.

McClintock, Inez, and Marshall McClintock. *Toys in America.* Washington, DC: Public Affairs Press, 1961.

McCloud, Scott. *Understanding Comics: The Invisible Art.* Northampton, MA: Kitchen Sink Press, 1993.

McDermott, Catherine. *Book of 20th Century Design*. New York: Overlook Press, 1998.

McGee, Mark Thomas. *The J.D. Films: Juvenile Delinquency in the Movies*. Jefferson, NC: McFarland, 1982.

McKeever, Porter. *Adlai Stevenson: His Life and Legacy*. New York: William H. Morrow, 1989.

McNeil, Alex. *Total Television: The Comprehensive Guide to Programming from 1948 to the Present*. 4th edition. New York: Penguin Books, 1996.

McShane, Clay. *Down the Asphalt Path: The Automobile and the American City*. New York: Columbia University Press, 1994.

Meeker, David. *Jazz in the Movies*. New York: Da Capo Press, 1981.

Melinkoff, Ellen. *What We Wore: An Offbeat Social History of Women's Clothing, 1950 to 1980*. New York: Quill, 1984.

Mendelson, Jack H., and Nancy K. Mello. *Alcohol: Use and Abuse in America*. Boston: Little, Brown, 1985.

Mergen, Bernard. *Play and Playthings: A Reference Guide*. Westport, CT: Greenwood Press, 1982.

Meritt, Jeffrey. *Day by Day: The Fifties*. New York: Facts on File, 1979.

Meyer, Susan E. *America's Great Illustrators*. New York: Galahad Books, 1978.

Meyerowitz, Joanne. *Not June Cleaver: Women and Gender in Postwar America, 1945–1960*. Philadelphia: Temple University Press, 1994.

Milbank, Caroline Rennolds. *New York Fashion: The Evolution of American Style*. New York: Harry N. Abrams, 1989.

Miller, Douglas T., and Marion Nowak. *The Fifties: The Way We Really Were*. New York: Doubleday, 1960.

Miller, William H. *The Last Atlantic Liners*. London: Conway Maritime Press, 1985.

Mintz, Steven, and Susan Kellogg. *Domestic Revolutions: A Social History of American Family Life*. New York: Free Press, 1988.

Mitchell, Curtis. *Cavalcade of Broadcasting*. Chicago: Benjamin Company/Rutledge Book, 1970.

Modell, John. *Into One's Own: From Youth to Adulthood in the United States, 1920–1975*. Berkeley: University of California Press, 1989.

Moline, Mary. *Norman Rockwell Encyclopedia: A Chronological Catalog of the Artist's Work, 1910–1978*. Indianapolis, IN: Curtis Publishing, 1979.

Monaco, James. *How to Read a Film*. New York: Oxford University Press, 1981.

Montgomery, John. *The Fifties*. London: Allen & Unwin, 1966.

Morgan, Hal, and Dan Symmes. *Amazing 3-D*. Boston: Little, Brown, 1982.

Morris, Kenneth, Marc Robinson, and Richard Kroll, eds. *American Dreams: One-Hundred Years of Business Ideas and Innovation from* The Wall Street Journal. New York: Light Bulb Press, 1990.

Mott, Frank Luther. *American Journalism, A History: 1690–1960*. 3rd edition. New York: Macmillan, 1962.

Mulvey, Kate, and Melissa Richards. *Decades of Beauty: The Changing Image of Women, 1890s–1990s*. New York: Checkmark Books, 1998.

Nabokov, Vladimir. *The Annotated Lolita*. Alfred Appel, Jr., ed. New York: McGraw-Hill, 1970.

Nachbar, Jack, and John L. Wright, eds. *The Popular Culture Reader*. Bowling Green, OH: Popular Press, 1977.

Nachman, Gerald. *Raised on Radio*. Berkeley: University of California Press, 1998.

Naifeh, Steven, and Gregory White Smith. *Jackson Pollock: An American Saga*. New York: Clarkson N. Potter, 1989.

Naremore, James. *More Than Night: Film Noir and Its Contexts*. Berkeley, CA: University of California Press, 1998.

National Association of Margarine Manufacturers. "History of Margarine." Available: http://www.margarine.org. (Accessed May 16, 2003).

"Native Dancer." Available: http://www.fortunecity.com/marina/commodity/nativedancer.html. (Accessed May 20, 2003).

Neuberg, Victor. *The Popular Press Companion to Popular Literature*. Bowling Green, OH: Popular Press, 1983.

Neumeyer, Martin H., and Esther S. Neumeyer. *Leisure and Recreation*. New York: Ronald Press, 1958.

Newhouse, Thomas. *The Beat Generation and the Popular Novel in the United States, 1945–1970*. Jefferson, NC: McFarland, 2000.

Nickens, Christopher. *Brando: A Biography in Pictures*. New York: Doubleday, 1987.

Nye, David E. *American Technological Sublime*. Cambridge, MA: MIT Press, 1994.

Nye, Russel, ed. *New Dimensions in Popular Culture*. Bowling Green, OH: Popular Press, 1972.

———. *The Unembarrassed Muse: The Popular Arts in America*. New York: Dial Press, 1970.

Oakley, J. Ronald. *God's Country: America in the Fifties*. New York: Dembner Books, 1986.

O'Brien, Richard. *The Story of American Toys: From the Puritans to the Present*. New York: Abbeville Press, 1990.

Olian, Joanne. *Everyday Fashions of the Fifties: As Pictured in Sears Catalogs*. New York: Dover, 2002.

Oliver, Valerie Burnham. *Fashion and Costume in American Popular Culture: A Reference Guide*. Westport, CT: Greenwood Press, 1996.

Olson, James S. *Historical Dictionary of the 1950s*. Westport, CT: Greenwood Press, 2000.

Osgerby, Bill. *Playboys in Paradise: Masculinity, Youth and Leisure-Style in Modern America*. New York: Berg, 2001.

O'Sullivan, Judith. *The Great American Comic Strip: One Hundred Years of Cartoon Art*. Boston: Little, Brown, 1990.

Outdoor Life Editors. *Outdoor Life: 100 Years in Pictures*. Denver, CO: Cowles Creative Publishing, 1998.

Packard, Vance. *The Hidden Persuaders*. New York: David McKay, 1957.

———. *The Status Seekers*. New York: David McKay, 1959.

Palladino, Grace. *Teenagers: An American History*. New York: Basic Books, 1996.

Panati, Charles. *Extraordinary Origins of Everyday Things*. New York: Harper & Row, 1987.

———. *Panati's Parade of Fads, Follies, and Manias*. New York: HarperCollins, 1991.

Parish, James Robert, and Michael R. Pitts. *The Great Gangster Pictures*. Metchuen, NJ: Scarecrow Press, 1976.

Passman, Arnold. *The Deejays*. New York: Macmillan, 1971.

Patterson, James T. *Grand Expectations: The United States, 1945–1974*. New York: Oxford University Press, 1996.

Patton, Phil. *Open Road: A Celebration of the American Highway.* New York: Simon & Schuster, 1986.

Peacock, John. *20th-Century Fashion: The Complete Sourcebook.* London: Thames and Hudson, 1993.

———. *Fashion Sketchbook: 1920–1960.* New York: Avon Books, 1977.

Pearce, Christopher. *Fifties Source Book.* London: Quantum Books, 1998.

Pendergrast, Mark. *For God, Country and Coca-Cola.* New York: Charles Scribner's Sons, 1993.

Persico, Joseph E. *Edward R. Murrow: An American Original.* New York: McGraw-Hill, 1988.

Peterson, Theodore. *Magazines in the Twentieth Century.* Urbana: University of Illinois Press, 1964.

Phillips, Lisa. *High Styles: Twentieth-Century American Design.* New York: Whitney Museum of American Art, 1985.

Pillsbury, Richard. *From Boarding House to Bistro: The American Restaurant Then and Now.* Boston: Unwin Hyman, 1990.

Pitz, Henry. *200 Years of American Illustration.* New York: Random House, 1977.

Pollay, Richard W., ed. *Information Sources in Advertising History.* Westport, CT: Greenwood Press, 1979.

Poppe, Fred C. *The 100 Greatest Corporate and Industrial Ads.* New York: Van Nostrand Reinhold, 1983.

Potter, David M. *People of Plenty: Economic Abundance and the American Character.* Chicago: University of Chicago Press, 1954.

Pottker, Jan, and Bob Speziale. *Dear Ann, Dear Abby: The Unauthorized Biography of Ann Landers and Abigail Van Buren.* New York: Dodd, Mead & Company, 1987.

Prendergast, Roy M. *Film Music, A Neglected Art: A Critical Study of Music in Films,* 2nd ed. New York: New York University Press, 1992.

Pulos, Arthur J. *The American Design Adventure, 1940–1975.* Cambridge, MA: MIT Press, 1988.

Rader, Benjamin G. *American Sports: From the Age of Folk Games to the Age of Spectators.* Englewood Cliffs, NJ: Prentice-Hall, 1983.

———. *In Its Own Image: How Television Has Transformed Sports.* New York: Free Press, 1984.

Radio Commercials. Available: http://www.old-time.com/commercials/. (Accessed March 27. 2003).

Rae, John B. *The Road and the Car in American Life.* Cambridge, MA: MIT Press, 1971.

Randel, William Peirce. *The Evolution of American Taste.* New York: Crown Publishers, 1978.

Reed, Walt, and Roger Reed. *The Illustrator in America, 1880–1980.* New York: The Society of Illustrators, 1984.

Reidelbach, Maria. *Completely MAD: A History of the Comic Book and Magazine.* Boston: Little, Brown, 1991.

Reisman, David, Reuel Denny, and Nathan Glazer. *The Lonely Crowd.* New York: Doubleday Anchor Books, 1953.

Remmers, Hermann. *The American Teenager.* Indianapolis, IN: Bobbs-Merrill, 1957.

Rhode, Eric. *A History of the Cinema from Its Origins to 1970.* New York: Hill and Wang, 1976.

Rice, Arnold S. *The Warren Court, 1953–1969.* Millwood, NY: Associated Faculty Press, 1987.

Rideout, Walter B. *The Radical Novel in the United States: 1900–1954.* New York: Hill and Wang, 1956.

Robbins, Dan. *Whatever Happened to Paint by Numbers? A Humorous Personal Account.* Delavan, WI: Possum Hill Press, 1998.

Roberson, John, and Marie Roberson. *The Complete Small Appliance Cookbook.* New York: A.A. Wyn, 1953.

Robinson, Jerry. *The Comics: An Illustrated History of Comic Strip Art.* New York: G.P. Putnam's Sons, 1974.

Rollin, Lucy. *Twentieth-Century Teen Culture by the Decades: A Reference Guide.* Westport, CT: Greenwood Press, 1999.

Rose, Albert C. *Historic American Roads: From Frontier Trails to Superhighways.* New York: Crown, 1976.

Rose, Brian G. *Television and the Performing Arts: A Handbook and Reference Guide to American Cultural Programming.* Westport, CT: Greenwood Press, 1986.

———, ed. *TV Genres: A Handbook and Reference Guide.* Westport, CT: Greenwood Press, 1986.

Rosenberg, Bernard, and David Manning White, eds. *Mass Culture: The Popular Arts in America.* Glencoe, IL: Free Press, 1957.

Ross, Andrew. *No Respect: Intellectuals and Popular Culture.* New York: Routledge, 1989.

Roth, Leland M. *A Concise History of American Architecture.* New York: Harper & Row, Publishers, 1979.

Rothman, Ellen K. *Hands and Hearts: A History of Courtship in America.* New York: Basic Books, 1984.

Rovin, Jeff. *Adventure Heroes: Legendary Characters from Odysseus to James Bond.* New York: Facts on File, 1994.

Rowsome, Frank, Jr. *They Laughed when I Sat Down.* New York: Bonanza Books, 1959.

———. *Think Small: The Story of Those Volkswagen Ads.* Brattleboro, VT: Stephen Greene Press, 1970.

Rubenstein, James M. *Making and Selling Cars: Innovation and Change in the U.S. Automotive Industry.* Baltimore, MD: Johns Hopkins University Press, 2001.

Rubinstein, Ruth P. *Dress Codes: Meanings and Messages in American Culture.* Boulder, CO: Westview Press, 1995.

Ruehlmann, William. *Saint with a Gun: The Unlawful American Private Eye.* New York: New York University Press, 1984.

Rutherford, Paul. *The New Icons? The Art of Television Advertising.* Toronto, Canada: University of Toronto Press, 1994.

Ryan, Thomas. *American Hit Radio: A History of Popular Singles from 1955 to the Present.* Rocklin, CA: Prima Publishing, 1996.

Samuel, Lawrence R. *Brought to You By: Postwar Television Advertising and the American Dream.* Austin: University of Texas Press, 2001.

Sandeen, Eric J. *Picturing an Exhibition: "The Family of Man" and 1950s America.* Albuquerque: University of New Mexico Press, 1995.

Sandler, Irving. *The New York School: The Painters and Sculptors of the Fifties.* New York: Harper & Row [Icon], 1978.

Sanjek, Russell. *Pennies from Heaven: The American Popular Music Business in the Twentieth Century.* New York: Da Capo Press, 1988.

Sann, Paul. *Fads, Follies and Delusions of the American People.* New York: Crown, 1967.

Savage, William W., Jr. *Comic Books and America, 1945–1954.* Norman: University of Oklahoma Press, 1990.

Sayre, Nora. *Running Time: Films of the Cold War.* New York: Dial Press, 1982.

Schaub, Thomas Hill. *American Fiction in the Cold War.* Madison: University of Wisconsin Press, 1991.

Schickel, Richard. *Brando: A Life in Our Times.* New York: Atheneum, 1991.

———. *The Disney Version.* New York: Simon & Schuster, 1968.

Schnurnberger, Lynn. *Let There Be Clothes: 40,000 Years of Fashion.* New York: Workman Publishing, 1991.

Schor, Juliet B. *The Overspent American: Why We Want What We Don't Need.* New York: Harper Perennial, 1998.

Schremp, Gerry. *Kitchen Culture: Fifty Years of Food Fads.* New York: Pharos Books, 1991.

Schreuders, Piet. *Paperbacks, U.S.A.: A Graphic History, 1939–1959.* San Diego, CA: Blue Dolphin Enterprises, 1981.

Schudson, Michael. *Advertising, the Uneasy Persuasion: Its Dubious Impact on American Society.* New York: Basic Books, 1984.

Schultze, Quentin J., et al. *Dancing in the Dark: Youth, Popular Culture, and the Electronic Media.* Grand Rapids, MI, 1991.

Sears, Stephen W. *The "American Heritage" History of the Automobile in America.* New York: Simon & Schuster, 1977.

Seidman, David. *All Gone: Things That Aren't There Anymore.* Los Angeles: General Publishing Group, 1998.

Seldin, Joseph L. *The Golden Fleece: Selling the Good Life to Americans.* New York: Macmillan, 1963.

Sennett, Ted. *Your Show of Shows.* New York: Collier, 1977.

Settel, Irving. *A Pictorial History of Radio.* New York: Grosset & Dunlap, 1967.

Settel, Irving, and William Laas. *A Pictorial History of Television.* New York: Grosset & Dunlap, 1969.

Sexton, Richard. *American Style: Classic Product Design from Airstream to Zippo.* San Francisco: Chronicle Books, 1987.

Seymour, Harold. *Baseball: The Golden Age.* New York: Oxford University Press, 1971.

Shapiro, Jerome F. *Atomic Bomb Cinema: The Apocalyptic Imagination on Film.* New York: Routledge, 2002.

Shaw, Arnold. *The Rockin' 50s.* New York: Hawthorn Books, 1974.

Silk, Gerald. *Automobile and Culture.* New York: Harry N. Abrams, 1984.

Silver, Alain, and Elizabeth Ward. *Film Noir: An Encyclopedia of the American Style.* Woodstock, NY: Overlook Press, 1992.

Silver, Alain, and James Ursini. *The Noir Style.* Woodstock, NY: Overlook Press, 1999.

Simon, George T. *The Big Bands.* New York: Macmillan, 1967.

Sklar, Robert. *Movie-Made America.* New York: Vintage Books, 1975.

————. *A World History of Film.* New York: Harry N. Abrams, 2002.

Skolnik, Peter L. *Fads: America's Crazes, Fevers & Fantasies.* New York: Thomas Y. Crowell, 1978.

Slide, Anthony. *The American Film Industry.* Westport, CT: Greenwood Press, 1986.

Sloan, Bill. *"I Watched a Wild Hog Eat My Baby!" A Colorful History of the Tabloids and Their Cultural Impact.* Amherst, NY: Prometheus Books, 2001.

Smith, Bradley. *The USA: A History in Art.* New York: Doubleday, 1975.

Smith, C. Ray. *Interior Design in 20th-Century America: A History.* New York: Harper & Row, 1987.

Smith, Ernest Allyn. *American Youth Culture: Group Life in Teenage Society.* New York: Free Press, 1962.

Smith, Jane Webb. *Smoke Signals: Cigarettes, Advertising, and the American Way of Life.* Chapel Hill: University of North Carolina Press, 1990.

Smith, Joe. *Off the Record: An Oral History of Popular Music.* New York: Warner Books, 1988.

Smith, Leverett T., Jr. *The American Dream and the National Game.* Bowling Green, OH: Popular Press, 1975.

Smith, Robert. *Pro Football: The History of the Game and the Great Players.* New York: Doubleday, 1963.

Smith, Wes. *Pied Pipers of Rock 'n' Roll: Radio Deejays of the 50s and 60s.* Marietta, GA: Longstreet Press, 1989.

Solberg, Carl. *Conquest of the Skies: A History of Commercial Aviation in America.* Boston: Little, Brown, 1979.

Solomon, Louis. *America Goes to Press: The Story of Newspapers from Colonial Times to the Present.* New York: Crowell-Collier Press, 1970.

Sorrell, Richard, and Carl Francese. *From Tupelo to Woodstock: Youth, Race and Rock & Roll in America, 1954–1969.* 2nd ed. Dubuque, IA: Kendall/Hunt, 2001.

Spectorsky, A.C. *The Exurbanites.* Philadelphia: J.P. Lippincott, 1955.

Spigel, Lynn. *Make Room for TV: Television and the Family Ideal in Postwar America.* Chicago: University of Chicago Press, 1992.

————. *Welcome to the Dreamhouse: Popular Media and Postwar Suburbs.* Durham, NC: Duke University Press, 2001.

Spivey, Donald, ed. *Sport in America: New Historical Perspectives.* Westport, CT: Greenwood Press, 1985.

Springer, John. *All Talking! All Singing! All Dancing!* Secaucus, NJ: Citadel Press, 1966.

Stearns, Marshall. *The Story of Jazz.* New York: Oxford University Press, 1958.

Stearns, Marshall, and Jean Stearns. *Jazz Dance: The Story of American Vernacular Dance.* New York: Schirmer Books, 1968.

Stedman, Raymond William. *The Serials: Suspense and Drama by Installment.* Norman: University of Oklahoma Press, 1971.

Steinberg, Cobbett S. *Film Facts.* New York: Facts on File, 1980.

————. *TV Facts.* New York: Facts on File, 1985.

Sterling, Christopher H., and John M. Kittross. *Stay Tuned: A Concise History of American Broadcasting.* Belmont, CA: Wadsworth, 1990.

Stern, Jane, and Michael Stern. *American Gourmet.* New York: HarperCollins, 1991.

————. *Auto Ads.* New York: Random House, 1978.

————. *Square Meals.* New York: Alfred A. Knopf, 1984.

Stern, Robert A.M. *Pride of Place: Building the American Dream.* Boston: Houghton Mifflin, 1986.

Stern, Sydney Ladensohn, and Ted Schoenhaus. *Toyland: The High-Stakes Game of the Toy Industry.* Chicago: Contemporary Books, 1990.

Stewart, Tony. *Cool Cats: 25 Years of Rock 'n' Roll Style.* New York: Delilah Books, 1982.

Stilgoe, John R. *Metropolitan Corridor: Railroads and the American Scene.* New Haven, CT: Yale University Press, 1983.

Stoddard, Bob. *Pepsi-Cola: 100 Years.* Los Angeles: General Publishing Group, 1997.

Stover, John F. *The Life and Decline of the American Railroad.* New York: Oxford University Press, 1970.

Strasser, Susan. *Never Done: A History of American Housework.* New York: Pantheon Books, 1982.

Street Swing [Dances]. Available: http://www.streetswing.com/histmain/. (Accessed April 2, 2003).

Summers, Harrison B. *A Thirty-Year History of Programs Carried on National Radio Networks in the United States, 1926–1956.* Columbus: Ohio State University Press, 1958.

Swanberg, W.A. *Luce and His Empire.* New York: Charles Scribner's Sons, 1972.

Sweeney, Russell C. *Coming Next Week: A Pictorial History of Film Advertising.* New York: Castle Books, 1973.

Symons, Julian. *Bloody Murder: From the Detective Story to the Crime Novel.* New York: Penguin Books, 1972.

Tannahill, Reay. *Food in History.* New York: Stein and Day, 1973.

Tanner, Tony. *City of Words: American Fiction, 1950–1970.* New York: Harper & Row, 1971.

Taylor, Ella. *Prime Time Families: Television Culture in Postwar America.* Berkeley, CA: University of California Press, 1989.

Taylor, John W.R., and Kenneth Munson. *History of Aviation.* New York: Crown, 1972.

Taylor, Joshua. *America As Art.* Washington, DC: Smithsonian Institution Press, 1976.

Tchudi, Stephen N. *Soda Poppery: The History of Soft Drinks in America.* New York: Charles Scribner's Sons, 1986.

Tebbel, John. *The American Magazine: A Compact History.* New York: Hawthorn Books, 1969.

Tebbel, John, and Mary Ellen Zuckerman. *The Magazine in America: 1741–1990.* New York: Oxford University Press, 1991.

Television Commercials. Available: http://www.usatvads.com/. (Accessed May 30, 2003).

Tennyson, Jeffrey. *Hamburger Heaven.* New York: Hyperion, 1993.

Terrace, Vincent. *The Complete Encyclopedia of Television Programs, 1947–1979.* 2 vols.; 2nd ed. New York: A.S. Barnes, 1979.

That's Dancing! Dir. Jack Haley, Jr. MGM, 1985. Videocassette.

That's Entertainment! Dir. Jack Haley, Jr. MGM, 1974. Videocassette.

That's Entertainment! Part II. Dir. Gene Kelly. MGM, 1976. Videocassette.

That's Entertainment! Part III. Dir. Bud Friedgen and Michael J. Sheridan. MGM/ UA, 1994. Videocassette.

Thomas, Bob. *Walt Disney, An American Original.* New York: Simon & Schuster, 1976.

Thompson, Don, and Dick Lupoff, eds. *The Comic-Book Book.* New York: Arlington House, 1973.

Thornburg, David A. *Galloping Bungalows: The Rise and Demise of the American House Trailer.* Hamden, CT: Archon Books, 1991.

Tichi, Cecilia. *Electronic Hearth: Creating an American Television Culture.* New York: Oxford University Press, 1991.

Time-Life Books. *This Fabulous Century.* Vol. V: 1940–1950. New York: Time-Life Books, 1970.

Time-Life Books. *This Fabulous Century.* Vol. VI: 1950–1960. New York: Time-Life Books, 1970.

Time-Life Editors. *The American Dream: The 50s.* Alexandria, VA: Time-Life Books, 1998.

Time-Life Editors. *Rock & Roll Generation: Teen Life in the 50s.* Alexandria, VA: Time-Life Books, 1998.

Tobler, John. *The Buddy Holly Story.* New York: Beaufort Books, 1979.

Toll, Robert C. *The Entertainment Machine: American Show Business in the Twentieth Century.* New York: Oxford University Press, 1982.

———. *On with the Show: The First Century of Show Business in America.* New York: Oxford University Press, 1976.

"Topher's Breakfast Cereal Character Guide." Available: http://www.lava-surfer.com/cereals/. (Accessed July 16, 2003).

Toth, Emily. *Inside Peyton Place: The Life of Grace Metalious.* New York: Doubleday, 1981.

Tracy, Marian. *Casserole Cookery Complete.* New York: Viking Press, 1956.

Trahey, Jane. *Harper's Bazaar: One Hundred Years of the American Female.* New York: Random House, 1967.

Truett, Randle Bond. *The First Ladies in Fashion.* New York: Hastings House, 1954.

Twitchell, James B. *Adcult USA: The Triumph of Advertising in American Culture.* New York: Columbia University Press, 1996.

———. *Lead Us into Temptation: The Triumph of American Materialism.* New York: Columbia University Press, 1999.

———. *Twenty Ads that Shook the World.* New York: Crown, 2000.

Van Dover, J. Kenneth. *Murder in the Millions: Erle Stanley Gardner, Mickey Spillane, & Ian Fleming.* New York: Frederick Ungar Publishing, 1984.

Variety Books. *The "Variety" History of Show Business.* New York: Harry N. Abrams, 1993.

Varnedoe, Kirk, and Adam Gopnik. *High and Low: Modern Art and Popular Culture.* New York: Harry N. Abrams, 1990.

Vinokur, Martin Barry. *More Than a Game: Sports and Politics.* Westport, CT: Greenwood Press, 1988.

Visser, Margaret. *Much Depends on Dinner.* New York: Grove Press, 1986.

Voight, David Quentin. *American Baseball: From Postwar Expansion to the Electronic Age.* University Park: Pennsylvania State University Press, 1983.

Wachs, Martin, and Margaret Crawford, eds. *The Car and the City: The Automobile, the Built Environment, and Daily Urban Life.* Ann Arbor: University of Michigan Press, 1992.

Wainwright, Loudon. *The Great American Magazine: An Inside History of Life*. New York: Alfred A. Knopf, 1986.

Wakefield, Dan. *New York in the Fifties*. Boston: Houghton Mifflin/Seymour Lawrence, 1992.

Walker, Lester. *American Shelter*. Woodstock, NY: Overlook Press, 1996.

Wallechinsky, David. *The People's Almanac Presents The Twentieth Century: The Definitive Compendium of Astonishing Events, Amazing People, and Strange-But-True Facts*. Boston: Little, Brown, 1995.

Wallis, Allan D. *Wheel Estate: The Rise and Decline of Mobile Homes*. New York: Oxford University Press, 1991.

Walsh, William I. *The Rise and Decline of the Great Atlantic & Pacific Tea Company*. Secaucus, NJ: Lyle Stuart, 1986.

Ward, Ed, Geoffrey Stokes, and Ken Tucker. *Rock of Ages: The "Rolling Stone" History of Rock & Roll*. New York: Summit Books, 1986.

Ward, Geoffrey C., and Ken Burns. *Jazz: A History of America's Music*. New York: Alfred A. Knopf, 2000.

Watkins, Julius Lewis. *The 100 Greatest Advertisements: Who Wrote Them and What They Did*. New York: Dover, 1959.

Watters, Pat. *Coca-Cola: An Illustrated History*. New York: Doubleday, 1978.

Weatherford, Claudine. *The Art of Queena Stovall: Images of Country Life*. Ann Arbor, MI: UMI Press, 1986.

Weibel, Kathryn. *Mirror Mirror: Images of Women Reflected in Popular Culture*. Garden City, New York: Anchor Books, 1977.

Weiskopf, Herm. *The Perfect Game*. Englewood Cliffs, NJ: Prentice-Hall, 1978.

Weiss, Jessica. *To Have and to Hold: Marriage, the Baby Boom & Social Change*. Chicago: University of Chicago Press, 2000.

Welch, Richard. "The Making of the American Dream: Rock 'n' Roll and Social Change." *History Today* 40 (February 1990): 32–39.

Wertham, Frederic. *Seduction of the Innocent*. New York: Rinehart, 1954.

West, Elliott. *Growing Up in Twentieth-Century America: A History and Reference Guide*. Westport, CT: Greenwood Press, 1996.

Whitcomb, Ian. *After the Ball: Pop Music from Rag to Rock*. Baltimore, MD: Penguin Books, 1972.

White, David Manning, and Robert H. Abel, eds. *The Funnies: An American Idiom*. New York: Free Press, 1963.

White, G. Edward. *Creating the National Pastime: Baseball Transforms Itself, 1903–1955*. Princeton, NJ: Princeton University Press, 1996.

White, Roger B. *Home on the Road: The Motor Home in America*. Washington, DC: Smithsonian Institution Press, 2000.

Whyte, William H., Jr. *The Organization Man*. New York: Doubleday Anchor Books, 1956.

Williams, Carol Traynor, ed. *Travel Culture: Essays on What Makes Us Go*. Westport, CT: Praeger, 1998.

Williams, Mark. *Road Movies*. New York: Proteus Publishing, 1982.

Williams, Martin T., ed. *The Art of Jazz*. New York: Oxford University Press, 1959.

———. *The Jazz Tradition*. New York: Oxford University Press, 1983.

Wilson, Elizabeth. *Adorned in Dreams: Fashion and Modernity*. Berkeley: University of California Press, 1985.

Wilson, Kemmons. *The Holiday Inn Story*. New York: The Newcomen Society, 1968.

Wilson, Sloan. *The Man in the Gray Flannel Suit*. New York: Pocket Books, 1955.

Winship, Michael. *Television*. New York: Random House, 1988.

Wittner, Lawrence S. *Cold War America: From Hiroshima to Watergate*. New York: Praeger, 1974.

Witzel, Michael Karl. *The American Gas Station*. New York: Barnes & Noble, 1999.

Wolfe, Tom. *The Kandy*Kolored Tangerine*Flake Streamline Baby*. New York: Farrar, Straus and Giroux, 1963.

Wood, James Playsted. *Magazines in the United States*. New York: Ronald Press, 1956.

———. *The Story of Advertising*. New York: Ronald Press, 1958.

Wood, Michael. *America in the Movies, or "Santa Maria, It Had Slipped My Mind!"* New York: Dell [Delta], 1975.

Woodham, Jonathan M. *Twentieth-Century Design*. New York: Oxford University Press, 1997.

Woodward, Helen. *The Lady Persuaders*. New York: Obolensky, 1960.

Wright, Bradford W. *Comic Book Nation: The Transformation of Youth Culture in America*. Baltimore, MD: Johns Hopkins University Press, 2001.

Wright, Gwendolyn. *Building the Dream: A Social History of Housing in America*. New York: Pantheon Books, 1981.

Wulffson, Don. *Toys: Amazing Stories Behind Some Great Inventions*. New York: Henry Holt, 2000.

Yaquinto, Marilyn. *Pump'em Full of Lead: A Look at Gangsters on Film*. New York: Twayne Publishers, 1998.

Young, Dean, and Rick Marschall. *Blondie & Dagwood's America*. New York: Harper & Row, 1981.

Young, William H. "Barbie." *Encyclopedia of American Studies*, Vol. 1. Ed. George T. Kurian, et al. New York: Grolier Educational, 2001.

Zinsser, William. *Easy to Remember: The Great American Songwriters and Their Songs*. Jaffrey, NH: David R. Godine, 2000.

Zuckerman, Mary Ellen. *A History of Popular Women's Magazines in the United States, 1792–1995*. Westport, CT: Greenwood Press, 1998.

Index

About the Authors

WILLIAM H. YOUNG is a freelance writer and independent scholar. He has recently retired from teaching English, American Studies, and popular culture at Lynchburg College in Virginia for 36 years. Young has published books and articles on various subjects of popular culture.

NANCY K. YOUNG is an adjunct professor for the Counselor Education Program in the School of Education and Human Development at Lynchburg College.

1-29-01